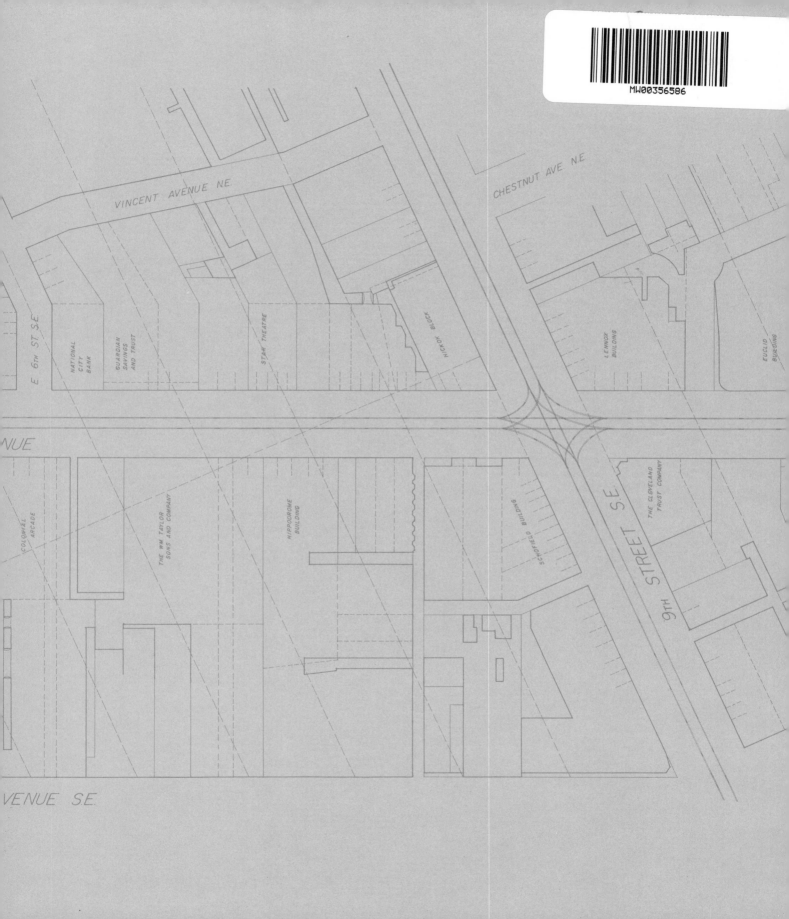

SHOWPLACE OF AMERICA

SHOWF

Clevelana

LACE *of* AMERICA

's Euclid Avenue, 1850–1910

JAN CIGLIANO

THE KENT STATE UNIVERSITY PRESS
Kent, Ohio, and London, England

In cooperation with The Western Reserve Historical Society

© 1991 by The Kent State University Press, Kent, Ohio 44242
All rights reserved
Library of Congress Catalog Card Number 91–9019
ISBN 0–87338–445–8
Manufactured in the United States of America

Published in cooperation with
The Western Reserve Historical Society.

Endpapers illustration by Thomas E. Johnson, AIA.

Library of Congress Cataloging-in-Publication Data

Cigliano, Jan.
    Showplace of America : Cleveland's Euclid Avenue, 1850–1910 / Jan
Cigliano.
        p.   cm.
    Includes bibliographical references and index.
    ISBN 0–87338–445–8 (alk. paper) ∞
    1. Euclid Avenue (Cleveland, Ohio) 2. Cleveland (Ohio)—Social
life and customs. 3. Upper classes—Ohio—Cleveland—History.
I. Title.
F499.C675E844 1991
977.1'32041—dc20   91–9019

British Library Cataloging-in-Publication data are available.

To the enduring legacy
of George Mountain Edmondson (1866–1948),
who captured the image and life
of Euclid Avenue best
through his photographic lens

Contents

Foreword

One of the most frequently asked questions about Cleveland's past is, "What was Euclid Avenue?" There is a seemingly insatiable interest in this street. Called the most beautiful street in the world by Bayard Taylor, a prominent travel writer at the end of the nineteenth century, Euclid Avenue was compared in its grandeur with St. Petersburg's Prospekt Nevsky, Paris's Champs Elysées and Berlin's Unter Den Linden. Today, less than a century later, Euclid Avenue is an essay in urban blight composed of decayed industrial buildings, abandoned hotels, seedy shops, and vacant lots. It has sunk to the depths of decay, and now there has begun to appear the signs of a new generation of institutional building to replace the derelict properties. Yet even the best of the modern structures cannot match the great houses that once stood on broad lawns behind the stately trees that bordered the Avenue and contributed to its sense of splendor and privilege.

Through the inexhaustible energies of Jan Cigliano we now have an answer to the question, "What was Euclid Avenue?" Over the past fourteen years she has devoted every spare moment from her Oberlin College days onward to delving into the street's history. The result is a thorough documentary of Euclid Avenue, its mansions, and the people who lived in them. It is more than that, however, because Jan has asked the basic questions of what caused the avenue to come into being and what were the roots of its decay. This is a comprehensive historical work that will provide its readers with many hours of richness and delight—compatible with the spirit of the avenue itself in its prime.

The Western Reserve Historical Society is pleased to have been part of this project and to have its name associated with it. The vast holdings of the Society's archives have provided the single most extensive source of primary material for Jan's historical study. The importance of both the Society's papers and Jan's historical analysis seem highlighted by the very topic of Euclid Avenue itself. America's cities are young, fast growing, and ever changing. Without these records and the scholarly interpretation of them, our restless nation would lose its collective memory. We need that memory as a measure of current values and a stimulus for civic pride. Jan Cigliano has reconstructed the story of a once-great street that brought international acclaim to the city of Cleveland. Its triumphant rise and tragic fall provide us with instructive lessons for the future.

Theodore Anton Sande
Executive Director
The Western Reserve Historical Society

Acknowledgments

This book, like the story it tells, has had many lives. I hope it will have many more. It started out fourteen years ago as my senior honors thesis at Oberlin College; the story was reconstituted and expanded a decade later to create this publication and the exhibition that complements it. In its making, I have had the good fortune of being assisted by many people. Without their help and generosity this book would have been a skeleton of what it is—or simply impossible.

In the spring of 1977, while a history major at Oberlin College, I decided to write my honors thesis on nineteenth-century Euclid Avenue—the families, the houses, the businesses, the architects, and the urban neighborhood. After all, for an Oberlin history student who then lived in Cleveland, I could dream of no better subject to ensconce myself in for the next year. I was right. But I had no idea the Avenue would continue to constitute such a major part of my life.

The initial research introduced me to the manuscript collection of the Western Reserve Historical Society, a tremendous archival resource by all measures. In the late 1970s, Virginia Hawley supervised researchers of these archival collections, including photographs, family records, journals, newspapers, biographical directories, and public documents. She knew as much about the contents of the collections as did the scholars; she managed both with an expert command.

I was also introduced to the Avenue's life and its residences by Ella Grant Wilson's two-volume publication, *Famous Old Euclid Avenue* (1932, 1937). For decades Mrs. Wilson's landmark work has been the basic reference source for Euclid Avenue history, as it was based on her personal acquaintance with many Avenue families through her florist business and on her own exhaustive research. This book is intended to complement her study. Two other important texts are *Beautiful Homes of Cleveland* (1917), which devoted a chapter to spectacular residences on the Avenue, and William Ganson Rose's exhaustive chronicle, *Cleveland: The Making of a City* (1950, 1990). Finally, the Sanborn insurance maps and Hopkins atlases, which documented the location, ownership, and size of property throughout the city from the 1870s through the 1950s, have been invaluable resources in piecing together Euclid Avenue's urban landscape.

The purpose of this book is to take the reader along the Avenue and inside the houses to present a vision of Euclid Avenue life in the nineteenth and early twentieth centuries. The ambitions and tastes of particular men and women living on the Avenue shaped its development. This book looks at places, people, and a way of life that are remote to us today. The houses have been demolished, the essence of the grand residential street has all but disappeared except in memory, and the customs and ceremonies seem as remote to us as those centuries past. The houses were built by and filled with real people—some extremely intelligent, some ignorant, some very kind, others mean, pompous, boisterous, unhappy, or toughened by situation and experience. The architects and builders were true craftsmen—some were revered for their talents, others were thought of as the patrons' hired agents.

We can still see the beautiful art that hung on the walls and the furniture and rare objects that stood in the rooms of Avenue homes in a tour through the Cleveland Museum of Art and the Western Reserve Historical Society's period rooms; they provide snapshots of the past. Through account books, diaries, letters, ledgers, newspaper articles, city and biographical directories, public records, architectural plans, renderings, and photographs, a fuller picture takes shape.

The Society's staff and manuscript collection have been the most valuable resources in the making of this book. Theodore Anton Sande, executive director, made the original commitment and has been supportive throughout the project. Kermit J. Pike, director of the library, and Ann Sindelar, reference supervisor, have been particularly helpful in assisting me with special manuscript requests and overall guidance. Eric Johannesen, the Society's preservation officer until his death in July 1990, provided me with a wealth of insight into the history of Cleveland's architecture based on his own work, chiefly *Cleveland Architecture, 1876–1976* (1977), as well as served as my friendly critic and sponsor throughout the writing of the book. Others at the Society to whom I am indebted for their able assistance include: Barbara Clemenson, reference assistant; John Grabowski, curator of manuscripts; Dean M. Zimmerman, chief curator; Michael G. McCormick, photographer; George Cooper, library page; and Sallie Chisholm, library volunteer. Others who assisted me in amassing the materials include: Sue Hanson, curator of special collections at Case Western Reserve University; William Becker, curator of the *Cleveland Press* library at Cleveland State University; Judith G. Cetina and Glenda Hopkins of the Cuyahoga County Archives; Martin Hauserman, archivist, Cleveland City Council; Janice H. Chadbourne, curator of fine arts, Boston Public Library; Mary Perencevic, keeper of the photograph collection in the Cleveland Public Library; Roland Bauman, archivist at Oberlin College; and Thomas Greer, William Barnard, and Becky Freligh of *The Plain Dealer.*

Among the most important resources for a book such as this are the private records, heirlooms, and memories of family and friends. Those who opened their personal archives and memories for my benefit include: Molly Mather Anderson, Charles P. Bolton, Mrs. Elsie Jaynes Cadwell, Mimi Carlin

Camp, Carl Boardman Cobb, Steven R. Ehrlich, Mrs. J. Henry Melcher, Roderick Boyd Porter, Constance Mather Price, Gary J. Reiter, Ivy Edmondson Starr, Clara and David R. Upson, Florence Chapin Waite, Barbara Brown Webster, Mr. and Mrs. Edward Everett Worthington, and Barbara Squire Vero. To each, I am very grateful.

Funds to sponsor the book and exhibition have come from many generous contributors over the years. In 1978, I received a Jerome Davis Scholarship Award to support the initial research at Oberlin College. During 1987–89, the Society and I were indebted to descendants of Euclid Avenue residents who supported the research and publication. These donors included Mr. and Mrs. Charles P. Bolton, Mr. and Mrs. Allen H. Ford, Mrs. A. Dean Perry, Mrs. Pamela H. Firman, Mr. and Mrs. Henry R. Hatch III, Mrs. Richard P. Nash, Mrs. J. Henry Melcher, Ms. Kathryn van den Eynden, Mr. and Mrs. David Upson, Mr. Corning Chisholm, Mr. and Mrs. Morris Everett, and Mr. and Mrs. Joseph A. Vero. The exhibition in the Society's museum was sponsored by major funding from The Cleveland Foundation and The George Gund Foundation.

I would also like to thank those individuals who critiqued the entire manuscript in its various stages. Jolie Solomon, reporter for the *Boston Globe,* suggested touches to enliven the story, based on her knowledge of Cleveland and of what readers enjoy. Dorn C. McGrath, Jr., professor of urban planning at The George Washington University, provided a national perspective of the urban grand-avenue phenomenon. Julianne Mueller, architectural historian in Washington, D.C., offered lively comments and excellent suggestions to ensure historical and architectural precision, as well as being an unfailing and interested listener throughout many hours of my prattling on about this subject. S. Frederick Starr, a historian of New Orleans life and architecture, and the grandson of Euclid Avenue photographer George M. Edmondson, devoted himself to a thorough and genuinely thoughtful critique of every paragraph and point. Throughout my writing, he offered a critical and knowing eye to the story that unfolded in each draft.

I would also like to thank Julia Pappas, my typist, who managed to turn around the numerous drafts with remarkable speed, ease, and accuracy. And I extend personal thanks to my friends, who did not abandon me during the necessary solitary days and weeks I devoted to this book or tire of my endless Euclid Avenue tales—particularly Julianne Mueller, Herta Burbach Feely, Sherry C. Birk, E. Rachel Kazan, J. Kevin Lawler, and Alan Greenspan. And to my parents, William and Gertrude Cigliano—thank you for supporting me in my desire to be a historian and for understanding my curious extracurricular work habits. I also extend a very special thanks to my mother, who happily went above and beyond the call of duty to assist me with archival research.

Finally, the one person who deserves more thanks than I can give in a few sentences is Geoffrey T. Blodgett, Danforth Professor of History at Oberlin College. As my teacher, thesis advisor, mentor, and critical reader, he deserves credit for much that is worthwhile about my history and writing. He has been among the most influential forces in helping me with the interpretation of this story, and his careful (and gently opinionated) reading of the manuscript has been invaluable, as it is based on his extensive knowledge of American urban, political, and architectural history and on his own scholarship in vernacular town building and major American architects.

Jan Cigliano
Washington, D.C.
January 1991

Illustration captions include dates of construction where known.
Dates in parentheses are when the photograph was taken.

SHOWPLACE OF AMERICA

Fig. 1. Euclid Avenue in the sleighing season (Western Reserve Historical Society, c. 1870s).

Cleveland's Grand Avenue

If you have ever met a Bufflander, you have heard of Algonquin Avenue. He will stand in the Champs Elysées, when all the vice and fashion of Europe are pouring down from the Place of the Star in the refluent tide that flows from Boulogne Wood to Paris, and calmly tell you that "Algonquin Avenue in the sleighing season can discount this out of sight." Something is to be pardoned to the spirit of liberty; and the avenue is certainly a fine one. It is three miles long and hardly a shabby house in it, while for a mile or two the houses upon one side, locally called "the Ridge," are unusually fine, large, and costly. They are all surrounded with well-kept gardens and separated from the street by velvet lawns which need scarcely fear comparison with the emerald wonders which centuries of care have wrought from the turf of England.

John Hay, The Bread-Winners

"Buffland" . . . Cleveland; "Algonquin Avenue" . . . Euclid Avenue; there is no question about Hay's inspiration (fig. 1). The masterful writer masked the identity of his resident city and its grand avenue no less successfully than he did his own identity as the anonymous author of *The Bread-Winners*.[1] A tale of the strife that swept through this and other American cities in 1873, the popular novel eloquently portrayed the elegant life of the Algonquin Avenue elite amidst the turmoil of labor unrest in the railyards and on the docks. Hay's perspective was that of an Avenue capitalist and resident. Like other writers who set their novels on America's grand avenues of the late nineteenth century, as Edith Wharton did for Fifth Avenue in the *Age of Innocence* and Agatha Young did again for Euclid Avenue in *Light in the Sky,* Hay marveled at the grandeur and tradition that engulfed the houses, grounds, and lives of Euclid Avenue patrons. He even pardoned "the spirit of liberty" that accounted for a slight unevenness in the overall patina.

This "liberty," which Hay all but casually dismissed, was a crucial birth-right of Euclid Avenue and other American grand avenues. Unlike their European counterparts in London, Paris, or Berlin, which were planned and built under authoritarian state edict, America's grand avenues were created out of the collective actions and interests of private individuals. The huge fortunes made from capitalistic endeavors and the aspiring cultural appetites of Avenue patrons created these residential showcases in Cleveland and elsewhere.

Exclusive residential streets were a phenomenon of nineteenth-century America, and especially of the emerging cities of the industrial midwest. Modeled after the boulevards of Baron Haussmann's Paris—the Champs Elysées was the ideal—such streets became public showcases of grandeur and acclaim. The families that transformed American cities into industrial centers in the post–Civil War decades built their residences, with few exceptions, on America's grand avenues—Fifth Avenue in New York, Prairie Avenue in Chicago, Woodward Avenue in Detroit, Summit Avenue in St. Paul, St. Charles Avenue in New Orleans. Among the country's finest and best-remembered was Euclid Avenue. Appropriately, it was also known as Prosperity Street and Millionaires' Row. Even the British writer Anthony Trollope, who stopped in Cleveland during his continental tour of the Americas in 1861–62, was particularly struck by Euclid Street, uniformly lined with large houses and shaded "on each side . . . by the beautiful American elm."[2] Trollope went so far as to recommend the city's handsome streets and "grand avenues of trees" over those of either Paris or London. This was an exceptional compliment, since the European boulevards had been created out of a unified vision while Cleveland's avenues evolved over many years out of numerous acts of independent citizens.

During the second half of the nineteenth century, Euclid Street—made an avenue in 1865—became one of the finest residential streets in America, distinguished for its architecture and the eminence of those who resided there. Extending four miles from downtown Public Square eastward to Ninetieth Street, the Avenue was a kind of linear roll call of the residences of Cleveland's business and cultural leaders. The houses lining the Avenue were stunning monuments to the city's, and country's, growing prosperity. In their massive size, opulent style, and rich materials, the residences of Euclid Avenue symbolized the wealth and energy of the age.

The houses lining this and other grand avenues often exhibited the highest caliber of architectural design, most having been built in the prosperous post–Civil War years between 1865 and 1910. The residents commissioned the finest architects of the period to design elegant mansions that would reflect and enhance their own economic and social positions. These residences constituted the finest ensemble of nineteenth- and early twentieth-century domestic architecture in the city (fig. 2). For Euclid Avenue patrons, the design arts were much more than a frill; they were an essential part of their everyday lives. In their houses, furniture, paintings, art objects, gardens, the commercial buildings they built, and the street itself, the Avenue's residents embraced the inherent value of great art and architecture.

The models for this acquisitive enthusiasm were clearly evident in the established eastern cities of New York, Philadelphia, and Boston, and abroad in London and Paris. But Cleveland patrons, like their Chicago and Detroit counterparts, built distinctly American "country houses" along their avenue. In contrast to the Eastern and European elite, whose streets were built on the London plan and lined with compact rows of brownstone and limestone fronts, Clevelanders, and most other late nineteenth-century grand-avenue patrons, built

large detached houses with expansive, landscaped lawns and sculptured gardens. Most of these patrons, who hailed originally from the country, created parklike environments within the city.

    The most interesting questions to pose about Cleveland's grand avenue are how it came to be and why it only survived for such a brief period in Cleveland's history. In the 1850s, Euclid Avenue still competed with Franklin Boulevard in Ohio City, west of the Cuyahoga River, as the premier address of Cleveland capitalists. Bankers, lawyers, and commercial entrepreneurs gravitated to the east side of the Cuyahoga River, while many of the leaders of Cleveland industry and shipbuilding settled on the west side.[3] Euclid Avenue triumphed in

Fig. 2. The finest ensemble of domestic architecture in the city (Western Reserve Historical Society, by I. T. Frary, c. 1900).

this competition largely because of its proximity to the downtown business district and Public Square offices and because it was the city's central spine. It was a magnificent neighborhood, architecturally and socially. The enormous resources invested in the creation of both the streetscape and the houses implied an enduring commitment to a special way of life. Yet the residential community that brought fame to Euclid Avenue really thrived for only sixty years, between about 1850 and 1910.

The progressive fortunes of capital and culture that built the residences and created the vision for this avenue were the same fortunes that drove the growth of the city. The commitment of money, energy, and creative vision by residents sprang from the same values that they invested in the city's development. The Avenue symbolized more than a monument to the personal fortunes and accomplishments of the families who lived there; it was also a monument to the strong and dynamic city they had created. Euclid Avenue was probably the most important integrating element in the city during the formative years of Cleveland's development. Commerce, however, expanded at the sacrifice of the residential neighborhood of its principal promoters. Cleveland had but one Euclid Avenue in the second half of the nineteenth century. No other street could take its place as a residential showcase. By the turn of the century, no other could rival it as the city's main commercial street. Even though Euclid Avenue entrepreneurs were sanguine about their triumphs, they did not envision further financial gains adversely affecting their private environment. But without municipal control of planning and development, the architectural glory of Euclid Avenue gradually faded and disappeared (fig. 3).

Euclid Avenue's place in the history of Cleveland's physical and cultural development is not diminished by its short life. It is really that much greater because of its remarkable presence, and now its absence. Its origins, its very reasons for being at all, were not remarkable. It was an urban neighborhood—the gathering of families who lived in one place for the purpose of reinforcing their collective activities. What is remarkable is who these people were, the size and style of the houses they built, and the central position their avenue had in the city's urban development. The street grew with the economic expansion of the village and city. Ironically, it was the tremendous success of Cleveland's industry and commerce that nurtured the rise and fostered the fall of this grand avenue.

The Economic Foundation

Over the century after its founding in 1796, Cleveland grew from a rural village of seven residents to a driven industrial metropolis of 381,000 people. The city's economic growth throughout the nineteenth century radically expanded its geographical limits (figs. 4, 5). The eastern boundary of the town had been extended from Fourteenth Street in 1796, to about 116th Street in 1896. It covered an area of 640 acres in 1830, twelve square miles in 1870, and over twenty-eight square miles in 1890. Its resident population increased in like measure from 1,075 people in 1830, to 92,829 in 1870, 261,353 in 1890, and

Fig. 3. The architectural glory of Euclid Avenue gradually faded and disappeared. Looking east from Eighteenth Street (Western Reserve Historical Society, 1940s).

over 560,000 by 1910, making it the sixth largest city in the nation. Cleveland's fortunate location at the center of trade routes from the East, the South, and the West enabled local entrepreneurs to exploit lake, canal, and rail trade and build the city's import-export industries from a deficit of over $80,000 in 1825 to a profitable $300-million business by 1896.

Cleveland's emergence as a major urban center during the nineteenth century was the work of innovative men transforming the potential wealth of the region's resources into tremendous profits. The waterfront area bordering Lake Erie and the Cuyahoga River was the focal point of the town's early commercial development. Shipbuilding and port trade were the principal industries in the 1810s and 1820s, thanks to the prosperity of import trading in such goods as furniture, stoneware, dry goods, livestock, groceries, and whiskey.[4] The financial houses founded on Bank Street during that period capitalized on lake and river businesses and rose and fell with the local economy and national money market.

The improvement of harbor facilities and the extension of transportation routes to other major ports in the 1830s and 1840s gave a big boost to Cleveland's growth. When the village became the northern terminus of the 309-mile Ohio Canal—opened to Akron in 1827, then Portsmouth on the Ohio River in 1832—Cleveland merchants could reach plentiful flour and wheat markets. By the early 1830s, steamers, schooners, and canal boats were traveling between

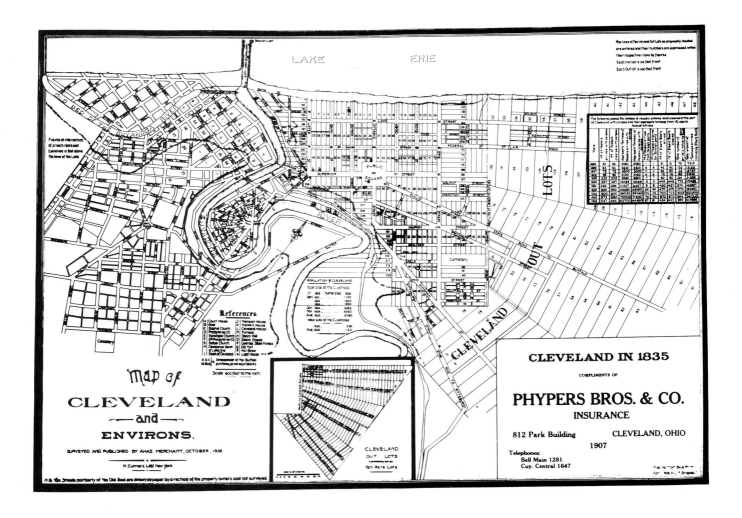

Fig. 4. Map of Cleveland and Environs, 640-acre radius (Western Reserve Historical Society, 1835).

Louisiana and Ohio, then on to New York and Pennsylvania. When the Pennsylvania and Ohio Canal opened in 1840, a more direct route was established with the Atlantic seaboard. Produce and shipping merchants, as well as grocers, ship chandlers, and lake suppliers, flourished on Bank Street and in the mercantile district along Superior Avenue. The Cuyahoga Flats were crowded with trade warehouses, retail and wholesale stores, and small industrial plants.

A second factor that spurred this urban port's development was the inception of railroad building in the 1840s and the discovery by Cleveland entrepreneurs of copper and iron deposits in the Marquette Range in the northern Michigan peninsula. The completion of the Cleveland, Columbus & Cincinnati rail line in 1852 and the Cleveland, Painesville & Ashtabula line the next year reinforced canal trade and stimulated the city's import-export business. By the mid-1850s, iron had become the chief import commodity, and coal supported the export industry. By the early 1860s, sixteen iron-ore manufacturing plants

occupied the river Flats, and fifty companies mined Michigan ore in the Lake Superior region (fig. 6).

The oil refining business joined this strong foundation in the 1860s, facilitated by the completion of the Atlantic & Great Western Railroad in 1863, then the Lake Shore and Michigan Southern in 1869. Cleveland's refineries processed one-third of all the crude oil drawn from Pennsylvania's rich fields. The Civil War created a large market for iron ore products and refined oil, and these industries soared thereafter. The decade between 1860 and 1870 set Cleveland's future course: the population more than doubled, from 43,417 to 92,829, and

Fig. 5. Map of the City of Cleveland, 28-square-mile radius (Library of Congress, Cramm Beers & Bennett, surveyors, *Atlas of Cuyahoga County,* 1892).

the value of the iron industry rose from $7.1 million in 1865 to $13.6 million by 1871. In 1867, Euclid Avenue resident and banker Randall Wade wrote his father, Union Telegraph founder Jeptha Wade, "Our City grows more elegant and lively every day."[5]

By 1870 the pressure of such rapid growth in Cleveland, and throughout the nation, had produced adverse consequences, notably chaotic financial markets and labor unrest. In 1873 unsound banking practices and overspeculation led to panic and depression, and in 1877 a nationwide rail strike blocked Cleveland's transportation facilities and choked manufacturing. For Euclid Avenue residents, many of whom represented the management and banking interests, the prosperous late 1860s and early 1870s turned into a period of stagnation and discord. Most of the city's entrepreneurs, however, looked upon all this as merely a cost of doing business and invested their energies in further expanding their commercial interests. In fact, the conditions of the 1870s foreshadowed those of the 1880s—spectacular prosperity and continued unrest. Both the ore and oil industries continued to flourish, as did railroads and shipyards. By 1890, iron producers and oil refiners both boasted $10-million industries, second only to those of New York.[6]

Since the 1840s, Cleveland thrived because of its geographical location and the entrepreneurial drive of individuals who took advantage of it. Most leaders of the city's commercial and banking interests came to Cleveland to capitalize on its access to natural resources. Such men as Samuel L. Mather, Amasa Stone, Henry Chisholm, George Worthington, Truman P. Handy, Jeptha H. Wade, Samuel Mather, John D. Rockefeller, Charles Brush, Ambrose Swasey, and Jacob D. Cox, Jr., recognized the city's potential. They established, through their business endeavors, the foundations of this Midwest industrial center. All of them lived on Euclid Avenue.

The Making of the Grand Avenue

The two chief neighborhoods in the city during the second half of the nineteenth century were the river district, where industry gathered, and Euclid Avenue, where affluent residents built their homes. In 1866, a reporter from the *Pittsburgh Commercial* summed up the face Cleveland presented to the outside world:

> A traveller approaching Cleveland is greeted by extensive manufacturing establishments. They are confined to one locality and so do not mar the beauty of the city. The streets are wide and cross each other at right angles. There appears to be no obstacle to improvements. Euclid Street can not be excelled for beauty, 3 miles or more are lined with elegant mansions. All in all, Cleveland is one of the most beautiful places, and intelligent appreciative people have turned its many material advantages into profit.[7]

Euclid Avenue's emergence as the city's premier thoroughfare was no accident and owed much to the ambitions and perseverance of its residents. They established a neighborhood whose purpose was to be—and to be known to be—the heart of the city's social, cultural, and material life. Euclid Avenue also

Fig. 6. The industrious urban port (Western Reserve Historical Society, 1853).

evolved into the main artery connecting the city's commercial and cultural centers, with Public Square on the west end and University Circle on the east. It also became the principal link between downtown and the growing eastern suburbs. When the village of East Cleveland was annexed in 1872, Euclid Avenue provided the pathway to future expansion. The city council, concerned over the possible opposition of Avenue residents, cautioned them and the public to "let no false and narrow policy stand in the way of [Cleveland's] unity and continued growth."[8]

There was even a movement in 1874 to widen the Avenue from seventy-six to 180 feet between Ninth and Fifty-fifth streets, with an eye to making it a paved boulevard after the European fashion. The plan never materialized but the city's outward growth, with Euclid Avenue as its spine, continued unabated and unguided. As in most American cities, no planning framework or official regulation of land use existed. The guiding spirit of urban development was money and the needs of commerce. Within this context, industry prospered, commerce prospered, and the city expanded eastward at an unrelenting pace. Smoke from nearby blast furnaces, factories, and oil refineries was seen not as a nuisance but

Fig. 7. A neighborhood of elegance and vitality. Looking east from Thirtieth Street on south side (Western Reserve Historical Society, c. 1890).

as a welcome sign of progress. By the early 1870s, Euclid Avenue residents—many of whom owned the polluting factories—were "compelled to breathe coal dust instead of pure air," according to a *New York Tribune* correspondent. A decade and a half later, the Avenue's most prominent writer and diplomat, John Hay, remarked in a letter to his friend Henry Adams, "The children are well and very grubby from coal-smoke."[9] The economic development that made Euclid Avenue also became its curse.

Even so, for decades house building on the Avenue remained desirable and more compelling than the unpleasant environmental conditions. Euclid Avenue grew from a cluster of fifty-eight houses in 1851 to a neighborhood of 126 residences in 1865 and 254 in 1881. It reached its peak of elegance and vitality in the 1880s and 1890s, even in the face of serious smog and commercial encroachments—its residents apparently believing that their homes provided them with a lasting way of life (fig. 7). Their persistence was evidence of their sense of permanence. Across an eighty-year period, about one-third of all the Avenue's residents lived there for twenty to forty years, and another one-third lived there for over forty years. Over the decades, fewer than one in six of the families who made their home on the Avenue stayed for less than ten years. This stability is remarkable given the high degree of mobility that existed among the

street's residents in the antebellum years. But as soon as the neighborhood's definition was clearly established, mobility diminished and long-term stability of residence became the norm.

Euclid Avenue's place in history stemmed from this extraordinary commitment. In its time, the street and community attracted national admiration. The name Euclid was used for towns in Pennsylvania and Minnesota in honor of the Avenue, in contrast to the usual practice by which streets were named for cities. Euclid Township in Norman County, Minnesota, for example, established in 1879, was named by landowner Springer Harbaugh "for the beautiful Euclid avenue in Cleveland where he had formerly lived."[10]

The street beloved by Harbaugh and his contemporaries underwent dramatic change over the years and today has disappeared. But the name and legend have endured. The purpose of this book is to recreate that neighborhood and the story of its making, development, and dissolution (fig. 8).

Fig. 8. Euclid Avenue changed dramatically over the years and today the grand residential avenue has disappeared. Looking east from Ninth Street (Lake County [IL] Museum, Curt Teich Postcard Archives, 1925).

Fig. 9. The Buffalo Stage Road.
Looking west toward Public
Square (Western Reserve His-
torical Society, 1838).

ONE

From Buffalo Stage Road to Village "Frog Pond," 1816–1860

Euclid Street was known in the early 1800s as the "girdled road," for the encircling markers around the bark of its trees, and as the Buffalo Stage Road, since it carried four-horse passenger coaches to and from Buffalo, New York. The name Buffalo Road prevailed through the mid-1840s (fig. 9).[1]

In their original 1796 survey of Cleveland, Amos Spafford and Seth Pease did not even chart a street for what became Euclid Avenue. In fact, it was not until twenty years later, in 1816, that Euclid Road was surveyed and platted on a map of the village, and at that it was a narrow dirt track leading at a diagonal eastward from Public Square. Cleveland's village board of trustees gave it the official local name, Euclid Road, because it led to Euclid Township, which was settled by the original surveyors in Moses Cleaveland's party and named in honor of the geometrician Euclid, the patron of surveying.[2] When Cleveland village was first platted, Superior Avenue was actually laid out as the city's main street. Its wide expanse and straight east-west route crossed Ontario, the principal north-south street, at the central ten-acre Public Square. The pioneer surveyors obviously intended Superior to be Cleveland's grand avenue.

Euclid Avenue emerged only gradually as the grand avenue of Cleveland, a rather uneventful and evolutionary process that extended through the first half of the nineteenth century. Its rise and recognition resulted as much from the city's urban development as it did from the road's natural topography and the collective actions of the day's leading citizens.

Cleveland was a compact wilderness village of virgin territory when Spafford and Pease laid out street lines and lots according to a strict grid plan. The village they mapped out was bounded by Lake Erie on the north, Fourteenth Street on the east, Ohio Street on the south, and the Cuyahoga River on the west. The original plan for Cleveland simply mirrored that of a New England village. The surveyors of the Connecticut Land Company returned to Cleveland in 1797 to lay out three highways through the rolling wooded terrain to the town center and the lake: North Highway, South Highway, and Central Highway. These later became St. Clair, Kinsman, and Euclid avenues.[3]

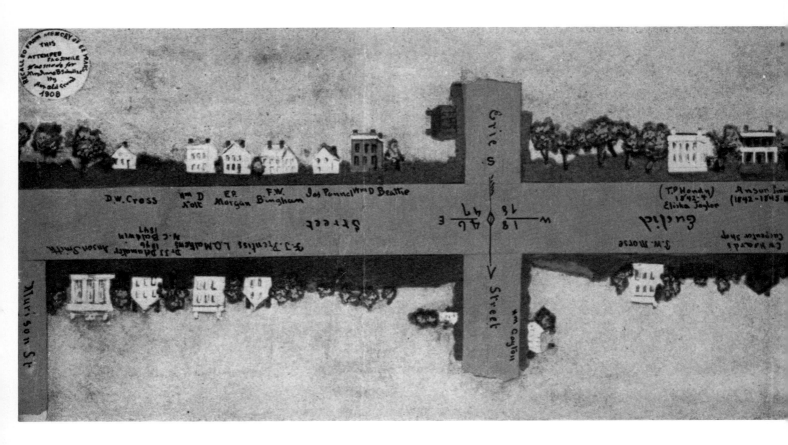

The Buffalo Stage Road

In its earliest days, Euclid Street was an unpaved, unlighted path through the woods. It was scarred and rutted by the wheels of stage coaches and frequented by wolves and other wild animals. By 1818, about thirteen log cabins stood along the four-block area east of Public Square, and a Virginia rail fence fronted the land on the north side for the next five-block stretch. A few of the cabins doubled as businesses, among them a malt brewery, a stoneyard for grave markers, a carpenter's shop, and a doctor's office. Beyond this district, only a few acres of the primeval forest had been cleared and fenced. A frame house in "a small clearing" stood at the present Fifty-fifth Street. A tannery stood a mile east of that, followed by Timothy Watkins's seventeen-acre farm and tavern at what is now Seventy-ninth Street. Otherwise, there was nothing but trees until one reached the crossroads at Doan's Corners, now 105th Street (fig. 10). Rufus Dunham was among the first to establish a foothold in this territory. In 1824 he bought a 140-acre farm at Sixty-seventh Street and opened his log tavern to stagecoach business.[4] The enormously popular lodge, frequented by locals and out-of-towners alike, offered food and drink for travelers on their way to and from Buffalo. Euclid Street's use as the road to Buffalo was memorialized in 1832 by the Ohio General Assembly, which declared it a public highway.[5]

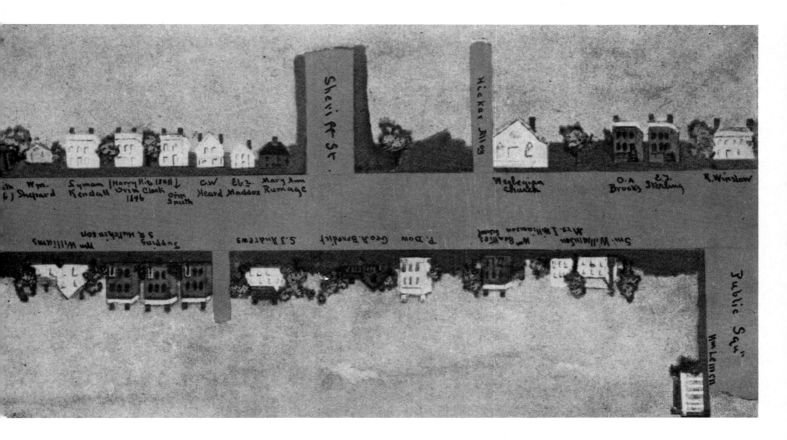

Superior Street, by contrast, remained the village's main business street, and Ontario was then the fashionable residential street.

An important turning point in Euclid Street's history came in the early 1830s when a dozen or so leading citizens built their homes along it. Most of them were canal merchants and attorneys who had offices on Public Square and nearby Superior. They apparently chose Euclid as their residence so they could live within walking distance of their businesses, yet distant enough from the mercantile activity around Superior, the river, and, increasingly, Ontario Street. One after the other they settled along Euclid Street. By the mid-1830s, it had become an enclave of leading lawyers, home to Judge S. O. Griswold (built c. 1830), Samuel Cowles (1834), Thomas Kelley (1834–35), Sherlock J. Andrews (1835), Samuel Williamson (1835–37), Harvey Rice (1837), Thomas Bolton (1835–37), and Flavel Bingham (1836). They were joined by a handful of the village's prosperous factors and financiers, among them Richard Winslow (1832), Anson Smith (1834), and Truman P. Handy (1837).

All these men came to Cleveland from upstate New York or New England. Most were from small farming and mercantile towns, though a few hailed from such urban centers as Boston, New Haven, Hartford, and Buffalo. At the time they moved onto Euclid, most of these men and their families had only recently

Fig. 10. The unpaved, unlighted road in 1846–47 (Western Reserve Historical Society, facsimile by Carlos A. Smith for Mrs. Anne Baldwin Schultze, 1908).

Fig. 11. The dirt road through the woods. Euclid Avenue at Superior Avenue (*Cleveland Plain Dealer*).

arrived in Cleveland. They worked closely with one another to lay Cleveland's economic and civic foundations and chose to live among one another, in keeping with the tradition of their native towns.

Fig. 12. Peter M. Weddell residence, 3333 Euclid Avenue; Jonathan Goldsmith, masterbuilder, 1832 (Lake *Atlas,* 1874).

These early settlers built their homes within a convenient two-block walk of the Square, most houses standing along the level south side of the street and set back about twenty-five feet from the curb. The undeveloped higher ground across the street on the north side presented a bucolic picture, "a pasture full of bushes and wild berry vines" where horses and cows grazed (fig. 11).[6] East of this small neighborhood, farther out beyond the developed edge of the village, even beyond the corporation limits, a few venturesome settlers built homesteads. These rural gentry laid the path for future eastward development by purchasing large tracts of wilderness and laying out extensive farms. Their 100- and 200-acre plots were later subdivided during the postwar years into valuable Euclid Avenue frontage. These early farms established the expansive, countrified character for which Euclid Avenue was famous in subsequent decades. The most notable were the landholdings of Nathan Perry, Peter M. Weddell, Samuel Dodge, and John M. Sterling—each man a Cleveland legend in his own right.

In 1824 merchant and fur trader Nathan Perry bought 100 acres of timbered land on the north side between Twenty-first and Twenty-eighth streets extending up to the Lake. He cleared a farm site and, about 1830, built a one-and-a-half story frame-and-brick house, possibly the work of masterbuilder Jonathan Goldsmith. Subsequent additions built between 1832–40 extended the main house to either side. The Perry residence was sited 300 feet back from the street on a natural rise.

Further east of Perry's land, merchant Peter M. Weddell bought 800 feet of frontage on the north side of the street in 1832. He had retained Goldsmith to build his country house, which was set back 250 feet from the street. The pastoral setting of Weddell's Euclid Street residence was almost a world apart from the city house, where he lived and worked during the week, a mile-and-a-half away at the corner of Superior and Bank Streets—later the site of the Weddell House hotel, 1847, and then the Rockefeller Building, 1903–5. He used the Euclid Street residence for weekend retreats. Considered pretentious in its day, the house was built of stone and noted for its low central block, balustraded wings, and deep, full-length windows (fig. 12).

To the west of the Perry property, carpenter Samuel Dodge was deeded 110 acres extending east from Thirteenth to Twenty-first streets as compensation for a barn he had built in 1804. Upon receipt of the land, Dodge built a cabin in the middle of the site, at what is today the center of Seventeenth Street. The Dodge family moved out to Doan's Corners during the War of 1812 and then returned to the city in 1838, at which time Samuel built a new house on the former cabin site. His son Henry built a brick house at the northwest corner of Seventeenth Street and, in 1846, his son George built his "Strawberry Hill" residence to the east of his father's at the northeast corner of Seventeenth Street. All of the Dodge houses were sited 150 feet back from the street.[7]

Three years after Dodge had resettled on Euclid, John M. Sterling bought 300 acres at the northeast corner of Thirtieth Street. His estate was located between Perry to the west and Weddell to the east. Dr. Sterling, a native New Yorker, set his house 250 feet back from the street. Decades later this location would become the site of the grand Gothic residence of Samuel Andrews. To improve access to his land, Sterling opened the sixty-six-foot-wide Sterling Avenue, now East Thirtieth Street.

By the mid-1840s, the two-mile stretch of land along the north side between Thirteenth and Fortieth streets was controlled by four men. The open vista of the Perry, Weddell, Dodge, and Sterling properties, and the deep lawns reaching out to the street, established a pattern that would characterize the Avenue in the decades following. Theirs were country estates, in keeping with the landscape at that time. Little did these men realize that by laying out countrified house lots, with expansive grounds and front lawns, they were creating the hallmark of Euclid Avenue.

The topography of the land surrounding the street also played a role in the Avenue's streetscape design. An east-west ridge rose gradually from Lake Erie and reached its peak elevation of about 100 feet above sea level on the north side, where the early houses were sited. The top of this ridge—overlooking the lake to the north and the Avenue to the south—provided a splendid site for palatial residences. This higher elevation distinguished Euclid from other city streets and over time attracted the prominent city residents who built their homes along it. Once established, by the early 1850s the principle of building on the ridge and away from the Avenue became an honored convention (fig. 13). Banker Randall Wade expressed scorn in a letter to his son in 1875 when some "insignificant individual" built his new house "so near the street that the rear of the house will be in front of Britton's house." Avenue residents were not

Fig. 13. *Opposite.* Building on the ridge became an honored convention. Looking east from William J. and Florance S. Boardman's lawn, 1303 Euclid Avenue (Western Reserve Historical Society, 1868).

the only ones who respected the advantage of Euclid's "summit." The 1879 *History of Cuyahoga County* noted that "a residence on Euclid Street, with a front yard of from two to five acres, soon became one of the prominent objects of a Clevelander's ambition."[8]

Euclid Avenue's position as Cleveland's premier residential street had been established by the early 1850s. By 1851, thirty-three houses lined the one-mile length from Public Square east to Eighteenth Street, and another twenty-five houses dotted the two-mile stretch between Eighteenth and Seventy-first streets. These individual residences and their owners had elevated Euclid Avenue to the finest address in the city.

The Village Frog Pond

Acclaim as Cleveland's best residential address did not come free of censure. Euclid Street's notable distinction was its residences. But as a grand avenue in the making, rather than one deliberately planned and promptly built, its attraction depended as much on piecemeal improvements by public powers as it did on independent enhancements by private property owners. The street's alter ego, the feature less appealing than the architectural masterpieces but equally notorious at midcentury, was the awful condition of the roadway itself (fig. 14).

The street's notoriety as the village "frog pond" was recounted by many, and became a public joke among city officials who were repeatedly visited by Euclid property owners requesting relief from the mud and flooding. An editorial in 1853 in the local daily, *The Daily True Democrat,* chided that "the city fathers intend taking a sail in one of the many lakes on Euclid Street." Residents in turn put up a headboard at the muddy and rutted intersection at Ninth Street that pointed an accusatory finger at the village street commissioner: "Here Lieth ye Street Commissioner, so called, who departed this life, May 6, 1853." In truth, residents shared the blame: Since improvements were paid for by property owners, residents frequently resisted the extent and cost of mandated projects, or did nothing.[9]

Indeed, the streetscape did not present a uniform picture of affluence and urbanity. Many of the earliest houses built in the late 1820s and early 1830s were modest frame structures. A schoolhouse, two boarding houses, a carpenter shop, a tavern and frequent vacant lots interrupted the continuity of the residential zone (fig. 15). It was still a village street, its character rough and uneven: cows and horses wandered in the street and the yards of owners and neighbors; burglaries for money, gold, saddles, and butter were commonplace.[10]

Periodic road improvements in the 1850s were as important to the Avenue's rising status as were the magnificent houses. Water runoff and the poor quality of the pavement were chronic problems. Deep puddles and ruts remained as troublesome in the 1850s as they were in the 1830s—impediments to easy and safe travel and to the street's reputation as a pleasant residential district.

The half-mile length east from Public Square had first been graded in 1837 to render it "passable and easy of ascent and descent." In 1838, twelve-

Fig. 14. The awful condition of the roadway was the street's alter-ego. Looking east toward Fourteenth Street (Western Reserve Historical Society, 1870s).

Fig. 15. A village street. Richard Winslow residence, Euclid Avenue at Public Square on south side; Levi Johnson, masterbuilder, 1831 (Western Reserve Historical Society, 1860).

foot sidewalks were laid and a culvert was built "to drain the water complained of from the south side." When this effort, paid for by Euclid Street petitioners, proved ineffective, a gutter was constructed during 1839–40 to direct the water flow into the culvert. Still, during the 1840s, the local paper frequently complained about the street's awful, swampy conditions. But property owners refused to pay the taxes required to do the needed work.[11]

While Euclid Street remained in poor condition, Superior Avenue gained on all fronts, as it was still Cleveland's chief mercantile street and the residential district for the affluent between Public Square and Ninth Street. The first attempt at street paving in the village not surprisingly occurred on Superior; planks were laid crosswise from the Square west to the river in 1842. Gas lamps were added in 1849, and the street was repaved in 1850, this time with the advanced technique of stone and plank boards coated with sand (fig. 16).[12]

In the meantime, boys were floating rafts down Euclid Street when it flooded. The only attempt to improve it in the early 1840s was the planting of fruit and ornamental trees in the hope they would absorb excess water and prevent flooding. Planting of the trees was also a gesture at village improvement, reflecting homeowners' reverence for the agrarian ideals that were an intimate part of their upbringing, in stride with a widespread horticultural enthusiasm of the time. The street itself was finally planked in 1848. Flooding persisted, however, and the wooden boards warped and made travel along the road just as difficult as it had been before. In 1852, Euclid Street's function as a well-used toll road to Buffalo prompted the laying of new log planks across the road, this time almost three miles east to Fifty-fifth Street.[13]

As the disparity grew wider between the street's poor condition and the fine appearance of the houses, residents became more troubled that Euclid Street was gaining architectural distinction while its surrounding landscape was deteriorating. An anonymous letter to the *Leader*'s editor in August 1855 posed the dichotomy: "Euclid is described as a beautiful street, but it is in need of repair. In wet weather it is full of ditches and puddles and in dry weather it is an elaborate Sahara, the dried up mud becoming dust and sand." The following month, Euclid Street residents and property owners were invited to meet with city officials to discuss recommended improvements for paved gutters, a lowered road bed, and extensive tree planting. Fifty residents—including major property owners Henry B. Payne, later U.S. Senator, and Horace P. Weddell, son of Peter M. Weddell—opposed the plan "because it wouldn't be permanent."[14] They instead proposed a less expensive program that would not inhibit travel and would allow water to drain off to either side of a single track of planks. Disagreement between public officials and private owners stalled any action for two years.

In the meantime, letters to the editor of the *Leader* abounded. "Euclid Street is worse than a mud hole—its a lake—an inland sea," one complained, "the whole thing is a credit to our city government." Another openly apologized to visitors for the dust and mud. Still another reported that "several buggies and wagons were capsized . . . in attempting to 'cross the waters' on Euclid

Fig. 16. Gas lamps were put up along Euclid Avenue in 1869 (Western Reserve Historical Society, 1880s).

Fig. 17. The most attractive avenue in the city. Looking east from Fortieth Street (Western Reserve Historical Society, steel plate, c. 1870s).

Street." After enough of this public outcry had drowned out the disagreement between the council and residents, the two-mile length between Public Square and Fortieth Street was replanked, sewered, lighted, and landscaped with trees on both sides. The work, paid for by the street's property owners, began in late 1857 and continued through 1859. The roadway was also widened from thirty to forty-one feet in 1860 to accommodate increased traffic.[15]

Following this major effort, another was soon begun in 1863 along the one-mile length of the principal residential district, between the Square and Twenty-first Street. Once again the sponsors' attention focused on improving the street's surface, this time with wood-block paving, which they believed was more durable through seasonal changes. Just four years later, property owners voted again to pave the street, this time as far east as the city limits at Fifty-fifth Street. They chose the new and superior Nicholson pavement—wooden blocks soaked with hot coal tar, for which the city had to acquire local rights. The Nicholson surface made for a smoother carriage ride and gave a more pleasing appearance. As a finishing touch, residents also put up gas lights for nighttime safety, then reflagged sidewalks in 1868–69.[16]

Minor as these improvements might seem today, they were all significant modernizations in the mid-nineteenth century. They greatly enhanced Euclid Avenue's riding surface and overall appearance. Even though poor drainage continued to plague the street and sidewalks well into the 1870s, it had become one of the most navigable roads in the city and an even more attractive avenue on which to build (fig. 17).

TWO

The Finest Avenue in the West, 1860–1875

The "noted street" had become the "pride of the city," exclaimed *Cleveland Leader* editorials.[1] If public concern for the street's condition appeared extraordinary, it simply reflected Euclid's extraordinary stature, locally and nationally. Cleveland's good standing among eastern and western critics ultimately focused on Euclid Street (fig. 18). By the early 1860s it had become home to many of the city's business and civic leaders, men who were central to the development of local canal trade, railroad transport, and iron-ore mining and manufacturing. The number of private residences had more than doubled since 1851, from fifty-eight to 136.

With this growth of the neighborhood also emerged apparent distinctions among the families and individuals who settled here. Some were already well established socially and financially in Cleveland's domain, like politician Henry B. Payne and merchant George Worthington, while others were of more recent arrival and affluence, like lawyer William J. Boardman and meat packer Herman Chapin. Among them were roughly equal numbers of trade merchants, industrialists, lawyers, and bankers. Unlike their counterparts in Boston, New York, and Philadelphia, where the esteemed professions of medicine, religion, and literature were well represented among the established elite families, Euclid Street's residents were mostly businessmen or lawyers, their enterprise the soul of the fast-growing city. The residences of such powerful industrialists as Jacob Perkins, Amasa Stone, and Charles Hickox and banker Hinman Hurlbut and lawyer Franklyn T. Backus contributed to the prestige of the street.

Local and out-of-town critics alike were noting its distinction by the late 1850s. One visitor in 1857 posed the rhetorical question, "Where is there a street west of a New York avenue, that can vie with Euclid?" A *Dayton Gazette* reporter announced that Euclid was "lined with splendid specimens of architecture, which betoken taste as well as wealth, and place it first among the handsome streets of Western cities." A *New York World* reporter suggested in 1863 that it was "the finest avenue in the west," distinguished by "a double row of charming villas and gardens where one might sigh to dwell." In 1866, another

Fig. 18. *Opposite.* The pride of the city. Looking west from Ninth Street on north side (Western Reserve Historical Society, late 1860s).

27

New York World reporter visiting Cleveland called Euclid "the Fifth avenue of the city"—a stunning compliment from a Manhattanite.[2]

These encomiums were voiced not only by itinerant American journalists whose job was to sell newspapers in their hometowns, but also by seasoned American and European travelers. Their testimony, broadened by experiences in other cities, lent credence to the view that Euclid Street was indeed a special place—a continuous cascade of spectacular houses, expansive sculptured lawns, and rows of elms. British novelist Anthony Trollope favorably compared the double row of "the beautiful American elm" that arched over the street to the "little paltry trees" that decorated Paris's boulevards. And while Charles Dickens was lauding New Haven's Hillhouse Avenue as the prettiest street in the nation, his literary counterpart, Mark Twain, singled out Euclid Street as "one of the finest streets in America"—praise not to be dismissed by this highly caustic novelist and reporter.[3]

In recognition of the street's prominence, Cleveland's city council dignified Euclid Street in 1865 by distinguishing it as one of Cleveland's seventeen avenues. This was a symbolic gesture, the ceremonial culmination of actions by property owners and city officials over the previous twenty years. The road was now framed on both sides by flagstone sidewalks, high sandstone curbs, and a double row of arching elms. Medina sandstone paving, the finest and most expensive road surface to be had at the time, was the unifying element of this urban landscape and a solution, finally, to the street's mud problems. The tawny brown sandstone was quarried in Medina, Ohio, exclusively for the Avenue, and the blocks were laid along its three-mile length to Fifty-fifth Street during 1873–75 when the street was widened to sixty feet. The superior road surface created an elegant approach for the residential grounds (fig. 19).[4]

The beauty of the Avenue cast a rosy glow over this landscape for many, especially outside observers. But within this "stirring, enterprising young city," as Twain had described Cleveland in 1868, a downtown neighborhood was exposed to certain dangers and intrusions. It was not an entirely magical environment. Like other inner-city streets, it was vulnerable to crime. The conspicuous wealth of its residents also made it an object of envy and trespass. Frequent reports in the newspapers through to the 1880s recounted details of each incident, mostly holdups and burglaries.

In the winter of 1859, "a valuable wolfrobe" was stolen from the house of George P. Smith; "an entire washing and half a barrel of flour" were stolen from S. N. Goodale's house; and Amasa Stone's residence was entered at dinnertime by a burglar who attacked his nephew and escaped. Andros B. Stone, brother of Amasa, was attacked on a spring evening in 1862 in his front yard at the northwest corner of Eighteenth Street. The assailant hurled a club at Stone's head and ran away, then returned later in the night and threw a large stone through the front window into the parlor. An account in 1868 told of "some dastardly wretch" who entered the grounds of a Euclid Avenue resident and "overturned and destroyed a fine life-sized statue of Mercury." The "wretch" also tried, without success, "to pry off one of the life-sized figures" on the

Fig. 19. A continuous, park-like vista of landscaped lawns, finely pruned shrubbery, and shaded walkways. Looking east from Eighteenth Street (Western Reserve Historical Society, 1880s).

entrance gateway.[5] Many such reports told of thefts of money, jewels, revolvers, clothing, and harnesses. Victimization by crime was one of the risks of this ostentatious life.

Cast-iron fences, uniformly installed by all Avenue residents, defined the boundary between public and private property and protected residents from intrusion by envious strangers and trespassers. These high iron bars screened the spacious, manicured lawns from the many passers-by who strolled along the Avenue, reinforcing the exclusiveness of the neighborhood. This barrier was further reinforced by the residents' propensity to erect these formidable fences along the sidewalk, but not between their homes. For four miles, from Public Square to Ninetieth Street, one yard flowed into another, interrupted only by side streets, the railroad crossing, and commercial blocks at Fifty-fifth Street. The result was a continuous parklike vista of landscaped lawns, finely pruned shrubbery, and shaded walkways (fig. 20).

The City Parade Ground

As the city's most elegant street, Euclid Avenue became Cleveland's parade ground, the place where ladies and gentlemen "turned out in crowds" to promenade in fine attire. Most political parades, military marches, victory processions, and holiday celebrations also centered on the Avenue. On one such

Fig. 20. Euclid Avenue was framed with flagstone sidewalks, high sandstone curbs, and a double row of arching elms. Looking west from Thirtieth Street (*Cleveland Plain Dealer,* 1870).

occasion, toward the end of the Civil War, Democrats of the city, with lanterns and banners and musical serenades, held a night victory march along the Avenue. They marched to Twenty-first Street to the home of the Avenue's most eminent politician, Henry Payne, where the band played "When the Cruel War Is Over" in his honor. After Payne congratulated the loyalists on the reduction of Abolition majorities in the South, the crowd marched on to the residence of

attorney Franklyn T. Backus at Twenty-ninth Street, where Backus held forth on a similar theme.[6]

A more somber occasion was the local funeral procession for President Abraham Lincoln in April 1865 when his casket came through Cleveland on the way to Illinois. Starting from the train station at Fifty-fifth Street, the slain President's horse-drawn hearse—covered with buntings, flags, and black plumes—led the way west along the Avenue, followed by a band playing Handel's *Funeral Anthem*. The silence of mourners was broken only by the rattle of the carriage wheels on the wooden block pavement and the even rhythm of the falling rain. As recounted by the *Leader*, "Thousands of people . . . stood almost motionless amid the pouring rain . . . their heads bowed." Just four years earlier President-elect Lincoln had toured the same route on his way from Illinois to the White House in Washington.[7]

Sleigh rides and races on the Avenue became the most popular tradition for which Euclid Avenue was known. John Hay's favorable comparison of the

Fig. 21. A winter pageantry of sleigh rides and races, showing residences of Charles Brush, no. 3725; T. Sterling Beckwith, no. 3813; and Randall H. Wade, no. 3903, in 1880s (Western Reserve Historical Society, painting by F. B. Egan).

Avenue to the Champ Elysées in the sleighing season warmed the hearts of Cleveland boosters. Sleighing became a seasonal event, beginning in the winter of 1867 when the street had been "blessed with the Nicholson pavement." Until the streetcar and automobile took over the road in the early 1900s, traffic and commerce deferred to the rhythm of afternoon sleigh races. Teams and spectators gathered from throughout the city as "gay equipages went dashing along the glassy street," at once a carnival, a spirited show, a dignified pageant.[8]

Races were so popular that the city council suspended the six-mile-per-hour speed limit during the winter season, and red flags went up at Ninth and Fortieth streets to suspend public travel on the two-mile course. Such Euclid Avenue luminaries as oil magnate John D. Rockefeller, railroad factor Jacob B. Perkins, industrialists Charles Otis, Leonard Hanna, Julius French, and Henry Blossom, and shipper Morris A. Bradley were frequent racers, turning out with their buffalo and fur robes, footmen, and charcoal footwarmers. Union Telegraph founder Jeptha H. Wade, another avid sleigher, had the finest cutter, a two-horse Russian sleigh mounted with a high dashboard and flaming red plumes (fig. 21).[9]

Harry Devereux, son of railroad magnate John Henry Devereux and a railway supplier himself, was Cleveland's premier horseman and the Avenue's finest racer. He planned his winter days around the races, working in his office until mid-afternoon, then taking out his mare, Kate Owen, for "several goes down the Avenue." He wrote in his diary one January day, "Found nobody who could head her, she went fast and steady." The next day, even with a "great crowd out," he again reported, "Found nothing the mare couldn't beat easily—'queen of the road.'"[10]

The best winters, in the view of one prominent Avenue resident, iron-ore entrepreneur Samuel L. Mather, were the "cold and stormy" ones when the Avenue was "lively every afternoon—a perfect Carnival." Since races during the sleighing season were such a favored enthusiasm among Avenue and city residents, in 1885 the city council detailed extra police patrolmen to keep "large wagons and carts" off the Avenue between two o'clock and five o'clock because they disturbed the race horses and caused accidents. In addition to this lively sport, leisurely or brisk sleigh rides were the foremost winter pastime among Avenue residents. Some liked an invigorating escapade, others a romantic sojourn. Emma and Fred Sterling especially enjoyed their moonlit sleigh rides together through the quiet nights, among snow-covered trees: "The whole landscape looked like a Fairy land" to Emma.[11]

The Street of Transit and Commerce

But the romance of this fairyland setting gradually gave way to progress on the city's chief transportation artery. A horse-drawn omnibus first traveled on Euclid in 1853, making two daily trips to the Fifty-fifth Street railroad station. In later years the omnibus ran more frequently and went out to Doan's Corners at 105th Street. Then came the trolly lines. When the East Cleveland Railway Company was formed in 1859, Euclid Street was slated as one of two

main streetcar routes. Service began in 1860, first taking passengers to Fifty-fifth Street, then out to Seventy-first Street by 1863. The cars were rather bare and primitive in the early days, fitted out only with wooden seats and insulated by straw-covered floorboards. But for most Clevelanders who did not own a private carriage or sleigh, the streetcar was a wonderful convenience (fig. 22).[12]

Avenue residents, most of whom did own at least one carriage and sleigh and had a live-in coachman to livery them around, were less enamored with the streetcar. They did not need it for practical purposes, and they opposed its routing down their grand avenue from the start. Resentment intensified as the trolly grew more popular and more crowded and expanded farther east along Euclid. In response to Avenue residents' protests, city council routed the tracks along Prospect between Twenty-first and Fortieth streets to bypass the most fashionable stretch of Euclid Avenue. Ironically, the companies that constructed the line and the iron tracks were owned by Avenue residents William Chisholm and his son Stewart.[13] Despite their neighbors' opposition, the Chisholms were instrumental in bringing mass transit to their residential street.

The Street Railway Company continued to press for permission from a majority of property owners to operate on the off-limits length between Twenty-first and Fortieth streets. The company circulated petitions, but those were only met with scorn. In fact, in the late 1860s, when plans were underway to resurface the street with the handsome Nicholson pavement, Avenue residents tried once again to remove the tracks between Fortieth and Fifty-fifth streets. They wanted their beautiful Avenue to be "free from obstructions" and less accessible to the transit-going public.[14] Their efforts failed to deflect the street's larger public purpose.

Inroads by mass transit lines on the city's grand residential street were not unique to Cleveland. The intrusion was also hotly debated in New York City and New Orleans in the middle of the nineteenth century. In Manhattan, the contest between Fifth Avenue residents and transit officials looked and sounded much the same as it did in Cleveland; this grand avenue was also one of the city's main traffic arteries. In New Orleans, the St. Charles Avenue steam street-car line was developed in the 1830s by private entrepreneurs to provide direct access between downtown and the resort hotel and gardens they had built on the Mississippi shore to the west. Affluent residents along this southern city's grand avenue objected to the steam engines' smoke and noise, a problem not completely rectified until the introduction of electric trolleys in 1893.[15] Grand avenue patrons in many cities came to regard the streetcar as a disdainful vehicle that served the needs of unwelcome outsiders but was of little use to themselves. Their isolationist sentiment arose not from uncharitable motives but from a firm interest in guarding the serenity of their urban neighborhoods.

Neighborhood Institutions

The dignity of the Euclid Avenue neighborhood was strengthened over the years by the erection of handsome churches throughout the residential area. After all, the Christian families of the Avenue regarded their churches as essential parts of the neighborhood, an extension of the home and of daily life.

The first to go up was the Wesleyan Methodist Church, built in 1839–40 just east of Public Square on the south side. This modest, one-and-a-half story frame building was razed in 1869 to make way for a commercial block. St. Paul's Episcopal parish was the next to build, having been organized in 1846 by Euclid Avenue residents Moses Kelley, Oliver Brooks, George Benedict, Thomas Bolton, Elisha Sterling, and David W. Cross. A Gothic frame structure for St. Paul's was started in the summer of 1848 at the southwest corner of Fourth Street, but it burned to the ground before construction was completed. The congregation then elected to build in brick and retained architect Charles W. Heard—who designed many of the fine residences on the Avenue in the 1860s and 1870s—and the new Gothic edifice opened in 1851. St. Paul's was home to the Episcopal congregation until 1874, when it moved up the Avenue to a new sanctuary on the corner of Fortieth Street.[16]

Following St. Paul's, the First Baptist (Plymouth Congregational) Church at the northwest corner of Ninth Street opened its doors to the congregation in 1855. Four years later the Euclid Presbyterian Church was completed at the southeast corner of Fourteenth Street. The "church of 40 corners," designed by architect J. J. Husband, was built by a splinter group of Avenue residents from the First Presbyterian Church, including Elisha Taylor, Zalmon Fitch, and George Worthington. They left the mother church to found a congregation closer to their homes (fig. 23).[17]

Church building along the Avenue resumed after the Civil War with the construction of the Second Baptist Church at Eighteenth Street in 1868. This grand sandstone structure, designed by Max Freiber and Alfred Green, was built

in the early Romanesque style and was dominated by a central entrance tower and 208-foot spire. The Methodists, meanwhile, had become increasingly cramped in their small church near the Square and in 1865 purchased the southeast corner of Ninth Street across from the First Baptist Church. They first built a chapel on the site in 1869; construction then began on the main building, which was dedicated in 1874. Designed by Alexander Koehler in the English Gothic manner and built of limestone quarried in Sandusky, Ohio, this largest of Euclid Avenue's early churches was graced by a soaring buttressed tower and a magnificent stained glass window from Munich.[18]

These church buildings were the first structures to be built along the Avenue for community functions rather than private residences. Their sheer scale and grand use of stone enhanced their visibility amidst the residential grounds and marked a departure in the Avenue's uniform streetscape. But they fit easily into the neighborhood's residential complexion.

Just as the church was part and parcel of the village neighborhood, so too were commercial buildings and retail shops. Business outlets came to this street to capitalize on the commercial value of a Euclid Avenue address. The residential area had become a magnet and status symbol for retailers. Starting in the mid-1850s, stores and offices replaced the early residences located between the Square and Ninth Street. Those that first went up congregated around Public Square and the intersection at Ninth Street. These establishments, evolving into multistory business blocks, changed the character of this part of the street from a distinguished residential neighborhood to a thriving commercial district (fig. 24).

The first large commercial building was Chapin's Hall, a three-story brick block located at the northeast corner of Euclid at Public Square. It was built by one-time Cleveland mayor Herman Chapin, a resident of the street, and opened New Year's Day 1855. Elegant millinery, music, and confectionery shops occupied the ground floor, offices were on the second floor, and a 1,200-seat concert and lecture hall was on the third floor. The Schofield Block followed in 1856. This three-story brick building at the southwest corner of Ninth Street was the work of masterbuilder William B. Schofield. Dr. Sapp's homeopathic office and a drugstore were at street level, with offices above.[19] In the years following, fine clothing and confectionery shops moved into many of the small frame and brick residences which had been built in the 1830s.

Following the Civil War, the pace of commercial building on the Avenue broke into a brisk stride. Leading off Cleveland's commercial development in 1873 was the Standard Block between Second and Fourth streets on the north side. It was built by John D. Rockefeller to house his Standard Oil offices. In 1874 came the Cushing Block, home of William Taylor's department store.[20] That same year the house next door to the Standard Block was sold, torn down, and redeveloped as a masonry business block. The most opulent building to go up in the commercial district during this period was the Euclid Avenue Opera House at the southeast corner of Fourth Street (fig. 25). Construction of the four-story sandstone building began in 1873, and the Opera House opened with

great fanfare with the hit musical "Saratoga" on September 6, 1875. The impressive French Renaissance–style mansarded opera house enhanced the Avenue's civic role. Rich with marble foyers, sweeping galleries, glittering chandeliers, and white-columned private boxes, the 1,200-seat theater was designed and built by the prominent Cleveland architectural firm of Charles W. Heard & Sons. Far from being an intrusion into the Avenue's established patterns, this palace of entertainment was financed by such staunch residents as Jeptha Wade and Horace Weddell. They sold it in 1879 to street railway financier and political captain Marcus A. Hanna.[21]

The Avenue's commercial footings were deepened when it established a direct link to Superior's mature business district in 1875 with the opening of Sixth Street between Euclid and Superior. Avenue resident Charles Otis and his partner Hubbard Cook seized the new commercial opportunity and, on their

Fig. 24. The thriving commercial district at Public Square (Western Reserve Historical Society, c. 1870s).

Fig. 25. The opulent Euclid Avenue Opera House, southeast corner of Fourth Street; Charles W. Heard and Sons, architects, 1873–75 (Western Reserve Historical Society, c. 1875).

property near Fourth Street, built the five-story Otis Block, which opened to rave reviews on New Year's Day 1876. Also designed by architect Heard, it housed a first-class café and Brainard's music store on the ground floor, a billiard parlor on the second floor, and apartments on the third and fourth floors.[22]

By the mid-1870s, the district between Public Square and Ninth Street was happily called "the business avenue east of the park." The shops and business blocks had created a new, young commercial district for downtown Cleveland, one that catered mostly to affluent shoppers and first-class business offices. Meanwhile the thirty-three private homes that lined this part of the Avenue in 1851 had diminished to just thirteen by 1877. The "unmistakable indications" of an expanding trading area aroused concern among only a handful of residents. For most, the nearby services were a practical amenity rather than an unwanted intrusion on their serenity. They adopted a benign ignorance about the commercial district's fabulous future success. Real estate investors, having a keen eye for value, were not at all ignorant and touted "the superior character of retail business . . . clustering about [Euclid's] terminus near the Square." To them, it was evidence of "marvelous changes" underway. They likened the Avenue to New York's Broadway.[23] Land prices on the Avenue in 1874 confirmed its commercial potential: Residential property on Prospect, one block to the south, sold for $300 per foot, while a similar location on Euclid Avenue commanded $1,000 to $1,200 per foot.

The immediate reward of prosperity blinded people to the long-term implications of this commercial development. As in other American cities, no official land use regulations existed to guide the city's expansion. Instead, the use of land was dictated by the interests of whichever owner could pay the price. The collective interests and actions of key residents certainly moderated this practical pursuit of individual profits and protected the area from more rapid change. But the individual and group interests of those involved with Euclid Avenue—residents, churches, commerce, the street railway—remained in a state of dynamic tension that was never fully resolved.

The civic pride invested in Euclid Avenue focused on the competing interests of the splendid residential streetscape and the business district. Commercial expansion proved to be relentless. When Cleveland residents voted in 1872 to annex the village of East Cleveland and extend the corporate limits two miles eastward from Fifty-fifth Street to Mayfield Road, the Avenue was viewed as the central spine that would make the annexation successful. The enterprising spirit that called voters to "let no false and narrow policy stand in the way of [Euclid's] unity and continued growth" in fact summoned people to put the interests of commerce above those of residential stability. A large majority accepted this proposition, and annexation occurred in October 1872.[24]

The rival interests of residential and commercial growth prospered through the turn of the century, competing in uneasy but happy coexistence for many years. But it was the dominance of Euclid Avenue's residential neighborhood throughout these years that enabled the architectural streetscape to flourish, making it one of the finest residential streets in late nineteenth-century America.

Fig. 26. Nathan Perry residence,
2157 Euclid Ave; Jonathan Goldsmith, masterbuilder, c. 1830
(Western Reserve Historical Society, by George Mountain Edmondson, 1930s).

THREE

Urban Townhouses and Country Villas, 1830–1865

The first houses built on Euclid Street were fairly modest frame dwellings. They were rooted stylistically in the plain vernacular of the villages in upstate New York and New England from which their owners had come. The home built for Nathan Perry around 1830 was typical: a gabled roof, clapboard siding, and little detailing to differentiate this house from any other (fig. 26). The architecture, like the road, was rustic and utilitarian. Most of these early houses were razed and replaced by more sophisticated ones in the 1840s and 1850s. In some cases, as with the Perry residence, the original house was modernized over the years by the addition of masonry wings, porches, and a rooftop cupola.

The Classical Tradition, 1830–1845

Like the early houses, those that followed in the 1830s and 1840s resembled the native architectural conventions familiar to the families that had recently come to the village from the Northeast. But by now the desire for a more urbane, classical format prevailed among the leading lawyers and merchants who built their homes on Euclid Street. Brick and stone, rather than wood, were used to capture the outlines of the Federal and Greek Revival styles. The houses were organized around a rectilinear plan and three- or five-bay facades, with the main entrance and hallway on one side or at the center. Typical of the period, the detailing that dressed these houses consisted of little more than stone lintels and sills around windows and doors, wooden shutters, and a columned porch or portico over the entrance (figs. 27, 28).

During the decade between the mid-1830s and mid-1840s, the number of houses on Euclid Street increased from twenty-five to forty-five.[1] The design and siting of the newer ones prepared the tone and scale for what would become Euclid Avenue after midcentury. The masterbuilders who shaped the street's architectural character during this time were all-purpose tradesmen who designed, built, and crafted the homes with their own hands. Their stylistic inspiration was limited to the few publications on building and architecture then available, most of them English works.[2] Among the most active craftsmen on

TABLE I
The Classical Tradition, 1830–1850

Patron/Resident	Address	Building Date	Masterbuilder
Nathan Perry	2157	c. 1830	[J. Goldsmith]
Richard Winslow	2	1832	L. Johnson
Peter M. Weddell	3333	1832–33	J. Goldsmith
Samuel Cowles	622	1833–34	J. Goldsmith
Sherlock Andrews	400	c. 1833–35	J. Goldsmith
Thomas M. Kelley	1723	1834–35	J. Goldsmith
William Williams	723	1835–36	J. Goldsmith
Thomas Bolton	1111	c. 1835	Unknown
George A. Hoadley	1201	c. 1835	J. Goldsmith
Samuel Williamson	9	c. 1835–37	Unknown
Truman P. Handy	800	1837	J. Goldsmith
Anson Smith	1167	1840–42	Unknown
Irad Kelley	3500	c. 1845	Unknown
Stillman Witt	1115	c. 1851–52	Unknown
George Worthington	3635	1852	Unknown

Euclid Street were Levi Johnson, Warham J. Warner, Charles W. Heard, and particularly Jonathan Goldsmith (see table 1). Goldsmith, often assisted by his son-in-law Heard, designed and built at least a dozen houses on the street during the 1830s, most notably for judges Samuel Cowles, Sherlock Andrews, and Thomas Kelley, for merchant Peter M. Weddell, mayor George A. Hoadley, and banker Truman P. Handy. The coincidence of each patron's position in the community and his choice of Euclid Street for his residence and Goldsmith for his builder reinforced the stature of the client, the street, and Goldsmith.

Goldsmith (1783–1847) had come with about sixty other family members to the Western Reserve in 1811 from a small town in the Berkshires. The clan settled in Painesville, where Goldsmith built a log cabin for his family and worked as a bootmaker, a trade for which he had apprenticed as a teenager in New Haven. He had also trained under a carpenter-joiner in that city, and within a decade of his arrival in Painesville he was building houses, stores, and taverns for the town.[3] The relative prosperity of Cleveland in the 1820s had inspired him to pursue business there. Goldsmith was not a formally educated man, but he had studied such reference sources of the building trade as Asher Benjamin's 1833 pattern book, *The Practice of Architecture*.[4] Even though he mostly adapted the designs he had seen in the carpenters' manuals, as most builders did, he was also known for developing innovative building techniques to express his emerging personal style. Goldsmith worked almost exclusively in Lake County and Cleveland, and he was recognized then, and later, as the leading masterbuilder of his era. Talbot Hamlin, the eminent critic of nineteenth-century Ohio architecture, praised Goldsmith's later work, of the 1830s and 1840s, for "a growing mastery of Greek refinement and Greek simplicity" to achieve "a consistently high level both in conception and execution."[5]

Fig. 27. William Williams residence, 723 Euclid Avenue; Jonathan Goldsmith, masterbuilder, 1835–36 (Western Reserve Historical Society, 1860s).

Fig. 28. Samuel Williamson residence, 9 Euclid Avenue, c. 1835–37 (Western Reserve Historical Society, c. 1870).

Fig. 29. Samuel and Cornelia Cowles residence, 622 Euclid Avenue; Jonathan Goldsmith, masterbuilder, 1833–34 (Western Reserve Historical Society, 1850s).

Goldsmith's Euclid Street residence for Samuel Cowles, built in 1833–34, exemplified this talent. The house, probably his second on the street, established his reputation as the builder of choice for the street's residents. Judge Cowles, a respected lawyer, had come to Cleveland from Hartford, Connecticut, fifteen years before at the age of forty-four to serve on the common pleas bench, and had married another recent arrival, Cornelia Whiting. The Cowleses were highly regarded in the village as distinguished hosts, and they acquired an expansive lot on the south side of Euclid Street, between Fourth and Ninth streets, with the purpose of building a distinguished residence (fig. 29).[6]

Thanks to surviving records, Cowles's personal involvement in the design of his house is known to be extensive, from laying out floor plans to specifying ceiling heights, construction materials, room dimensions, and decorative features. He had a clear image of what he wanted his residence to look like. Among the items Cowles instructed Goldsmith to incorporate into the design were brick partitions, a rooftop cupola, and a floor plan "to admit a free circulation of the lake breezes in the summer through all apartments."[7] Cowles allowed Goldsmith to make the decision whether to build the house of brick or stone. Goldsmith chose brick.

The 5,000-square-foot residence, with its columned portico facing Euclid Street and gardens and stables at the rear, was known to be the most expensive dwelling in the city at the time. Judge Cowles died only three years after his

house was completed. His widow lived there until 1842, when she sold it to telegraph agent Anson Smith for $7,000, a fabulous sum at the time. Smith lived there until 1845–46 while his own substantial residence was being built at the northwest corner of Twelfth Street. The Cowles residence was sold in 1850 to Bishop Amadeus Rappe for the Catholic Ursuline Convent and boarding school. The convent added a third story and flanking pavilions and occupied the enlarged residence until it was razed in 1906 to make way for William Taylor's department store.[8]

About the same time that the Cowles residence was being built, Goldsmith was working on the Andrews and Weddell houses—the former located nearby at the northwest corner of Second Street and the latter beyond the town line at Thirty-third Street. For Judge Andrews's house, Goldsmith employed carpenter and son-in-law Charles W. Heard as "boss journeyman," or construction manager. The close attention that both architect and builder devoted to the job clearly delighted the patron; so pleased were the Andrewses with the result that they gave Goldsmith an imported silver watch and a "heavily-chased ornamental gold key for his services."[9]

After 1835, Goldsmith's work and house design on Euclid Street generally turned to a larger, more refined profile. The residences built for Judge Thomas M. Kelley (1834–35) and banker Truman P. Handy (1837) were benchmarks in this evolution. Judge Kelley, a native of Middletown, Connecticut, had prospered by shipping meat to Montreal and the South.[10] He retained Goldsmith to design and build a house at the northwest corner of Eighteenth Street in the form of a Greek Revival temple heralded by a two-story portico, Ionic columns, and one-story lateral wings (fig. 30). In keeping with the emerging pattern for the street, the house was set back about 100 feet from the curb on the Euclid ridge.

The village's leading banker, Truman P. Handy, retained Goldsmith in 1837 to design the most splendid residence yet to grace Euclid Street (figs. 31, 32). Handy, who had arrived in Cleveland from Buffalo five years earlier, quickly established himself as a central figure in the business community through his position as cashier of the Commercial Bank of Lake Erie and as a factor in lake and canal trade. When the Commercial Bank's charter expired in 1842, Handy moved into the void and established the private banking house of T. P. Handy and Company. And when the State Bank of Ohio was organized in 1845, Handy became the largest stockholder and served as its chief executive until 1865, when he then became president of the Mercantile National Bank. Banking was the mainstay of his enterprise, but like many of his colleagues, he had diverse interests—railroads, mining, and manufacturing among them. He was also a pillar of many of the village's cultural and educational enterprises, having been inspired early in his career by the eminent historian George Bancroft. He advocated free public education; he founded the YMCA with fellow banker Daniel Eells; he presided over the Cleveland Mozart Society, the Mendelssohn Society, and the Children's Aid Society. Among his close friends were other leading businessmen—bankers Eells and Hinman Hurlbut, oil king John D. Rockefeller, railroad magnate John Henry Devereux, and industrialist Stillman Witt—all of whom later built on Euclid Street.[11]

The residence Goldsmith designed for Handy reflected this patron's affluence and cultural breadth. It was located immediately west of Samuel Cowles's property on a publicly owned lot that Handy had bought at a sheriff's auction during the 1837 financial panic. The Handy house, built of brick, was dominated by a two-story portico supported by stone Ionic columns. It stood out as a refined and even erudite rendition of the Greek Revival ideal. Notwithstanding this, after only four years in the house Handy moved up the street to the north side just east of Eighteenth Street. His new residence, a first in Italianate design on the street, again placed Handy at the vanguard of architecture and location. He had sold his Goldsmith-designed residence in 1841 to drygoods merchant Elisha Taylor, who later sold it to Cleveland mayor George B. Senter. In 1872, the former Handy residence was purchased for an impressive price of $160,000 by "a group of companionable and cultivated gentlemen," better known as the Union Club. After a long and distinguished life as the club's headquarters, the Handy house was sold in 1902 for $400,000 and demolished to make way for the Hippodrome Building.[12]

The subsequent residences built during the mid-1840s and early 1850s by merchants Irad Kelley and George Worthington and industrialists Stillman Witt and Anson Smith continued the stylistic trend set earlier by Cowles, Kelley, and Handy (figs. 33–35). The size of their houses and grounds reinforced Euclid Street's emerging grand architectural stature. Smith and Witt built their residences in town, next door to one another at the northwest corner of Twelfth Street, while Kelley and Worthington went out to Euclid Street's borderland, about a mile east beyond Thirty-fifth Street. Their residences extended the street's existing boundaries, and the neighborhood was broadened by the quality

Fig. 31. The village's leading banker, Truman P. Handy (Western Reserve Historical Society; oil painting by Jarvis Hanks, 1838).

Fig. 32. Truman P. Handy residence, 800 Euclid Avenue; Jonathan Goldsmith, masterbuilder, 1837 (Western Reserve Historical Society, 1900).

Fig. 33. Irad Kelley residence, 3500 Euclid Avenue, c. 1845 (Western Reserve Historical Society).

Fig. 34. Stillman Witt residence, *left*, 1115 Euclid Avenue, c. 1851–52; Anson Smith residence, *right*, 1167 Euclid Avenue, 1840–42 (Western Reserve Historical Society).

of each residence and each family's position in the business and cultural affairs of the village.[13]

The Gothic Country House, 1845–1865

By the mid-1840s, the severe classicism that had shaped the street's appearance over the past fifteen years began to give way to an enthusiasm for more picturesque forms in the architecture of the new houses. While the square plan still remained the organizing unit, it was now garnished with central pavilions, arched window moldings, bracketed eaves, corner quoins, and rooftop

Fig. 35. George Worthington residence, 3635 Euclid Avenue, 1852 (Western Reserve Historical Society, by G. M. Edmondson).

Fig. 36. The garden, the white picket fence, the natural landscape. Alonzo P. Winslow residence, 7102 Euclid Avenue, c. 1860–65 (Lake *Atlas,* 1874).

balustrades and cupolas. House design followed two rival models: the Italianate villa and the Gothic country house, both more romantic in their inspiration and appearance than the austerity of earlier residences. The Italianate, or Tuscan, villa was exceptionally popular among Euclid Street patrons from the 1840s through the 1860s. Gothic styling, however, was much less so and was usually adopted by residents whose farmhouses dotted Euclid Street's woodland region beyond the village's eastern boundaries.

Most of the houses designed in the rusticated Gothic manner owed their birthright to the continental English cottage of the early nineteenth century, introduced into the American vocabulary by the popular pattern books of Alexander Jackson Downing, *Cottage Residences* (1842) and *The Architecture of Country Houses* (1850). Most of the Gothic cottages built on Euclid Street mimicked Downing's models as well as the contextual genre of rural virtue that he advocated as being part of the fabric of the cottage shelter—the garden, the white picket fence, the natural landscape (figs. 36–38). The cottages on Euclid Street, like those in Downing's designs, were not always small, but they were simple and pristine. Their frame structures were distinguished by expansive gable roofs, scroll-sawn gingerbread eaves, an occasional off-center cupola or

Fig. 37. A Gothic cottage on Euclid Avenue's borderland. Hylas Jaynes residence, 8221 Euclid Avenue, 1845 (Lake *Atlas*, 1874).

Fig. 38. Downing's cottage villa in the rural Gothic style (Plate 128, *The Architecture of Country Houses*, 1850).

TABLE 2
The Gothic Country House, 1845–1865

Patron/Resident	Address	Building Date	Masterbuilder
William Baley	4560	c. 1845–50	Unknown
Ira Adams	8903	c. 1845	Unknown
Hylas Jaynes	8221	1845	Unknown
Henry B. Payne	2121	1849	C. W. Heard
Thomas Bolton	7030	1848–49	Unknown
Moses Kelley	6908	1850–52	Unknown
Alexander Sackett	6700	1852	Unknown
Herman M. Chapin	4307	1857	Unknown
Capt. Alonzo P. Winslow	7102	c. 1860–65	Unknown
Henry C. Rouse	3826	1866–67	Unknown

tower, large porches, and many lancet-arched windows and doors opening on the land (figs. 39, 40). The modesty of these houses amidst the street's grandeur was apparently guided by the rural environment that surrounded them and the character of their owners (see table 2). Such was the case of the residences of law partners Thomas Bolton and Moses Kelley, who settled next door to one another.

Bolton and Kelley, both natives of small towns in upstate New York, were classmates in high school and Harvard Law School and came to Cleveland together in 1836 to establish their law practice. Their move to this young, aspiring market proved a good one as the firm thrived during the financial dislocations of the late 1830s and early 1840s when land companies dissolved and banks went bankrupt. In 1848, once their practice and their personal fortunes were established, Bolton and Kelley were able to recapture the leisure of their native rural homes by buying seventy-two acres of the old Giddings farm in Euclid Street's borderland outside the city's center. The property was covered with orchards and fields and extended almost a mile along the south side between Sixty-ninth and Seventy-first streets. Bolton was the first to build, moving into his Gothic country house around 1849, and Kelley moved into an identical residence around 1852 (fig. 41). Like many borderlanders on this street, and elsewhere around the country, the two friends surrounded their handsome homes with a horticultural panoply of shrubs, fruit trees, and ornamental plants. Gardening became as much a retreat from the demands of work as the borderland was from the pressures of urban living. They separated their houses by a high orange hedge, a wheat field, and an apple orchard, and each landscaped his lawn with winding walks, shade trees, flower gardens, and a wooden picket fence along Euclid Street. Together they traveled three miles downtown to the courthouse each day and, also together, hired gardener Henry Tegrafe to tend the fields in their absence (fig. 42).[14]

While most of the Gothic landscapes on the Street were located in the rural area beyond Fifty-fifth Street, a few urban dwellers—notably Henry B.

Fig. 39. Alexander Sackett residence, 6700 Euclid Avenue, 1852 (Lake *Atlas,* 1874).

Fig. 40. Gothic country house, Ira Adams residence, 8903 Euclid Avenue, c. 1845 (Western Reserve Historical Society).

Fig. 41. Judge Bolton's country house, 7030 Euclid Avenue, 1848–49 (Western Reserve Historical Society).

Fig. 42. The Bolton farm (*Cleveland Plain Dealer,* by H. M. Albaugh, c. 1900).

Payne, Herman M. Chapin, and Henry C. Rouse—surrounded their English country houses, which were closer to the village center, with highly structured "naturalistic" landscapes. Senator Payne's cut-stone residence was among the finest and was considered to be at the leading edge of house design in the city when it was built in 1849 (fig. 43). But the romantic architectural idiom was not new to architect Charles W. Heard, as evidenced by his powerfully Gothic St. Paul's Episcopal Church at Euclid and Fourth streets (1848–51). Heard, who

Fig. 43. Senator Payne's Gothic cottage was acclaimed for its steep-pitched roof and wooden eaves, 2121 Euclid Avenue; C. W. Heard, architect, 1847–49 (courtesy Bolton Family, by G. M. Edmondson, 1935).

two years before had taken over Goldsmith's practice when his classicist mentor died, showed the breadth of his artistic talent in his design for the Payne residence. That design supported the view later voiced by architect Frank Barnum that the "refined and scholarly" work of the city's preeminent builder architects before midcentury could "easily put to shame most of the work that immediately followed it." Upon completion of the stately Payne residence, a reporter of Cleveland's *Daily True Democrat,* the public forum for the Democratic senator, extolled Heard's accomplishment as "the best . . . among the fine houses put up in this city for the last few years." The reporter went on to explain, "Its outer proportions and appearance are admirable; its style of architecture massive and enduring—its finish beautiful, and all interior arrangements, for elegance, comfort, convenience and health, equal to any residence we have ever seen."[15] Recognition for this and the St. Paul's commission secured Heard and partner Simeon C. Porter's position as the leading architectural and building firm in Cleveland and on Euclid Street in the 1850s.

Notwithstanding the acclaim and success of the architect's completed design, Senator Payne departed from the mainstream when he decided to build a Gothic villa. Considering that his neighbors Anson Smith, who built his house three years before, and George Worthington, who built three years later, both chose the conventional lines of the Greek Revival period, the senator's choice of style appeared quite bold. It made an important contribution to the street's role as a showcase for leading architectural design. Payne's choice of site, which was set back 300 feet from the street, was not surprising; it was next door to the family home of his wife Mary Perry Payne, where the couple had lived since their marriage in 1836.[16]

The commanding positions of the senator and his wife in the community assured that their residence would be noticed by all. Payne's stature and influential career as an attorney, railroad entrepreneur, and politician reinforced an emerging pattern of leadership and ambition among Euclid Street residents (fig. 44). While his wife, the daughter of Nathan Perry, had been raised on the street, Payne was among the day's young migrants to Cleveland who rose to riches by his own enterprise. He arrived here from the small town of Hamilton, New York, in 1833 and opened a law office with his Hamilton College classmate H. V. Willson. His successful practice representing business clients and his direct ties with industry enabled Payne to found the Cleveland & Columbus Railroad in the mid-1840s. His railroad interests then drew him into state politics, an environment which captured his attention. By the late 1840s Payne was well on his way to a distinguished career as the street's most highly placed elected official—an Ohio Senator (1849–51), Democratic Congressman (1874–85), and U.S. Senator (1885–91).

Payne's appearance and personal style departed from the stereotypical brash politician of his day; his clerical-cut coats and soft-spoken manner made him more like a preacher than a savvy public leader. But he succeeded in politics because of his drive and his skill in advancing the interests of local industry. This alliance was Payne's greatest asset, and ultimately his greatest liability. His

Fig. 44. The Honorable Henry B. Payne (Western Reserve Historical Society).

many years of public service ended with mixed reviews stemming from the allegation that his son, Oliver, treasurer of Rockefeller's Standard Oil Company, spent $100,000 to secure his father's U.S. Senate seat. While a Senate investigation of the charge was inconclusive, the "absence of satisfactory denials" led many to believe that loyal business interests had bought his seat and that Payne had capitalized on his ties with private industry to achieve his public ambitions. But among his friends in business and in politics—Jeptha Wade, Truman Handy, John Devereux, and U.S. President James Garfield—he was respected as a judicious man and trusted confidant.[17]

Following construction of Senator Payne's villa, the next Gothic house to be built on the street came eight years later in 1857, evidence of Payne's advanced taste relative to the conservative preferences of his neighbors. It was commissioned by one-time Cleveland mayor and meat-packing entrepreneur Herman M. Chapin, who built his residence two houses east of Fortieth Street (fig. 45). Chapin soon discovered that this pastoral location was too remote for easy travel downtown each day and sold his residence within two years to Marine Bank president Edwin B. Hale. Hale and his wife Susan raised their seven children here, married many of them off to the sons and daughters of other residents of the street, and lived in the residence until their deaths in 1891 and 1904, respectively (fig. 46).[18]

Gothic villa design did not really become popular on the Avenue until the 1870s, when it flourished in the more grandiose form of the high Victorian period. The style's cool reception from Euclid patrons contrasted with the its

Fig. 45. Herman Chapin's folly, 4307 Euclid Avenue, 1857; bought by Edwin B. Hale in 1859 (courtesy Mrs. J. Henry Melcher, by G. M. Edmondson, c. 1930s).

Fig. 46. The Hales' library (courtesy Mrs. J. Henry Melcher, by G. M. Edmondson, 1930s).

TABLE 3
The Italianate Villa, 1845–1865

Patron/Resident	Address	Building Date	Architect
Truman P. Handy	1829	1841–42	Unknown
Edwin C. Rouse	1208	c. 1840–45	Unknown
S. B. & F. J. Prentiss	1107	c. 1843–45	Unknown
Samuel Dodge	1621	1846	Unknown
Joseph Perkins	2719	1851–53	R. Upjohn
Jacob Perkins	2605	1851–53	R. Upjohn
Henry Gaylord	833	c. 1854–55	Unknown
Moses C. Younglove	1921	1857	Unknown
George E. Herrick	2435	1856–57	Unknown
Amasa Stone	1255	1858	Unknown
Edmund P. Morgan	1784	1858–59	Unknown
William B. Castle	1211	c. 1855–60	Unknown
James J. Tracy	1225	c. 1855–60	Unknown
Dr. Henry Kitchen	3134	c. 1855–60	Unknown
James F. Clark	1415	c. 1855–65	Unknown
Fayette Brown	3210	1865–66	Unknown
Stephen V. Harkness	6508	1866	S. C. Porter

endorsement elsewhere in the developing nation, especially in the northeast. By definition and origin, the Gothic villa fit in with the English cottage landscape theme that won favor around midcentury as part of Anglo-American enthusiasms in art and architecture. And while Euclid Street residents shared this preference of design for their street and grounds, they shunned the Gothic style for their residences, perhaps because most who built during this period defined success by the classicism in their upstate New York and New England hometowns. For them, a Gothic cottage belonged in the rural village and farm, not on an urbane city street; the classically inspired Italianate and Tuscan styles seemed more fitting.

The Italianate Villa, 1845–1865

The Italianate villa style preferred among the street's residents from the 1840s through 1860s respected the clear rectilinear forms of the Greek Revival while employing more freedom with exterior embellishments. It permitted a predictable format at one level and individual interpretation at another. The large number of houses built in this style was evidence that these characteristics appealed to the temperament of both the patrons and the architects (see table 3).

The earliest versions of the Italianate villa retained the three-bay facade and two-story massing of the Greek Revival, usually with the main entrance and hallway to one side. Bracketed eaves, molded window surrounds, polygonal bays, an entrance porch, and a flanking wing to one side were characteristic features (figs. 47, 48). Rooms of modest size, decorated with a modicum of wooden molding and marble decor, contrasted with the interior extravagance of residences built later on.

Fig. 47. Henry Gaylord residence, 833 Euclid Avenue, c. 1854–55 (Western Reserve Historical Society).

Fig. 48. Edwin C. and Mary M. Rouse residence, 1208 Euclid Avenue, c. 1840–45 (courtesy Julia Raymond, Western Reserve Historical Society, 1943).

Fig. 49. Truman P. and Harriet Handy residence, 1829 Euclid Avenue, 1841–42 (Western Reserve Historical Society, 1870s).

The style's evolution on the street presented two variations on the basic theme—the one a sophisticated version of the Italianate country villa, the other a full-bodied version of the Tuscan villa. The Italianate villa, also popularized by the pattern-book designs of Downing and his design partner Andrew Jackson Davis, introduced asymmetrical massing while retaining a fairly strict rectilinear presentation. Full play was given to round-arched windows and doors, prominent towers, and deep, airy verandas (figs. 49, 50). The finest examples were the residences built between 1851–53 for the brothers Joseph and Jacob Perkins west of Thirtieth Street (figs. 51, 52). Unlike nearly all their neighbors before them, the Perkins brothers went beyond Cleveland for their architect to the eminent professional of the day, Richard Upjohn of New York City. Upjohn's design for Joseph Perkins's residence was similar to others the architect was working on at the time, notably the Edward King house in Newport, Rhode Island (1845–47), the Seth Adams house in Providence, Rhode Island (1852–54), and the J. H. Birch house in Chicago, Illinois (1852–53). The common theme shared by these residences was the prominent second-story balcony hooded by an elaborate canopy.[19] The balcony was featured on Joseph's house, though without a canopy (fig. 53).

Once Upjohn had completed the drawings and sent them off to Perkins in Ohio, the client managed the execution, retaining the city's leading building and architectural firm of Heard & Porter to construct the architect's design. Joseph Perkins personally purchased the stone, brick, lumber, nails, glass, and window

Fig. 51. Jacob Perkins residence, 2605 Euclid Avenue, 1851–53 (Western Reserve Historical Society, 1890s).

Fig. 52. Joseph and Martha Steele Perkins residence, 2719 Euclid Avenue; Richard Upjohn, architect, 1851–53 (Western Reserve Historical Society, 1890s).

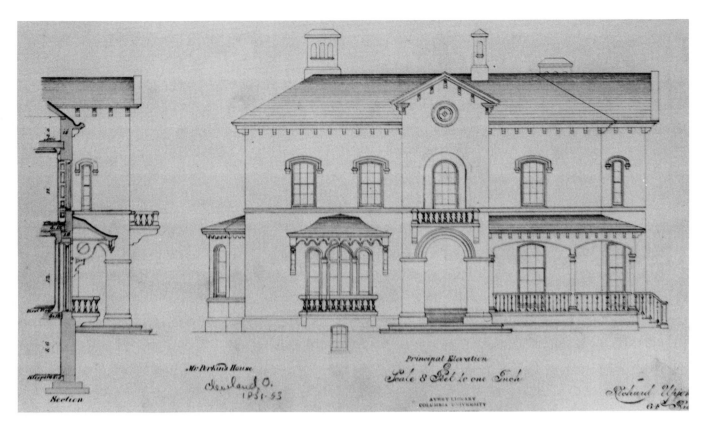

Fig. 53. Richard Upjohn's original rendering of Joseph Perkins house, 1851–53 (Avery Architectural and Fine Arts Library, Columbia University, New York City).

frames and negotiated the contracts for the stone mason and day laborers. Labor and materials cost Perkins $30,150, and Heard & Porter's services for the eighteenth-month construction job, from summer 1852 through winter 1853, were $17,430—at the time an extraordinary total of $47,580. Upon its completion, one local observer commented that the Perkins residence resembled "the comfortable country home of a family of wealth and taste in England"—just as Downing had envisioned and Upjohn had made possible through his exceptional talent.[20]

The residence fit well with the sophisticated pursuits of its occupants. Joseph and Martha Steele Perkins had purchased the Euclid Street lot and commissioned Upjohn prior to moving to Cleveland from Warren, Ohio, in 1852. Once here, they became active leaders in Cleveland charities and the women's temperance movement. Joseph, a son of the wealthy General Simon Perkins family of Warren, had graduated from Marietta College and worked in his father's railroad businesses before arriving in the city. He came to preside over the Bank of Commerce, a position he held for two decades (1852–72), and, with his brother Jacob, built the Cleveland & Mahoning Valley Railroad, which opened the plentiful Mahoning valley coal fields to the city's industrialists beginning in 1852. Perkins also had expansive civic interests and was a founder of the Western Reserve Historical Society and Lake View Cemetery, a long-time

trustee of Western Reserve College, a central figure in the Ohio Board of State Charities, and a participant in the country's jail system reforms. For her part, Martha Perkins led hundreds of women in the organization of the local Women's Christian Temperance Union in 1874. In her mission to abolish alcohol abuse, she went frequently to the River Street district in the Flats to counsel those in impoverished homes, sailors' saloons, and boarding houses—places quite different from her pleasant Euclid Street surroundings.[21] The Perkinses' refined external environment, while the more public, was in no way a barrier to their pious commitments to social and educational welfare.

House and grounds were only part of the enthusiasm for the design arts that residents of the street shared with their neighbors. Avenue families took as much pride and pleasure in the manner of life they led within their homes as they did in their public architecture. A variety of interior motifs played behind the reserved uniformity of exterior facades. The interior domain became as much a focus of the owners' and designers' attentions as the exterior. In the 1850s, a liberated enthusiasm for things sculptural in rooms and furnishings anticipated lavish post–Civil War taste. Rooms were decorated with deeply molded cornices and carved woodwork, not to mention the clutter of furniture and artifacts. Free from the constraints of classical orders, marble fireplaces displayed bold arched openings and stairways swept openly from one floor to the next—all characteristic of Italianate interior designs (figs. 54–56).

Fig. 55. A liberated enthusiasm for things sculptural in Italianate rooms and furnishings. Herrick residence (Western Reserve Historical Society).

Tuscan villa facades, a close cousin of the Italianate, adopted this high-relief look as an exterior hallmark. The residence was treated as one big sculptural piece; it was made of textured building materials and surmounted by magnificent rooftop embellishments of cast iron balustrades, cupolas, and gable pediments. The orchestrated use of different kinds of masonry became popular during this period of early romantic design, thanks in part to bounteous regional reserves of clay and sandstone available to Cleveland builders.[22] These malleable materials enabled the architect and builder to introduce intricate detailing into the Tuscan's otherwise strict symmetrical format.

Fig. 56. A variety of interior motifs played behind a reserved uniformity of exterior facades. Moses C. Younglove residence, 1921 Euclid Avenue, 1857–58 (Western Reserve Historical Society).

TABLE 4
The Tuscan Villa, 1855–1865

Patron/Resident	Address	Building Date	Architect
Henry Chisholm	653	1857–58	Unknown
Hinman Hurlbut	3233	1855–58	Heard & Porter
Zenas Kent (Samuel L. Mather)	1369	1858	Thomas & Sons
William Bingham, Sr.	2843	1858	Unknown
Franklyn T. Backus	2921	1858	Unknown
Joseph G. Hussey	3411	1859–60	Unknown
L. J. Pier	6407	c. 1855–60	Unknown
Rollin C. White	6619	c. 1865	Unknown
George S. Russell	7003	1863–65	Unknown
Leroy Chadwick	8204	c. 1860–65	Unknown
Randall Wade	3903	1865–66	Unknown
Jeptha Wade	3917	1865–66	Unknown

The residences of industrialist Henry Chisholm, banker Hinman Hurlbut, investor Zenas Kent, merchant William Bingham, Sr., and attorney Franklyn T. Backus were superb renditions of refined Tuscan villa design (figs. 57–59). Charles Heard and Simeon Porter were likely responsible for much of this work, although they can be attributed with the design of only a few houses (see table 4). Heard's design for the residence of Hinman Hurlbut, as well as those for James Mason and Charles Hickox, prompted the *Leader* to announce that "Cleveland is emphatically a city of beautiful residences. . . . The designs of [these houses] are beautiful indeed and will add greatly to the already splendid appearance of that part of the city."[23] The Hurlbut house, distinctive for its unusual facade, was sheathed with decorative tiles applied with a mastic cement. According to the *Leader*, it cost an estimated $13,000, a price tag about ten times greater than the average cost of a new house in Cleveland at the time (fig. 60).

The artistic appearance of Hurlbut's residence at the northwest corner of Thirty-third Street spoke to both the architects' ambitions and the patron's expensive taste. The prosperous banker was lionized for his private art collection, as he was for his horticultural talents. His magnificent art pieces, acquired over years of extensive travel in the U.S. and abroad, became a nucleus of the Cleveland Museum of Art's permanent collection, when Hurlbut willed them to the city for the establishment of a public art gallery after his death in 1896.[24]

His decorative Euclid Avenue garden, a proclamation of his commitment to his property, with its well-groomed flower beds and Greek marble statuary, created a pictorial frame around Heard & Porter's elegant design. The ornamental plants and fruit trees gave Hurlbut a pleasurable outlet from the urgent claims of his business. Like many businessmen of his day and stature, he enjoyed the quiet leisure of gardening, and the fruits of his labor were a source of

Fig. 57. William and Elizabeth Bingham, Sr., residence, 2843 Euclid Avenue, 1858 (Western Reserve Historical Society).

Fig. 58. *Below left.* Henry and Jean Chisholm residence, 653 Euclid Avenue. Built by Nelson Monroe in 1857–58, "adding to the grand appearance of that noble avenue"; bought by Chisholm for $29,025 in 1863 (Western Reserve Historical Society, 1870s).

Fig. 59. *Below right.* Intricate details dressed up the Tuscan Villa's strict symmetrical facade. Timothy and Eliza Otis Crocker residence, 3111 Euclid Avenue, 1870 (Western Reserve Historical Society).

Fig. 60. Hinman Hurlbut residence, 3233 Euclid Avenue; Heard and Porter, architects, 1855–58 (Western Reserve Historical Society, by G. M. Edmondson, c. 1900s).

Fig. 61. *Opposite.* Samuel L. and Elizabeth Gwinn Mather residence, 1369 Euclid Avenue. Built by Zenas Kent; Thomas & Sons, architects, 1858 (Western Reserve Historical Society).

enormous pride. When Hurlbut took his prize grapes to the Ohio state fair in 1859, they were acclaimed as some "of the finest ever seen," each grape judged to be a "masterpiece of ripe luscious fruit."[25]

The grounds of the Samuel L. Mathers, about a mile west from the Hurlbut property, did not receive such care and attention from the owner, but the gardens and residence were a handsome contribution to the street's elegance after midcentury. The house had been built in 1858 for real estate investor Zenas Kent, serving as the home of the Mather family for sixty-four years thereafter. Its design was a bellwether in the street's development, as it introduced a romantic stylism and mechanical excellence that became standard fare. This sandstone Tuscan villa was designed by the New York architectural firm of Thomas and Sons, and built by William McIntosh, an Irish immigrant who built many houses in Cleveland around midcentury (fig. 61). Its Corinthian-columned entrance porch and Doric-styled rooftop observatory, according to one observer, commanded "a view of the Lake and entire city and the country for miles in

every direction." The interior was just as elegant, featuring a large reception hall, parlor, dining room, bedroom, and bath on the first floor, and the kitchen, laundry, and servants' quarters in a rear wing. Elizabethan-style carved pine trimmed the hallway doors, ceiling panels, and cornice brackets. The sweeping

Fig. 62. Samuel L. Mather, the city's leading iron ore entrepreneur (Western Reserve Historical Society, by James F. Ryder, c. 1870s).

staircase leading to the second-floor bedrooms and roof-top cupola opened up the house's circulation flow and improved "upon the old fashion of boxing up stair-cases," according to the *Leader.* Each room was fitted with such modern comforts as piped hot and cold water and central heating from the basement furnace.[26]

One of the street's most active entrepreneurs, Samuel L. Mather bought the house at the close of the Civil War, seven years after it was built by Kent (fig. 62). The senior Mather moved to Euclid Avenue in 1865 from his nearby Superior Avenue home with his wife Elizabeth and children Samuel, Katharine, and William. He had come to Cleveland more than two decades before, in 1843, to manage his father's 3,000 acres of Western Reserve land, and early on he entered the iron-ore industry. Mather established the Cleveland Iron Mining Company in 1852, the first in the city to take up the business.[27] He brought his sons into the company when they were still teenagers and remained their associate and companion throughout their lives. Son Samuel lived in his parents' home until he married Flora Stone at age thirty and moved in with Flora's parents, the Amasa Stones, three doors down the street. Son William stayed on with his mother after his father's death in 1890 and maintained the family residence for his city house until 1909, when it was acquired and razed by the Higbee Company.

The Mather residence, as a family landmark of sorts, symbolized a major period in the development of the street, whose number of houses more than doubled between 1851 and 1866—the period during which the house was built

and then acquired by the Mathers. Most of the new residences were also designed in the Tuscan villa genre, each one distinguished from the other by various stone blockings, towers, cupolas, and polygonal bays. By far the most opulent of these, which fully garnered the craftsmen's resources, was the residence built for Mather's in-law Amasa Stone in 1858 (fig. 63).

Railroad entrepreneur Amasa Stone, Jr., a native of Worcester, Massachusetts, chose in 1858 to have his Italian-style villa built on the most urban

Fig. 63. Amasa and Julia Stone residence, 1255 Euclid Avenue, 1858 (Western Reserve Historical Society).

stretch of the Avenue's residential community. He chose an architectural idiom fully influenced by the European tastes that his neighbors sought in the boulevarded street plan after midcentury. An innovator in all respects, Stone was among the earliest architectural patrons on the Avenue to dismiss all American tendencies—he and his fellow patrons now seeking to emulate highly regarded Continental models. Stone's house, inside and out, also reflected the patron's background as a carpenter, contractor, and bridge builder. At the time his house was designed and built, Stone was forty years old, at the peak of his career and one of the most successful railroad builders in the country. His house seemed to reflect his penchant for highly complex creations. It represented the state-of-the-art in architectural design, from its highly stylized romantic details to its structural system and mechanical devices. The 8,500-square-foot residence took over 700,000 bricks to construct and had 23-inch-thick walls. An eight-inch hollow space in the outside walls insulated rooms from wide temperature swings, a technique the *Leader* recommended as "a great improvement in the construction of brick exterior walls." The roofs were sheathed with painted tin and the basement was constructed of stone and brick—both intended as fireproof measures to protect against the disasters that destroyed so many American houses during the nineteenth century.[28]

The interior, praised by a *Leader* reporter who visited the house upon its completion, was centered around a grand mahogany hallway with an open staircase to the second-floor bedrooms. The family's private parlor, nursery, and a "bathing-room" were to one side of the hall, with a public reception room, library, and dining room to the other. The kitchen and pantry, housed in the rear wing, were "conveniently fitted up" with piped water and gas. All the main rooms were graced by elegant paneled ceilings and molded cornices, rosewood or oak doors, and fireplace mantels sculpted out of "the very finest Vermont statuary." Stone's personal library, designed to accommodate his business activities, was noted for the fireproof recess where his desk, bookcase, and safe stood. Each room was piped with running water, and the house was centrally heated by the basement furnace, encased in a masonry fortress to inhibit explosions. A "model" laundry and coal room were also located in the basement.

Upon completion, the Stone residence was hailed for its "novel and imposing" presence. It outshined all other Italianate residences along the street, such as the houses of neighbors James J. Tracy and James F. Clark (figs. 64–68). Amasa Stone himself cut no less a "novel and imposing" figure in the community (fig. 69). As a hard-nosed businessman he had few equals; yet a sequence of tragedies shadowed his life. Three particular events ultimately brought him to ruin. The first occurred in 1865, when his only son, Adelbert, drowned in the Connecticut River while swimming with his schoolmates.[29] Stone never recovered from the grief he suffered from this death. Then in 1876 an iron truss bridge which Stone had designed and built over the Ashtabula Gorge—a design which violated his engineer's advice—collapsed in a sixty-mile-per-hour windstorm while a ten-car train was traveling over the main arch. Only eight of the 159 passengers survived the accident. Stone was subjected to an investigation

Fig. 64. James J. Tracy residence, 1225 Euclid Avenue, c. 1855–60 (Western Reserve Historical Society).

Fig. 65. Dr. Henry Kitchen residence, 3134 Euclid Avenue, c. 1855–60 *(Cleveland Plain Dealer)*.

Fig. 66. James F. Clark residence, 1415 Euclid Avenue, c. 1855–65 (Western Reserve Historical Society).

Fig. 67. *Below left.* An Italianate villa. Unidentified house; Levi T. Scofield, architect (Western Reserve Historical Society).

Fig. 68. *Below right.* Edmund P. Morgan residence, 1784 Euclid Avenue, 1859 (Western Reserve Historical Society).

by the state, which held its hearing in his personal library because he was "too ill" to leave his home. The state maintained that Stone's Lake Shore & Michigan Southern Railroad had not regularly inspected the precarious bridge, and the court ordered the railroad to pay damages of $600,000. Stone was unable to shake his guilt over the disaster. He fled to Europe for a brief respite. Then, in 1883, the nationwide financial panic bankrupted three iron and steel companies in which he held a controlling interest. His physical and spiritual constitutions were now completely broken. He ended his misery that year by shooting himself through the heart.[30]

Upon his death, friends and associates, in testimonials in the local papers and personal letters, affectionately recounted the contributions he had made to the city and the railroad industry. One such tribute came many years later, in 1902, in a simple note from prominent Cleveland photographer James F. Ryder to Stone's younger daughter, Flora Stone Mather. Ryder captured the generous spirit that underlay Stone's stern and controversial manner. He wrote:

> A man to whom your father had been kind in a business matter, desired to do something to mark his gratitude [and] commissioned me to procure a marble bust portrait. This work was to be done without your Father's knowledge and placed in the family home as a pleasant surprise. . . . I invited Mr. Stone by letter to an appointment for sitting for photographs without naming the purpose for which they were to be used. . . . As he was starting to leave I said it was possible I might wish to repeat the sittings and if so would he give me another chance. He said "Yes, Ryder, I would do anything you would ask. . . . Remember this," and went his way. I was a younger man then, and construed his meaning to be a thought that I was, in my business, carrying a heavy load, and was I liable to want a helping hand. I thanked him most earnestly in my heart and have never forgotten. . . . It was a help to me more than he understood.

Ryder's remembrance reflected the traits in Stone that were carried on in the community work of his two daughters, Clara Stone Hay and Flora Stone Mather. Clara lived next door to her parents' residence with her husband, John Hay, in the house Stone built for them. Flora and Samuel Mather lived in the Stone house until Flora's death in 1909. The family home was razed that year to make way for Higbee's department store.[31]

While Amasa Stone chose to build on Euclid's central parade ground, his friend and business associate Jeptha Wade chose instead to build on its borderland. In 1866 Wade, who built his prosperity as the preeminent innovator of the nation's telegraph network, created adjoining estates for himself and his son, Randall, at Fortieth Street (fig. 70). Wade had been familiar with Cleveland since 1850, when he brought the telegraph to the city. In 1866 he moved his family to town from Columbus, choosing Euclid Avenue as the locale from which he and his family would "not wish to move." Father and son, both artists, jointly planned and built their residences, each at a cost of $200,000. They chose the prevailing Italianate manner for the designs—the senior Wade's a conventional Italianate villa and Randall's a Tuscan country villa—and surrounded them by vast sculptured landscapes in keeping with the Downing ethos. The grounds, professionally laid out by the Wades' gardener, a Mr. Graham, displayed a luxurious array of statuary, shade trees, a pear orchard, a Malaga grape arbor—Jeptha Wade's hobby—stone walkways, and a frontyard pond with a spray fountain and stocked fish.[32]

While the senior Wade paid the bills, Randall took responsibility for managing the construction of the houses, making progress reports by letter and telegram to his father, who was traveling throughout the country on business. Randall arranged for a sandstone quarry to be opened near Akron to supply

the stone and worked directly with the builder Kirby, the frescoer, the stair-builder, painters, and more than a dozen carpenters. His management clearly had its rewards, as it did its trials. During the final weeks of construction some of the workmen pressured him to raise their wages. Infuriated, he wrote his father, "I find this system of paying a profit on each man leads to a system of robbery—All boss painters are getting rich because they are all dishonest—We have been swindled probably less than many others but I have stopped it." The laborers' demands were strengthened by the fact that they were also working on Franklyn Alcott's and Ralph Harman's Euclid Avenue houses and making up to a-dollar-a-day more than on the Wade job. But Randall held firm, discharged the "boss" contractor, and replaced him with a new man who finished out the job.

The resulting lavish interiors—parlors, drawing and reception rooms, and hallways—were as much a product of the Wades' artistic vision as they were of architect and craftsmen. The customized spaces became a showcase for the Wade family's exquisite art pieces acquired in world travels. The rooms and halls were dressed with gilt molding and elaborate frescoes (fig. 71). The third-floor ballroom of Jeptha's house doubled as his private picture gallery. And

Fig. 70. The Randall and Jeptha H. Wade estate, 3903 and 3917 Euclid Avenue, 1865–66 (Lake Atlas, 1874).

Fig. 71. The grand music room, Randall and Anna Wade residence (Western Reserve Historical Society).

masterpiece paintings by Reynolds, Turner, Renoir, and Monet lined the walls of the great hall and music room in Randall's house. His dining room was custom designed for the carpet, sideboard, gilded chairs and tables, gold mirrors, and chandelier. It was the first room completed, and he was so pleased with the effect that he exclaimed to his father, it "goes off in good style, *very nice.*"[33] All furniture and carpets were personally selected by the Wades from the finest New York houses and designers, notably Bruner and Moore.

Beyond this decorative finery, each residence incorporated current advances in central steam heating, running water, and gas fixtures. Bathrooms were built for each bedroom; large closets had built-in drawers; and a temperature-controlled wine cellar was built in Jeptha's basement. The Wade families moved into their newly completed residences in October 1866. Randall, flushed by the fruits of his family's affluence, wrote his ailing father in New York, "*Elegance above, beneath, and all around. We ponder = can it be true that its all ours and permanent, or is it a fairy dream?*"[34]

Thirty-one-year-old Randall had not always known such comfort; only in the last ten years did his father become a wealthy man, and money was neither plentiful nor certain before then. Fifty-five when he built his Euclid Avenue estate, Jeptha had been the youngest child of a large, impoverished, fatherless household in upstate New York. Forced to support himself at an early age, he had worked as a shoemaker, carpenter, mechanic, and portrait painter over the years. Poor health moved him from one occupation to another, but his talents and perseverance enabled him always to succeed. Such was his fate and fortitude when in the mid-1840s he happened upon a job building a telegraph line. The telegraph industry was young and few knew anything about it. Wade promoted this industry for its wonderful possibilities. He took risks when others, including his own Western Union board, thought him foolish; he triumphed while others thought the task impossible.[35]

Wade's business success was evidence of his mechanical and financial acumen, as it was of his anxious pursuit in all he did. Upon retiring from the presidency of Western Union the year after his Cleveland residence was completed, Wade convalesced for a time and then involved himself in the affairs of the major railroads headquartered in Cleveland, not to mention gardening, world travel, and civic activities. Jeptha's strong character and wide-ranging commitments positioned the Wades as one of the richest and most influential families in the city in the second half of the nineteenth century. He and his wife Sue carried on a grand lifestyle in their Euclid Avenue residence, welcoming into their home such diverse people as President Ulysses S. Grant, a personal friend, and homeless orphans whom Sue and Jeptha took in as their own.[36] Jeptha's most notable gift to Cleveland was eighty-two-acre Wade Park, located at the far eastern end of the Avenue. He amassed and landscaped this property at a cost of one million dollars before giving it to the city. It later became the nucleus of University Circle and the terminus of the Euclid Avenue neighborhood.

Jeptha Wade was an exceptionally talented and complicated personality. His aptitude for artistic expression—portrait painting, building and playing musical instruments—and his avid interest in occult spiritualism reflected a sensitive, less strictly material dimension of his mind. So vulnerable were his sensitivities that in 1874 he paid $1,500 to St. Paul's Church, which stood across the street from his house, to stop tolling its bells. The piercing bells never rang until after his death in 1890. His many encounters with spirits, especially that of his first wife Rebecca, led him to fear that his own spirit would be "earthbound and trapped in his house." Wade was equally disturbed by the growing commercial presence on the Avenue and feared that his home would be entrapped by these forces. He therefore stipulated in his will that his house was to be razed within a month of his death.[37] His wish was granted, and in 1890 newly widowed Sue Wade moved next door to live with her daughter-in-law Anna and her grandchildren; her son Randall had died of pneumonia in 1876, having lived only ten years in his Euclid Avenue residence. Randall's villa became the surviving Wade homestead, surrounded by the beautifully landscaped grounds and a tall cast-iron fence—a country estate within the city.

After Randall's death, his son, Jeptha Homer Wade II, had succeeded him as master of the house and family. Nineteen years old at the time, the young Homer became a son to his grandfather and an intimate associate in business and civic affairs. An executive in forty-five companies and principal benefactor of the Cleveland Museum of Art, Homer carried on the family traditions of professional diversity and patronage of the arts. He continued to live in the Avenue residence with his own family, having married his childhood sweetheart Ellen (Nellie) Garretson in 1878, daughter of Avenue residents Hiram and Ellen Garretson. Like his parents before him, and many of his neighbors, his household clan spanned three generations of family—he and Nellie, their three children, and their widowed mothers Anna Wade and Ellen Garretson.

Homer enlarged the house over the years to accommodate the extended family's needs. A music room and piazza were built around 1890 and designed by Cleveland architects Coburn & Barnum, and a stable, designed by Hubbell and Benes, was built at the rear of the property in 1901. The Wade family vacated the residence after Homer's death in 1926, and occasionally reopened it for public art exhibitions in the great hall and ballroom. Within eight years, however, tax assessments for the house and land became so burdensome that the property was sold and razed in 1934.[38]

The street on which Wade chose to build his estate in 1866 was the finest residential avenue in Cleveland at that time, the home of many of the most opulent residences and leaders in the city. But even then, had the Euclid Avenue story ended in 1866, it would not have been worthy of grand avenue fame. That coveted status was still being shaped, rising to its heyday in the postwar decades.

Fig. 72. One of the most beautiful residential streets in America. Looking east from Fourteenth Street (Western Reserve Historical Society, 1880s).

FOUR

The Great Age of the Grand Avenue

The 1893 edition of Baedeker's guide to the continental United States recommended Euclid Avenue as "one of the most beautiful residence-streets in America."[1] No other street in this 500-page traveler's bible had such an honor bestowed on it. Baedeker based its praise on the sheer visual impact of the residences and the tree-lined avenue as a whole. Euclid Avenue was one among a few urban streets in the country whose property owners respected three basic design features over a fifty-year period, features which produced the character that made the Avenue famous (fig. 72). One of these was the continuous, four-mile panorama of residences, which began at Public Square and over the years moved progressively eastward along the Avenue toward Wade Park. Another characteristic was the open landscape of expansive grounds, one residence after the other, which created a parklike vista of country houses. And a third feature was the quality and variety in the design of the residences, which produced a living museum of nineteenth- and early twentieth-century architectural styles.

John Fiske, internationally acclaimed scholar, best captured the Avenue's special qualities in a lecture to the Royal Institution of Great Britain in June 1879. He observed that "in Cleveland . . . there is a street some five or six miles in length and five hundred feet in width, bordered on each side with a double row of arching trees, and with handsome stone houses, of sufficient variety and freedom in architectural design, standing at intervals of from one to two hundred feet" along the entire length of the street. "The effect," he concluded, "was very noble indeed. The vistas remind one of the nave and aisles of a huge cathedral" (fig. 73).[2] Fiske's measurements were actually grander than the Avenue's—eighty feet wide rather than 500 feet—but his conclusions were quite valid. His speech, entitled "American Political Ideas," described how the value and development of property affected political and social systems. Euclid Avenue exemplified, for Fiske, the New England village ideal, wherein abundant land and private ownership created a more fluid political and social structure than the feudal system in England. Artemus Ward and Mark Twain, among others, had no difficulty arguing that Euclid Avenue was not the country's best example of an open social system, but Fiske, undaunted by contrary evidence, serenely viewed it as representing the epitome of the system's success in America.

Most of the houses which gave notice to this architectural showcase were built during the great age between 1850 and 1910, while Cleveland was being transformed by tremendous industrial growth. The city's grand avenue was built by the new money of capitalists who shaped Cleveland into a midwestern industrial trade center. The elegant residences can be seen as proud statements of their owners' individual involvement in the city's economic growth, in many cases becoming personal portraits of economic and social stature. Undoubtedly, more than a few were pretentious, a reflection of the patrons' aspirations. But if the architecture was bold and flamboyant, it was no more so than the patron's business style. If rooms were big and ceilings high, they were no less so than the occupants' realized ambitions.

The Eastward Procession, 1850–1910

The residential development of the street began around Public Square in the 1820s, moving eastward toward Ninetieth Street and Wade Park as the century matured. This procession generally followed major street improvements over time and the extension of sewer and water lines. The chronology is not exact, however. More than a few individuals built their residences "way out," east of the corporation limits, beyond the core of the residential area and in advance of public improvements. Also, "infill" development occurred frequently throughout the nineteenth and early twentieth centuries when residents built as close to the Square as the availability of property permitted. The reason for this was that the premier residential area remained west of Fifty-fifth Street, even though most of the vacant house lots after 1870 were east of Fifty-fifth Street.

Most early Euclid Avenue houses were built within a ten-minute walk of Public Square. Among the few residents who built east of the village boundary at Fourteenth Street before 1840 were Nathan Perry and Peter Weddell. Even fewer found their way into the wilderness beyond Weddell's vast holdings around Thirtieth Street. An eastward shift gradually occurred over the decades. Two-thirds of the twenty-three houses built between 1845 and 1860 were located between Twelfth and Thirtieth streets, residents lured by the newly widened and wood-planked roadway.[3] One could now have a country house and still enjoy most of the city services available to their downtown counterparts (see table 5).

Thanks to the grading and widening of the Avenue to Fortieth Street in 1860, the building of the Fortieth Street sewer in 1866, and the laying of a new water main from Twenty-first to Fifty-fifth streets in 1867, about half of the stately residences built in the late 1850s and 1860s were located beyond Thirtieth Street. The other half were located within the established boundaries between Ninth and Twenty-first streets. The six-year period 1860–66 witnessed the building of ten houses each year, the residential community solidifying its shape and scale during this time (see table 6).

Fig. 73. *Opposite.* "The nave and aisles of a huge cathedral." Looking east from Twelfth Street (Western Reserve Historical Society, 1870s).

TABLE 5
Residential Building, 1840–1860

Patron/Resident	Address	Building Date
Anson Smith	1167	1840–42
Truman P. Handy	1829	1841–42
Samuel Dodge	1621	1846
Henry B. Payne	2121	1849
George Worthington	3635	1852
Stillman Witt	1115	c. 1851–52
Jacob Perkins	2605	1851–53
William J. Boardman	1303	1856
Zenas Kent (Samuel L. Mather)	1369	1858
Franklyn T. Backus	2921	1858
William Bingham, Sr.	2843	1858
Amasa Stone	1255	1858
Charles H. Hickox	2727	1855–59

The eastern end of the Avenue to about Eightieth Street was opened up to new development during the 1870s and 1880s by the extension of sewer and water lines beyond Fifty-fifth Street in 1870–71 (fig. 74).[4] Even so, at least one-third of the residents who built during this time located in the central stretch of the Avenue west of Fifty-fifth Street. The Cleveland & Pittsburgh Railroad that crossed the Avenue at Fifty-fifth was an impediment to the flow of eastward development. The railbed had been laid in 1850, long before the residential district had moved that far east. But the iron turntable in the middle of the intersection, the car barns and depot to the side, the loud harness bells,

TABLE 6
Residential Building, 1860–1870

Patron/Resident	Address	Building Date
Herman M. Chapin	4307	1857
Hinman Hurlbut	3233	1855–58
Fayette Brown	3210	1865–66
Anson Stager	3813	1866
Randall & Jeptha Wade	3903/3917	1866
George A. Garretson	3716	c. 1865–67
Charles S. Bissell	4611	1866–67
John D. Rockefeller	3920	1866–68
Harry E. Myer	2263	c. 1866–70
Samuel Williamson	3609	c. 1865–70
Timothy Crocker	3111	1870
Charles A. Otis, Sr.	3133	1868–72

sooty debris, and commercial blocks that surrounded this corner were nuisances to be avoided; they were incompatible with the developing neighborhood and remained so until the late 1880s (fig. 75).

Fig. 74. Millionaires' Row. Looking west from Thirtieth Street (Cleveland Public Library, 1880).

By the early 1890s, however, a number of prominent Clevelanders had crossed the railroad line and built spectacular residences between Fifty-fifth and Ninetieth streets (see table 7). Most who built in this eastern district did so because they were limited in their choice of Avenue sites. The large tracts of property on the north side between Twenty-first and Fifty-fifth streets were by this time either spoken for by others or very expensive. If a family wanted to establish their residence on the grand avenue, their choice was to buy a smaller tract on the south side in the established residential district or a larger tract in the area east of Fifty-fifth Street where they could lay out a conventional large estate. The community of families who built beyond the Fifty-fifth Street rail line and those who lived along the traditional Millionaires' Row extended the geographic boundaries of the original Euclid Avenue neighborhood to the far eastern edges. The length between Fifty-fifth and Ninetieth streets had grown

TABLE 7

Residential Building, 1875–1900

Patron/Resident	Address	Building Date
Liberty E. Holden	7809	1875
Joseph W. Britton	7817	1875
David Z. Norton	7503	1884–85
Morris A. Bradley	7217	1886
George H. Worthington	6603	1888
William J. Morgan	8615	1889–90
Worcester R. Warner	7720	1891–92
John L. Severance	8811	1891–92
Samuel F. Haserot	7224	1892–93
Arnold C. Saunders	7407	1892–94
Henry Hatch	8415	1892–94
Dan R. Hanna	7404	1895
Mary L. Severance	8821	1899–1900

from a virtual wilderness in 1877 to a neighborhood of forty houses by 1886, and 122 residences by 1896 (fig. 76).

The entire length of Euclid Avenue reached its zenith as a showcase for architecturally grandiose residences in the late 1890s, when nearly 260 houses lined the four-mile processional between Ninth and Ninetieth streets. By the first decade of the twentieth century, the continuity that was the principal theme in the design and development of this residential street would be challenged by contrary forces. Irreversible changes would be set in motion to bring the Avenue's great age to a close within fifteen years.

The Urban Landscape

A carriage ride or stroll along Euclid Avenue during its great age was on every visitor's list of things to do during a stay in Cleveland. The Avenue was a spectacle to behold for visitors and residents alike. The most striking impression was the grandeur and obvious expense of the houses and lawns. The residential grounds on the Avenue's north side, and in a few sections on the south, were closer in overall presentation and plan to the country estates of Great Britain and France than to such American enclaves of wealth as those of Philadelphia's Rittenhouse Square, Boston's Back Bay, or New York's Fifth Avenue. Most of the streetscape on the south side, however, resembled the denser urban patterns of the Avenue's eastern counterparts (figs. 77, 78).

The park-like character of Euclid Avenue even contrasted with Cleveland as a whole. The American correspondent for the *London Standard* was confused by Cleveland's nickname of the Forest City, as he could find in his 1865 visit no "trace of forest for miles around." For him, the term "Forest City" made no sense, though "Empire City" did make sense for New York and the "Grain City" for Chicago. He decided that the name derived not from the city overall but from "the shady avenues and neat pleasure grounds" along Euclid Avenue

Fig. 75. The Cleveland and Pittsburgh Railroad at Fifty-fifth Street impeded the grand avenue's development (Western Reserve Historical Society, 1890).

Fig. 76. The eastern end of the Euclid Avenue neighborhood, around Eighty-sixth Street (Cleveland Public Library, c. 1900).

Fig. 77. The country estates on the north side, showing the residences of Charles W. Bingham, no. 2445; Harry Devereux, no. 2525; Samuel Mather, no. 2605; and Leonard Hanna, no. 2717 (Western Reserve Historical Society, by I. T. Frary, c. 1900).

and Prospect Street, which he believed set Cleveland apart from other American cities. The origin of the Forest City name is obscure. It was attributed to William Case, who as mayor in 1850–51 encouraged the planting of shade and fruit trees along Cleveland's principal streets, including Euclid Avenue.[5] The Avenue's property owners avidly sustained the tree-planting tradition. Like other American villagers and urban businessmen at midcentury, they apparently sought to create a quiet, countrified environment inside the city. They also fancied that the trees might improve drainage on the street.

The street's pastoral landscape emerged not just from this linear row of trees. The early settlement habits of Perry, Weddell, Dodge, and Sterling in the 1820s and 1830s were actually more influential. The broad expanses of their vast holdings were in character with a country road surrounded by a virtual wilderness; the countrified scenery of their properties were quite natural creations on this Avenue. Those residents who built here in the early decades of the century, and those who amassed farms and garden estates beyond Thirtieth Street around midcentury, actually were located in the country. It was the intent of such people as Thomas Bolton, in 1850, and Jeptha Wade, in 1866, to live on Euclid's borderland, beyond the reach of the city's mercantile center.

As John Stilgoe has portrayed in his survey of the American borderland, a bucolic location in the city's outskirts freed urbanites for a leisurely, casual pace of life compatible with the landscape. Borderland districts across the country, Stilgoe writes, pictured open expanses "where houses are so far apart that even in winter they cast shadows only on their own lots . . . houselot size makes continual casual conversation between neighbors difficult."[6] This was the life that many Avenue patrons enjoyed, contrary to most grand avenue settlers elsewhere in North America. These wealthy Clevelanders, many of them natives of rural villages, established a precedent for the Avenue's countrified development for the rest of the century. Euclid Avenue had the added feature of the rolling ridge upon which to site a house.

The set-back convention, distancing one's residence from the street by a generous 100 to 300 feet of rolling lawn, was a serious matter for those who built on the Avenue. A few observers wondered if Euclid Avenue residents aspired to a European tradition by copying the British and French practice. The humorist Artemus Ward suspected that the depth of the Avenue set-backs was artfully measured to pronounce "the length of the owner's pedigree." A case in point, Ward mockingly noted, was "one resident who discovered the other day that

Fig. 78. The dense urban pattern on the south side of the street, showing the residence of M. P. Ranney, no. 2734 (Western Reserve Historical Society, 1880s).

his maternal grandfather, six times removed, was associate master-of-the-mews in the household of the third Duke of Gillyflower" and was preparing to move his house back fifty feet. The design of the grounds and houses on the Avenue, in Ward's view, were "calculated to strike awe to the plebeian heart."[7] This observation is hard to quarrel with, for the size of most Euclid Avenue houses exceeded all others in the city. Even though many housed two and three generations and up to ten or more family members, who frequently entertained out-of-town guests for long stays, only the very affluent could afford the great size of the rooms in these grandiose homes.

One could chart Cleveland's increasing prosperity by the increasing bulk of the residences on the Avenue. Those built in the 1840s and 1850s rose to two-and-a-half stories and enveloped 3,500 to 5,000 square feet of living space, compared to those on adjacent side streets that enclosed up to 1,000 and 2,000 square feet under two stories. By the late 1850s, and well into the 1870s, most of the Avenue's houses had grown up to three stories, many with soaring towers and turrets, and were as large as Amasa Stone's 6,500-square-foot residence (1858) or Anson Stager's 10,000-square-foot manse (1866). In the decades following, the houses of Samuel Andrews (1882–85), Sylvester T. Everett (1883–87), Charles F. Brush (1887–88), and Samuel Mather (1907–9) were among the largest, housing 17,000 to 50,000 square feet in three floors of private rooms, public halls, and grand stairways. Meanwhile, their neighbors on Prospect Street were building houses one-fifth that size.

The expansive grounds, the vast houses, the attention to the street's landscaping—one has to ask why Avenue residents over more than five decades devoted themselves so consistently to the creation of these estates and their overall panorama. Why did the early pattern of large property holdings persist? It prevailed because of patrons' intent to preserve it. If they had not, had a denser urban pattern been introduced in Euclid's development, it would certainly have been more in keeping with the grand avenues of New York, Boston, New Haven, Charleston, and other eastern cities, which these Clevelanders had undoubtedly seen.

The vision that took shape on Euclid Avenue, first voiced by residents as early as 1855, was that of a European "garden, boulevard, or promenade." It was to be "a continuous avenue of shade running like the Boulevards of Brussels, . . . a drive and a promenade of about 5 miles." This explicit form and function, a broad tree-lined processional, was quite sophisticated for its day. It predated by more than a decade the completion of the great scheme fabricated for Paris by Napoleon III and Baron Haussmann. Haussmann's boulevard plan for Paris, which had just gotten underway in 1852 and would not be completed until 1870, firmly set the stage for both European and American grand avenues. Even though most European cities had developed a central promenade by the mid-nineteenth century—the Unter den Linden in Berlin, Regent's Street in London, Nevsky Prospekt in St. Petersburg were among the finest—most paled by comparison to the grand avenue Haussmann created in the Champs Elysées. In this spirit, a decade later in the mid-1860s and again in 1874, Avenue residents sustained the dream of a boulevard for Cleveland, to "make Euclid avenue the finest thoroughfare in the world."[8] The strongest push by private citizens to make the Avenue the central spine of a city-sponsored boulevard scheme occurred in the mid-1890s, but it too ultimately failed. At no time was the idea of a European boulevard adopted as a formal policy of Cleveland's public officials. Rather, the park-like setting was created by the coordinated actions of residents. The grandeur of Euclid Avenue certainly enhanced Cleveland's reputation, just as it did that of its residents. This is apparently why the vision triumphed. It helped to glorify the names of its families over many generations to come as unmistakable symbols of prosperity and cultural leadership.

For most, these extraordinary houses, crafted out of tons of masonry, were designed and built to last. As it is, the legacy of these residences and the families who built them has endured for decades beyond the physical life of the grand avenue and the houses themselves. Such men as Jeptha Wade, Charles Hickox, Louis C. Severance, Samuel Mather, and Charles Brush built their modern fortunes and Euclid Avenue estates with the belief that they would be passed on to their children and grandchildren to preserve.[9] The houses, and the street alike, were for many residents personal monuments, even though blatantly public in character; the close involvement by patrons in the design and building of their residences was testimony to this monument-building. These people, unlike the established gentry in New York or Charleston, were not aggrandizing deep-rooted family wealth with their new Euclid Avenue residences; they were nouveaux riches, and they needed roots. Their desire to center themselves along four continuous miles of the city's principal parade ground reflected the prestige of an Avenue address and indicated a commitment by the family to its residence and its street.

This unusually deep loyalty is why when pressure for commercial development on the Avenue intensified in the 1890s, and came to appear all but unstoppable, many residents fought it hard. A few—including Union Telegraph founder Jeptha Wade, General Electric founder Charles Brush, Standard Oil founder John D. Rockefeller, and architect Harry Myer—simply refused to sacrifice their homes to such development. Their residences belonged to Cleveland's grand residential street, not its commercial main street. And rather than have them subdivided into rooming houses or offices, each man specified in his will that his home be demolished when he died.

The Architectural Wonderland

The families who built Euclid Avenue were builders of property. It is an understatement to say that these entrepreneurial individuals were materialists; they thought and acted mostly on the basis of concrete interests rather than philosophical ideas. Few of the men were artists, writers, or scholars; most were capitalists engaged in such lifelong concerns as canal routes, railroad tracks, telegraph lines, ore and copper products, electric dynamos, oil, turrets and lathes, and nuts and bolts. As innovators in their respective fields, they set precedents and influenced what others thought and did, for better or worse. In architecture, as in business, they recognized the value and influence of physical property and of their own leadership in advancing striking architectural form. Many patrons did indeed play an important role in the design and construction of their houses. They energetically participated in the entire process, from the rendering of the original plans to the management of contractors and the selection of Tiffany skylights and dining room furniture.[10] The end results were often as much a product of the owner's tastes as those of the builder or architect.

The constant arrival of new wealth and the economic advance of the city fueled a succession of architectural styles between 1840 and 1910. Patrons showed themselves to be pliant stylists; they accepted the new and did not cling to the old. But they did not set trends either. Their residences generally conformed to prevailing architectural tastes in vogue nationally at the time of design and construction. Inasmuch as they and their architects and builders applied currently popular styles in expensive, magnificent forms did they influence local residential design.

The conventional aesthetic leanings of these patrons were entirely consistent with their traditional values and formal lifestyles. Novelties and innovations in structural and mechanical systems were what distinguished these houses from others being built in the city. This was quite consistent with patrons' wealth and their innovative and entrepreneurial characters. Money was the greatest obstacle to advancing domestic technology: most people were unable to afford new, improved devices. But money was rarely an obstacle for Euclid Avenue patrons. In fact, their progressive, even inventive, attitudes about the vast possibilities available in material resources inspired them to encourage their builders and architects to incorporate the most modern structural, plumbing, heating, lighting, and power devices available. Euclid Avenue houses led the way in Cleveland in introducing the first running water, central ventilation, electric lighting and wiring, and the first elevator and steel-frame construction in a residence. These patrons and their residences helped advance the art and science of Cleveland house construction, ultimately raising the quality of life for others, as such innovations subsequently became standardized and affordable to the larger population.

Over the sixty years in which the Avenue rose and gained its reputation as an architectural wonderland, over 250 houses were built along Euclid. During the same period, residential design witnessed the rise and fall of four major stylistic periods: the Italianate and Gothic revivals in the 1840s–70s; the Victorian and English manor house influences of the 1880s–90s; the Romanesque revival in the 1880s–90s; and the neoclassical revival in the 1890s–1910s. These stylistic idioms provide a logical framework in which to organize the development of Euclid Avenue's architectural streetscape. Yet no sooner does one apply this overall chronology than a myriad of exceptions and the absence of a rational sequence appear in the choice of style from one house to the next, one patron to the next. It is helpful to remember that pluralism of styles and ideologies was the natural state of affairs in a diverse and complex society. In the end it was individual preferences, more than national or international fashions, that

Fig. 79. *Opposite.* The architectural wonderland. Looking west on the north side from Twenty-first Street (Western Reserve Historical Society, c. 1890).

Fig. 80. The houses of Euclid Avenue created a superb survey of nineteenth- and early twentieth-century building tastes (Western Reserve Historical Society, by I. T. Frary, c. 1910).

dictated which architectural style would prevail at any one time and for any one house on Euclid Avenue. The inconsistencies among styles as they appeared in each residence reflected differences in tastes and talents of the patrons, architects, and builders. Just because of this human variety, the houses of Euclid Avenue created an architectural ensemble that represented a superb survey of nineteenth- and early twentieth-century building tastes (figs. 79, 80).

Fig. 81. Post–Civil War grandeur. Mrs. T. Sterling Beckwith and her friends on the lawn, 3813 Euclid Avenue; Joseph Ireland, architect, 1866 (Western Reserve Historical Society, early 1870s).

FIVE

Post–Civil War Grandeur, 1865–1885

The house was "like a grand lady in a new gown." She stood three stories tall, her front was a profusion of wooden decoration, and she was crowned by an ornate cupola of lacy ironwork. A rich red carpet flowed down her broad front steps to the sweeping carriageway. Such was the elegance and grandeur of the fictitious Euclid Avenue house of John Fenno, the surly industrialist who rose to riches and fell to ruin in Agatha Young's novel *Light in the Sky*.[1] The house, allegedly built in 1872, could have been modeled after any one of a number of residences that went up along the Avenue in the 1870s.

On Euclid Avenue, and throughout the country, the decades following the Civil War were an exceptional time of buoyant prosperity and intense building activity (fig. 81). In just fifteen years, between 1865 and 1880, 130 new houses appeared on the Avenue, more than doubling the size of the neighborhood. Income tax–free affluence, most of all, fed the Avenue, enhancing the design and bulk of its residences. Anthony Trollope had been "particularly struck by the size and comfort" of these houses when he visited Cleveland in 1862. From this he concluded that Americans generally lived "in better houses than Englishmen," but that the English probably spent more on wine, entertainment, horses, and other amusements.[2] Perhaps so, but Euclid Avenue residents, who were not wanting for these other pleasures either, would have reveled in the thought that they had surpassed their English peers in domestic comforts.

Comfort was an important element of postwar house design, outside and inside, and was an outgrowth of the popular romanticism of the time that dominated American life. While strict historic precedents and principles formed the basic text of earlier design theories, the dialect of these decades was full of oblique and eclectic references to classical orders and Gothic and Romanesque details. Rich, warm architectural images coalesced into several fashions. There was plenty of pastiche, nationally and locally, and more than a few critics found this troublesome. Cleveland architect Frank Barnum, who entered the field in the late 1870s, thought his colleagues' determination to be original really produced unseemly incongruities and buildings worth little praise.[3] But designers and patrons alike admired romantic and free-spirited forms and furnishings.

The human qualities fondly used to describe Euclid Avenue residences and rooms indicated how residents thought about their houses in the postwar era. Young's portrait of the fictitious Fenno house was one such expression. Another was John Hay's personal references in *The Bread-Winners* to his own Euclid Avenue library, which, like himself, was "marked . . . with a kind of serious elegance—one of those apartments which seem to fit the person like a more perfect dress." This octagonal room was designed by Hay and his architect, Joseph Ireland, to create an overall expression of "warmth and good manners."[4] Carved oak bookcases, cordovan leather walls and chairs, a patterned ceiling in deep blues, browns and golds, and incidentals of Owari pots, Barbediene bronzes, and Limoges and Lambeth vases produced a chamber of total comfort for its occupant. Hay and his neighbors on the Avenue introduced personal pleasure into the decor and design of their rooms—a lively production of dark, rich colors, natural materials, and sincere sculptural detailing. Such curios as Japanese fans, brilliant peacock feathers, eggplant-colored drapes, maroon-lacquered woodwork, and embroidered upholstery in cobalt, plum, crimson, purple, and oxblood red enforced the fashion of the day. Residents were limited only by their acquisitive tastes, their travels, and their incomes. The results were sometimes awesome, sometimes gaudy, and quite often elegant.

The Mansard Manse, 1865–1875

In house design the outstanding feature of the era was the French-inspired mansard roof, which enabled Avenue patrons to build upward and outward (figs. 82–84). A third story could be added simply by introducing the steep-pitched roof. While Amasa Stone's 1858 house was over thirty feet from ground to rooftop, Dr. Worthy S. Streator's mansard-styled residence, built in 1864, rose to new heights and measured forty feet from foundation wall to the peak of his "new French concave style" roof. Streator started out in the spring of 1864 planning just to enlarge his old farmhouse at Sixty-ninth Street, but finally built a substantial new residence instead. He retained Cleveland architect Joseph M. Blackburn and builder J. Slatt to create his 10,000-square-foot "model of comfort and elegance." Akron brownstone blocks gave the house its antique appearance, and the square sixty-foot tower to one side and round fifty-five-foot water tower to the other promised a picturesque effect. Streator's own design for the landscaped grounds completed the composition. The house's mechanical system was anything but fashioned after this natural, romantic image, as it was recognized for its state-of-the-art gas- and water-line system and modern central steam heating (fig. 85).[5]

The mansard roof was the chief hallmark of the houses that went up along the Avenue in the 1860s, and they crowned country villas like Dr. Streator's as well as the urban townhouses built closer in (see table 8). Among the most stately was the residence of John D. Rockefeller, who purchased a brick mansion for $40,000 from builder Francis C. Keith in 1868, two years before the twenty-nine-year-old entrepreneur founded the Standard Oil Company. Designed by Cleveland architect Simeon Porter in 1866, Rockefeller's res-

Fig. 82. The French-inspired mansard roof. William J. and Florance Sheffield Boardman residence, 1303 Euclid Avenue, 1855–56; remodeled and enlarged with new roof and rear wing by Heard and Porter, architects, 1860–61 (courtesy Carl Boardman Cobb, by G. M. Edmondson, c. 1910).

Fig. 83. *Below left.* William P. and Louisa Southworth residence, 1218 Euclid Avenue, 1860–61 (Western Reserve Historical Society).

Fig. 84. *Below right.* George A. Garretson residence, 3716 Euclid Avenue, c. 1865–67 (Western Reserve Historical Society).

Fig. 85. The new French concave style roof, on Dr. Worthy
S. Streator's residence, 6903 Euclid Avenue; Joseph M. Blackburn, architect, 1864 (Lake *Atlas,*
1874).

TABLE 8
The Mansard Manse, 1865–1875

Patron/Resident	Address	Building Date	Architect
Charles H. Hickox	2727	1855–59	Heard & Porter
William P. Southworth	1218	1860–61	Unknown
William J. Boardman	1303	1856; 1860–61	Heard & Porter
Dr. Worthy S. Streator	6903	1864	J. M. Blackburn
James Parmelee	3036	c. 1865	Unknown
Zenas King	4719	1865–66	Unknown
Stephen V. Harkness	6508	1866	S. C. Porter
John D. Rockefeller	3920	1866–68	S. C. Porter
Ralph Harman–Earl W. Oglebay	1815	1866	Unknown
Anson Stager–T. S. Beckwith	3813	1866	J. Ireland
Charles S. Bissell	4611	1867	J. Ireland
George Hall	3146	1869–70	Unknown
George Hoyt	3112	c. 1865–67	Unknown
George A. Garretson	3716	c. 1865–67	Unknown
Samuel Williamson	3609	c. 1865–70	Unknown
Alexander E. Brown	2626	c. 1866–70	Unknown
John H. Devereux	3226	1873	J. Ireland

idence was distinguished by a precise symmetrical plan, deep Italianate moldings, and a columnar porch. Eleven years after settling into his residence, in 1879, Rockefeller bought the adjacent house at the southwest corner of Fortieth Street from Levi Burgent for $60,000. The combined lots gave him two acres of land and 231 feet of linear frontage on the Avenue. By securing control of the corner and moving the second house, Rockefeller enhanced the visibility of his residence and created a landed estate within the city.[6] The Rockefeller residence struck a high profile on the Avenue, for it commanded a prominent intersection and was sited uncharacteristically high on its deep, rolling grounds (fig. 86). It was long identified with the ambitious endeavors of its nationally acclaimed owner.

Fig. 86. The Rockefeller residence struck a high profile on the Avenue, overlooking the intersection at Fortieth Street and sited uncharacteristically high on its deep rolling grounds on the south side of the street, 3920 Euclid Avenue; Simeon C. Porter, architect, 1866–68 (Cleveland Public Library).

Rockefeller was closer to being a native Clevelander than most of his neighbors—he had lived and worked in the city since age fifteen, and many of his family's deepest roots were planted in the Cleveland community. Here he met and married Laura Spelman, a schoolteacher, in 1864, and he started the oil refining business of Rockefeller & Andrews with Samuel Andrews in 1865 and then the Standard Oil Company in 1870. Once he had embarked on his drive to consolidate and control the region's oil refineries, Rockefeller fast became known as a tough and often ruthless entrepreneur. But as he was a man with a vision, he was also a man of contrasts: he was respected for his accomplishments and for his temperate Christian manner, but not for his disturbing, enigmatic business methods.[7] He would not hesitate to pressure a competitor or associate into selling out to him, even if he were a Euclid Avenue neighbor. At the same time, Rockefeller did more than any other parishioner to support the Euclid Avenue Baptist Church, and did so out of a piety that appears genuine. He saved this institution from financial ruin on more than one occasion, and later built a new building to house it at Ninth Street. He was a devout member of the congregation until his death.

Aside from their church activities, the Rockefellers socialized little with others on the Avenue (figs. 87, 88). They had a fondness for simple living, in contrast to many of their neighbors. Within their plainly appointed residence, John and Laura Rockefeller quietly raised their four children—Elizabeth, Alta, Edith, and John, Jr.—employing two live-in maid servants and a coachman to care for the family and home. The children had private tutors, and Laura Rockefeller entertained only when it furthered her own work with the Plymouth Congregational Church and her husband's involvement with the Baptist Church. Rockefeller maintained close friendships with only a handful of men, namely business partners Henry Flagler and Stephen V. Harkness, Flagler's stepbrother. Flagler lived across the Avenue, and the partners enjoyed walking or riding together to and from the downtown Standard Block each day. Harkness also bought property on the Avenue at Sixty-fifth Street and in 1866—the same year Porter built the house Rockefeller later acquired—hired architect Porter to design for him "an elegant residence."[8]

After a decade on the Avenue, the Rockefellers vacated the Euclid Avenue house for their seventy-nine-acre Forest Hill estate. Rockefeller had originally developed this property around 140th Street in 1877 as a sanitarium; that endeavor failed, so he remodeled the main building for his new residence. Then in 1884, the family bought its New York City townhouse and divided time between it and the Forest Hill estate. Meanwhile, the house on the Avenue stood as a grand residence occupied only by a maid. Decades later, around the turn of the century, Rockefeller leased it as a sanitarium for alcoholics, which neighbor Edward A. Merritt disparaged as the "drunk cure establishment" and Homer Wade, son of Randall Wade, dubbed the "liquor effect eliminator establishment."[9]

Rockefeller maintained a few ties among his Euclid Avenue neighbors, most of them parishioners of the Baptist Church, to which he traveled by car-

Fig. 87. John D. Rockefeller, the richest man in Cleveland (Cleveland Public Library, by G. M. Edmondson, 1910).

Fig. 88. Laura Spelman (Mrs. John D.) Rockefeller (Cleveland Public Library, by G. M. Edmondson, 1908).

riage from Forest Hill every Sunday when he was in town. Charles Otis, Sr., was a friend, steadfast in good times and bad. The two men would sit and talk for hours on the Otises' front porch during the time when Rockefeller was building his Standard Oil empire; Otis would drive an hour-and-a-half in his Victoria out to Forest Hill after Rockefeller had lost favor among many of his Cleveland neighbors. Worcester L. Warner was another constant friend to Rockefeller, and he even built a country retreat near his former Avenue neighbor at Pocantico Hills in Tarrytown, New York. During Rockefeller's celebrated 1905 Ohio income tax case, in which he was assessed $2.5 million on all his intangible property in both Cleveland and New York, Warner defended the credibility of his former neighbor by decrying as "malicious" the assault on Rockefeller's character printed in the *Cleveland Leader*. He and Otis rallied support from a group of chamber of commerce members, most of whom lived on the Avenue, who tried to convince Rockefeller to stay in Cleveland. But this episode over the state taxes, which he refused to pay, and his beratement by neighbors and Clevelanders—stemming from his shrewd character and apparent cunning in business dealings—turned the oil magnate against Cleveland. His love for his adopted hometown was dead. Even though he was "grateful beyond expression for all the kindness" shown him by Otis and others, he decided to leave his Avenue home. The family maintained the residence until Rockefeller's death in 1937, after which it was razed in accordance with his will.[10] The cleared property was sold and redeveloped as a parking lot and gas station.

In the years before the Rockefeller residence was razed, many noted the disparity between its unpretentious design and its owner's extraordinary affluence. This disparity was magnified when the house was compared to those of industrialists Charles H. Hickox and Ralph Harman, attorney Samuel Williamson, and entrepreneurs Anson Stager and Charles S. Bissell, whose homes were all built around the same time. Each of these homes was more artistically stylized with towers, arches, and lavish details to enhance the picturesque effect. As impressive as these features was the force of each house's overall size and masonry construction. The architects chiefly responsible for creating this higher level of design were Heard and Porter, who had dissolved their ten-year partnership in 1860, and New York émigré Joseph Ireland, who decided to open an office in Cleveland in 1865. Their patrons, all prosperous businessmen, many of them active connoisseurs, shared credit for advancing the scale and drama of architectural design on the Avenue (figs. 89–92).

The increased mechanical and structural complexity of these residences also distinguished them from their predecessors. They required teams of ten to fifteen skilled laborers and craftsmen to construct and decorate. The mechanical systems, designed to provide maximum comfort and convenience for their wealthy occupants, demanded greater technical knowledge of the most innovative devices from the designers and builders. And the great height of these new houses, up to seventy and eighty feet, posed occupational hazards for builders—hazards which were less dangerous before soaring towers and steep-pitched roofs were introduced. When Charles Bissell's house was under

Fig. 89. Charles Hickox residence, 2727 Euclid Avenue; Heard and Porter, architects, 1855–59 (Western Reserve Historical Society, 1880s).

Fig. 90. Samuel Williamson residence, 3609 Euclid Avenue, c. 1865–70 (Western Reserve Historical Society).

Fig. 91. Zenas King residence, 4719 Euclid Avenue, 1865–66; later the home of Lester M. Coe (Western Reserve Historical Society).

Fig. 92. Ralph H. Harman–Earl W. Oglebay residence, 1815 Euclid Avenue, 1866 (Western Reserve Historical Society, 1900s).

construction, for example, one of the workmen, Henry Dawson, "met with a serious accident" while at work on one of the towers; Dawson slipped and fell, "striking on the cornice and bounding off to the ground below." Seventy feet and a moment later, he found himself with a broken arm and lacerated head and face.[11] Growing complexity in architectural design challenged builders' abilities in more ways than the dangerous new heights (fig. 93).

But neither the builders nor the architects complained, for the prosperity of Cleveland industry in the postwar years endowed the design and building trades with more and even larger commissions. The *Plain Dealer* reported in March 1866 that "the architects tell us that building in Cleveland will be unusually brisk the coming summer." The house that caught the reporter's special attention was the residence of Colonel Anson Stager, an associate of Jeptha Wade in the Western Union expansion and, most recently, the supervisor of Northern troops during the war. Stager's "magnificent brick and stone residence" was designed by young Ireland, only twenty-two years old at the time,

Fig. 93. The heightened scale and drama of architectural design on the Avenue. Charles S. and Cynthia Wick Bissell residence, 4611 Euclid Avenue; Joseph Ireland, architect. Original rendering, 1867 (courtesy Carl Boardman Cobb, Western Reserve Historical Society).

with its three stories encompassing over 10,000 square feet and costing $60,000 to design and build (fig. 81). Such opulence was without peer beyond the Avenue: the best houses going up on Prospect Street and to either side of the Avenue were no more than 4,000 square feet and cost up to $3,500 to build.[12]

Such grandeur bought superior comforts, as it did functional discomforts; the size and sophistication of these fine residences depended increasingly on the smooth operation of highly technical mechanical systems. The so-called "modern conveniences" of the Ireland-designed Stager manse were not yet operational when the family first occupied its big villa in October 1866, making for obvious discomforts during Cleveland's late-autumn chill. Observing this, their neighbor Randall Wade told his father of how Mrs. Stager had "just cause for her fears about going into their new house before it [had] ever been warmed and no prospect of steam for months—no gas, no conveniences, nothing finished." Having just moved in to their own new house and concerned for Mrs. Stager's distress, the Wades prepared a generous dinner for the family and servants, Randall remarking, "they will be uncomfortable for a long time yet . . . confusion generally."[13]

The Stagers lived in their new residence for only eight years, a short stay for Euclid Avenue families. They sold it in 1874 to Cleveland's premier dry goods and interiors merchant, Thomas Sterling Beckwith. Beckwith's professional propensity for designing and furnishing interiors took hold immediately in his own home as he set about frescoing and recarpeting the place, retaining local frescoers Cook, Kroger & Company to design and execute the "manner and style" for each room. On the main floor, they covered the walls and ceilings of the double drawing room, reception room, and library on the west side and the living room, dining room, and kitchen on the east side. On the second floor, they frescoed the two large bedrooms facing the Avenue and the three smaller rooms for the children at the back. On the third floor, under the mansard roof, the ballroom and billiard room received new decors.[14] In the backyard, Beckwith built a snow slide down the sloping rear lawn for his children, creating a wonderful winter sport for them and their playmates.

The year Beckwith bought the Stager mansion marked an important advance in his life: he had moved both his residence and his thirty-year-old carpet and interiors store, Beckwith, Sterling & Company, to the Avenue, his store now located in the ground level of the new Euclid Avenue Opera House. Among his business partners were neighbors Alexander Sackett, Peter Weddell, Dudley Baldwin, and Frederick A. Sterling, all of whom built on the Avenue. Hard work came naturally to Beckwith and his wife, Sarah, who were pious Christians devoted to the Bethel, which provided welfare assistance to seamen, widows, and orphan children. Within two years of his arrival on the Avenue, however, Beckwith died of Bright's disease. His widow and their four children—two sons and two adopted daughters—lived in the residence for another twenty-five years, until Mrs. Beckwith's death in 1900. At that time their neighbor to the west, Charles Brush, bought the home to ensure that it would be well maintained as a private residence and not diminish the value of his own estate. When the University Club first approached Brush to buy the former Beckwith house for their club, he initially hesitated but finally agreed to sell in 1913. The University Club retained architects Milton Dyer and Henry H. Walsh to remodel and enlarge it, an investment that ensured the mansion's preservation well beyond the Avenue's residential life.[15]

The Victorian Villa, 1875–1885

The Beckwith house and many of its companion mansard-styled villas displayed pronounced High Gothic features, a shift away from the strict Italianate design of the antebellum years to the grandiose sculptural forms of the age of postwar prosperity (figs. 94, 95). This grandeur culminated in the 1870s and early 1880s in the form of a High Victorian Gothic indulgence, an unabated freedom by architects and patrons in picturesque design. Many of the decorative features that became popular echoed the furniture of British designer Sir Charles Eastlake: spindle columns supporting porches resembled legs of chairs, and geometrical cornice motifs were reminiscent of ornamental borders on beds and mirrors. Interiors, more so, were designed by patrons and architects with "sincere" Eastlake furniture, bookcases, and doors. "Sincerity" was an important design virtue in this period because eclecticism was so rampant that specific styles were sometimes impossible to identify.

Interiors also emphasized density in the appearance of rooms, moldings, and furnishings—heavy, over-stuffed, and colorful. Organized clutter became the order of the day. Hours of furniture shopping must have been a common pastime for Euclid Avenue residents, both husbands and wives—first to make rooms functional, then to fill them up. The *Leader* observed in 1878 that

> every department of house furnishing and interior decoration has undergone a change, which implies a higher standard of art culture among our people. The "Eastlake" and "Queen Anne" furniture and upholstery, the wallpapers of such elegant designs and texture that fresco has gone out of use, and the course, clumsy shapes and patterns of gas fixtures are being replaced by the most elegant and artistic designs, in which polished brass is combined with baunce, crockle, and other porcelain vases of antique shape.[16]

Interior decor had become as much an art form as architectural design, and decorators and furniture designers rivaled architects in the creation of the Avenue's showcases. The prosperity of these years, and all the opulent mansions it underwrote, created a lucrative market for the "celebrity designer," the best of whom made a fortune organizing and decorating the new homes of the new millionaires. Euclid Avenue patrons often bypassed local decorators to go to the finest New York studios of Herter Brothers, Louis C. Tiffany, and John La Farge for their furniture and tapestries. They coordinated their personal tastes and collections with those of the interior designer on one side and the architect, who created the spacious stagesets, on the other (figs. 96–100).[17]

Fig. 94. *Above left.* Henry H. and Alexander E. Brown residence, 2626 Euclid Avenue, c. 1866–70 (Western Reserve Historical Society).

Fig. 95. *Above right.* George Hall residence, 3146 Euclid Avenue, 1869–70 (Western Reserve Historical Society, c. 1910).

Fig. 96. Charles A. and Ann Otis, Sr., residence, 3133 Euclid Avenue, 1868–72 (Western Reserve Historical Society, c. 1880).

Fig. 97. Otis–Sanders residence, living room. Looking east through front hall to parlor (Western Reserve Historical Society, by G. M. Edmondson, 1933).

Fig. 98. Charles A. Otis, Sr.–William Sanders residence; renovated and enlarged by daughter Annie Otis and her husband, William Sanders (Western Reserve Historical Society, by G. M. Edmondson, 1933).

Fig. 99. Otis–Sanders residence, backyard. Looking north to gardener's cottage and coachman's house at far left (Western Reserve Historical Society, by G. M. Edmondson, 1933).

Fig. 100. Otis–Sanders residence, southwest bedroom. Looking through dressing room to west bedroom (Western Reserve Historical Society, by G. M. Edmondson, 1933).

TABLE 9
The Victorian Villa, 1865–1885

Patron/Resident	Address	Building Date	Architect
Orlando Hall	2638	1865–66	Unknown
Franklyn L. Alcott	4820	1866	[J. Ireland]
Harry E. Myer	2263	c. 1866–70	H. E. Myer
Alanson T. Osborn	2317	c. 1870	Unknown
Charles A. Otis, Sr.	3133	1868–72	Unknown
Liberty E. Holden	7809	1875	Unknown
Joseph W. Britton	7817	1875	[L. T. Scofield]
George H. Ely	4203	c. 1874–75	Unknown
Ahira Cobb	6305	c. 1870–75	Unknown
Levi H. Malone	5004–12	c. 1875	Unknown
John Hay	1235	1875–76	J. Ireland
Daniel P. Eells	3201	1876	J. Ireland
Col. William Harris	1167	1877	J. Ireland
Rufus K. Winslow	2409	1878	L. T. Scofield
A. W. Blann	4712	c. 1875–80	Unknown
William T. Corlett	1953	c. 1882–85	[L. T. Scofield]
George W. Stockley	2343	1885–86	L. T. Scofield

Patrons also devoted abundant resources to their grounds, which became outdoor museums for decorative whims. The deep, landscaped lawns took on a furnished look with larger-than-life iron statuary—cherubs, goddesses, deer, and classical serpents (figs. 101–2). In exterior architectural arrangements, symmetry was now the exception rather than the rule, and when it did appear—as in the Daniel P. Eells residence designed by Joseph Ireland—it was overshadowed by pointed towers, decorative eaves, spacious porches, and arched windows and doors. Among the master designers of these houses were Cleveland architects Ireland, Levi T. Scofield, and, later, Forrest Coburn and Frank Barnum (see table 9).

Architects worked hand in hand with patrons to endow the Avenue with a sculptural elegance. Among the many residences built in this spirit, the finest were those of banker Eells, writer and diplomat John Hay, shipping magnate Rufus Winslow, and business manager George W. Stockley (figs. 103–5).

The Hay house, designed by Ireland, distinguished itself with its luxurious Eastlake-inspired traceried front. It was built as a wedding present to John and Clara Hay from Clara's father, Amasa Stone, and stood next door to the Stone residence, where the couple had lived during construction. Building of the new house began within "an hour or so" of the couple's arrival from New York City in 1875, Hay reported to his friend Whitelaw Reid, and "ever since my ears have been full of the muffled click of the chisels of some half hundred workmen on the soft yellow stone."[18] Surely he exaggerated the size of the crew, industrious as the masons might have appeared, but Hay enjoyed good drama and clearly the construction of his grand sandstone house captured his imagination.

Fig. 101. Ella Grant Wilson and goddess. Randall Wade residence, 3903 Euclid Avenue (Western Reserve Historical Society).

Fig. 102. *Opposite.* Outdoor museums of iron statuary; life-sized iron deer that graced the grounds of the Edwin B. Hale residence, 4307 Euclid Avenue (courtesy Mrs. Henry B. Melcher, by G. M. Edmondson, 1930s).

Fig. 103. George H. Ely residence, 4203 Euclid Avenue, c. 1874–75 (Western Reserve Historical Society).

Fig. 104. Alanson T. Osborn residence, 2317 Euclid Avenue, c. 1870 (Cleveland Public Library).

Fig. 105. Ahira Cobb residence, 6305 Euclid Avenue, c. 1870–75; later The Kensington hotel, c. 1907–10 (*Cleveland Plain Dealer,* c. 1910).

Father-in-law Stone, the creator of decorative woodwork, lavished upon his daughter and son-in-law's house the finest woodcarving and cabinetwork he could buy. He hired the talented German artisan John Herkomer, who was well known locally for his handcrafted workmanship. The presence of skilled immigrant German and Scottish carpenters and masons in Cleveland, as in other major cities, contributed to the distinctive detailing of the Hay house and others along the Avenue in the 1870s and 1880s (fig 106).[19] Herkomer memorialized

Fig. 106. John and Clara Stone Hay residence, *left,* 1235 Euclid Avenue; Joseph Ireland, architect, 1875–76. Residences of Amasa Stone, no. 1255, and William Boardman, no. 1303, *right* (Western Reserve Historical Society, 1920s).

the Stone and Hay union in the main hall of the residence by inscribing the elegant floral *S* and *H* on the newel posts of the black walnut staircase. He surmounted one of the newel posts with a life-size wooden owl, which became a secret cove where Hay hid marshmallows to amuse his children. Years later, his son Clarence recalled that his first introduction to bribery was when his father would "miraculously extract from the bird's ear a marshmallow," bait used to entice him and his sister to go to bed (fig. 107).[20]

Hay was one among the truly great figures who lived on the Avenue. His blue-ribbon résumé portrayed a man of unique intellect and energy—the private secretary to President Abraham Lincoln, an editor of the *New York Tribune,* coauthor with John Nicolay of the masterful biography of Lincoln, ambassador to Great Britain, and secretary of state under Presidents William McKinley and

Theodore Roosevelt. By temperament he was very much a scholar; by profession he was the perfect diplomat—handsome, disarming, witty, brilliant, a charming cosmopolitan. After his marriage to Clara Stone, he came to Cleveland to appease her father and to write Lincoln's biography (fig. 108). As a man of relative leisure who was mildly amused by his newfound affluence and glamourous life, he became a wonderfully astute observer of Cleveland society, and of his own household in particular. This all began with the design and building of his residence.

The long and lively correspondence he maintained with his sister-in-law Flora Stone, who was traveling abroad at the time, traced the progress of home construction. After one of his daily site visits, just before the completion of the house, Hay happily remarked that it was "getting on beautifully." He was particularly pleased that the drawing room suite was all but ready to receive

Fig. 107. Hay residence, main stairhall (rebuilt from Euclid Ave. house in Western Reserve Historical Society, 1990).

Fig. 108. John Hay (Western Reserve Historical Society, by Bach Brothers, c. 1900).

guests, except for "the gilding of the black dado and woodwork of the parlor." The west parlor, a "perfectly lovely" room that was unequaled by any other Hay had seen, he privately named "the Pavilion de Flore," an endearment meant to flatter his sister-in-law. The gilded and paneled interiors, still being executed a year after the family had moved in, commanded Hay's personal attention. John and Clara worked closely with their New York interior designer, Herter Brothers, in selecting all fireplace mantels, carpets, and furniture to achieve a "sincere" but comfortable Eastlake ambiance in each room. Hay seemed to enjoy his working relationship with architect Ireland, as he had previously with architect Richard Morris Hunt during design of the Tribune Building in Manhattan in 1873, and as he would later with Henry Hobson Richardson while his Lafayette Square house in Washington, D.C., was under construction during 1884–86. So enthusiastic was his involvement that he was cheered when he could present Ireland with the drawing room mantelpiece two months ahead of schedule, enabling the architect to design the room's wainscoting with this centerpiece in place.[21] Hay respected Ireland's professional skill and greatly admired his indispensable contribution to the project.

Some of Hay's neighbors, however, had more confidence in their own artistic abilities and paid less respect to the architect's talent. This was specifically true of Colonel and Mrs. William Harris, who retained Ireland in 1877 to remodel the Anson Smith house, located down the street from Hay and one door east of the home of Mrs. Harris's own family, the Stillman Witts. The Harrises hired Ireland to transform the 1842 Greek Revival residence by tearing away the classical portico and replacing it with a decorative front of handcrafted scrollwork (fig. 109). Hay was exasperated when the Harrises gave Ireland "no credit for it—the Colonel calmly says that he and Mrs. Harris planned it—told Ireland just what they wanted, etc." Hay's irritation was increased by what he viewed as Ireland's splendid design for the apron-like facade: "I have rarely seen a prettier front," he wrote Flora.[22]

The traceried fronts of the Hay and Harris residences were among the few that engaged such carpenterlike detail, adding a light and playful touch to the Avenue's bold streetscape (figs. 110, 111). Most of the residences of this period, rather, held to the more serious High Victorian manner, a style influenced by the 1876 World's Centennial Exhibition in Philadelphia, to which many Clevelanders traveled, which gave fresh impetus to the city's building arts. The Daniel P. Eells residence, designed by Ireland and built in 1876–77, was one of the finest. The central tower, together with the mosaic tiled roof and carved window ornament, amplified the presence of the Eells house upon the ridge. The fireproof interior featured Eells's black ebony library, inset with white ivory, and a spacious center hall brilliantly lit by gas jets and a colorful skylight three flights above. During construction in late 1876, Daniel and Mary Eells hosted a grand supper party for the craftsmen who worked on their house—a rare event for the city. The 100 dinner guests were evidence of the massive scale and complexity of this residence (figs. 112, 113).[23]

Eells showed himself to be a sophisticated and thoughtful patron in his choice of an architect who was known as a brilliant stylist of grandeur and in his respectful appreciation of the tradesmen who built his residence. As the youngest son of a Presbyterian minister, and descended from almost two centuries of New England ministers, Eells's pious and traditional principles gave rise to uncompromised quality in all he did. He made his own fortune and main-

Fig. 109. Colonel William Harris residence, *right,* 1167 Euclid Avenue; originally Anson Smith house (1840–42), rebuilt by Joseph Ireland, architect, 1877. Stillman Witt residence, no. 1115, *left* (Western Reserve Historical Society, 1870s).

tained throughout his life—from college student to elder entrepreneur—a constant faith in innovation and intellectual honesty. By selecting for his residence a high-style design showcased to American viewers only that year in Philadelphia, Eells affirmed his astute cultural awareness.

He was one of the few college-educated men among the first-generation entrepreneurs of Cleveland. He had come to Ohio from upstate New York in 1836, first settling with his parents in Amherst and then Elyria. He went on to Oberlin College and finally to Hamilton College, where he graduated in 1844. When he arrived in Cleveland three years later, he started out in a trade commission house, and then Truman Handy appointed him bookkeeper for the State Bank of Ohio's commercial branch in the city. He advanced over the next two

Fig. 110. Levi H. Malone residence, 5012 Euclid Avenue, c. 1875 (Western Reserve Historical Society, 1889).

Fig. 111. Franklyn L. Alcott residence, 4820 Euclid Avenue, 1866 (Western Reserve Historical Society).

Fig. 112. Daniel P. and Mary Witt Eells residence, 3201 Euclid Avenue; Joseph Ireland, architect. Original perspective drawing, May 1876 (Western Reserve Historical Society).

decades to become president of the Commercial National Bank. At the time he built his Euclid Avenue residence, Eells had taken the place of his neighbor Handy as Cleveland's premier banker. From this position, he became a principal force in the formation of such diverse industries as railroads, iron and steel foundries, and the Sandusky Portland Cement Company, which sold products to over ninety countries. He also wielded impressive political influence. One of his many accomplishments was convincing William McKinley, with Marcus A. Hanna at his side in a meeting in Eells's Euclid Avenue library, to run for president.[24]

Beyond business and politics, Eells joined his wife, Mary Witt, a daughter of the Stillman Witts, in devoting hundreds of hours to the founding and growth of the city's YMCA and YWCA. Their charitable interests extended to the Presbyterian and Baptist churches and to other such major Christian insti-

Fig. 113. The Eells residence (Western Reserve Historical Society, 1880s).

tutions as the Children's Aid Society, the Home for Aged Women, and the Protestant Orphan Asylum. When their daughter Eliza, known as Idaka, died in a steamer explosion on Chautauqua Lake in 1871, they erected the Idaka Chapel for First Baptist Church in her memory.[25]

With their three other children, the couple built their Beach Cliff country estate in Rocky River about a decade after completing the Euclid Avenue house. Their many in-town interests and friends, however, tied them to their Avenue residence until the turn of the century, even though they lived most of the year ten miles out in Rocky River. They eventually sold the downtown house to Warren Corning, who then sold it to Price McKinney. Spencerian College occupied it for two decades, 1922–42, but thereafter it stood empty until it was razed in 1959 to make way for a hotel.[26]

Within a few years after Daniel Eells built his residence at Thirty-second Street, Liberty Holden, Rufus Winslow, George Stockley, and Dr. William Corlett commissioned Cleveland architect Levi T. Scofield to design and build elegant sandstone residences styled in the High Victorian dialect. Each of these patrons had achieved a leading position in his profession—real estate, shipping, electric utilities, and medicine—and each aspired to build on the city's main promenade in the fashion of the day. Their residences took on a Romanesque spirit through their coarse sandstone walls, crenelated roof eaves, and cathedral windows (figs. 114–18).

One of the more interesting of them was the house built in 1885 by Brush Electric general manager George Stockley, later the home of Tom Johnson during his five terms as Cleveland's controversial Progressive mayor (fig. 119). Johnson made a number of changes in the house—as he did with just about everything with which he was personally involved—and one of the most significant was the west wing addition, which he reportedly washed with a soot solution to make the pale new sandstone blocks complement the decade of built-up grime on the original house. In the backyard he built an indoor skating rink, which became a stage for his large and raucous political gatherings. Down in the basement, the former street railway magnate experimented with his visionary "slip-slide" street car that was designed to increase the speed of public travel. Relying on the extraordinary structural strength of his house, Johnson suspended the car from steel shoes running along upper and lower tracks along the ceiling and floor. It was designed to lift off the tracks and float through the air when energized with electrical current. General Electric made plans to build a test track for the car at its Schenectady plant, a promise forestalled by the 1907 financial panic. Even so, Johnson believed that his "Greased Lightning" train could make a trip from Chicago to New York in four to five hours and from New York to Philadelphia in thirty minutes.[27] The real mystery was not perhaps the viability of Johnson's invention, but how the railway car was moved in and out of the Euclid Avenue house.

Even though Johnson lived in opulence on the Avenue, he was unquestionably a populist at heart (fig. 120). Henry George was his philosophical mentor, William Jennings Bryan a good friend. In many respects the mayor was an anomaly among his neighbors. He lacked finesse and refinement, though he possessed a brilliant mind and enormous wealth and was a savvy politician. Some of his neighbors, like Charles A. Otis, Jr., were invigorated by his lively and unpretentious character; others thought him brash and unbridled. His archenemy Mark Hanna, for one, claimed he was a "socialist—anarchist—nihilist." One biographer, Carl Lorenz, nicely summed up Johnson's personal reputation with the comment that he was "greatly hated and greatly loved."[28]

Fig. 114. A. W. Blann residence, 4712 Euclid Avenue, c. 1875–80; later Edward H. Cushing house (Western Reserve Historical Society, 1880s).

Fig. 115. J. W. Britton residence, 7817 Euclid Avenue, 1875; possibly Levi T. Scofield design (Western Reserve Historical Society, 1889).

Fig. 116. A series of Syrian arches. Liberty E. Holden residence, 7809 Euclid Avenue, 1875; later Feargus B. Squire house, 1905 (Western Reserve Historical Society).

Fig. 117. William T. Corlett residence, 1953 Euclid Avenue; possibly Levi T. Scofield design, c. 1882–85 (Western Reserve Historical Society, 1890s).

Fig. 118. Rufus K. and Lucy
Clarke Winslow residence, 2409
Euclid Avenue; Levi T. Scofield,
architect, 1878. Winslow built
his eighteen-room house when
the family's old Euclid Avenue
home at Public Square was
razed; later Herman Frasch
house (Western Reserve Historical Society).

Fig. 119. Tom Johnson, who lived on Euclid Avenue during his five-term populist mayoralty (Cleveland Public Library, by G. M. Edmondson).

Fig. 120. Mayor Johnson's campaign entourage and the original Red Devil, in front of Johnson and Frasch residences (*Cleveland Plain Dealer*, 1902).

For all his progressive activism in the public arena, he lived a conservative, reposed life in his Avenue residence. Although an innovator of mechanical and political machines, he was content to *acquire* an Avenue residence rather than building his own, accepting a conventional rather than personal architectural statement (fig. 121).

Fig. 121. George Stockley residence, 2343 Euclid Avenue; Levi T. Scofield, architect, 1885–86. Bought by Mayor Tom L. Johnson in 1892 (Western Reserve Historical Society).

Fig. 122. The robust Romanesque Revival. Sylvester T. and Alice Wade Everett residence, 4111 Euclid Avenue; Charles F. and Julius Schweinfurth, architects, 1883–87 (Western Reserve Historical Society, 1890s).

SIX

The Age of Robust Prosperity, 1880–1895

The picturesque traits that had first appeared on Euclid Avenue residences in the late 1840s—notably Senator Payne's Gothic villa—were by the 1880s in full play, patterned after the buildings of eminent Eastern architects widely published and admired in the trade press (fig. 122). The best of these landmarks was the robust Romanesque 1874 design for Trinity Church in Boston by Henry Hobson Richardson, undoubtedly the starting point of the Romanesque revival in the States. The residences designed by Levi Scofield for his financially and culturally prodigal patrons, designs which drew on Romanesque and English influences, had previewed the full thrust of design on the Avenue in the 1880s. The pointed and playful demeanor of architect Ireland's earlier Gothic villa designs had evolved into bolder, more masculine forms. Over 100 Avenue residences were built in the fifteen years between 1881 and 1896; most were constructed of sandstone and most were designed in either the English manor house or Romanesque revival style.

The English Manor House, 1880–1890

The Hay house of 1875 had favored the use of wood and stone to enhance the composition. But few other Avenue patrons then shared the Stones' and Hays' view that dressing up a facade with wooden carpentry was elegant. Instead they preferred the presence of a uniform family of masonry materials for both walls and ornament; the more substantial English manor house, descended from early eighteenth-century British country house precedents, became popular among Avenue residents in the 1880s and changed all this (see table 10). The use of the so-called "honest" building materials of stone and wood now prevailed, though accented by carved wooden tracery, tall and slender chimneys, and airy front porches (figs. 123, 124).

The architects who designed these manor houses were principally the same elite group who were most active in the late 1870s, among them Joseph Ireland, Levi Scofield, and the young partnership of Forrest Coburn and Frank Barnum. George H. Smith, recently arrived from Pennsylvania, made his debut as a major contributor to the Avenue's venue during this period. To turn out

Fig. 123. Frederick A. and Mary Betts Sterling residence, 3447 Euclid Avenue; George H. Smith, architect, 1881 (Western Reserve Historical Society, 1900).

Fig. 124. *Below left.* Hiram H. Little residence, 7615 Euclid Avenue; Coburn and Barnum architects, 1881–82. The Amherst sandstone house cost $25,000 and was noted for its unusually steep roof (Western Reserve Historical Society).

Fig. 125. *Below right.* Judge W. W. Boynton residence, 8021 Euclid Avenue; Coburn and Barnum architects, 1884 (Western Reserve Historical Society, 1889).

TABLE 10
The English Manor House, 1880–1900

Patron/Resident	Address	Building Date	Architect
M. P. Ranney	2734	1878	Unknown
Frederick A. Sterling	3447	1881	G. H. Smith
Lee McBride	6107	1882	Coburn & Barnum
J. H. McBride	6111	1882	Coburn & Barnum
Samuel Andrews	3033	1882–85	Walter Blythe
William J. Rainey	7418	1882	Unknown
S. J. Miller	7103	1881–82	J. Ireland
Hiram H. Little	7615	1881–82	Coburn & Barnum
William L. Miller	7335	1882	J. Ireland
Stevenson Burke	4811	c. 1882–83	Unknown
Thomas H. White	8220	1883	Unknown
W. W. Boynton	8021	1884	Coburn & Barnum
David Z. Norton	7503	1884–85	[Coburn & Barnum]
Charles C. Bolton	7016	c. 1885	Unknown
Morris A. Bradley	7217	1886	Unknown
Lester A. Cobb	6211	c. 1885	Unknown
James B. Savage	3410	c. 1882–87	Unknown
Charles W. Moses	9301	c. 1885–89	Coburn & Barnum
Edwin R. Perkins	8011	1891	Unknown
John J. Stanley	8411	c. 1893–95	Meade & Granger
George P. Welch	8806	c. 1893–95	Meade & Granger

their designs, the architects called on a large and growing field of local builders, painters, and craftsmen, most of whom had, within the decade, emigrated to the city from Ireland, Scotland, and the British Isles.

The Frederick A. Sterling house, designed by Smith, who was only thirty-two years old at the time, exemplified the new style (fig. 125). Smith's towering stature and broad girth must have been inspiration for the scale of his buildings. He was a designer who usually shunned understatement of any kind and was best known as the architect of the magnificent residence of Charles F. Brush (1887–88). He liked to create buildings with full-fledged Romanesque detailing rendered in husky stone forms, which can still be seen in his design for The Arcade (1890) linking Euclid and Superior avenues. In the Sterling commission he was less bold, probably because he accommodated the desires of the patron, represented by lady of the house Emma Betts Sterling, who involved herself directly in the design process. She oversaw the work of the painters, selected the "speaking tubes," the furnace, the tiles and patterns for the bathroom tubs, and the wooden mosaic for the vestibule floor. She also chose the stained glass for the library, hall, and dining room. Characteristic of her personal touch, "appropriate" mottoes hung in certain rooms, such as that for the dining room: "Eat at Pleasure; Drink by Measure."[1] Others were strategically placed in the hall, kitchen, and bedrooms.

The Sterlings' involvement with the architect and contractor matched that of others who built on the Avenue in the 1880s and 1890s. Fred Sterling's ascension to financial and professional success also paralleled the path of other new residents during this period, men who worked their way to comfortable positions from fairly modest beginnings. Sterling had begun his career as a day clerk in the carpet and interior decorating firm of T. S. Beckwith, becoming Beckwith's partner around 1876. By the late 1880s he had become senior partner in the successor firm of Sterling, Welsh & Company.[2]

By the time the Sterlings could afford to build a stately residence on the Avenue, their stature in Cleveland business and society was such that they built the house just one block from their current home on Superior. The new Euclid residence rose up as a handsome public flagship of the Sterling family. But the Sterlings' arrival on the Avenue, as exhibited in the house they built, was modest when compared to the effusive statement of their neighbor Samuel Andrews, who began design of his mansion one year later. He retained the lesser-known local architect Walter Blythe, a former partner and son-in-law of Charles Heard. Andrews, who was previously a member of Rockefeller's close-knit Standard Oil clan, stood out against the Avenue's self-consciously genteel social landscape. His residence had the same impact.

Like most of his peers, Andrews rose to affluence from near poverty; unlike them, he enjoyed a brash and pretentious way of life in Cleveland, a chapter that closed behind a veil of mystery. He had started out as a mechanic and chemist, before joining Rockefeller in the oil refining business. In fact it was Andrews who developed the lucrative process to extract kerosene from crude oil. But in 1874 Rockefeller bought out Andrews's stock for about $1 million because of irreconcilable differences, and the two men parted. He then went to work for neighbor Charles Otis, Sr., at the American Wire Company.[3]

At the time he retained Smith to design his grand English Gothic mansion at the northeast corner of Thirtieth Street—formerly the John Sterling estate—he was living two doors west at Twenty-eighth Street. William Bingham, Sr., was living in a stone house on the old Sterling estate. They exchanged properties in 1882 and Andrews began the three-year project of building his residence. An Englishman who had come to this country in 1857, he clearly looked back across the Atlantic to his native land for inspiration in the style of his residence. One account claims that an actual English mansion that Andrews knew from his boyhood was used as the model to guide Blythe's design (fig. 126). Plans were reportedly drawn up in London and sent to Cleveland, along with two dozen joiners, wood carvers, and other craftsmen.[4] Whether this is fact or fiction, the thirty-three-room Andrews house represented a scholarly and mature rendition of the highest High Victorian Gothic manor. Set back 280 feet from the street, surrounded by deep lawns, and approached by a serpentine carriage drive, the residence housed 18,000 square feet on three floors. The basement was equipped with kitchen, furnace, and store rooms, and the six first-floor chambers surrounded the central skylit court, which was opulently furnished with black onyx mantels and gilt-framed mirrors. The centerpiece of the house

was a broad circular staircase, winding from two sides of the foyer up to thirteen bedrooms on the second floor. The Andrewses' five daughters and two sons all had their own rooms, some with carved bird's-eye maple four-poster beds and dressing tables, designed to match the woodwork. The servants' quarters and a large ballroom occupied the third floor. It was the first Cleveland house to have an elevator, an extraordinary convenience in 1885; it ran from the basement to the third floor (fig. 127).

Fig. 126. An English manor house. Samuel Andrews residence, unbuilt design; original rendering, Walter Blythe, architect (Western Reserve Historical Society, rendering by Otto Kuetenik, c. 1882).

Fig. 127. Samuel Andrews residence, 3033 Euclid Avenue; Walter Blythe, architect, 1882–85 (Western Reserve Historical Society, by G. M. Edmondson, 1889).

After three years of building and decorating, the Andrews family moved into their Avenue residence in 1885. They moved to New York three years later, leaving the Euclid Avenue house vacant. For all its haunting opulence, the Andrews house was a catastrophe for its owners in its operations and maintenance, but also for its meaning. It was only a monument, not a home. The sandstone pile stood furnished but mostly unoccupied for thirty years. Andrews's son,

Horace, made occasional visits and even lived there from time to time. The great house was as enigmatic as it was bold; no explanation at the time or since could account for Andrews's ambitious decision to build such a fabulous palace and then leave it to ruin. The house was immortalized as a dramatic stage set for three movies filmed in Cleveland: *House Without Children*, *Women Men Love*, and *Dangerous Toys* (fig. 128). Fifty years after it was built, the furnishings were put up for public auction and the building was razed.[5]

Other Avenue patrons who built residences inspired by eighteenth-century British country houses aligned more with the moderation of the Sterlings than the grandeur of the Andrewses. All except one of these residences, the Judge Stevenson Burke house, were built on the south side of the Avenue or east beyond Fifty-fifth Street on the north side, where land was less expensive. They were smaller as well, about half the size of their north-side neighbors. Of the

Fig. 128. Andrews's folly cum movie stage set. Scene from *House Without Children*, filmed in the Andrews residence in 1919 (Western Reserve Historical Society).

several architectural images that were fashioned after English domestic design, "Queen Anne" was liberally used to refer to a variety of classical types and designs. The free association of big and small bay windows, gables, dormers, cantilevers, and detailing inspired one contemporary critic to observe that the Queen Anne fashion was "very much like cabinet maker's work translated into architecture."[6] The furniture analogy was a good one, for it seems that these residences, inside and out, were conceived more for comfort than for show (figs. 129, 130).

This was not to say that they were inexpensive, however. Ella Grant Wilson described the spiraling cost of rebuilding the highly ornate Queen Anne manor house of Stevenson and Ella Burke in her book, *Famous Old Euclid Avenue* (1937). Judge Burke complained to Mrs. Wilson that the architect had originally estimated the cost around $12,000, but after the bill had exceeded $40,000, Mrs. Wilson wrote that "the Judge advised the architect that he would have to get future orders from Mrs. Burke for he was ready to throw up his hands." While the Judge had cause to be annoyed by the three-fold increase in cost, he appar-

Fig. 130. David Z. and Mary Castle Norton residence, 7503 Euclid Avenue; possibly the work of Coburn and Barnum, 1884–85 (Western Reserve Historical Society, c. 1885).

ently was proud of the outcome, for he selected an etching of his residence in place of a personal portrait to illustrate his biography in the *National Cyclopedia of American Biography*. This was only one of two residential portraits in the 560-page volume (fig. 131).[7]

Burke was a dignified and prominent lawyer. He came to Cleveland in 1869 after graduating from Ohio Wesleyan University in 1846 and serving on the Lorain County common pleas bench since 1861. Among his most notable cases was the Oberlin-Wellington slave rescue, which, due in large part to his ruling, strengthened abolitionist sentiment in Ohio. His Cleveland practice, in partnership with neighbors Franklyn T. Backus and E. J. Estep, centered on a number of railway consolidations and arbitrations, notably William Vanderbilt's 1882 purchase of the New York, Chicago & St. Louis Railroad. As legal counsel to railways, Burke knew the industry well and became a successful entrepreneur in his own right. He was president, chief executive, or director of many rail and steel companies, among them the Cleveland & Mahoning Valley, the Canadian Copper Company, and Republic Coal. The Burkes built their Euclid Avenue residence shortly after their marriage in 1882—Burke's second marriage following the death of his wife of three decades, Parthenia Poppleton. Ella

Fig. 131. Stevenson and Ella Burke residence, 4811 Euclid Avenue, c. 1882–83 (*Cleveland Plain Dealer*).

Fig. 132. *Opposite above left.* Isaac N. Topliff residence, 6602 Euclid Avenue, c. 1885 (Western Reserve Historical Society, 1889).

Fig. 133. *Opposite above right.* Edwin R. Perkins residence, 8011 Euclid Avenue, 1891 (Western Reserve Historical Society, c. 1891).

Fig. 134. *Opposite below.* Morris A. Bradley residence, 7217 Euclid Avenue, 1886 (Western Reserve Historical Society, 1889).

Burke, a Chicago native, was clearly the artistic one in the family. Her influence was as strong in the design of their house as it was in the organization of the Cleveland School of Art.[8]

The Burke residence was one of the Avenue's finest Queen Anne designs, many details of which were emulated in the houses of iron ore shipping magnate Morris Bradley and banker Edwin R. Perkins. Later versions of the Queen Anne style retained the broad gables and dynamic massing but strengthened the "stickwork" motif by symbolically echoing on the exterior facade the diagonal wooden members of the hidden structural frame. Later residences also departed from earlier models in their evocation of Tudor manses and Swiss chalets. Such was the case with the homes of merchant George P. Welch (c. 1890–95) and investment broker Charles A. Otis, Jr. (1900) (figs. 132–36). Another variant of the English manor house in the mid-1880s and early 1890s was the shingle style, named for the extensive use of shingle siding. Broad porches and gables, multistory bays and towers, and numerous windows reaching out to the open landscape were carried over from the Queen Anne, but in a much more simplified format. Coburn & Barnum and Charles F. Schweinfurth were the architects of record for the dozen or so residences designed in this style on the Avenue (see table 11). Though few in number, these houses added a comfortable warmth to the street's grandiose presence. The natural freedom and simple beauty of the house of lumberman George Pack, who remodeled and enlarged the 1833 Weddell house, was among the finest.[9]

Fig. 135. P. S. Jennings residence; Coburn and Barnum, architects, 1895 (*Cleveland Plain Dealer*).

Fig. 136. George B. Welch residence, 8806 Euclid Avenue; Meade and Granger, architects, c. 1893–95 (*Beautiful Homes of Cleveland*, 1917).

TABLE 11
The Shingled City House, 1885–1905

Patron/Resident	Address	Building Date	Architect
Isaac N. Topliff	6602	c. 1885	Unknown
George H. Worthington	6603	1888	C. F. Schweinfurth
George W. Pack and Amos B. McNairy	3307/3333	1887–89	C. F. Schweinfurth
Ralph Cobb	6203	1889	C. F. Schweinfurth
George W. Morgan	8302	1889	Coburn & Barnum
William J. Morgan	8615	1889–90	Coburn & Barnum
W. H. Van Tine	8120	1889–91	C. O. Arey
William H. Boardman	3608	1891–92	C. F. Schweinfurth
Arnold C. Saunders	7407	1892–94	C. F. Schweinfurth
George B. Christian	7341	c. 1894	Coburn & Barnum
Dan R. Hanna	7404	1895	C. F. Schweinfurth
William A. Price	7801	1903	Unknown

Pack retained Schweinfurth in 1887 to redesign the two houses on the Weddell estate, one for himself and one for his daughter and son-in-law, Mary and Amos McNairy (figs. 137, 138). The result was a combined thirty-room house centered around Schweinfurth's large living hall with a sitting area and open stairway to the second floor. It featured twelve fireplaces and a third-floor ballroom. The architect resurfaced the exterior skin with blue sandstone blocks on the ground level and cypress shingles on the upper story and roof. He also sheathed interior walls and floors with natural woods—oak on the first, cherry on the second, and Norway pine on the third floor—and designed furniture, fixtures, and hardware to complement the woodwork.[10] The architect revived subtle American colonial traits in the Pack-McNairy residence in the Palladian window in the front gable and the Tuscan pillars of the open porch. These features hearkened back to New England house design of the eighteenth century, which Schweinfurth would fully incorporate in his subsequent Euclid Avenue houses of the 1890s.

The Avenue's shingled residences formed an understated, quiet interlude in residential design, but not a sustained or popular one. By its very nature, the style lacked the urbane appearance favored by most Euclid Avenue patrons. This preference certainly was not unique among Clevelanders; shingle-style residences were typically found throughout the country in more countrified settings, like the suburbs and along the seashore. Euclid Avenue had long since lost its bucolic ambiance. It was now very much an urban city street and the stage for large, expensive city houses. Instead, the more elaborate Romanesque revival manner captured the attention of most patrons, becoming the preeminent style on the Avenue during the active building period of the 1880s and 1890s (figs. 139–46).

Fig. 137. Amos B. McNairy residence, 3333 Euclid Avenue. Originally Peter M. Weddell house, renovated and enlarged by C. F. Schweinfurth, architect, 1887–89 (Western Reserve Historical Society, 1890s).

Fig. 138. Residences of George W. Pack, *left,* and Amos B. McNairy, *right,* 3307 and 3333 Euclid Avenue; C. F. Schweinfurth, architect, 1887–89 (Western Reserve Historical Society, 1890s).

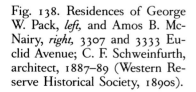

Fig. 140. George W. Morgan residence, 8302 Euclid Avenue; Coburn and Barnum, architects, 1889 (Coburn and Barnum, *Folio,* 1897).

Fig. 141. *Above*. William J. Morgan residence, 8615 Euclid Avenue; Coburn and Barnum, architects, 1889–90 (*Inland Architect and News Record*, April 1890).

Fig. 142. *Right*. William A. Price residence, 7801 Euclid Avenue, 1903 (*Beautiful Homes of Cleveland*, 1917).

Fig. 143. *Above.* W. H. Van Tine residence, 8120 Euclid Avenue; Clarence O. Arey, architect, 1889–91 (*Inland Architect and News Record,* May 1891).

Fig. 144. *Left.* William H. and Augusta Bissell Boardman residence, 3608 Euclid Avenue; C. F. Schweinfurth, architect, 1891–92 (Western Reserve Historical Society, 1910).

Fig. 145. George B. Christian residence, 7341 Euclid Avenue; Coburn and Barnum, architects, 1894 (Western Reserve Historical Society).

Fig. 146. Arnold C. Saunders residence, 7407 Euclid Avenue; C. F. Schweinfurth, architect, 1892–94 (Western Reserve Historical Society).

The Romanesque Revival Arrives

Euclid Avenue patrons were among good company in their growing fondness for revived Romanesque forms; not only their American contemporaries but also their European ancestors took a liking to this masonry style. Montgomery Schuyler, a leading architectural critic in the 1880s, noted that it was the merchants rather than the princes who built the original Romanesque palaces in the medieval commercial republics of Venice, Florence, and Genoa, "as plainly as that story is told by Fifth Avenue and Commonwealth Avenue and Michigan Avenue and Rittenhouse Square."[1] Schuyler might well have added Euclid Avenue to this list of urban showcases.

Sandstone was a principal ingredient in the Romanesque recipe. This stone was particularly appropriate for the high style favored by Euclid Avenue patrons since it was the source of one of Ohio's largest industries. Sandstone was the building material of the age and Ohio quarries and flagging plants were the chief providers of it to the rest of the nation. Cuyahoga County contained the largest stonecutting plant in the country, the Independence Stone Company,

Fig. 147. Sandstone quarries in Independence, Ohio, supplied the Romanesque rage on Euclid Avenue. William and Mary Stone Chisholm residence, 2827 Euclid Avenue; C. F. Schweinfurth, architect, 1887–89 (Western Reserve Historical Society, 1889).

TABLE 12
The Romanesque Revived

Patron/Resident	Address	Building Date	Architect
Sylvester T. Everett	4111	1883–87	C. F. & Julius Schweinfurth
Charles W. Bingham	2445	1883	Peabody & Stearns
William Chisholm, Sr.	2827	1887–89	C. F. Schweinfurth
P. M. Spencer	6513	c. 1885–90	Unknown
Rev. William A. Leonard	3054	c. 1885–90	Coburn & Barnum
French-Devereux	2525	1889–91	C. F. Schweinfurth
Charles F. Brush	3725	1887–88	George H. Smith
Stewart H. Chisholm	3730	1891	Unknown
William Chisholm	3618	1895	Unknown
Samuel F. Haserot	7224	1892–93	C. F. Schweinfurth
Henry Hatch	8415	1892–94	C. F. Schweinfurth
John L. Severance	8811	1891–92	C. F. Schweinfurth
Albert L. Withington	7111	1898	C. F. Schweinfurth
Luther Allen	7609	1896–97	Meade & Granger
David Z. Norton	7301	1897–98	C. F. Schweinfurth
Cox-Prentiss	3411	1898–99	C. F. Schweinfurth
Mary L. Severance	8821	1899–1900	F. S. Barnum
Henry W. White	8937	1901	F. B. Meade

and the quarries near the northern Ohio town of Independence were the main reserves for the sandstone shipped by the B&O Railroad to the East and Midwest (fig. 147).[12]

This period in the architectural development of Euclid Avenue was particularly significant to Cleveland's building trades in that it welcomed out-of-town artisans, craftsmen, and architects in greater numbers than ever before. Through the residences built for Avenue patrons, Cleveland decisively joined the national architectural scene. Located midway between Chicago and cosmopolitan Eastern urban centers, Cleveland designers drew stylistic inspiration from both the rustic bent of their fellow midwesterners, with whom they felt a natural affinity, and their sophisticated Atlantic seaboard mentors, whose high-style taste they greatly admired. The fully mature Romanesque style arrived on Euclid Avenue with the arrival in Cleveland in 1883 of architect Charles F. Schweinfurth from Boston. Such local architects as Levi Scofield, George H. Smith, and the firm of Coburn & Barnum had already worked in the style, and even influenced Schweinfurth to some extent, but Schweinfurth's arrival inaugurated a grander phase in which the best ideas nationally inspired the city's best architects (see table 12).

The designs of Richardson and his followers in the 1880s and 1890s emphasized a rational approach to building through dense shapes and forms calculated to create bold impressions of strength (figs. 148, 149). While the trademarks of the style were to be found in asymmetrical massing, foliated carvings,

Fig. 148. P. M. Spencer residence, 6513 Euclid Avenue, c. 1885–90 (Western Reserve Historical Society).

Fig. 149. Bishop William A. Leonard residence, 3054 Euclid Avenue; Coburn and Barnum, architects, c. 1885–90 (Coburn and Barnum, *Folio,* 1897).

high-pitched roof lines, towers, turrets, and obtuse bays, its most distinct attribute was its sheer massiveness, which reflected the robust taste of the day. Romanesque forms nicely mirrored the era's complex commercial growth, aggressive politics, and heady social spirit.

It is appropriate that the patron responsible for introducing the mature Romanesque revival style to Cleveland was foremost banker and railroad entrepreneur Sylvester Everett. A man of diverse talents and interests, Everett had lived in Cleveland since boyhood and had gained his prominent position in the business, culture, and politics of the city through his leadership of some of its most dynamic institutions. In the spring of 1883, he retained Boston architects Charles and Julius Schweinfurth to design a grand manor house in the style pioneered in Boston by Richardson (fig. 150).

Everett prepared carefully. First he purchased the northeast corner of Fortieth Street across from the family homestead of his wife, Alice Wade, granddaughter of Jeptha Wade. Then he razed the existing house on the site and engaged the architect and sculptor Levi Scofield to draw up plans for a new house. It soon became clear to Everett that Scofield could not meet his rising expectations. Having toured the European continent, having close ties with an extraordinary array of business and political leaders in New York, Washington, D.C., Philadelphia, and Boston, and being a voracious reader of world history and literature (he was said to have memorized all of Shakespeare's major plays), Everett was acquainted with many of the great works of contemporary art and architecture and was a demanding and well-versed patron. He sought out architects active in the East Coast cities and chose the Schweinfurth brothers of Boston to see if they could produce a superior design. Their first rough sketches for him indicated they could indeed "make a much more substantial looking house" than Scofield could. Everett dropped Scofield, hired the Schweinfurths, and instructed them to "go ahead as fast as possible with the work."[3]

Everett's Hummelstone palace took four years (1883–87) to design, construct, and furnish. It had four-foot-thick exterior walls and housed over 20,000 square feet on three floors. Romanesque motifs of the medieval and Renaissance eras appeared in the round and polygonal towers, crenelated porte-cochere, and massive twin Corinthian columns supporting the front porch. The specific influence of the Louisiana-born Boston architect Richardson was to be seen in the strong, controlled emphasis on contrasting vertical and horizontal elements, the richly carved rounded windows and arches, and the polychromatic stonework (figs. 151, 152). When his former Boston associates completed the Everett house, Richardson gave their design his "high commendation."[4]

It was as grandiose as it was handsome. The mansion had thirty-five principal rooms and forty fireplaces. The great hall, the center of the first floor, opened out to the living room, dining room, library, music and reception rooms (figs. 153, 154). Immense stained glass windows inlaid with images of Richard the Lion-Hearted and the Everett coat of arms dominated the broad stairway and the hall. The family's second-floor living quarters and guest rooms, includ-

Fig. 150. Charles F. Schweinfurth was the medieval Romanesque master on Euclid Avenue. Unidentified residence; C. F. Schweinfurth rendering, 1892 (Western Reserve Historical Society).

Fig. 151. Everett residence, 4111 Euclid Avenue; Charles F. and Julius Schweinfurth, architects, 1883–87 (Western Reserve Historical Society, by G. M. Edmondson).

Fig. 152. Everett residence (*Beautiful Homes of Cleveland*, 1917).

Fig. 153. Everett residence, second-floor landing (courtesy E. E. Worthington, by G. M. Edmondson, 1937).

ing fifteen bedrooms and twelve bathrooms, were designed to accommodate Everett's three daughters from his first marriage, his and Alice's four children, and their frequent houseguests. Besides Japanese and Scandinavian themes for some bedrooms, the black ebony guest room—reserved exclusively for visits by U.S. presidents—received extraordinary design care (fig. 155).

The most unique room was surely that built for Everett's young wife Alice, who had a deathly fear of thunderstorms. Always protective of her comfort, he ordered the architects to add a windowless and soundproofed sitting room to which she could flee during rough weather. Alice's "hostess balcony," at the head of the central stairway on the third floor, was another customized amenity designed to honor her status: to enable her to view and be viewed by guests as they passed into the ballroom. For his daughter Allie, a secret stair-

Fig. 154. Everett residence, grand hallway (courtesy E. E. Worthington, by G. M. Edmondson, 1937).

Fig. 155. Everett residence, ebony bedroom of the U.S. presidents (courtesy E. E. Worthington, by G. M. Edmondson, 1937).

way from the front hall to her second-floor bedroom enabled her to escape from the public rooms on the first floor. For himself, Everett had the architects face the den fireplace with hand-painted tiles depicting twenty of his favorite Shakespearean plays (fig. 156). So for a man who had grown up on a modest Trumbull county farm in a family of eleven children, he had achieved a distinction far exceeding even his own expectations. Alice Wade, however, twenty years her husband's junior, was quite accustomed to such elegance. She "expected everything but the moon" from Everett, according to their daughter Ruth, "and he nearly always could supply it."[5] Certainly he did so with their new home, which rivaled the splendid Wade residence in which she had been raised.

The Everetts' residence was a baronial pile with its huge rooms and high ceilings, which some found gloomy and forbidding and all viewed as awesome.

It was a legend in its time and was widely believed to be among the most expensive homes in Cleveland. Everett, who may have known more business and political leaders than did most U.S. presidents, hosted such eminent industrialists as J. P. Morgan and Andrew Carnegie—who stayed here during his infamous custody trial with Cassie Chadwick—and a virtual pageant of presidents: Grant, Hayes, Harrison, McKinley, Taft, and Harding.[16] He was one of Cleveland's most highly respected citizens, really among the capitalist royalty of the city. Everett was lured into the center of Republican politics through his business interests in banking, iron ore, and street railways, but he preferred to work on the sidelines rather than on the public stage. Alice Wade Everett, the only daughter of the Wade dynasty, was equally esteemed, respected especially for her commitment to the Cleveland Orphan Asylum.

Fig. 156. Everett residence, Moorish wishing-well room with inlaid tile mosaic, sandalwood paneling, and star-shaped fountain (courtesy E. E. Worthington, by G. M. Edmondson, 1937).

Fig. 157. Bingham residence, library (courtesy Bolton Family, by G. M. Edmondson, c. 1930s).

Schweinfurth's design for the Everett residence—in which the family lived for over thirty-five years—was a landmark in the Avenue's architectural development. It introduced the stylistic bent of Richardsonian Romanesque to Cleveland and expanded the vision of grand house design beyond the city's venue. Standard Tool Company president Charles W. Bingham shared Everett's astuteness for high style and also tapped the East Coast architectural establishment when he hired Peabody & Stearns of Boston to design his Avenue residence (figs. 157, 158). Over the years, Bingham maintained a close association with these prominent architects, who designed his Avenue house in 1883 and his Glenville country cottage in 1887–88. The refined talent apparent in their work prompted Bingham to retain the architects again in the 1890s when he came into possession of his wife's family home, the old Nathan Perry house, and

asked them to design extensive interior alterations and a wing and stable at the rear. While Bingham's houses were the architects' only residential commissions in Cleveland, they designed palatial residences on the grand avenues of Philadelphia, New York, and Newport, with the majority of their private clients similar in stature and affluence to the Binghams of Cleveland (figs. 159, 160).[17]

Quite possibly, Peabody & Stearns's work directly inspired one of Schweinfurth's finest house designs, which was commissioned by William Chisholm, Sr. (fig. 161). The architect's design for this house, built in 1887–89, was disarmingly similar to Peabody & Stearns's design for the Binghams in the massing, the broad front gable, open entrance porch, and the rounded front bay. Schweinfurth kept a photograph of the Bingham house in his office portfolio. In an 1897 profile of the architect in *Architectural Reviewer,* critic Charles Jenkins commended Schweinfurth's "air of proportion" for the Chisholm residence as "one of the very best examples of this style" that he had produced.[18] Certainly

Fig. 158. Charles W. and Mary Payne Bingham residence, 2445 Euclid Avenue; Peabody & Stearns, architects, 1883 (courtesy Bolton Family, by G. M. Edmondson, 1930s).

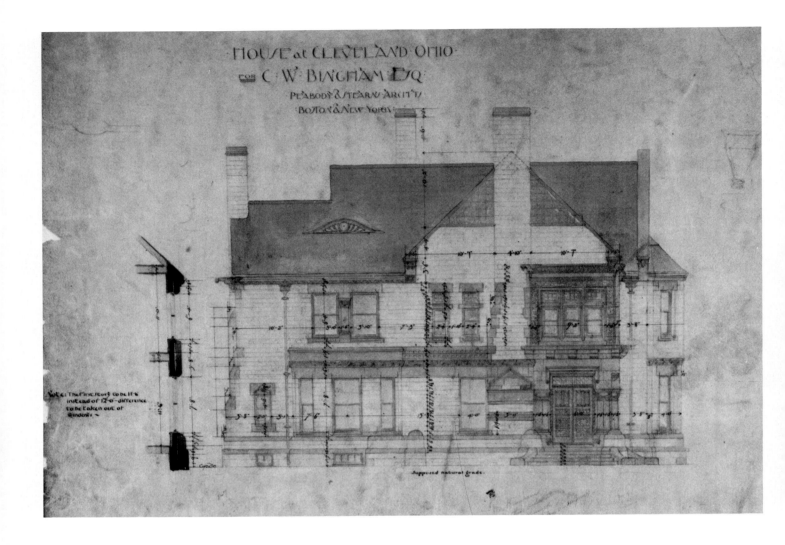

Fig. 159. Bingham residence, original rendering of front elevation, Peabody & Stearns, 1883 (Boston Public Library).

it memorialized the architect's great talent for invigorating a design with well-chosen materials. For the Chisholms he selected a Lake Superior red granite for the body of the house (shipped by freighter from Minnesota) and black slate from the Maine coast for the roof tiles. The interior was paneled with natural hardwoods.

Client William Chisholm was a wealthy industrialist, and he and his wife Mary were both midwesterners. Chisholm had grown up on the Avenue, son of Scottish parents, Henry and Jean Chisholm, who had made their way in Cleveland after arriving in America at midcentury. William trained as a mechanical engineer at the Philadelphia Polytechnic College and later went off to manage one of his father's rolling mills in Chicago, the native city of his wife, Mary Stone. Upon their return to Cleveland in 1879, Chisholm took over the presidency of his father's firm, the Cleveland Rolling Mill Company, and the couple

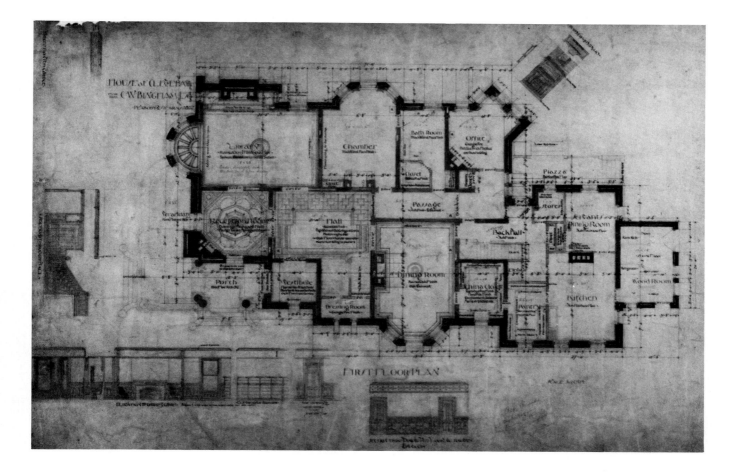

FIRST FLOOR PLAN

and their three children set up housekeeping in the former Avenue residence of William B. Castle. In their mid-forties when they built their Schweinfurth-designed residence, the Chisholms chose the grandest style of their day, the cultural symbol of commercial success in this age of capitalism.

Other Avenue capitalists who retained Schweinfurth to design handsome sandstone residences were Julius French, Henry R. Hatch, Dan R. Hanna, and Albert Withington (figs. 162–64). Schweinfurth was the architect of choice for the fashionable Romanesque revival, and Euclid Avenue was Cleveland's main showcase, as were Prairie Avenue in Chicago, Delaware Avenue in Buffalo, and Vandeventer Place in St. Louis.

The Refined Romanesque Villa

But not everyone who built a Romanesque mansion on this grand avenue sought to emulate the robust Richardsonian mold or retained Schweinfurth to design it. Other patrons preferred the sculptural definition of Italianized Renaissance forms. The enormous mansion of Charles F. Brush, the inventor of electric arc lighting, was one of the finest in this vein.

Fig. 160. Bingham residence, original rendering of first floor plan, Peabody & Stearns, 1883 (Boston Public Library).

Fig. 161. William Chisholm, Sr., residence, 2827 Euclid Avenue; C. F. Schweinfurth, architect, 1887–89 (Western Reserve Historical Society).

In 1887 Brush bought and demolished the former residence of Henry M. Flagler, which was three doors west of Fortieth Street, and retained architect George H. Smith to design a Romanesque villa to take its place (fig. 165). (He and neighbor John Severance would next commission Smith in 1889 to design their commercial development on Euclid Avenue, The Arcade.) The Brush house was built during 1887–88 by local contractors William B. McAllister and Andrew Dall, both Irish immigrants, and the Brooks Building Company.[19] To no one's surprise, the inventor's residence was the first in the city to be wired for and lit by electricity. Like Brush himself, who was broad-shouldered, deep-chested and stood over six feet tall, his house was massive in size and encompassed almost 40,000 square feet on three floors and was set back 160 feet from the Avenue. To the rear stood the largest windmill in the world; it had a sail area of 1,880 square feet and generated the power to fuel the house's ten tons of storage batteries. It must have appeared in this late nineteenth-century setting as the satellite dish does in late twentieth-century backyards (fig. 166).

Fig. 162. Julius E. French–
Harry K. and Mildred French
Devereux residence, 2525 Euclid
Avenue; C. F. Schweinfurth, architect, 1889–91. Mirrored the
overall design of the Everett
house (Western Reserve Historical Society).

Fig. 163. Henry K. Hatch residence, 8415 Euclid Avenue;
C. F. Schweinfurth, architect,
1892–94. Original perspective
drawing, 1892 (Western Reserve
Historical Society).

Like many of their neighbors, Charles and Mary Brush shared in the planning of their residence, especially the interior, to make sure the look and function of each room matched their tastes. Brush worked closely with the prolific New York furniture design house of Herter Brothers and the brilliant decorative artist Louis Tiffany, who designed all the lighting fixtures, stained glass windows, transoms, and skylights. Brush also guided the woodcarver, fireplace builder, and other craftsmen. In one instance, he returned Herter's dining room drawings edited with "pencil memoranda on some of them" and told him to "please note carefully." He admonished Herter for the design of the table, which was too small: "Now this top must be not less than 10' in diameter. . . . This was carefully considered when the drawings for the sideboard were made. I enclose tracing from drawing of sideboard and surroundings, indicating how Mr. Smith and I proposed to arrange the high narrow door . . . so as to admit the 10 foot top easily." Brush, never known to be reticent with his opinions, went on at length to comment on every detail of the rosewood furniture for the library and reception room.[20]

Undoubtedly at Brush's request, Smith's grandiose design for the house was a kind of revival showcase for Romanesque and Italian Renaissance styles. The rough sandstone blocks, excavated in Amherst, Ohio, were set to recall certain Romanesque traits: the checkerboard pattern at the gables, straight-topped windows, and beautifully carved moldings. The house's vertical thrust and use of the stylized domed tower and Ionic capitals lent a Renaissance flavor.

But contrary to historical tradition, Smith and Brush incorporated such current advances in domestic technology as fireproof construction and a comprehensive electrical wiring system. The somber, though luxurious, interior was paneled with carved oak from England in the dining room and Japanese rosewood in the family's library and reception rooms. At the foot of the circular mahogany staircase in the main hall stood the central attraction: Brush's enormous pipe organ, which reached up three floors to the ballroom.[21]

Fig. 165. An Italianized Romanesque palace. Charles F. and Mary Brush residence, 3725 Euclid Avenue; George H. Smith, architect, 1887–88 (Western Reserve Historical Society, by G. M Edmondson).

Fig. 166. The largest windmill in the world, built by Charles F. Brush in his Euclid Avenue backyard (Western Reserve Historical Society, 1889).

It is appropriate that this Renaissance man had a Renaissance house (fig. 167). He was a genius. At age twenty-seven, Brush invented the first electric open-coiled dynamo. Within three years, in 1879, he threw a switch which dramatically illuminated the Public Square with twelve dynamo-powered arc lamps, thus inaugurating electric streetlighting throughout the world. His was an invention that profoundly transformed the quality of urban life in this country, chiefly because of his own facility in its use and promotion. Brush founded

Fig. 167. The Renaissance inventor, Charles F. Brush (Cleveland Public Library, by G. M. Edmondson, 1909).

the Brush Electric Light and Power Company in 1881 to build central power stations and arc lamps for Cleveland and such other major cities as New York, Boston, Philadelphia, Baltimore, Montreal, and San Francisco. The firm consolidated with Edison Electric in 1892 to form the General Electric conglomerate.[22]

Brush's ceaseless laboratory work, centered in the basement of his Euclid Avenue residence since the late 1880s, led to more than fifty inventions. Following his retirement from active businesses in 1891, his residence became his headquarters; after the death of his wife, Mary, his research became his companion and his laboratory his retreat.[23]

He also presided over his property with vigor—by day and in perpetuity. The Everett girls, who lived about a half-block east at Fortieth Street, called him "the wolf" because he would stand in his backyard cracking a long horsewhip to scare their horses away if they dared to ride on the trail through his property. He expanded his private domain by acquiring the property of his next door neighbor Mrs. T. Sterling Beckwith upon her death in 1900. Brush kept the Beckwith house for thirteen years until the University Club convinced him that it would be a good neighbor. Notwithstanding his concession in this case, Brush was generally more gloomy than many of his neighbors about the Avenue's residential future. As a native Clevelander, he had watched the changes on the grand avenue over an eighty-year period, from its rise in the 1850s to the onset of its fall in the 1920s. He resolved that his own home would not be left to developers after his death. Like Rockefeller, Brush ordered in his will that his

house be demolished after his death. The sandstone residence and its fabulous windmill came down in 1929.[24]

The Brush mansion's version of the Romanesque appealed to few others along the Avenue during the age of Richardson (figs. 168, 169). But whatever the particular strain, the Romanesque in all its various forms remained the prevalent fashion of the day among Euclid Avenue patrons. In the 1890s the preeminent Avenue architects, Schweinfurth and Coburn & Barnum, introduced yet another variation on the basic theme by emphasizing angular Tudor references—prominent gables, crenelated roofs, and slender, capped chimney stacks. Among the finest renditions were the manor houses commissioned by industrialists Luther Allen, Samuel Haserot, and David Z. Norton, financiers Louis H. Severance and his brother Solon, and dry goods merchant Henry K. Hatch. The architecture of these residences marked a clear departure from that of the more robust and pure pedigree of the earlier Everett and Chisholm residences (figs. 170, 171).

The Severance houses, for example—one authored by Schweinfurth in 1891 and one by Frank Barnum in 1899–1900—blended the refined touch of

the Tudor with the solid weight of the Romanesque. Schweinfurth even showed his affection for early nineteenth-century Puginesque motifs in the foliated carvings he designed for the great staircase in Severance's main living hall. And it was Schweinfurth, an avid collector of European pattern books, who brought the Tudor tendency to its highest level on the Avenue. The architect's schematic designs for the double residence commissioned by Jacob Dolson Cox, Jr., in 1898 revealed a further turn in Schweinfurth's artistic development.[25] He drew up two design schemes for Cox and his wife, Ellen: one was a romantic interpretation of the English Tudor half-timbered fashion, and the other, the design actually built, was a strict Romanesque design blended with Tudor details. The

Fig. 169. William Chisholm residence, 3618 Euclid Avenue, 1895; acquired by Dr. William T. Corlett in 1911 (Western Reserve Historical Society).

Fig. 170. Tudor chivalry meets Romanesque revival. John L. Severance residence, 8811 Euclid Avenue; C. F. Schweinfurth, architect, 1891–92 (Western Reserve Historical Society).

Fig. 171. Luther and Julia Allen residence, 7609 Euclid Avenue; Meade and Granger, architects, 1896–97 (*Beautiful Homes of Cleveland*, 1917).

half-timbered cottage might have been ideal for a country residence, but apparently the Coxes preferred the stronger Romanesque presence for their Euclid Avenue city house (figs. 172, 173).

The differences between the two designs were purely stylistic. Both plans were guided by the prominent twin gables and triple-arched central entrance on the front and a U-shaped floor plan, to achieve a division between the Cox family quarters on the west and the apartment for Lucretia Prentiss, Mrs. Cox's unmarried sister, on the east. Lucretia had a separate entrance with a connecting door to the Cox quarters. The first-floor layout of each household's "apartment" was quite similar, except for a family den and a larger octagonal-shaped dining room in the Cox quarters. All the main rooms were finished with white pine, with a more modest Georgian pine in the servants' quarters at the rear.[26] Schweinfurth also designed the stables to complement the main house. The entire estate was finished and ready for occupancy on Thanksgiving Day of 1899, just in time to celebrate the fiftieth wedding anniversary of Cox's parents.

The handsome residence, really an artful and academic study of romantic principles, must have provided the senior Jacob Dolson Cox—Civil War general, former Ohio governor, and an honorary member of the American Institute of Architects (AIA)—with a nice stage for his anniversary celebration. His son

Fig. 172. The architect's proposed half-timbered country house. Original design scheme for Jacob D. Cox–Lucretia Prentiss double residence, 3411 Euclid Avenue; C. F. Schweinfurth, architect. Original rendering, 1898 (Western Reserve Historical Society).

Fig. 173. The client's preferred Romanesque mansion. Design scheme as built for Cox–Prentiss residence; C. F. Schweinfurth, architect, 1898–99. Original rendering, 1898 (Western Reserve Historical Society).

was also an architecturally astute client, having been informally educated in the subject by his father. Architecture was the main occupation of neither man—Jacob, Jr., was founder and president of the Cleveland Twist Drill Company—yet both respected the culture of the building arts. In fact, the younger Cox's Schweinfurth-designed residence was just one of the major architectural projects in which he was involved. He built his family's first house on the Avenue in 1882, next door to the residence of his wife's parents, the Samuel B. Prentisses, and he and Schweinfurth collaborated again in 1900 when the architect designed the corporate offices for his business. Cox later worked closely with the gifted New York architect Cass Gilbert during the design and construction in 1915 of Cox Administration Building at Oberlin College, a building named for his father, the general, on a campus once presided over by his grandfather, Charles G. Finney.[27]

Cox might have been a demanding patron for Schweinfurth, but so were many of the architect's Euclid Avenue clients, among them David Z. Norton. Schweinfurth's responsiveness to his clients' tastes—designing a Romanesque rather than Tudor style residence in Cox's case—was one of his distinctive talents. For Norton's Euclid Avenue residence, Schweinfurth went through the

same process with the client as he had in the design of the Cox–Prentiss house. Banker and iron merchant Norton, who had first built on the Avenue in the early 1880s, retained Schweinfurth in 1897 to design a new residence to match the new wealth he had achieved as co-owner of Oglebay, Norton & Company. The first plans the architect turned out were in the academic Adamesque manner, a style revived by the major architects in this country in the late 1890s (fig. 174). Schweinfurth's genteel, high-style design showed the principal facades draped with lavish carved swags and classical ornament. Nothing of its kind, so delicate and refined, had yet been built on the Avenue, and Norton rejected the scheme.[28] Instead, the iron ore entrepreneur, a native Clevelander attuned to the prevailing taste among his grand avenue neighbors, chose a more conventional Romanesque Tudor manor house (fig. 175).

The residence, which faced the northeast corner of Seventy-third Street, proclaimed itself to the Avenue by the imported Venetian stone lion statues that stood on either side of the arched doorway (fig. 176). This masculine theme

Fig. 174. The architect's proposed Adamesque manor house for David Z. and Mary Castle Norton, 7301 Euclid Avenue; C. F. Schweinfurth, architect. Original rendering, 1897 (Western Reserve Historical Society).

Fig. 175. The client's preferred Romanesque villa; design scheme as built. David Z. and Mary Castle Norton residence, 7301 Euclid Avenue; C. F. Schweinfurth, architect, 1897–98. Original rendering, 1898 (Western Reserve Historical Society).

Fig. 176. Venetian lions in repose. Norton residence, front porch facing the northeast corner of Seventy-third Street and Euclid Avenue (*Cleveland Plain Dealer*).

was carried into the interior in the heavy use of dark wooden wall panels, thick ceiling beams, and raised doorway moldings. The "Napoleon Room," the finest chamber on the main floor, showcased David Norton's exquisite Napoleona collection and revealed his and his wife's fondness for the romance of chivalry. The medieval armored statues that stood guard in the main hall reflected the same enthusiasm.[29] Upstairs, as was the custom in many Euclid Avenue houses, the master's bedroom and private bath were at the front of the house overlooking the Avenue and taking in the southern sun. The three children—Miriam, Robert, and Laurence—enjoyed the luxury of their own private rooms, and a bath shared among them. The billiard room for Norton and his sons was also on the second floor, while the ballroom was located among the public rooms on the first floor rather than the third (figs. 177, 178).

The Nortons, cosmopolitan in their interests and activities, thrived in their Euclid Avenue residence. Having lived in only this city and on the Avenue for

Fig. 177. A romance for chivalry. Norton residence, main hall (Western Reserve Historical Society, by G. M. Edmondson, 1939).

Fig. 178. A passion for Napoleon. Norton residence, Napoleon Room, recreated from family home of Mary Castle Norton and dedicated to the memory of her father, William B. Castle (Western Reserve Historical Society, by G. M. Edmondson, 1939).

Fig. 179. Norton residence (Western Reserve Historical Society, by G. M. Edmondson, 1910).

decades, both David Norton and his wife Mary—who was the daughter of Cleveland's former mayor, William B. Castle—were established figures in the city's downtown cultural and social institutions. David was entrenched in many fraternal and sports clubs, among them the Union and University clubs, the Country and Castalia Sporting clubs. Mary Norton, who was unique among her neighbors for her schooling in Lausanne, Switzerland, and at Vassar College, was founder of the Musical Arts Association and an officer of the Cleveland Institute of Music and Fortnightly Club. Their sons, Robert and Laurence, who reveled in the leisurely pleasures of their parents' Euclid Avenue life, lived on in the family home long after their parents' deaths in January 1928. In 1937, forty years after the Nortons first occupied it, the family home was one of only eight private residences remaining on the Avenue (fig. 179).[30]

The Romanesque houses of the 1880s defined the architectural design theme of this grand avenue, with their stones and bricks in contrasting colors, wide arches, and massive turrets. They were showy and clever, full of plays on shallow niches and unexpected spaces in unexpected shapes. But after the 1890s, patrons showed diminished enthusiasm for the romance of Romanesque forms and, instead, a heightened interest in revived classical and Renaissance styles. This ushered in a new era in residential design on the Avenue. Around the turn of the century, the street itself entered a new era. It was during this period that the long and delicate balance between the forces advancing the grand residential avenue and those promoting the commercial main street tipped to favor commerce.

Fig. 180. Downtown Cleveland's grandest promenade. Euclid Avenue looking west from Ninth Street toward Public Square, Permanent Block, *left foreground;* Ursuline Convent, *second from left;* Hickox Building with C. A. Selzer china store on ground, *right foreground* (Cleveland Public Library, 1892).

SEVEN

Imperial Elegance, 1895–1910

Downtown Cleveland had become a major city by 1895—active, dense, and populous. It was alive and well and thriving. Euclid Avenue was centered at the very heart of this activity as the city's premier residential street and also its best business address. On the Avenue itself, and on the parallel streets of Prospect and Superior avenues, retailers, showrooms, and small industries moved in to capitalize on the crowds of people, carriages, and trolley cars. Downtown businesses sought to establish a presence on the city's grandest promenade (fig. 180).

These commercial pressures prompted Euclid Avenue residents to think about the civic function of their street as both a place of private homes and a park-like boulevard developed according to a unified vision. Residents manifested their interests and concerns in several ways, most obviously in their protests against commerce, transit, and high property assessments. Yet a more conservative, even subtle, response appeared in the shifting architectural preferences of those who built on the Avenue around the turn of the century. If the Romanesque spirit portrayed the Avenue in its finest hour, the imperial classicism of the following decade would come to symbolize the neighborhood's peak of elegance and the beginning of its decline.

The art and architecture of European capitalism as expressed in Romanesque triumphs in the previous decades turned in the 1890s to embrace the Renaissance traditions of the finest high-style art forms. Italian palazzos, French chateauxs, and Grecian mansions replaced Romanesque palaces as the new cultural monuments. The imperial classicism of Italy, France, England, and Greece grew in favor among both architects and patrons: the architects, because the influential Ecole des Beaux-Arts in Paris and the American architectural schools were teaching formal design based on historical precedents; the patrons, because European high culture was viewed as the successful model for restoring order to the changing city. Grand avenue patrons, who avidly embarked on continental grand tours to satisfy their cultural appetites, promoted the genteel traditions of European art and architecture to elevate the American public's artistic standards. Having seen the grandeur of massive, state-initiated grand avenue projects in the European cities they toured, they hoped that such uniform classicism could ennoble their own neighborhood streets. It mattered less to them which stylistic reference was used, only that European historicism prevailed.

When English Tudor motifs were first imposed on the Avenue's Romanesque forms in the 1890s they brought a touch of refinement to these rough-hewn masses. They signaled the start of the move away from picturesque exuberance toward more subdued, classical motifs. By the late 1890s, the Eastern architectural establishment had fully embraced Renaissance influences. In Cleveland, however, patrons advanced more cautiously beyond their Romanesque allegiance. David Norton's resistance in 1897 to classical formality in the design of his Euclid Avenue mansion was a case in point.

It took the building of monumental civic and commercial projects designed by nationally prominent architects to turn the tide. A big step toward full acceptance of the new style was the Group Plan of 1903 formulated by the great Chicago architect and planner Daniel Burnham. The plan grouped the city's major municipal buildings around a ceremonial mall, all designed in the classical Beaux-Arts style. In this visionary civic setting, the new architecture was very popular. The broad appeal of the Chamber of Commerce Building in 1897, designed by Boston architects Peabody & Stearns, the Williamson Building in 1900, by New York architect George B. Post, and the Cleveland Trust Building in 1905, also by Post, further established the Renaissance and classical forms.

Among Euclid Avenue patrons, this revision in architectural taste occurred at a time when residential building on the Avenue was ebbing, and stylistic changes were therefore much more noticeable. In the fifteen years between 1895 and 1910, only sixty houses were built on the Avenue, far fewer than in earlier decades. The architects were also largely a new group. A younger generation of Cleveland architects entered the Avenue's building scene at this time, designers professionally trained in the classics and well-equipped to respond to the fresh tastes of the Avenue's clientele. Among the architectural newcomers were J. Milton Dyer, Frank Meade, Abram Garfield, and the firm of Hubbell & Benes. Meanwhile, Schweinfurth, the Romanesque master, remained in the forefront by shifting his design style in response to the changing tastes of his Euclid Avenue clients.

Some patrons bypassed local talent to call on the services of prestigious out-of-town architects, now a customary practice on this grand avenue as on others. The best known were New York architects Richard Morris Hunt and Stanford White, of McKim, Mead & White, and Boston architects Peabody & Stearns, who had worked with Charles W. Bingham in the 1880s. Their residential commissions were chiefly supported by grand avenue patrons—in New York, Boston, Newport, Washington, and Chicago, as well as Cleveland. The selection by Euclid Avenue patrons of nationally recognized talent reflected residents' insistence on the finest caliber of design. Sylvester Everett had done just this in 1883 when he chose Boston's Schweinfurth over the Clevelander Scofield.

TABLE 13
Academic Elegance, 1895–1910

Patron/Resident	Address	Building Date	Architect
Ambrose Swasey	7808	1891–92	R. M. Hunt
Worcester R. Warner	7720	1891–92	R. M. Hunt
Alfred A. Pope	3648	c.1895–1900	Unknown
George W. Howe	2248	1892–94	Coburn & Barnum
Charles A. Otis, Jr.	3436	1900	Unknown
Otto Miller	3738	1904	Unknown
James J. Tracy	3535	1904–5	Charles Hopkinson
Lyman H. Treadway	8917	1904	J. Milton Dyer
Samuel Mather	2605	1907–12	C. F. Schweinfurth
Francis E. Drury	8625	1910–12	Meade & Hamilton

Imperial Elegance

In 1891, engineers Ambrose Swasey and Worcester R. Warner further advanced the Avenue's artistic standards when they retained the eminent New York architect Hunt to design their adjacent houses just west of Seventy-ninth Street (fig. 181). Friends and business associates since age nineteen, Warner and Swasey were both fairly modest, genial characters—Swasey even timid—and prudent in their personal expenditures. Hunt, by contrast, born into the monied elite of old New York, was admired as the most prolific and talented designer of the Eastern establishment and was the family architect of such munificent clients as the Vanderbilts, Marquands, and Astors. The choice of Hunt by the more frugal Warner and Swasey, then, might have appeared a surprising one except for the fact that Hunt and Warner had previously worked together. They first met in 1886 when each had been retained by the federal government to collaborate on the design of the U.S. Naval Observatory in Washington, D.C.—Hunt for the observatory buildings and Warner for the mountings of the telescope. The architect was then commissioned in 1889 by Adelbert College of Western Reserve University, of which Warner was a trustee, to design Clark Hall and the president's house.[1]

Similar to much of his residential work at this time, especially the New York City commissions, Hunt's city houses for Warner and Swasey were modeled after the chateaux of the English Tudor and early French Renaissance periods. Unlike much of the expensive extravagance found on a Vanderbilt or Astor Fifth Avenue mansion, these Euclid Avenue townhouses lacked grandiose pretentions, as did their patrons. Hunt created the two residences to be viewed as one composition, symmetrical about a central driveway and Warner's observatory to the rear. They presented a brief but authentic continental facade to the street (fig. 182).

Fig. 181. The twin city houses of Ambrose Swasey and Worcester R. Warner, 7808 and 7720 Euclid Avenue; Richard Morris Hunt, architect, 1891–92 (Case Western Reserve University, by G. M. Edmondson).

Independent and yet related, the two houses reflected their owners' attitudes toward one another. Warner and Swasey's fifty-year partnership, which began back in Exeter, New Hampshire, when they lived in the same boarding house, grew into an "intimate business association," founded in mutual respect and trust. A decade before they built their residences on the Avenue, they came to Cleveland together from Chicago to establish their engineering company of Warner & Swasey, an international leader in the design and manufacture of telescopes and astronomical instruments. Their best known commissions were the huge telescopes for the Lick and Yerkes Observatories.[2]

Fig. 182. The magnificent observatory in Warner and Swasey's backyard (Case Western Reserve University).

Their scientific and business successes were no accident: each was a talented mechanical engineer with an eye for invention and profit. Warner was the more gregarious of the two, a great storyteller with many friends. He and his wife, the former Cornelia Blakemore, coprincipal of Miss Mittleberger's School, devoted their energies to Cleveland's cultural and educational affairs and to world travel. After thirty years in the city, in 1911, they and their daughter Helen built a country house north of New York City in Tarrytown-on-the-Hudson. Even at age sixty-five, Warner was unsure about the promised advantages of a leisurely life away from the city during the spring and summer months, in spite of his new proximity to Manhattan and his old Euclid Avenue friend John D. Rockefeller. But Warner, like so many Avenue contemporaries, came to enjoy a life split between city and country, not to mention excursions abroad. On their nineteenth European tour, in June 1929, Warner died of a stroke in Eisenach, Germany, marking an appropriate end to his cultivated life.[3] Within a period of ten days in 1929, Cleveland, and Euclid Avenue, lost two of their most distinguished inventor residents—Worcester Warner and Charles Brush.

Warner's partner, Ambrose Swasey, maintained a quieter existence in Cleveland. Unlike the Warners, he and his wife, Lavinia, traveled and entertained little and devoted themselves to the Euclid Avenue Baptist Church, to such educational institutions as Case School of Applied Sciences, and to their close friends, the Brushes, Garfields, Nortons, and Westinghouses. Swasey, the son of an affluent New Hampshire farmer, was an accomplished scholar, a creative scientist, a passionate inventor, and a homebody extraordinaire. He lived eighty of his ninety-one years in Exeter and Cleveland, staying on in his Euclid Avenue home long after the Warners' departure in 1911 and his wife's death in 1913.[4] Swasey was a modest man liberated by his earned wealth, his love of the inventive age in which he lived, and his faith in scientific and cultural progress. His residence was testimony to the fruits of the affluent society he admired, as were the profound technical advances he witnessed during his lifetime (1846–1937): the invention of the automobile, the airplane, the submarine; the development of the telephone, the radio, photography, and electricity; and the refinement of steam and electric railways and machine production. On his own Avenue, as an old man, he observed the consequences of this progress. It was cause for pride as well as chagrin. At age ninety-one, he returned to his parents' former farm in Exeter, New Hampshire, to die amidst the peaceful countryside of his childhood. Two years later his Euclid Avenue house was razed, the symbolic close to his and Warner's remarkable partnership.

When their residences were built almost a half-century before, they had introduced the continental strain of American classic design to the Avenue. Another contemporary strain, more eclectic in its origins, revived such Mediterranean and Roman concepts as flatter roof slopes and boxier shapes, which presented a blunt and rectilinear face to the street. These residences, in their understated elegance, departed from the complexity of either the English or French styles and certainly from the picturesque forms of earlier decades.

Fig. 183. Alfred A. Pope residence, 3648 Euclid Avenue, c. 1895–1900 (*Cleveland Plain Dealer*).

Fig. 184. Otto and Elizabeth Clark Tyler Miller residence, 3738 Euclid Avenue, 1904 (*Cleveland Plain Dealer*).

Fig. 185. Lyman H. Treadway
residence, 8917 Euclid Avenue;
J. Milton Dyer, architect, 1904
(*The Brickbuilder,* March 1904).

Among the Avenue patrons who built in this simplified genre were bankers
George W. Howe, Otto Miller, Lyman H. Treadway, and James J. Tracy. The
conventional character of each residence was simply a product of the vernacular. Their residences were more restrained in appearance than many of their
neighbors' houses, perhaps reflecting the conservative mood of each client (figs.
183–85).

George Howe's brick and terra-cotta house was completed in 1894, just
seven years before he died at age sixty-nine (fig. 186). Howe had come to
Cleveland forty years before to sell sewing machines produced by his uncle,
inventor Elias Howe. He turned to banking, following Civil War service, as an
officer of the Citizens Savings and Banking Company and then the Guardian
Trust Company. He and his wife Kate, whom he married in 1853, had lived
most of their married life on Prospect Street. In 1892 they retained the popular
Avenue firm of Coburn & Barnum to design for them an 11,000-square-foot
Euclid Avenue house one door east of Trinity Cathedral. The architects' clean
design provided a nice complement to Trinity Chapel's highly ornate facade.
The yellow Roman brick walls were simply trimmed, the most decorative displays being the fanciful cherubic-faced capitals on the front porch and second-
story balcony. Coburn & Barnum made up for any scarcity of exterior grandeur, however, by installing elaborate marble and tile fireplaces in the public
rooms. And even though the Howes had no children, their house had five bedrooms, noted for their "modern improvements" of walk-in closets, marble wash

basins, and connecting baths. The area for the four servants' rooms at the rear of the second floor had a separate bath and a private stairway down to the kitchen.[5]

Howe's neighbor, banker and real estate investor James J. Tracy, built a Renaissance-inspired mansion on the Avenue a decade later, in 1903–4 (fig. 187). Tracy, like Howe, had a long view of the Avenue's grand past and its likely commercial future. He had come to Cleveland in 1835 and was among the few Clevelanders who enjoyed a seventy-five-year acquaintance with the city's development. One local chronicler of the day wondered why Tracy, at age eighty-five, had to build a large and expensive Euclid Avenue residence. Why, indeed? He had lived on the Avenue for twenty years after his marriage to Jane Foote, yet as late as 1903 Tracy decided he wanted to build his own Euclid Avenue legacy. The residence, designed by Charles Hopkinson, was completed

Fig. 186. George W. and Katherine Howe residence, 2248 Euclid Avenue; Coburn and Barnum, architects, 1892–94 (Western Reserve Historical Society).

Fig. 187. James J. and Jane Foote Tracy residence, 3535 Euclid Avenue; Charles Hopkinson, architect, 1904–5 (Western Reserve Historical Society).

in 1904. Tracy died in 1910, and the house was leased within a decade to the Cleveland Women's Club.[6]

Architect Hopkinson, who had trained in the academic manner at Cornell University and traveled extensively throughout western Europe in the late 1880s, was a steadfast practitioner of the traditional European orders. In fact his best known work on the Avenue prior to the Tracy residence was the Georgian revival Colonial Club, built in 1895–96.[7] The Tracy house recalled subtle Renaissance traits in a brick and terra-cotta classical rendition, and it introduced such modern mechanical innovations as indirect electrical cove lighting in the living room. A sumptuous classicism sheathed the interior rooms, from the marble mantels and hand-carved mahogany woodwork on the first floor to the

cornice swags in the third-floor ballroom, which was added to the architect's plans at Mrs. Tracy's request.[8]

The Tracys' life in their mansion, though brief, befit their stature. Mrs. Tracy was an energetic hostess; she often invited notable speakers to entertain her dinner guests, or held forth herself with illustrated lantern slide talks on her travels. She was an enthusiastic supporter of Cleveland's musical and arts institutions, and with her friend Flora Stone Mather she co-founded the Cleveland Day Nursery and Free Kindergarten Association. The two women, neighbors for two decades on the Avenue, also served together on the advisory council of Flora Stone Mather College for Women.[9]

Fig. 188. A grand Tudor townhouse. Samuel and Flora Stone Mather residence, 2605 Euclid Avenue; C. F. Schweinfurth, architect, 1907–12. Formerly a portion of the site of Jacob Perkins residence (Cleveland Public Library, 1932).

The Tracy and Mather families were among the venerable institutions of the Avenue, judged by longevity and seniority. Even though Samuel and Flora Mather lived only about half the year in their Avenue residence after their summer house, Shoreby, in Bratenahl, was completed in 1891, their ties with the Avenue remained as strong as ever. Such commitment was cause for the Mathers, having lived on the Avenue for forty-four years, to decide in 1907 to build a house of their own making, for Samuel continued to enjoy the convenience of walking each day to his office in the Western Reserve Building at Water and Superior. The Mathers commissioned Charles Schweinfurth to plan their American classic residence, an imperial Tudor Gothic design for house and grounds that marked their view of the grand avenue and the family's place on it (fig. 188). By this time, Samuel Mather was recognized as the architect's chief client after having worked with one another on several projects. Thanks to his influence in the building of University School, Trinity Church, Kenyon College, and Western Reserve University, Mather had brought Schweinfurth a number of major commissions. His choice of architect for his Euclid Avenue residence was therefore not at all surprising; the fact that he decided to build a $3 million residence on the Avenue as late as 1907 was much more so.[10] But Mather was not one to accept passively the momentum of commercial change that was bearing down on the residential neighborhood. Rather, he strove to educate others by the force of his own actions. He thus bought the residence originally built by Jacob Perkins in 1853, demolished it, and retained Schweinfurth to design a new city manor house in its place.

This turned out to be Schweinfurth's largest residential commission, and the largest house ever built on the Avenue. The house and grounds encompassed a formal composition that was unprecedented in scope. The architect's scheme took in the entire man-made landscape, covering 2.4 acres of formal gardens, squash courts, an eight-car garage, and a forty-three-room residence (figs. 189, 190). The house, sited against a deep 600-foot front lawn, was the centerpiece of this highly structured composition, deliberately measured in the best Renaissance fashion to enhance its impact along the grand avenue. It was a triumphant display of architecture, landscape, and civic art. For Schweinfurth, the Mather commission represented the climax of his artistic development; it combined his natural talent in the anticlassical, Mediterranean dialect with his developed skill in academic forms.

Schweinfurth was in the midst of design development for Trinity Cathedral at the same time he was at work on the Mather residence. The two buildings shared common traits in their traceried windows, deep-set doorways, and stone battlements—delicacies that over the years had garnered Schweinfurth's loving attention. He perfected their details through his many trips to Spain and England and his volumes of sketches of things medieval. Even in the early 1890s, when the architect was still preoccupied with the Romanesque, *Plain Dealer* reporter S. J. Kelly, who visited Schweinfurth at work, was struck by his medieval

vision. Describing the drawings spread out on drafting tables throughout Schweinfurth's office, Kelly wrote, "All revealed that the designer's mind dwelt on days of chivalry, cloistered monks, and high arched churches of medieval times."[11] Schweinfurth's architectural signature was indeed drawn from the "days of chivalry."

Schweinfurth had another celebrated trait that endeared him to clients and gave pause to his contractors: He was a stubborn perfectionist in the execution of his plans and the choice of materials. As he told it, he superintended his work like a hawk, "knowing what I want, and recognizing it when seen." And

Fig. 189. Mather residence, landscaped backyard showing squash courts, *left rear* (Western Reserve Historical Society).

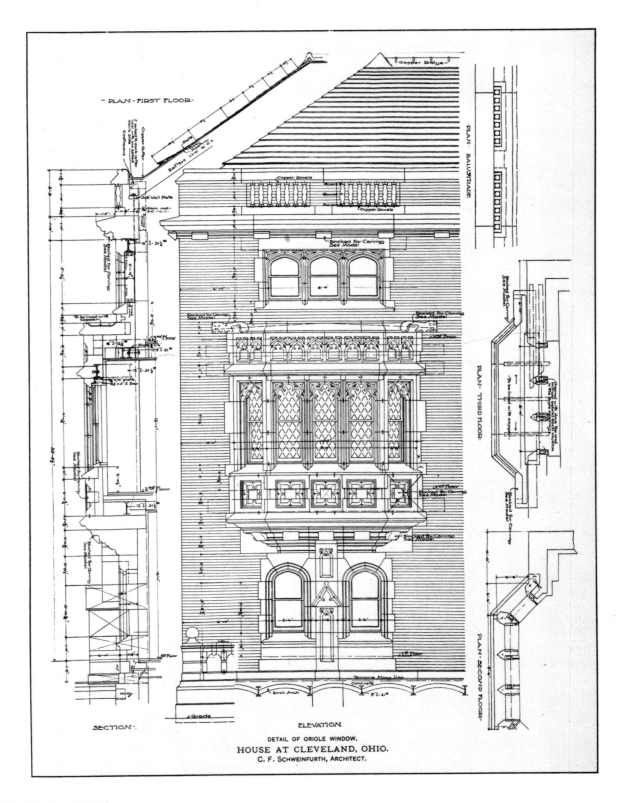

- PLAN - FIRST FLOOR -

PLAN · BALUSTRADE ·

PLAN · THIRD FLOOR ·

PLAN · SECOND FLOOR ·

SECTION·

ELEVATION

DETAIL OF ORIOLE WINDOW.
HOUSE AT CLEVELAND, OHIO.
C. F. SCHWEINFURTH, ARCHITECT.

when he did not see "it" executed as he had envisioned in his design, he became enraged, even to the point of demolishing a craftsman's work. Within the trade, Schweinfurth was revered and feared as "a terror to contractors who varied a hair's breadth from his designs." In one of his more dramatic outbursts, in 1915, he axed and destroyed a gold leaf ceiling in the making in the Cuyahoga County Court House. The workman on the job, surprised and angered, struck Schweinfurth across his face with a monkey wrench and blinded him in one eye. Years later, young Philip Mather asked his father which of the architect's eyes was the glass one, and his father replied, "Look for the gleam of human kindness; that is his glass eye."[12] Schweinfurth's volatile temperament always protected his clients' best interests and was little hindrance in the fine camaraderie he enjoyed with the Mathers. In fact, Flora Mather greatly enjoyed her partnership with Schweinfurth during the house's design and construction, even though she was terminally ill at the time.

The plans for the residence were shaped by Samuel and Flora's personal interests. Samuel had the dark red bricks of the exterior custom ordered and fired in Gonic, New Hampshire, to duplicate those of Harvard's main gates and Yard buildings, which he admired. Flora's personal study was located beyond the first-floor public rooms, adjacent to an elevator for her use. Next came Samuel's billiard room and den, handsomely fitted out with oak paneling and moldings carved in Flemish motifs. The kitchen, pantry, and servants' dining and sitting rooms were across the hall, just another part of the family's private domain. On the second floor, Samuel and Flora's spacious bedrooms, joined by marble baths, looked out to the Avenue, while the other bedrooms for guests and the Mather children—Constance, Philip, Amasa, and Livingston—had views of the gardens. Seven servants rooms were on the third floor, as was a ballroom that seated 300.

Schweinfurth hired a contractor and a team of craftsmen, carpenters, and sculptors to carry out the plans, as was his practice. His contractor, J. Wentworth Smith, who built many homes for affluent Clevelanders, was responsible for construction management and carpentry. William B. McAllister and his chief sculptor handcrafted the Ionic capitals and pilasters in the drawing room, the lion finials of the main staircase newel post, and the Flemish carvings in Mather's billiard room. Sculptors Thomas C. B. Reardon and Karl F. Broemal worked under McAllister's direction on the stone figures, gargoyles, Gothic tracery, and the clustered chimney stacks. Construction began in 1909. Three years later in the autumn of 1912, the house was finally ready for the Mather family (fig. 191).[13]

The family had changed in important ways during these three years. Their new home had been conceived as a public reception hall and private sanctuary for the Mathers—Flora Stone Mather, the youngest daughter of Amasa Stone and a leading benefactress of the city, and Samuel Mather, chairman of Pickands, Mather & Company, one of the largest shippers of iron ore, and also a leading benefactor. But Flora Mather, the family's gracious matron and mother of four children, who had personally outlined much of the original house plans

Fig. 190. *Opposite*. Mather residence, detail of oriel window on front elevation (*The Brickbuilder,* November 1909).

with Schweinfurth, never saw her contribution to the Avenue rise above ground level. She died of breast cancer in the fall of 1909 at the age of fifty-seven.[14] Her daughter, Constance, became the lady of the house, taking over her mother's responsibilities as hostess for her father's social gatherings (fig. 192).

Samuel Mather, a native Clevelander, had moved onto the Avenue with his parents forty-five years before, then had lived with Flora and their children in the Stone residence after their marriage in 1881 (fig. 193). He was sixty-two years old in 1912 and was recognized as the city's first citizen. Like his father before him, he invested as much in local and national civic institutions as he did in his own businesses. He had been seriously injured at age eighteen by an explosion in one of his father's Michigan mines, a misfortune which prevented him from entering Harvard College but enabled him to get an early start in his profitable career. By the turn of the century, Mather was one of the city's most active corporate capitalists; he was the officer of at least nine companies and a director of more than two dozen iron, banking, and transportation concerns.

Thanks to his wealth, and his respect for the building arts, he made an indelible mark on the city through the building programs he spearheaded: the Western Reserve Building, designed by Daniel Burnham of Chicago; his own

Fig. 192. Flora Stone Mather (Cleveland Public Library, by G. M. Edmondson).

Fig. 193. Samuel Mather (Cleveland Public Library, by G. M. Edmondson, 1911).

residence; and buildings for Kenyon College, Trinity Cathedral, and Western Reserve University. Mather promoted the stature of each institution by retaining the finest architects—usually Schweinfurth—and demanding first-class design and construction. The value of his work endures almost a century later, as most of the buildings he sponsored are still standing. His own residence on the Avenue passed to the Cleveland Institute of Music when he died in 1931, then to the Cleveland Automobile Club in 1940. The state acquired the property for Cleveland State University in 1969 and restored the residence in 1978.[15]

Classical Elegance

Mather's faith in the durability of his Avenue residence spoke through the magnitude of his investment and the strength of the reinforced concrete and steel-frame structure. His august view of the Avenue and his place on it was evident in the magnificent residential campus expressed in the classic English manor house tradition (figs. 194, 195). With their celebration of European roots, the Mathers and other Avenue residents also rediscovered the classic symbols of their own New World culture. Similar to such early builders on Euclid as Truman Handy and Thomas Kelley in the 1830s, who aspired to the conventions of cultural success that could be found in their native regions, the last generation of Euclid Avenue patrons looked back and paid homage to the most sophisticated features of the American Georgian and Greek revival periods. Ironically, these classic residences built during the grand avenue's final decades were designed in a genre similar to those of the Avenue's first decades, though they were clearly built on a much grander scale (figs. 196–99). Staunchly conservative in conception, the residences of attorney Andrew Squire, industrialist Leonard C. Hanna, banker Henry C. Wick, and investor Anthony Carlin celebrated the grandeur of classical design principles (see table 14).

Among the first patrons to return to the classical orders was Andrew Squire, a founding partner of the corporate law firm of Squire, Sanders & Dempsey. In 1895 Squire went to Charles Schweinfurth for the design of his residence on Euclid Avenue, the home to which he would take his second wife Eleanor after their marriage in 1896. Schweinfurth had previously built only one other strictly classical residence, for Charles B. Parker in 1892, yet Squire retained the Avenue's preeminent architect to design a residence in the Greek manner. The patron's inspiration and point of reference might very well have been his own family's classical New England home in Hiram, Ohio, which he had helped build in 1863. And Schweinfurth's design bore a strong resemblance to Jonathan Goldsmith's work of a half-century before in its great Ionic portico and the strict symmetry of its center-hall plan, even if the scale was very much of its own day. Squire chose a site that was four houses east of his law partner William Sanders's residence—originally built by Sanders's father-in-law, Charles Otis, Sr.—and he tailored the interior design of the new twenty-seven-room house to luxurious living and his and Eleanor's personal enthusiasms. A large library housed the attorney's law books and Eleanor's rare book collection, and the handsome recreation room was Squire's retreat where he played

Fig. 194. Francis E. Drury residence, 8625 Euclid Avenue; Meade and Hamilton, architects, 1910–12 (*Architectural Record*, December 1915).

TABLE 14
Classical Elegance, 1890–1910

Patron/Residence	Address	Building Date	Architect
Charles B. Parker	1521	1892	C. F. Schweinfurth
Robert H. Clark	3450	1895–96	A. H. Granger
Andrew Squire	3443	1895	C. F. Schweinfurth
William L. Harkness	3634	1895–98 (remodel)	Meade & Garfield
Charles W. Bingham	2157	1901–2 (remodel)	Peabody & Stearns
Leonard C. Hanna	2717	1901–2	McKim, Meade & White
Henry C. Wick	3515	1904	Meade & Garfield
Anthony Carlin	3233	1911–12	Adolph Sprackling

Fig. 195. Drury residence, main hall (*Architectural Record*, December 1915).

Fig. 196. Charles B. Parker residence, 1521 Euclid Avenue; C. F. Schweinfurth, architect, 1892 (Western Reserve Historical Society).

Fig. 197. Charles W. Bingham residence, 2157 Euclid Avenue. Original Nathan Perry house (c. 1830); renovated and enlarged by Peabody & Stearns, 1901–2 (courtesy Bolton Family, by G. M. Edmondson).

Fig. 198. Robert and Julia Bissell Clark residence, 3450 Euclid Avenue; A. H. Granger, architect, 1895–96 (courtesy Carl Boardman Cobb).

Fig. 199. Bingham–Perry residence, living room (courtesy Bolton Family, by G. M. Edmondson).

billiards with his male companions. For Eleanor, Schweinfurth built a private gymnasium where, anticipating the habits of the late twentieth century, she donned her rubber suit and exercised away excess weight on a stationary bicycle. The grand reception hall, entered through a screen of Ionic columns, and the basement wine cellar were upstairs-downstairs companions, each designed to produce conviviality at the couple's social gatherings (fig. 200).[16]

They, like so many of their grand avenue neighbors, were active in the city's cultural and political life and frequently hosted large events in their home. As the senior partner of one of Cleveland's largest law firms and counsel to major businesses, Squire served on many bank and corporation boards and was a trustee of Western Reserve University and of Hiram College, his alma mater. He also became involved in Republican politics through his law practice,

Fig. 200. Andrew and Eleanor Squire residence, 3443 Euclid Avenue; C. F. Schweinfurth, architect, 1895 (Western Reserve Historical Society, 1920s).

Fig. 201. William L. and Edie Harkness residence, 3634 Euclid Avenue. Original James M. Hoyt house (1864–65); remodeled by Meade and Garfield, architects, 1895–98 (Western Reserve Historical Society, c. 1900).

staunch conservative that he was. He was a personal friend of James Garfield and a delegate to the 1896 national convention that nominated William McKinley. His energetic and witty wife pursued her own career in the arts and horticulture and was the founder of the Fine Arts Garden at the art museum and a leading organizer of the Cleveland Garden Center. Eleanor also devoted her talent to cultivating herb gardens and orchards on the 275-acre Chagrin Valley estate, Valleevue Farm, that she and Squire built for their summer residence. The estate went to Flora Stone Mather College upon their deaths. They too gave their Euclid Avenue house to Western Reserve University. It promptly became the Red Cross headquarters in 1938 and then the home of the Knights of Columbus in 1950.[17]

In its time, the Squire residence represented the best of classical elegance on the Avenue. Within ten years, however, such formalism had taken on a whole new meaning, becoming more sophisticated and even decadent. The residences built for Leonard Hanna, Henry C. Wick, and Anthony Carlin were stunning portraits in the sumptuous high-style Georgian manner with their two-story porticoes graced with broad fluted columns and rooftop balustrades (fig. 201). They were all the more remarkable given the millions of dollars invested in their design and construction and the care taken in every carved detail. The patrons exercised no apparent reserve, which, in retrospect, is astonishing, in view of the late period in which they built and their houses' proximity to the expanding eastern edge of the Avenue's commercial district. Leonard Hanna, brother of political mastermind Marcus A. Hanna, even went so far as to commission the famed New York architect Stanford White of McKim, Mead & White to design his new residence in 1901 (figs. 202–4).

Hanna, who took over leadership of the M. A. Hanna Company after his brother's death in 1904, knew McKim, Mead & White's work in Washington and New York, just as he was well acquainted with their clientele, the urban establishment of grand avenue patrons, national institutions, and the federal government. He undoubtedly brought White to his hometown of Cleveland to bestow upon its grand avenue, through his own residence, some of the same artistic splendor the architect had created in New York, Washington, and Boston. The firm's work during the first decade of the twentieth century included such commissions as the Joseph Pulitzer house on Fifth Avenue in New York City, the Mrs. William K. Vanderbilt house, also on Fifth Avenue, the new East Wing of the White House, and the Washington residence of Payne and Helen Hay Whitney, daughter of John and Clara Stone Hay. The firm had also designed the Farmington, Connecticut, summer home of Euclid Avenue resident Alfred A. Pope in 1898–1901. The Hanna residence was completed in 1904 after two years of construction. Within fifteen years the Hanna family left the Avenue, and the house was turned over to the Cleveland Museum of Natural History.[18] It was razed in 1958 to be replaced by the freeway overpass just east of the Mather mansion.

Foundry entrepreneur Anthony Carlin built the last house on the Avenue in 1910–12, marking the end of the age of elegant building (fig. 205). The

Fig. 202. *Opposite above*. Leonard C. and Caroline Hanna residence, 2717 Euclid Avenue; McKim, Meade & White, architects, 1901–2. Formerly a portion of the site of Jacob Perkins residence (Western Reserve Historical Society).

Fig. 203. *Opposite*. Hanna residence; original rendering of south front elevation, McKim, Mead & White, 1902 (courtesy of The New-York Historical Society, New York City).

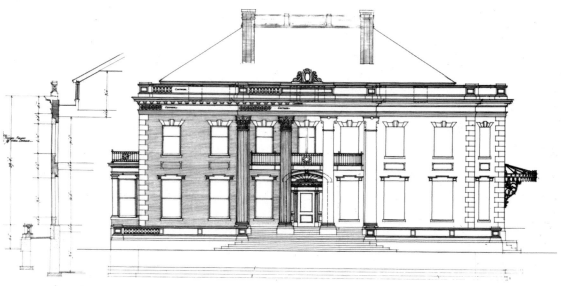

Fig. 204. Hanna residence; original rendering of east side elevation, McKim, Mead & White, 1902 (courtesy of The New-York Historical Society, New York City).

grandeur of architect Adolph Sprackling's design was enhanced by the 600 feet of rolling lawn—formerly occupied by Hinman Hurlbut's handcrafted garden and statuary—which set off the semicircular portico and giant Ionic columns. Continuing the sweep inside, the Carlins' entrance foyer opened onto an imperial staircase that was dominated by a magnificent Tiffany window at the landing. The Carlins, deeply religious Irish Catholics, arranged for a small marble chapel to be built next to their bedroom. In the rear sun room, they installed a fish pond mounted on an ornate cherubic pedestal, with electric lights in shades of green, blue, red, and yellow dramatically illuminating the pond and fountain.

In the basement, Carlin built a large wine cellar of thick masonry walls and padlocked steel doors for his valuable liquor supply, a bounty left over from the days when he owned the Euclid Hotel. Indeed, this potent reserve, if known about, would surely have been cause for some comment among his neighbors, for while many Avenue residents were connoisseurs of fine wines, many others were uncompromising advocates of the temperance movement. The entire liquor issue was politically controversial, especially during Prohibition. But Carlin was certainly not the sole purveyor of good cheer during these years. His neighbor Charles Otis, Jr., also had a secret wine cellar out in his Waite Hill residence, which was considered a happy oasis among friends. Like Carlin, he stored hundreds of cases of fine liquor behind old bank vault doors.

The main legacy of Carlin's house was that it was the last residence to be occupied in the Avenue's grand tradition. Carlin's son John and his wife, who lived there after his parents had died, remained on the Avenue as long as possible—until the noise, traffic, and soot became unbearable. The Carlins recognized their distinction as the last residents of this remarkable street and

memorialized their departure in 1950 by opening up their house to a formal farewell party for Euclid Avenue. One hundred guests attended the notorious "last dinner dance" in the Carlins' second-floor ballroom. Those who came celebrated, and those who watched saluted for the final time the Avenue's most genial ritual.[19]

Fig. 205. Anthony and Mary Carlin residence, 3233 Euclid Avenue; Adolph Sprackling, architect, 1911–12. Formerly the site of Hinman Hurlbut residence (courtesy Mimi Carlin Camp).

Another photo of the Wade's front gate & house

and "Stir" Beckwiths lonely spot.

EIGHT

The Architects and Builders

The grand avenues of America distinguished themselves from other city streets by the sheer number of architectural masterpieces that lined them. Since an early time, Euclid Avenue was the spine of Cleveland and the place for builders and their patrons to show off. Such opulence arose from the wealth of the city and that of its Avenue residents, but opulence was ultimately the creation of a personal commitment by the street's patrons to superior design. They, like most grand avenue patrons around the country, commissioned only the prominent masterbuilders, architects, and artisans of the period to create these magnificent dwellings, these centers of private living and public socializing (fig. 206).

The story of the architects and builders on Euclid Avenue is as much a tale of the artisans who were chiefly responsible for fabricating the architectural streetscape as it is one of the dynamic relationship that existed between the architects and their patrons. The houses on Euclid Avenue were products of the talent and skill of their designers and craftsmen blended with, or in some cases dominated by, the wealth and tastes of their clients. An important role of the architect was to act as a filter, to absorb and cleanse everything the client requested. For some architects, then as today, their need for a personal signature came at the expense of their clients' desires or tastes. Those architects who prospered on Euclid Avenue satisfied both the divergent needs of their clients as well as their own artistic reputations, and doing so without completely blurring the message.

Over the decades, from the first house built on the Avenue to the last, the role of the masterbuilder and architect, and his relationship to his clients, changed in important ways. Architectural practice during most of the nineteenth century, and even into the twentieth, was not trammeled by definite rules and regulations or established levels of expertise and training. The trade was open virtually to anyone who wished to practice. The relationship between the architect and patron, too, was defined by each individual patron. Many patrons, especially those early in the life of the Avenue, charted the direction of the builder's or architect's design and managed all facets of construction. Others were passive participants and retained a masterbuilder or architect for their comprehensive services.

Fig. 206. *Opposite.* A showcase for architectural patrons. Scene of Euclid Avenue, residences of Beckwith, no. 3813, and Wade, no. 3903, *top*; Beckwith residence, *bottom* (Edward Merritt letter, June 1912, Western Reserve Historical Society).

Euclid Avenue patrons worked with an elite group of architects throughout the Avenue's development, a remarkable fact considering the openness of the field. The tradition was established early on when Jonathan Goldsmith was brought to Cleveland in 1833 by Nathan Perry and Peter Weddell. The success of these residences and Goldsmith's relationship with his clients provided good references for his next commission, and subsequent jobs were important references for future commissions. A half-century later, the same process secured the Euclid Avenue career of Charles Schweinfurth. The reputation of any one architect was thus subject to both objective and subjective forces: the architect's design skill and the reception of his work by his clients and prospective clients.

These informal criteria were as prevalent in the 1830s as they were in the 1890s, and as they still are in the 1990s. But unlike today, up until the 1880s an architect's or builder's references and the quality of what he produced were the only basis for determining his competence. The building industry and the patrons engaged throughout the century in an often difficult search to establish criteria for evaluating an architect's capabilities, and hence to define his role and reputation in design and building. It was precisely this dilemma that forced the creation in 1857 of the American Institute of Architects (AIA), the parent association of the profession. The AIA was organized to establish national standards that would be recognized by architects, builders, and patrons alike. Such groups as the Western Association of Architects, formed in 1870, the Cleveland Architectural Club, formed in 1880, and the subsequent Cleveland chapter of the AIA in 1887, were created to administer professional standards and practices at the regional and local levels (fig. 207). They also responded to the architects' desire for better communication among themselves. Architectural journals, both national and regional, were another important medium. Among those with the largest circulation in northeast Ohio and the Midwest were the *Inland Architect,* the *American Architect and Building News, Architectural Record,* and the *Ohio Architect, Engineer and Builder.* The Avenue's architects contributed illustrations and photographs of their major commissions, as did their colleagues in other cities, each looking at what and for whom the others were designing. The journals helped to advance the art and promote the practices of contributing architects.[1]

The influence of the AIA and its associated networks was one of many factors that promoted and stabilized the architect's status. But probably the single greatest element in elevating the masterbuilder and hired draftsman of the early nineteenth century to the status of a professional architect by the last quarter-century was the awareness by patrons—and the self-awareness by architects—of the architect's critical position in an increasingly technical and publicized design and building process. Greater recognition rose out of the specialized services the architect provided the client, particularly such clients as those who lived on Euclid Avenue, as well as the commercial value and civic contribution of each architect's commissions. They increasingly needed better, more thorough training to design and build the most advanced mechanical and building systems in the large and complex designs that lined the Avenue.

Catalogue *of the* Architectural Exhibition *of the* Cleveland Architectural Club

¶ Held in the ROSE BUILDING   October Fifteenth to Twenty-Eighth   -   Nineteen Hundred and Nine

Up until the 1880s, all the successful practitioners on the Avenue were apprentices rather than formally educated. Their knowledge was gained from experience, study of technical trade books, and communication with one another. A few even benefited from the rare and challenging experience of working with such progressive clients as Amasa Stone and Charles Brush, who assisted the architect in engineering the technical systems of their houses. And while informal preparation generally sufficed in meeting the client's needs, by the mid-1880s academic training and AIA certification became trademarks of competence and earned architects a professional reputation previously unknown. When Sylvester Everett chose Schweinfurth over Scofield in 1883, his decision was based on the Boston architect's schematic design. But he also could be confident in Schweinfurth's overall capabilities because of the fact that the architect had studied seven years in the Office of the Supervising Architect of the Treasury, a traditional training ground for bright young architects in the late nineteenth century. The awareness by Euclid Avenue patrons of these professional matters originated in the responsibility they vested in the architect: to memorialize their stature for all to see in these spectacular residences while at the same time creating a stylized artistic form. Beyond the money invested or the bricks and mortar laid, these were the flagships of eminence for these great urban home builders. This was a big motivation for living on the grand avenue and one reason why the streetscape became an architectural museum. As the creator of these showcases, the architect claimed greater importance and authority with his clients.

The patron, however, ultimately controlled the choice and expression of style and the design and building process, for he held the money. But over the decades the recognition of expertise and the management of the process shifted from the client to the architect as the architects came to be respected as the creative and technical intelligence behind "the most beautiful street in the world." Until near the end of the nineteenth century, most of the architects and masterbuilders were employed as just one of the patron's many hired contractors. This limited position and the client's dominance of the process was exactly the issue that exasperated John Hay in 1877, when his neighbors Colonel and Mrs. William Harris demeaned architect Joseph Ireland as simply the delineator of their own ideas. That was, as Hay remarked, "as much as if I should say of one of [Edgar] Decker's photographs, 'I made it, that is I furnished the wife and baby for it.' "[2] Hay's point was that without the architect's artistic and technical ability to translate concepts into form, the client's design ideas would be nothing but unshaped images.

By the end of the century, the practicing architect, especially those who worked on the country's grand avenues, had become the artistic and technical manager. He now usually directly hired contractors and draftsmen of his own choosing, rather than having to accept those retained and managed by the patron. As late as 1906, though, Euclid Avenue architect J. Milton Dyer still believed that Cleveland architects had not yet "obtained to the same extent [as Eastern architects] a position of sufficient authority in respect to his clients." Dyer felt that Cleveland was twenty-five years behind New York in this respect. Money, and the availability of it, separated Cleveland from New York or Boston, Dyer believed, since architects "have rarely been allowed to do just what their preferences would have dictated."[3] Dyer's view may have been limited by his six years of practice in Cleveland; a contemporary in New York or one of Dyer's local predecessors might have disagreed. In truth, when compared to the situation a half-century before, the architect's authority was far greater and his professional stature more revered. Dyer—like most architects then and today—whose chief interest was to preserve his design in its translation from paper to built form, rebeled against the constraints imposed by finite budgets.

Emergence of the Architect, 1850–1875

In the 1837 city directory, Charles W. Heard was listed as a "carpenter and joiner," then working for masterbuilder Jonathan Goldsmith. By 1845, Heard had the title of "master builder," and in the 1850 directory he listed himself for the first time as "architect." In fact, Heard and his current partner, Simeon C. Porter, were the only architects who identified themselves as such in the 1850 directory; all others, such as William Schofield and Warham J. Warner, both of whom worked on Euclid, were listed among the city's twenty-one masterbuilders. Two years later, in 1852, the city directory listed five architects, and then nine in 1859. There were by now twenty-eight to thirty "builders" and seventy-two "carpenters" working in Cleveland.[4] These numbers and titles indicated the increased size and specialization of the local trade and the clearer distinction between the architect and other specialists.

Even so, the Cleveland architect was still viewed as the patron's hired hand, and with just cause. His knowledge of architectural style was derived mainly from trade publications and observations of other buildings. The leading architects and masterbuilders around midcentury, notably Heard and Porter, had only rudimentary training in the basic skills of carpentry and joinery. They certainly had no rigorous academic preparation, nor apprenticeship with a sophisticated architect; they learned their trade under the guidance of an elder carpenter or builder, such as Goldsmith. The Euclid Avenue houses these architects designed, while the best in the city, were still vernacular interpretations of the high-style buildings designed by eminent architects practicing in New York, Philadelphia, and Boston. These were the nation's centers of culture and commerce. The most a builder in Cleveland could hope to do was emulate the classic masterpieces, but it "often produced curious effects," according to architect I. T. Frary in his landmark publication, *Early Homes of Ohio*. The buildings "were crude," Frary concluded, because the proportion and balance so crucial in the execution of classical details were "often painfully misunderstood."[5]

Cleveland might have been an enterprising industrial center in the 1850s and 1860s, but it was still a young Western city and the caliber of its architects and architectural design reflected this fact. Many Euclid Avenue patrons were familiar with the work of Eastern architects from their travels, yet only a few, such as Jacob Perkins, who retained New Yorker Richard Upjohn, went beyond Cleveland's coterie. Architect Joseph Ireland, recently arrived from New York City in 1865, advertised the opening of his Cleveland office by capitalizing on this Eastward-looking bent. He promoted his "large experience of several years" with R. G. Hatfield and offered his "professional services in the practice of Modern Architecture as an Art."[6] The patrons who retained Ireland, Heard, or others commissioned the architects exclusively for their design services, maintaining complete control of the execution of that design. They rarely engaged an architect to orchestrate the entire design *and* construction job.

The architect and masterbuilder might have been frustrated or demeaned by this limited role, but others in the community thought better of their talents. An editorial in the *Leader* in 1855 gave just recognition to the hands responsible for Cleveland's "beautiful residences, handsome churches and, indeed, splendid buildings of all kinds." The writer concluded, "Architecture here is treated as a science, and an art worthy of the best mind, the soundest judgment and the most refined taste. It is, indeed, one of the noblest, if not the noblest of all arts. . . . Honor, we say, to the builder."[7] These were not just nice sentiments. The writer's esteem was borne out in the public acclaim Heard received for his major commissions, as well as for the company he kept. His Cleveland career spanned a forty-two-year period, from 1833 to 1875, and the strength of his work, his energy, and his personal forbearance secured an ascendant position in the community for himself and his peers.

Since his arrival in Cleveland, first as Goldsmith's foreman, then partner, Heard had expanded Goldsmith's reputable practice after his father-in-law's death in 1847 by joining forces with architects whose strengths complemented his own (fig. 208). His partnerships with Warham J. Warner (1847–49), Simeon C. Porter (1850–60), Walter Blythe (1864), and his own sons (1873–76) enabled him to secure a diverse portfolio of the finest commissions in the city— residences, churches, commercial buildings, and civic structures. His partnership with Porter was such a case in point, a liaison that proved quite profitable for both architects. When William J. Boardman retained them to design the addition to his Euclid Avenue house in 1860—paid for by Florance Boardman's father, Joseph E. Sheffield of New Haven—Boardman boasted to his father-in-law, "We consider ourselves very fortunate in receiving aid from two such fine architects."[8] Heard and Porter's partnership ended just as the Boardman job was getting underway, and Porter stayed on with the commission, much to the client's satisfaction. The young Porter's own practice, which began in Heard's office as a masterbuilder and draftsman, flourished after they parted, because of his own skill and his former partner's established reputation among the Avenue's clientele.

Heard was the first fashionable architect in Cleveland who moved easily in the exalted circles of commerce, culture, and politics, winning him exposure and respect among the city's influentials. His founding work with Leonard Case for the Cleveland Academy of Natural Science undoubtedly strengthened his chances to design the Case Block in 1875. And his active involvement with the local Democratic party brought him into an arena frequented by his friend and client Senator Henry Payne. Payne was one of his most celebrated patrons. After they had completed Payne's Avenue residence in 1849, the senator again retained him and his partner Porter in 1855 to design the Payne & Perry block,

Fig. 208. Charles W. Heard (Western Reserve Historical Society).

an important project for both men. Besides the eight Avenue residences he is known to have designed, of Heard's major commissions all were sponsored by Euclid Avenue residents: St. Paul's Episcopal Church on the Avenue (1848–51); the Euclid Avenue Opera House (1873–75); the Arlington Block (1875) for Charles Otis, Sr.; and the Ohio Centennial Building (1876) at the World's Centennial Exposition in Philadelphia.[9]

Heard collaborated with a number of different carpenters, contractors, stonemasons, frescoers, and tradesmen on his jobs. By the end of his career, having accrued superior credentials, he usually served as the client's construction superintendent as well as designer. Because of his personal stature, Heard led the way in advancing architectural practice locally from an artisan trade in the 1840s to a commercial business by the 1870s. Even so, Heard was among a generation of architects whose reputations were entrenched in a larger field of provincial builders, agents to their clients' tastes and authority.

Promotion of the Architect, 1875–1900

The architect's limited role in the fabrication of his building plans, and the client's prerogative to select and manage the builders and craftsmen regardless of their judgment in such matters, opened up vast opportunities for revisions, mistakes, and pirating of designs. The architects, after all, did not own their plans; these belonged to the clients who had paid for the product, and they rightfully could share their architect's designs with others. "The practice of persons going into half-finished homes in the absence of owners and noting such good points as may be obtained from plans and specifications lying around is to be condemned," the *Leader* admonished in 1875. "This is done by parties high in social standing and it accounts for the marked similarity in our houses, while it keeps alive second rate architects and builders, who were never guilty of an original idea."[10] Plagiarized designs showed a lack of respect for an architect's singular creative intelligence and effectively made a commodity out of both architect and plans.

These soft artistic standards improved in the last quarter-century as local architects came to be respected as members of the national profession. Architect Levi T. Scofield, especially, whose career overlapped Heard's last decade of practice, brought national recognition to Cleveland architects through his involvement with the central AIA and acquaintance with those at the top of the field. Scofield's work on the Avenue began in the late 1860s, and his background was as modest as the senior Heard's; he was a builder and engineer trained by his father, William B. Schofield, whose German origins he chose to Anglicize by dropping the *h* in Schofield (fig. 209). True to this American spirit, Scofield made a conscious effort to be recognized among his peers nationally, and he became the first local architect certified by the AIA in 1870 and elected to the AIA Board of Directors in 1892 and again in 1894–97. This brought him into contact with leading practitioners in other cities, and gave him the confidence to demand greater recognition by his local clients. Scofield was also a retired Civil War general, a favored status that he shared with several Avenue residents and clients. The one important difference between them, however, was that the Euclid Avenue patron bought architectural services, while Scofield provided stylistic design as defined by the client.

Any such tension between Scofield and his clients ended with his greatest and most difficult commission, the Soldiers' and Sailors' Monument on Public Square (1887–94), for which he served as architect, engineer, sculptor, and patron. He worked on the monument for over seven years without compensation. When the county commissioners refused to pay the total construction cost, Scofield made up the $57,500 balance out of his own funds. With this investment he became a patron of his own work and of Cleveland's most visible public works project.[11] Scofield's authoritative position in this instance and his sound reputation generally earned for him and his colleagues a greater measure of professional respect. To be sure, no single act or commission guaranteed complete success; it was an uneven process hindered by the hurdles a young, emerging profession frequently encounters.

Self-promotion was one worthwhile activity that architects nationally came to realize would bring wider public acclaim. As they gained professional stature they took more interest in artistic recognition, as individuals and as a group. Their first collective effort was the short-lived Cleveland Draftsmen's Association, which was founded in 1871 and chaired by Forrest A. Coburn for the purpose "of mutual improvement and the promotion of their profession and the branches of fine arts, sciences and mechanics." Two decades later, in 1894, fourteen of the city's leading architects formed a second Cleveland Architectural

Fig. 209. Levi T. Scofield (Western Reserve Historical Society, by Decker and Wilbur, c. 1870s).

Club, independent of the local AIA chapter, "to stimulate the public mind to a keener appreciation of Architecture in all its varied forms."[12] Their mission, in contrast to the AIA, was to educate the public through lectures, papers, competitions, and exhibitions. The Club thrived for over a decade, thanks to a strong core group intent on promoting the profession.

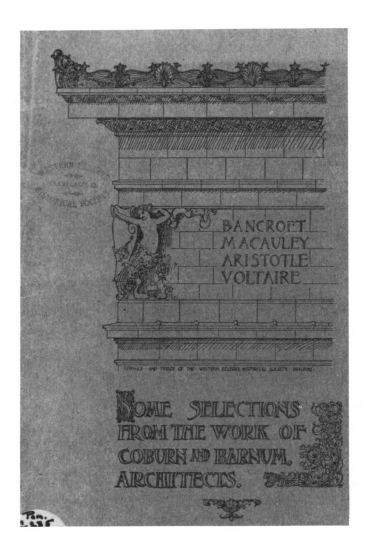

The firm of Coburn & Barnum, which designed at least twenty-two residences on the Avenue in the 1880s, was a master of the art of advertising (fig. 210). Forrest Coburn and Frank Barnum established their twenty-year partnership in 1878, Coburn having been apprenticed to Richard Morris Hunt in New York and Barnum to Joseph Ireland in Cleveland. Both were active AIA members, and through their association with the national organization they gained an astute understanding of the value of marketing. The firm devoted considerable resources—as much as anyone—to making their clientele aware of its design work. Judged by the number of commissions the firm built on the Avenue, this promotion paid off handsomely and enabled the architects to shape a good portion of Euclid Avenue's streetscape.[13] Charles Schweinfurth was probably the only other architect who could claim as strong a signature. Coburn and Barnum's clients, including merchant George Morgan, banker George Howe,

Fig. 211. Charles F. Schweinfurth (Western Reserve Historical Society).

and the Reverend William Leonard, largely recognized the architects as the central authority in the design and construction of their residences. These clients engaged them and referred them to others precisely because of the successful relationship they enjoyed and the quality of Coburn and Barnum's work. An important element to their success was their ability to bring together a team of the finest carpenters and craftsmen with whom they worked frequently. This practice produced not only quality workmanship but a loyal team of artisans. The firm excelled in managing both the client and the contractors and in ensuring that the original designs would be executed as planned, thus securing their reputation.

Charles Schweinfurth also built his architectural practice in the 1880s and 1890s on the strength of excellent client management (fig. 211). His distinction centered on his "uncompromising determination to secure for his clients that to which, by reason of their contracts, they were justly entitled," according to his younger colleague Benjamin S. Hubbell.[14] That was why Schweinfurth was so highly regarded by his clients and feared by his subcontractors; he demanded the best and would not rest until his vision was realized. As the favored architect of such eminent Euclid Avenue families as the Mathers, Hannas, Nortons, and Hatches, Schweinfurth was commissioned to design eighteen residences, two churches, and two institutional buildings on the Avenue, as well as summer houses and buildings for Western Reserve University and Kenyon College. This celebrity status grew out of his special talent for translating personal aspirations into meaningful architectural form while always retaining his own unique style. This is why Sylvester Everett initially brought him to Cleveland and why he prospered among the affluent and exhibitive people who resided on the city's grand avenue.

Schweinfurth had received a valuable education in design and client skills from experienced masters, whom he regarded with the "deepest respect." His first was a "prominent Boston architect" who worked in New York during 1872–74, possibly H. H. Richardson. He then spent the next seven years as a draftsman for James Hill, the Supervising Architect of the Treasury, and then two years with New York architect Edward Kendall. His apprenticeship in the Supervising Architect's Office at the Treasury enabled him to work on major public building projects around the country and engage in the arena of high period styles. Kendall's New York office assigned him to the ostentatious Fifth Avenue residence of industrialist Robert Goelet, a grand avenue patron of that city. When Schweinfurth moved to Boston to form a partnership with his brother Julius, he was well prepared to manage a practice that, in his words, brought him into "contact with the ablest New York and Boston practitioners" and patrons, such as the Everetts of Cleveland.[15]

Schweinfurth's Cleveland career ultimately distinguished itself by his many commissions for Euclid Avenue patrons, whose own stature secured the same for the architect. Just as he influenced their living standards and the street's architectural presence, their tastes and cultural initiatives shaped his personal design style.

The size and organization of his practice also grew in response to his clients' large projects. In contrast to the offices of Levi Scofield or Joseph Ireland in the 1870s and 1880s, he managed all the design and construction phases, acting as his client's developer and consulting with them only as necessary on schematic plans and final finishes. The technical proficiency of his operation required that he, not the patron, manage the entire process. At the peak of his practice Schweinfurth employed eight to nine draftsmen and managed a select group of subcontractors. J. Wentworth Smith, his building contractor, built the basic structures and stepped in as Schweinfurth's ad hoc chauffeur, driving him around to their job sites in the absence of a car and driver's license of his own. The McAllister & Company Woodcarving firm crafted most of the woodwork in his Euclid Avenue houses, and sculptor Thomas C. B. Reardon executed many of the carved details. McAllister employed the two gifted craftsmen, German immigrants William Schurmer and Karl F. Broemel, who built the clay models and sculptures of medieval and Renaissance motifs which became Schweinfurth's trademark.[16]

His practice was not on the scale of the corporate offices of Richard Morris Hunt or McKim, Mead & White, to be sure, but around the turn of the century it was among the largest and most productive in Cleveland. The younger generation of architects who were beginning their careers at this time believed that Schweinfurth, because of his practice and perfectionism, did more "to raise the standard of architectural design and construction in Cleveland" than any other architect, according to Hubbell.[17] His designs, his striking personality, as well as his reputation nationally as a director of the AIA (1894–97), greatly strengthened the architectural profession in Cleveland.

The Architect Elevated, 1900–1915

This "gradual invasion" of Western cities, such as Cleveland, by architects "whose standing and training are the best" was seen as the chief improving element for local professionals around the turn of the century by the young architect J. Milton Dyer, designer of Lyman Treadway's Euclid Avenue house. Dyer also believed that the clearer distinction between the architect and the builder had helped to promote the architect to a status superior to that of craftsmen and carpenters.[18] In his judgment, the early twentieth-century architect was now the ultimate interpreter and manager of the client's functional and aesthetic building needs (fig. 212).

Architects also stood at the top of a large industry. In Cleveland, as throughout the country, exponential growth of people and commerce in the second half of the nineteenth century was reflected in the building trade alone. By 1900, sixty architects and 570 carpenters had their businesses in Cleveland. This compared to only nine architects and seventy-two carpenters in 1860. The Cleveland AIA had twenty full members and five associate members, and the Cleveland Builder's Exchange, founded in 1892, numbered over 300 tradesmen and architects.[19] Remarkable differences existed between the industry at midcentury and that at the turn of the century: The building arts had grown 700 percent in forty years, and management of design and construction had wholly passed from the patron to the architects and largest contractors. An organized industry had risen to professional stature.

A successful architect needed as much talent in managing the client and his subcontractors as he did in designing the building. Such architects as Dyer and Frank B. Meade, who established a foothold on the Avenue in these years, also had appropriate social and educational credentials. When Meade, a graduate of the Massachusetts Institute of Technology (MIT), opened his Cleveland office in 1893, he set out to establish a practice that specialized in houses for such affluent Clevelanders as Euclid Avenue residents Henry C. Wick, William L. Harkness, Luther Allen, and Henry White. All in all, he designed sixteen houses on the Avenue and was commissioned by former Avenue families to

Fig. 212. The patron and his architects. Letter from Charles W. Bingham to Peabody & Stearns, architects, May 3, 1883 (courtesy Bolton Family).

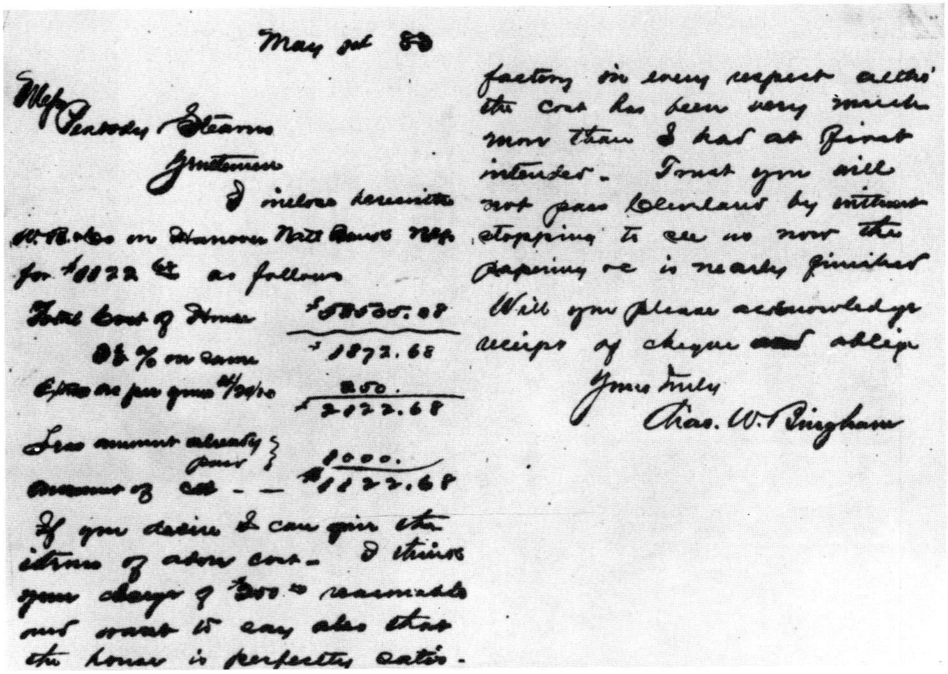

	May 3rd 83
Messrs	
Peabody & Stearns	
Gentlemen	
I enclose herewith	
C. W. B. & Co. on Hanover Natl Bank N.Y.	
for $1122.68 as follows:	
Total cost of House	$53505.38
2½ % ON SAME	$ 1872.68
Extra as per your [ltr] 4/24/83	250.
	$ 2122.68
Less amount already paid	1000.
Amount of [check]	$ 1122.68

If you desire I can give the
items of above cost. I think
your charge of $250.00 reasonable
and want to say also that
the house is perfectly satis-

factory in every respect altho'
the cost has been very much
more than I had at first
intended. Trust you will
not pass Cleveland by without
stopping to see us now the
papering etc is nearly finished.
Will you please acknowledge
receipt of cheque and oblige

    Yours truly
      Chas. W. Bingham

design more than a dozen country and suburban estates (fig. 213). He moved easily among these people, as one of their own. He lived on the Avenue, was a member of the Union Club and the Chamber of Commerce, and was the founding president of the Hermit Club.[20] His extensive acquaintances with his clientele together with his design talent enabled his practice to flourish.

Professionally, Meade was among the best trained of his colleagues. After his classical training at MIT, he worked four years in the offices of Jenney & Mundie of Chicago, a national corporate practice, then returned home to Cleve-

Fig. 213. Frank B. Meade (Western Reserve Historical Society).

land. Here he combined his own resources and revenues with those of his various partners, Alfred Granger, Abram Garfield, and James Hamilton, all graduates of MIT's architecture school. Meade's ultimate achievement was his appointment as secretary to the Group Plan commission, the imperial civic building project that envisioned Euclid Avenue as the grand processional to the city's center. He served on the commission with Frederick Law Olmsted, Jr., son of the eminent landscape architect of Boston, and New York architect Arnold Brunner.

Meade and those of his colleagues who prospered on Euclid Avenue in its declining decades—Dyer, Charles Hopkinson, Abram Garfield—carried on the old traditions of architectural design being foremost, a service that respected the clients' tastes and aspirations. They succeeded as much because they were talented artists as because they affirmed the view that the architect should protect his patrons' needs by managing both design and construction. As certified members of the AIA, they also had the strength of the national organization backing their professional credentials. This did not create a perfect world for them, as Dyer indicated in 1906, but it did lend enormous credibility to their positions. On the Avenue, architectural design and building was really neither better nor worse for this change over the last quarter-century. Even so, it secured well-earned recognition for the professionals who were chiefly responsible for the design of the masterpieces that made up this architectural showcase.

THE PERILS OF SOCIETY

A PHOTOPLAY
IN FOUR ACTS
— ENACTED BY —
CLEVELAND PEOPLE

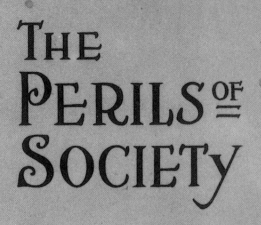

METROPOLITAN THEATRE
JUNE 26-27-28

MATINEES – TUESDAY & WEDNESDAY

THE MORGAN LITHO. CO., CLEVELAND.

NINE

A Neighborhood of Families

We can all cheerfully admit Euclid Street is a justly celebrated thoroughfare. Some of our best folks—mostly residents of the street in question—go so far as to say that Cleveland's proud highway is several rods ahead of the well-known 'Unter der Limburger' in Berlin, or the equally celebrated 'Roo de Boolfrog' in Paree, Fr-r-rance. The hoy-poloy visitor to the street, by wiping his feet on the mat at the lower end of the thoroughfare and showing a certificate of good moral character, will be permitted to traverse the sacred precincts free of charge.

Artemus Ward, 1860

Ward's characterization of this "sacred precinct," though tongue-in-cheek, touted the exclusiveness of the street and its residents. The opulence of the sweeping landscape reinforced the distinction of the Euclid Avenue neighborhood and raised economic and social barriers far more forbidding than any signpost or place name. Affluence, rather than aristocratic origins, was the cost to enter this society, which Mark Twain described in 1868 as a neighborhood unpenetrable by "poor white trash."[1] Twain's and Ward's descriptions were harsh, and in keeping with their caustic natures; but they aptly portrayed the profile of the Avenue after midcentury, once its stature had been established (fig. 214).

The lives of the people who made up this neighborhood, carried out in their homes, clubs, churches, and social activities, defined the character of this grand avenue as clearly as their residences did.[2] Their lavish ways might have appeared products of self-indulgent upbringings, yet the values of most families were really quite conventional, born out of a self-made New England austerity that seemed genuine. The same fresh wealth that financed the building of the homes defined the social life of the Avenue's residents. This new money created a fluid society that welcomed newcomers and was less tied to the rigid observances that molded the established domains of "proper" Boston and "old" New York.

Since Cleveland had only really begun to prosper in the 1840s and 1850s, it was without an entrenched elite tradition in the postwar decades. The residents of Euclid Avenue created this tradition, but they were nouveaux riches when placed beside the denizens of New York's Fifth Avenue, Boston's Back

Fig. 214. *Opposite.* The pretty perils of grand avenue society. *The Perils of Society* movie playbill, June 26–28, 1916 (Western Reserve Historical Society).

Bay, or Philadelphia's Rittenhouse Square. An Avenue resident was not apt to utter, "We're all as like each other as those dolls out of the same folded paper," as Edith Wharton's central character, Newland Archer, commented about Fifth Avenue society in *The Age of Innocence*. Instead, the society that grew up with the building of Euclid Avenue, more akin to its counterparts in Chicago, Denver, or San Francisco, was of recent arrival and wealth and was untrammeled by generations of molded traditions. The lives of the eastern elite, however, were charged by the cumulative effect of social habits bred over multiple generations. Taste was divine and style was structured. Affluent Clevelanders were influenced by such customs in fashioning their own culture. With the rise of Cleveland's commercial society in the 1860s and 1870s, families on the Avenue—more interconnected with one another now by blood, business, and matrimony than their predecessors had been—appeared to accept imposed modes of class distinction and standards of cultural excellence. This could be seen in their residences, dress, style of life, patronage of arts and letters, and acquisition of old masters and manuscripts—the narcotics of New York, Boston, and Philadelphia society.[3] Formality increasingly marked convivial occasions, and fashion became a vice-regent of form.

Over the decades, intermarriage, friendship, social affairs, and clubs bonded affluent Clevelanders with one another; most resided on Euclid Avenue after midcentury. The 1916 movie entitled *The Perils of Society* presented a parody of these people and showed the degree to which certain customs had crept into their manner of life. Filmed in Avenue homes, clubs, and Cleveland country estates, and starring Avenue residents Harriet Eells, Charles Otis, Jr., Robert Norton, Amasa Mather, and Leonard Hanna, the movie dramatized the trifling tactics an English earl and countess used to work their way into this society and mocked the ambitions that drove some among the Euclid Avenue community. But it also portrayed the values that these Cleveland people held sacred by contrasting the success that came to one of "sterling worth" against the vanity of inherited "royal blood." This linear neighborhood came to respect certain social conventions, to be sure, but it was chiefly governed not by decorum and pretense but by a regard for earnestness and generosity.[4]

The pomp and circumstance portrayed in *The Perils of Society*, as well as in John Hay's *The Bread-Winners* and Agatha Young's *Light in the Sky*, were the symbolic trademarks of good breeding, according to these authors. Randall Wade affirmed this view in his essay "Fashion," regarding this lofty concept as the "moulder of habits, the manners and the public opinion of the world." He believed that "fashion" was so highly esteemed as to dictate the form of "the palace, the temple, the cottage, the house-furnishing, the apparel, food, drink, amusements and all, even to the handling of a fork, and the tip of a shirt-collar." He concluded that "fashion governs the taste, morals, and in no small degree the religion of the age. She and not commerce is queen."[5] But just like architectural style, social fashion was subject to individual tastes, ambitions, and personal values.

The People of Euclid Avenue

The values that reigned supreme on the Avenue over three generations can be traced to the modest and pious origins of many first-generation families. They were hard-working and pious Yankees for whom the virtues of Puritanism still held real meaning in their conduct and ways of life. Most who settled the Avenue in the 1840s and 1850s had been born into working-class families from villages and farming communities in upstate New York, Connecticut, Massachusetts, Vermont, and Ohio. Only a few hailed from the urban centers of New Haven, Hartford, or Buffalo, and none had lived among the cosmopolitan gentry of such cities as New York or Philadelphia. Their early lives were without luxury and social graces. When they arrived in Cleveland, most in their twenties and thirties, they set out to capitalize on the business opportunities available in this small port city.

Private enterprise was the chief occupation of the men, most being merchants, manufacturers, shippers, and bankers. The professionals, mostly lawyers, also dealt extensively in real estate, railroads, and commerce.[6] They were capitalists; not one among them was a clergyman, journalist, writer, or artist. The financial and professional strength of such industrialists as Samuel Mather, Amasa Stone, and John D. Rockefeller, lawyers Samuel Cowles and Thomas Bolton, banker Truman Handy, and merchants Peter Weddell and William Bingham grew enormously from the time of their arrival in Cleveland. Each worked relentlessly to build his fortune. A college degree was a rare credential among them, and most had little exposure to the cultural and physical horizons they ultimately set for themselves and their city.

Their successors among the second generation who lived on the Avenue in the postwar decades were more accustomed to the manners and traditions of the emerging culture. Most were natives of Cleveland or Ohio, some even having lived on the Avenue since childhood. Only a few were migrants to the Cleveland area from such distant regions as rural Connecticut, upstate New York, and southern Ohio. Some Avenue residents even enjoyed common heritage with one another, certainly more than their elders could draw on, through intermarriage, education, business, or simply similar upbringings. Most had grown up in middle-income or affluent families; at least one out of four men were college-educated, and more than half of the women had attended boarding school. This second generation was better acquainted with the cosmopolitan ethos of Euclid Avenue life and fit comfortably into the collegial environment fostered by the grand avenue.[7]

The first-generation wealth of the antebellum years had shown its modest origins in its restrained expenditures. But the second generation, children of one of the most prosperous periods in the city's history, transcended the austerity of their predecessors by indulging in lavish material luxuries. Affluence had become a criterion of stature and residency on the Avenue. And while New York's polite society often shunned hard-driving entrepreneurs, and the tradition-bound patricians of Boston and Philadelphia lived in a less splendid manner—

feeling that material luxury created vulgar impediments to social and cultural duties—Euclid Avenue patrons apparently felt no schism between physical comfort and social responsibility.[8] They had inherited the Puritan values of their predecessors along with their wealth and enterprise.

Family firms prevailed in industry and trade—the Wades, Devereuxs, Chisholms, Mathers, Boardmans, all of whom resided on the Avenue.[9] Their occupations were as diverse as their origins; it mattered not at all that one family represented industry and another banking, law, oil, or railroads. Merit was gained by conduct rather than one's specific business or patriarchal bonds. The home, the family, was the core of this universe, the cultivator of the values and culture that perpetuated a pluralistic urban leadership over several generations.

The Family

Intermarriages, cross-family friendships, and front-porch meanderings knit this linear neighborhood together, as they did the smaller, divergent groups within it. Most everyone knew everyone else, at least casually, and each family belonged informally to at least one of the many coteries that distinguished one block from the next. Even John Rockefeller, the infamous loner, had Henry Flagler, William Harkness, Charles Otis, Jr., and Ambrose Swasey for friends. And it is not surprising that if a Mather, Wade, Chisholm, Devereux, Boardman, or Norton lived on one street—even in one house—for decades and through multiple generations he or she would be bonded, for better or worse, with neighbors and rooted in the pace and patterns of the place. Because the grand avenue itself loomed so large among these people, their lives were oriented outward to the street and their visibility on it. It was a picture window on their world (figs. 215–17).

Marriages among the families were the strongest link in the Euclid Avenue chain of social bonds. The marital ties abound: Antoinette Devereux and Horace E. Andrews; Harry K. Devereux and Mildred French; William H. Boardman and Augusta Bissell; Howard Eells and Alice Stager; Samuel Mather and Flora Stone; Amasa Mather and Catherine Hoyt; Mary Payne and Charles W. Bingham; Frances Bingham and Chester C. Bolton; Harvey Brown and Elizabeth Hickox. And there were many more. These couples apparently were brought together by their common set of values, social activities, family ties, and daily proximity. Charles Otis, Jr., who married Lucia Edwards of Prospect Street in 1895, concluded that he had chosen Lucia for his bride not only because "she was about the best looking girl in the country, and I had known her since we were 1 and 2 years old," but also because "our friendship and our families' friendship soon pointed to the fact that we would be congenial people in matrimony."[10] To keep the newlyweds close by, Mrs. Edwards and Mr. Otis, who had built his residence on Euclid in 1868–72, rented them a house on the Avenue located between the two family homes, where Charles's widowed father lived from time to time (figs. 218, 219).

Charles W. Bingham and his wife, Mary Perry Payne, had also grown up with one another, as children of neighboring Avenue families, the William and

Fig. 215. *Opposite.* Offspring of intermarriages on the avenue. Children of Samuel and Flora Stone Mather and Samuel and Emma Stone Raymond, *left to right:* (top row), Livingston Mather, Henry Raymond, Mary Raymond, Amasa Mather, Hilda Raymond; (bottom row), Julia Raymond, Constance Mather, Edward Raymond (Western Reserve Historical Society, by Edgar Decker, c. 1880).

Fig. 216. The David Z. Norton family (Western Reserve Historical Society).

Elizabeth Binghams and Senator Henry and Mary Payne. Bingham went off to college at age eighteen; after eight years away at Yale and on a European tour, he returned to Cleveland and settled into a courtship with Mary. Their two-year affair tested the patience of both young lovers, who yielded to their parents counsel to wait an extra year, "to look out upon this world a little longer unbound," rather than make an impetuous decision. Mary, known as Molly by family and friends, was slower to come to her love for Charles, or Charley, as she called him, but when she did she "absolutely worshipped him from the very depths of her soul and heart." They were engaged in February 1876 and married that June. The couple rented a house on the Avenue until they built their own Euclid residence in 1882–83. Their five children became the stewards of four generations of Perrys on the Avenue, from Nathan Perry in the 1830s to Elizabeth Beardsley Bingham Blossom in the 1910s (figs. 220, 221).[11]

The liaison between William H. Boardman and Augusta Bissell might well have been forgotten among the many conventional Avenue courtships except for their shocking marriage. Born into established families and groomed for twenty years through prep school and college, boarding and finishing school, both were thoroughly versed in the rituals of their parents' lives. But at age twenty-two, when William was a first-year law student at Trinity College and home for spring vacation, and Augusta was scheduled to sail the next morning with her mother on a grand tour of Europe, the couple turned their backs on the conventions of their society and rode off on William's bicycle to elope. No engraved invitations, no wedding parties, no church. The spirited newlyweds returned to Hartford, Connecticut, together so that William could finish law school, and then came home to the Avenue a year later and lived with the

Fig. 217. Alice Wade Everett and daughters. *Left to right:* Ruth, Alice, and Esther (Cleveland Public Library, by G. M. Edmondson, 1904).

Fig. 218. *Page 236.* Charles and Lucia Edwards Otis family (Cleveland Public Library, by G. M. Edmondson, 1906).

Fig. 219. *Page 237.* A grand old patriarch, Charles A. Otis, Sr. (Cleveland Public Library, by G. M. Edmondson, 1905).

Bissells until their Schweinfurth-designed home was completed in 1892. And
here the couple remained for the rest of their lives, a marriage that produced
four children and lasted over thirty years.[12]

These and all the other Avenue intermarriages had the drapings of extended institutions: they bonded two Avenue families, sometimes more, to per-
petuate through another generation the values and property of their parents and

the neighborhood. But the Boardmans clearly did not marry to pacify their parents' institutional interests. They married out of passion, because they loved one another, as did Charles Otis and Lucia Edwards, and Sylvester Everett and Alice Wade, whom Everett took on picnics and sleigh rides and simply idolized (fig. 222).[13] Love, that ideal of marital union, was not elusive or unimportant in many Avenue courtships. Choice of a spouse, whether self-initiated or by parents, might have considered the other family's financial or social status—as Sylvester Everett did when reviewing the bidding for his own daughters—but these factors were not always the exclusive criteria.

Jeptha Wade counseled his son, Randall, before his marriage to Anna McGraw, a woman of no wealth and little social schooling, that the "selection of a wife will be the most important event of your life, an event involving all your worldly happiness." Drawing on his own twenty-five years of marriage, he reminded his twenty-one-year-old son that "mutual worth and moral purity are first in order. Beauty soon fades, and while it lasts may only be a source of

Fig. 221. Mary Perry Payne (Mrs. Charles W.) Bingham (courtesy Bolton Family, by G. M. Edmondson).

jealousy—a beauty is generally a vain and worthless helpmate." Randall indeed chose his wife for her character rather than her wealth. He challenged her own sense of self-worth, telling her, "You call the lack of wealth a fault, that is *no* fault, only a circumstance—I think not of it—I have always said that I would never marry for money." Theirs was truly a marriage of love, according to their youngest daughter Ruth. Randall doted on Anna to such an extent that she never rode in a carriage until he had first tested the seats to make sure she would be comfortable (fig. 223).[14]

Fig. 223. The Wade household. Randall and Anna Wade with children (Cleveland Public Library, by Greene and Williams, c. 1860s).

John and Clara Stone Hay's marriage was another Avenue union founded on love and respect. Hay, gifted writer that he was, spoke with genuine affection about his wife and children. Before his marriage to Clara, he wrote his coauthor John Nicolay, "She is a very estimable young person—large, handsome and good. I never found life worthwhile before." After seven years of marriage Hay's esteem for his wife had only grown. He spoke of this to Whitelaw Reid at the time of Reid's engagement: "My heart is full of your happiness. . . . The best thing has happened to you that could happen. You will be at peace the rest of your life so far as the greatest of all questions is concerned. You will have a good wife—good through and through—and I can tell you what that amounts to."[15] Hay's happiness for Reid arose out of his pleasure in his own marriage. The Hays shared a mutual enthusiasm for literature, travel, Cleveland's social life, and the company of their three children. Clara was the manager of their home. She cared for the children, served as her husband's personal secretary, tended his needs during his frequent illnesses, and was his loving companion (fig. 224).

The marriages of the Hays, Wades, and Everetts appeared to be more common than rare. Clara Hay's sister Flora, who married Samuel Mather in 1881, was just as fond of her husband as her sister was of Hay. She pined to Samuel in one of her hundreds of letters to him while he was away on his frequent business journeys, this one in 1884: "Sam, dear, I think of you, and dream of you and want you every hour." And Cornelia Brown wrote her husband, Fayette, who was away on banking business for Mygatt & Brown during an apparent time of trial in their marriage, "I can truly my own dear husband say that I have at many times realized all my fondest dreams of happiness with you." She had faith that their marriage would emerge stronger from their current difficulties, as it had from others. Harry Devereux, the lively reinsman, lounged away one Saturday morning in 1885 by "reading, smoking and making love to [his wife] Pet." Molly Payne Bingham, on one of her frequent journeys to New York City, pined to her husband Charles, "My happiest time is when I dream of you. . . . Oh if I could only be with you this evening! So I say every evening." And Cornelia Warner, wife of engineer Worcester R. Warner, told friends at the time of her husband's death that "the hardest thing I have to face now is the emptiness of the office where unfailingly heretofore I have met the greeting 'come in, my lady—come in'—a smiling welcome warm with love."[16]

The long and frequent separations brought about by the demands of business strained more than a few marriages—the wives having the responsibility of caring for the household and children alone, arranging social engagements, and having to bear a necessary but disquieting loneliness. Daily letters to and from one another, regardless of a trip's length, helped to bridge the distance. But written between the lines, and in the words themselves, many couples expressed the frustrations and practical problems that arose from husbands being away so frequently and for such long periods. In one vivid testimonial, Randall Wade wrote Anna from Washington, D.C.:

> I don't remember of ever leaving you on the sidewalk but of course the people all know that you was trying to get something that would stick closer to you than I—but I will show you when I get home how close I can stick to you—my muscular system is all in a cramp *now* to think how I will

Fig. 224. The Hay clan. *Left to right:* Helen, Adelbert, and Alva (Western Reserve Historical Society, by E. Decker, 1870s).

grab at you, hug you and squeeze you. I am afraid your poor bones will ache when I finally get through . . . such sweet thoughts make me homesick. Oh I wish I was with you even for a little while.[17]

Such intimacies came through in other letters between husbands and wives—candid, affectionate avowals.

Even so, many Euclid Avenue couples did have separate bedrooms, usually adjoining one another by a common bathroom or sitting room (fig. 225). In an unguarded moment, Ella Squire, wife of lawyer Andrew Squire, who was telling museum director William Milliken about the ever-present dirt in Avenue houses in the early 1900s, remarked in the same breath, "Even when I go from my bed to Andrew's, my little feet get dirty, too."[18] Most husbands and wives also had their own private sitting rooms to which they could retreat alone to read, work, sew, or simply enjoy a quiet moment. These affluent families in their big houses could afford the personal luxury of spatial privacy, a room or two of their own in the midst of very public and active social lives. Such comforts were unattainable by most Clevelanders.

The children also enjoyed the luxury of private bedrooms. Many also had playrooms and large ballrooms where they passed the time, sometimes in the company of their parents and sometimes their nursemaids. The household servants were responsible for tending the children's practical needs and amusements, yet their parents, their closest companions, were the important cultivators of "proper" behavior. Fathers took chief responsibility for instilling in their sons the dos and don'ts of social customs and personal conduct, and the mothers groomed their daughters. The senior Wade's attention to his teenage son was exemplary; he told Randall that his keenest desire was to see him "fully grown up, with a healthy constitution, good habits and good education." Under these circumstances, his father concluded, "I shall feel that you have a good fortune to commence the world with." Samuel L. Mather, another father who readily disciplined his sons Samuel and William when he noticed the slightest sign of weakness in their characters, gently but firmly told Samuel, who was on an eighteen-month European tour, to curtail his trip because he was concerned about him being "away any longer from Home influences." His father feared that his Catholic traveling companion was overpowering him with inappropriate influences. Mr. Mather reinforced his action by adding, "Your mother fully agrees with me, and so I know does your Grandmother."[19]

Discipline was a duty of parenthood for the wealthy and poor alike. But Avenue parents took special care to prime their children—their sons especially—to carry forward the family's financial and cultural fortitude (fig. 226). This was why the famed scientist Charles Brush urged his son, Charles, Jr., to delay his decision about his college major until they could "talk it over together" during spring vacation. His father viewed it as an important decision that would affect his son's future distinction. In a similar vein, Jeptha Wade impressed upon his grandson Homer that he was now the senior Wade's "successor"—following Randall Wade's early death in 1876 just before his 41st birthday—and was charged with all the "duties, cares, and responsibilities" of such a position. Signifying for the eleven-year-old's benefit the importance of his family role, Wade informed Homer that he expected the young man "may prove worthy of the trust" and secure "the confidence and esteem" of all who knew him and knew of him. Wade concluded his bequest with the warning, "The fortune . . . that I leave so largely to you, with so much satisfaction and

hope, will most likely prove a blessing or a curse, according to the way you take care of and use it, and take care of yourself, and others that may be dependent upon you."[20] The Avenue's other heirs—among them offspring of the Boltons, Chisholms, Fords, Nortons, Paynes, Severances, and Worthingtons—inherited their parents' Avenue residences, joined their fathers' companies, and assumed the families' positions in business and philanthropy.[21] The character and values that parents sought to instill in their children in part rose out of an interest to conserve these substantial fortunes and public positions.

The Household Servants

Most Avenue households were large, active places. They were more than just private domains, more than four walls protecting a family from the elements and the public eye. They doubled as hostelries for visiting relatives and friends, social centers for intimate and gala dinners and dances and concerts, and domiciles of the resident families—often extending to include married children, grandchildren, in-laws, and other distant relatives. Hotels and restaurants would come into vogue as places of rest and entertainment for affluent Clevelanders after the Avenue's heyday.

Amasa and Julia Stone lived with their married daughter Flora and her husband Samuel Mather and their four children, and Clara and John Hay stayed with them for over a year while their own house was being built next door.

Charles and Laura Hickox made a home for three of their unmarried adult children, as well as their daughter Elizabeth and her husband Harvey Brown. Homer and Nellie Garretson Wade's household was made up of their three children and two widowed mothers, Grandma Garretson and Grandma Wade.

A total of eight people resided in a "typical" Avenue residence in the postwar decades, including live-in servants. In a day when all meals were eaten at home, hand-drawn hot tubs supplemented central plumbing, and kerosene room heaters were indispensable for such voluminous rooms, servants were the linchpins in the smooth operation of both mansions and families. After midcentury few Euclid Avenue households were without a cast of servants. Most had at least one man, twenty to thirty years old, who was the family's coachman, gardener, and chief butler. Only such families as the Thomas Boltons and Horace Weddells employed more than two male servants to tend their large estates and working farms. The two or three female servants, seventeen to twenty-five years of age and dressed in starched uniforms, tended the family's cooking, housekeeping, errands, and children, really running these houses. The butler or cook, chief of the internal hierarchy, was responsible for managing the staff and arranging menus and schedules with the lady of the house.

Over the decades, the number and native origins of household servants changed along with the affluence of Avenue families and the complexion of the city's foreign-born population. In 1850 most families employed two to three housekeepers, most of them Irish or German immigrants—Cleveland's largest foreign population. A few had come from England, Scotland, Holland, and France, and some even came from Louisiana and Illinois. By 1880, and continuing through the early 1900s, three or four servants were required to maintain the larger residences of the postwar decades. English-speaking Irish immigrants now constituted the large majority of the Avenue's servants, even though Germans dominated the city's growing foreign-born population. English, Scottish, Swedish, and German housekeepers were employed by some households, as were American-born natives of Ohio, New York, and Virginia. All Euclid Avenue servants were Caucasians, except Edwin B. Hale's cook.[22]

The relations between family members and their servants encompassed the full spectrum of emotions, from affection to indifference to insolence. Servants depended on their employers for their financial security, and their schedules and duties were tied to family members' personal demands. They lived amidst an affluence that they personally would never enjoy, and their stations in life were to serve, and observe, luxurious living. Some were no doubt envious and frustrated by their liberal servitude, giving rise to what many employers considered the problems of impudence. Such inevitable tensions were intensified by family and servants living together under one roof.

Those servants who virtually became members of the family were far fewer than those who were employed only one or two years and became a source of discord. At one end of the spectrum, Martha Steele (Mrs. Joseph) Perkins, a leader of the Women's Christian Temperance Union, enjoyed the "warmest affection" from her housekeepers because she took care of their

Fig. 226. *Opposite.* Three generations of Otises. *Left to right:* Charles, Jr., William, Charles, Sr. (Cleveland Public Library, by G. M. Edmondson, 1905).

comfort and happiness. Augusta Bissell (Mrs. William H.) Boardman was also loved by all her servants because she, an avid gourmet herself, fed her housekeepers the finest food. But John and Antoinette Devereux dismissed several coachmen and maids for impudence, and Cornelia (Mrs. Fayette) Brown prohibited her maid Kate from her bedroom for fear that she "would soon spoil it." Likewise, Fred and Emma Sterling had a perpetual problem with keeping good cooks, maids, and coachmen in residence. In the end, Fred himself mowed the large lawn and Emma canned and baked special treats for her family. Flora Stone Mather also felt beset by an incompetent maid and a troublemaking nursemaid; the children's nursemaid fabricated menacing stories about the other three girls in their employ, which caused the cook to leave "in tears" and Flora to fire the nursemaid. Mrs. Mather concluded that it would be less work to take care of the children herself than to referee quarrels among her housekeepers.[23]

In spite of these internal dramas, Euclid Avenue servants nevertheless enjoyed a good deal of freedom to come and go as they pleased. They had their own entrance at the back of the house which went directly into their downstairs living quarters and a private stairway to their upper-floor bedrooms. Many had their own dining and sitting rooms, conveniently located next to the main kitchen. The bedrooms were as far removed as possible from the family's bedrooms without being two floors below in the basement, which none were known to be. In most of the houses built before 1880, servants' rooms were located on the same floor as the family's in the rear section, and they were on the third floor in later residences. Only a few servant households enjoyed such privacy as living in a small house at the rear of the property.[24]

As with each servant household, Euclid Avenue life was full of variety—different people, interests, and activities. The picture does not add up to a uniform set of values or just one vision of domestic life on the Avenue. The diversity among generations and families made life interesting and kept the Avenue a lively place. It was still a neighborhood, though, connected by four miles of a continuous processional of grandeur, one that residents recognized they were a part of, whether they lived down around Twenty-first Street or up at Eighty-ninth Street.

Fig. 227. A dinner party in the grand style, in Marcus Hanna residence; Marcus A. Hanna, *far left*, and President William McKinley, *fourth from right* (courtesy Ivy Edmondson Starr, by G. M. Edmondson, c. 1900).

TEN

Life on the Avenue

New York society was led by grand dame Mrs. Astor. Chicago was presided over by the McCormicks and Fields. But Cleveland had no singular arbiter who dictated and organized the comings and goings of the city's affluent families. Instead, a distinct coterie of people, most of whom lived on the Avenue, embodied Cleveland high society. The visual continuity of the long street undoubtedly concealed differences among the various households, yet there was much that bound these personalities together in a common life. Indeed, camaraderie seeded this linear neighborhood and perpetuated it over time (fig. 227).

Friendships

Family clusters and friendships were the moving forces that cemented the Euclid Avenue neighborhood and joined it with its kind in other cities. Those who grew up on the Avenue came into these acquaintanceships quite naturally. Many went to school together, attended the same parties, joined the same clubs, and dined with one another. Business was another gathering force. Many of the men worked with one another in the same industry or joint ventures, often meeting in the crossover between professions. Such close entrepreneurial ties guaranteed both rewarding benefits and unpleasant consequences. When Worcester Warner and Ambrose Swasey arrived in the city to set up their Cleveland business, they received generous assistance from banker David Z. Norton, hardware supplier William Bingham, fellow scientist Charles Brush, and machinist Francis F. Prentiss—all of whom became lifelong friends and neighbors. Charles A. Otis, Jr., made a fast and profitable entry into the stock brokerage and banking business, thanks to his father's fine connections. Otis's ability to expand his own commission house into one of the largest in the country was facilitated, according to him, by the senior Otis having had a finger in a number of pies—newspapers, telephone lines, steel plants, and others.[1]

Business conflicts, on the other hand, were unavoidable with so many ambitious capitalists living in the same neighborhood. One of these, between Randall Wade and Fayette Brown, came to a head when Brown refused to pay a stock call of Wade's on time. After a number of requests, Wade finally confronted Brown at a social ball. Brown "hastily replied" that he would pay the debt, "turned upon his heel," and walked away. Wade felt that his neighbor was "one among many, several of whom were my friends with claims to partiality" who took advantage of his good will. The two men soon came to an amicable understanding and, to preserve the friendship of the two families, Wade personally apologized to Mrs. Cornelia Brown for any social embarrassment she might have suffered.[2] Numerous disputes, of greater and lesser degrees, arose frequently. Few Avenue residents, however, could claim the notoriety of John D. Rockefeller. He was probably the most controversial business figure on the Avenue, having courted many neighbors for venture capital when he was building the Standard Oil empire. In the process, he befriended and enriched Daniel Eells, Truman Handy, John Devereux, and Feargus Squire and estranged Samuel Andrews, Amasa Stone, and Jeptha Wade.

Whatever the circumstance, social or professional, from childhood through old age, these people assumed they were inevitably connected with one another in a distinct community.[3] Such ties constituted invaluable bonds, worthy of careful cultivation, at home and elsewhere. Charles Brush reminded his son, Charles, Jr., then a freshman at Harvard, that "if Aunt Alice tries to involve you in Boston Society, let her do it by all means. Nothing will keep you socially in Cambridge quite so much as an acqaintance with some of the *best* society of Boston (nothing but the best is worthwhile) and social standing is of very great importance in college and even afterward."[4]

Brush and his affluent neighbors believed that social connections were necessary to establish one's foothold in the world. Samuel L. Mather expressed despair when his son Samuel, then traveling in Paris, failed to deliver the letters of introduction he had written on his son's behalf to continental friends. He reminded Samuel, "they may have introduced you to many agreeable people and thereby you would have extended your acquaintances." His son apparently agreed, for he preceded his subsequent trips to Europe and the Far East by letters of introduction from his diplomat brother-in-law John Hay to such well-placed individuals as James Russell Lowell and the U.S. representatives in Teheran and Peking. Hay provided similar introductions for his neighbors Homer and Nellie Wade upon their temporary move to Washington, D.C., in 1889.[5] Such efforts to win the society of one's social peers, not at all to be disparaged, were simply considered "good, tactful diplomatic management," in Worcester Warner's view.

Daily Conventions

Just as the protocol of society respected certain conventions, so too did daily life. Glimpses into Avenue homes portray a picture of both the banal and glamorous, taking in a full array of rituals from daily trips to the market to evening soirees and dinner dances.

While the men worked in their offices around Public Square and in the river district during the day, the women managed the affairs of the household. From the 1840s through the 1890s, Avenue wives and mothers went almost every day to purchase the family groceries at nearby markets, down on Ontario Street or up on Doan's Corners at 105th Street. Sometimes the coachmen drove

them, but quite often they took the carriages out themselves (fig. 228). Personal diaries and letters are filled with such practical anecdotes as that written by Emma Sterling, who one day mentioned that she had taken "the carriage and went alone to market." Augusta Bissell Boardman, an avid cook and recipe collector who was known to induce the Waldorf Hotel's headwaiter Oscar to give her recipes of her favorite dishes, was prized for her special oysters, black bean soup, and Canadian nut bread. In a manner that would have been unthinkable in the more elitist Eastern cities of Boston, Philadelphia, and New York, these Avenue ladies assisted their maids with such chores as cleaning, washing, cooking, and sewing. In one instance, Samuel L. Mather apologized to his son Sam, who was at school, for his mother's and sister Kate's tardiness in writing because they had "been so busy . . . with housecleaning and dressmaking, that they say they have had no time to write you or anybody." Almost thirty years later, Samuel's own wife, Flora, wrote him that she had spent the afternoon before "in a sort of housewifely puttering; looking over drawers and putting away winter clothes."[6]

Outside of the home, shopping trips provided pleasant forums for casual socializing—taking a carriage ride down the Avenue and then walking about around the Square from one store to another (fig. 229). Out-of-town excursions

Fig. 228. Coupe of Mrs. Amasa Stone and Mrs. Samuel Mather; George Dudgeon, family coachman for many years. Stone stable at rear (Western Reserve Historical Society).

Fig. 229. Euclid Avenue's shopping district. Looking east from Public Square (Cleveland Public Library).

were even better. Though Cleveland proprietors could lay claim as purveyors of the best china, hardware, furniture, and clothing, Avenue patrons traveled frequently to New York City for the very latest in design and fashion. This was the place to go to indulge their highest form of acquisitive activity. They often stayed at the Waldorf and The Plaza on Fifth Avenue, lunched at Delmonico's, spent the day shopping, being fitted, and going for an afternoon drive in Central Park, then taking in a recent Broadway opening in the evening. But for all of the glamorous trappings of a Manhattan shopping trip, more than a few wealthy Clevelanders tired from such grueling schedules. Clara Stone Hay had enough after one week and wanted to come home, but her husband John urged her to stay until she had "done all her errands and made all her visits." Flora Stone, Clara's sister, went off with her neighbor Laura Barnett on a customary bridal spree to the big city in preparation for her wedding to Samuel Mather. Her days were filled with "busy, happy" times, she told her husband-to-be, despite the intense shopping. She defended her activities to her skeptical fiancé, claiming that in spite of what most men thought, "the average woman does *not* like shopping."[7] Maybe so, but Avenue women—as well as men, girls, and boys—did a lot of it to fill their houses, closets, and leisure hours.

Calls and visits also consumed many hours with leisurely carriage rides, or strolls along the Avenue from one house to the next during the day or in the evening. Dismissing such rigid rules for "at home" days, these people apparently enjoyed the simple pleasures of calling on one another unannounced. Impromptu house visits and summer evenings on the piazzas were refreshingly informal. Mr. and Mrs. Amasa Stone and Mr. and Mrs. John H. Devereux, two couples who were close friends, frequently dined and spent an evening together at a moment's notice. Antoinette Devereux kept a copious record of these visits in her diary, and in the summer of 1873 she wrote:

> Mr. Stone returned to-night. A pleasant portico full—and a merry time [July 25th]; Saturday night finds us with Sallie and Bessie and Mr. and Mrs. Stone [July 26th]; Bessie, Sallie and I down town to see Mrs. Stone who showed them pictures of Mr. Amasa Stone—then down to the Stones and home to dinner [July 30]; Mrs. Stone came up to tea and to spend the evening and when we were seated at the tea table Mr. Stone surprised us by coming in upon us—had a merry time. Mr. William Bingham and Mr. Armstrong came during the evening [July 31st].

Emma Sterling and Flora Mather, two others who religiously recounted their daily meanderings, often mentioned how pleasant it was for their acquaintances—the Boltons, Hurlbuts, Raymonds, Nortons, Paynes, Binghams, and Samuel Andrews—to stop in for an evening game of whist or whickham or an afternoon of tea and chatting.[8] Until around the time of World War I, an informal dinner with a game of bridge afterwards made for a popular, pleasant evening.

Food, drink, and good cheer had a conventional role on the Avenue. To consume it, digest it, and savor it suggested that the rituals of hospitality were carefully minded to keep an evening an orderly event. Once dinner and dessert were over, the women retired to the living room for a cup of coffee or tea, and the men retreated to the library for a glass of port and cigars. After a brief respite, the gentlemen rejoined the women in the living room and the evening's activities resumed. This practice, tacitly understood by everyone, occurred as just another course in an evening's menu, as it did among most wealthy Americans and Europeans. It enabled the men to speak candidly with one another about business affairs—which they would not have done with their wives present—and permitted the women to talk among themselves about such personal matters as their children, the household, and other "private" subjects deemed inappropriate for mens' ears. Children sometimes joined their parents on their evenings out; but more often they stayed at home in the company of their own guests or their maids. Their parents' active socializing gave rise to the frequent practice of inviting the children's friends to stay overnight at the house.

Avenue families and friends also enjoyed going out together to an evening lecture on a host of "improving" topics, much the same as going to the movies in the twentieth century, then often went out afterward for dessert or a light repast. The lectures were often held in the Avenue's churches, in keeping with their function as the custodians of social values. Up to the 1860s, abolitionism was the hot topic on the lecture circuit. One held at the Wesleyan Methodist Chapel in 1856 featured Anthony Burns, "a well-known fugitive slave who has cost the United States more than any other slave in the land." Another, in 1862, at the First Baptist Church, was sponsored by the National Freedmen's Association and featured contraband William Davis. In the 1870s and 1880s, popular topics were temperance and spiritual salvation. The First Baptist Church was "crowded to excess" one evening in 1875 for a mass meeting on temperance. Many Avenue families were especially interested in what a Dr. Bryce had to say about "Saving the Young in These New Country Houses" at the Third Presbyterian Church on an evening in 1885. And Miss Mittleberger often invited a small group of Avenue parents over to her school for an afternoon or evening lecture on a notable American author. But, on the lighter side, living rooms and ballrooms along the Avenue resounded many an evening with singing, dancing, and concerts by small musical ensembles.[9]

Afternoon teas were another favored ritual among friends, some being informal at-homes, where anyone could stop by, while others were by invitation only (fig. 230). A tea hosted by Mrs. Henry Gaylord and attended by such established couples as the Paynes, Masons, and the Newberrys, introduced John and Antoinette Devereux to the Avenue upon their arrival in 1873. Out-of-towner John Hay was accorded the same welcome when he brought his new wife, Clara Stone, back to her native Avenue in 1876. Hay, not one to buck the pagentry of tradition nor miss the opportunity to observe social nuances in action, soon became acclimated to his neighbors' love of socializing over tea and pastries. But as he told his sister-in-law Flora, "the rebellious Adam" in him rose up against the extravagance of such frequent gatherings. He cited the physical consequences of too much indulgence: "Sam Raymond weighs 164 and visibly gains. . . . Alfred is bursting his jacket buttons off. Schneider threatens momentarily to bloom out into the fuzzy splendor of pop-corn."[10] He could not understand how the neighborhood could eat so much and yet stay so healthy.

The fit constitutions of many Avenue residents may partially be attributed to their extensive outdoor activities—gardening, walking, gaming, or driving about. Carriage drives through the parks and further out into the countryside were a universal favorite among the Avenue residents. During the second half of the nineteenth century, families, friends, and lovers spent many a balmy evening or weekend afternoon in refreshing outings. Fayette Brown enjoyed one such pleasant Sunday with the Henry Chapins and Charles Bradburns in the spring of 1854. Starting out early in the morning, they rode their horses out to a "wild

Fig. 230. The tea group, fifteenth anniversary celebration, May 29, 1926 (Western Reserve Historical Society).

lovely stream" about three miles outside the city, where they found a grove of elms and sycamores to lay their spread. They spent the day walking, talking, rambling along the stream, and picnicking on cold meats and bread. Similarly, Samuel Mather and his family often rode out to their property in the Bratenahl woods, where his boys could enjoy a splendid time swimming and his family could picnic by the lake.[11]

Driving was a source of calm for some and a hearty sport for others. Such avid horsemen as Samuel L. Mather and Harry K. Devereux took great pleasure in a good, swift tour along the Avenue. After one of these impulsive outings, Mather felt re-invigorated—the world was a better place: "I took a long drive yesterday afternoon and feel better today."[12] But Avenue residents' love for the horse and carriage quickly gave way to the motorized vehicle when it appeared on the scene in the 1890s. These affluent families avidly acquired the latest models of automobiles for their use and play, as fast as the dealers could roll them out on the showroom floors (fig. 231).

Florence and Mary Brown, two of the city's maiden grande dames, continued the custom of Sunday afternoon drives well into the 1910s, having exchanged their carriage for an automobile. As told by William Milliken in his book *A Time Remembered,* the Brown sisters drove down the Avenue "sitting very erect, high in the tonneau of their Pierce-Arrow, their big hats tied under their chins, the ends of their veils floating about their heads." Samuel Mather, who, as early as 1907, built an eight-car garage at the back of his new Avenue home, took pleasure in driving his Baker electric car up and down the Avenue after 1900. Even if the batteries did run out after only twenty minutes, he was not chagrined; he would simply leave it in the street and wait for his chauffeur to pick him up. James J. Tracy, Jr., also enjoyed parading along the Avenue in his 1903 White touring car, which was hard to miss with its high-gloss aluminum red finish and steam-powered engine. Worcester R. Warner, inventive engineer that he was, proudly displayed Ohio's 341st driver's license as early as 1908.[13]

While motion seemed to capture the fancy of this society, stationary pleasures were not without their place. Among the fondest of these was the photographic sitting. It was a national enthusiasm to be sure, for the affluent and middle class alike, and Euclid Avenue residents had a special penchant for recording their images on paper. They approached the photographic sitting with the vigor of a social event. Thanks to the wealth of photographs they left behind, the visual picture of the Avenue's life is all the more vivid today. For them, it was another way of memorializing their lives, along with their houses, diaries, and art collections.

Among the talented photographers of the period, the most popular were James F. Ryder and Edgar Decker in the 1860s through the 1880s, then George M. Edmondson in the late 1890s through the 1930s (fig. 232). Edmondson, who inherited Decker's business, became part of the fabric of this society. When his clients came to his Euclid Avenue studio to spend an afternoon sitting for their portrait, he entertained them with tea and sherry. He was an amiable character

Fig. 231. A drive on the Avenue (Lake County [IL] Museum, Curt Teich Postcard Archives, c. 1909).

Fig. 232. The photographers. Edgar Decker, *left,* and George M. Edmondson, *right* (courtesy Ivy Edmondson Starr, 1898).

Fig. 233. Posed for action, Livingston and Amasa Mather (Western Reserve Historical Society, by E. Decker, 1880s).

Fig. 234. The lawyers, *left to right:* Andrew Squire, William Sanders, and James H. Dempsey (Cleveland Public Library, by G. M. Edmondson, 1907).

and everyone loved him; residents invited him to their parties and their homes and enjoyed stopping by just to sit and chat with him and Mrs. Edmondson. Of course his greatest legacy was his photographs—precise and beautifully composed—of people, residences, and gatherings. But he was also remembered for his Christmas gifts of thick leather photograph albums, embossed in gold and bound with brass hardware, a tradition from the Edmondson studio (figs. 233–35).[14]

Ambrose Swasey, one of the photographer's frequent subjects, treated his birthday sitting with Edmondson as a sacred ritual. Swasey was a modest man in other respects, but he went out of his way to be in town on his birthday to have his annual portrait taken. Year after year, it was "almost a religious ceremony," according to his biographer (fig. 236). Swasey's enthusiasm might have been extreme, but Cleveland society believed that "if you hadn't got that studio portrait done by Edmondson of Euclid Avenue you just hadn't been photographed."[15]

The Church

Religion strengthened the ties among Avenue families and affluent Clevelanders through common membership in select churches and sectarian charities.

In the spirit of the neighborhood, the comity of churches on the Avenue engendered cooperation among the different Christian denominations. And so it was among residents, devout and agnostic alike. Even within such households as the Rockefellers and Mathers, where husband and wife were leading members of different churches, diverse church affiliations and religious beliefs were peacefully respected as long as they worshipped the Christian faith.

Early on in the Avenue's life, in the antebellum years, the church became the established center of both social and religious values. Built by pious faithfuls in the 1830s and 1840s, the churches were integral to the residential street. This role was sustained through the Avenue's heyday. In 1881 five churches stood along the Avenue; by 1906 there were eleven. Among the most exclusive were Old Stone Church on the Public Square, St. Paul's Episcopal, Euclid Avenue Presbyterian, Euclid Avenue Baptist, First Methodist Episcopal, Calvary Presbyterian, and Trinity Cathedral. Leading Avenue residents were trustees and officers of these institutions, and their clergy had intimate ties with the families. Sunday morning services were a ritual, the likely origin of Sunday parading

Fig. 235. *Opposite.* Lady of the parlor, Nellie Garretson (Mrs. Jeptha H.) Wade II (Cleveland Public Library, by G. M. Edmondson, 1900).

Fig. 237. St. Paul's Episcopal Church, southeast corner at Fortieth Street (Western Reserve Historical Society, 1888).

along the Avenue. Fashionable carriages driven by liveried coachmen in long-processions deposited elegantly dressed ladies and silk-hatted gentlemen at the parish house curbs. For one member of Trinity Episcopal's parish, the Avenue's fashionable churches had been reduced to social clubs and the weekly service a

Fig. 238. Trinity Cathedral, southeast corner at Twenty-second Street (Western Reserve Historical Society, 1920).

species of entertainment—a poor Sunday show, he believed, which the theaters very easily outrivaled.[16] But for most the church carried an important religious function, and their commitments were intended to promote good works rather than colorful pageantry.

This is why many Avenue residents invested so much money and time in the building of their parish houses (fig. 237). Donations to Old Stone Church for land and building in 1834 came from such early Euclid Avenue residents as Samuel Cowles, Nathan Perry, John Sterling, and Peter Weddell; and the church's restoration after the great fire of 1884, which destroyed the interior and spire, was led by Avenue residents John Hay and John A. Foote and financed by Flora Mather, among others. Euclid Avenue Baptist Church was built by Rockefeller, William and Stewart Chisholm, and eight others who gave their assets to save the church that became the downtown Baptist stronghold until the early 1900s. Calvary Presbyterian Church at Seventy-ninth Street was completed in 1890 and officially organized in 1892 by 308 members of Old Stone Church, many of them Avenue residents, to serve the growing area east of Fifty-fifth Street. Moreover, the magnificent campus for Trinity Parish House and Cathedral was built on the Avenue at Twenty-second Street, 1890–1907, thanks in large part to the leadership and gifts of Samuel Mather and William J. Boardman. Trinity's move to the Avenue was motivated by a desire to have it stand within the residential district of its principal parishioners, to remove it from the darkened shadow of new, domineering business blocks going up on Superior (fig. 238).[17]

Since money was plentiful among these families, and building handsome structures was an obvious interest, it is not surprising that many focused their denominational devotion in major architectural projects (fig. 239). But their formative work for many of the city's welfare institutions, sponsored by these Christian churches, arose not from affluence or a sense of noblesse oblige, as it did among Chicago's elite who resided on Prairie Avenue, but from a deep belief in Puritan ethics. Such charitable interests—akin to those that consumed Boston's and Denver's society reformers—arose from a genuine Yankee sense of duty to improve the public welfare.

Each church had a ladies' society that raised money for health care and job counseling for the city's poor and aid for orphans and the elderly. The women, often assisted by their daughters, also organized food and clothing drives, the bounties distributed personally to impoverished families in the river district. In 1879 alone, the society of Old Stone Church raised $334, made 160 house calls, and supported sixteen families. All the women responsible for the work lived on the Avenue, among them Mrs. Amasa Stone and Mrs. Sherlock J. Andrews.[18] Old Stone Church parishioners were among the most active public servants in Cleveland, founding such major welfare institutions as the Home for Friendless Children, Lakeside and Willson Street hospitals, the Cleveland Orphan Asylum, the Women's Christian Association (later the YWCA), and the Goodrich House social settlement.

The Euclid Avenue Baptist Church was another stronghold of social works. Among its members were the Chisholm family, John D. Rockefeller, Samuel Andrews, and Mrs. Levi T. Scofield, wife of the eminent architect. These Avenue residents led the missionary spirit to collect money, food, and clothing for the church-sponsored homes. Mrs. Alanson T. Osborn (née Katherine Chisholm) was the chief inspiration for the ladies and their projects: the sewing circle, cook committee, Sunday picnics, and mission study classes held at her Avenue home. This queenly woman engendered a happy camaraderie that all admired, her successes evident in the rapport among her loyal cooks: entrance to her inner circle was jealousy guarded by the incumbents and sought after by those who desired to partake of meal preparations for the missions. Mrs. Osborn also spearheaded the Eaton Mission Band of little girls (the Sunbeams

after 1902) to fit them up to preside over meetings and prayer sessions among the Avenue's senior society.[19]

The church offered these people a pleasant respite from the demands of fashionable society. Mrs. Henry B. Payne reminded her daughter Mary in 1875 that "society has a pleasure and a claim, but only to an extent." Excess in dress and fashion, she believed, should be tempered with the genuine Christian ethics that suggest "everything good and noble and rational in man or woman."[20] But solemnity was not all the church offered its members: dinners, picnics, and musicales were as much a part of the ritual as Sunday services and good works. The Avenue's churches were social clubs of sorts: neighborhood institutions of like-minded people who shared the comfort of deep religious beliefs and values.

Parties

The exhibitionist traits that were apparent in the photographic and architectural enthusiasms of Euclid Avenue families also revealed themselves in their savoir faire in formal affairs. They heartily enjoyed good cheer and embraced social events with the kind of serious management that could rival professional business. The extravagance that others noted, and some even criticized, simply reflected a joy for formal celebrations. As the century matured and the affluence grew, so did the size and grandeur of events. Dinner parties in the 1860s and 1870s for six to ten guests expanded to twelve to twenty guests in the 1880s and 1890s. Guest lists of up to 700 for an evening of dancing were not unheard of. In the 1860s and 1870s, summer lawn concerts staged on the large residential grounds became quite popular. Whether a fundraiser for a charitable cause, as many were, or just an outdoor musicale, all were organized to draw Avenue people out of their homes for an enjoyable evening together under the stars. Edwin B. Hale hosted a lawn social in 1874 to honor the ladies of Trinity Church and celebrate the completion of the Home for Friendless Children. D. K. Clint sponsored a "lawn fete" on his grounds in 1875 to raise money for the Huron Street Hospital. In 1878, Charles Hickox and Amasa Stone were among the Avenue residents who offered their lawns for a series of concerts by the Germania Band and Mendelsohn Quartette.[21]

Holiday celebrations were also times for bringing Avenue families together with ebullient open-house parties that turned the street into a garlanded aisle of reception rooms. Among the most festive was New Year's Day; more calling cards were dropped in entrance hall baskets on this day than on any other throughout the year. The houses were opened to callers, and residents went from one to the other to visit friends and meet neighbors. The Devereuxs, who frequently opened their home to guests, were avid New Year's Day hosts. Antoinette Devereux mentioned in her diary on the eve of 1875 that she was "busy today getting ready for calls tomorrow." She was a success. The next day, one of her admiring guests, John Hay, told Flora Stone that Lady Devereux had entertained all her callers "with perfect dignity and self possession."[22]

The Charles Brush family also made the most of their elegant residence. In 1901, the *Leader* reported that among those on the Avenue who observed the great day, the Brush home, "which is so handsomely appointed for entertaining," was thrown open for one of the largest receptions in the neighborhood, "and the good cheer of the New Year's Day reigned everywhere." When the *Leader* distinguished the Brushes' party as one of the largest, one can only surmise the number of callers they received. In a house about half the size of the Brush manse, Mr. and Mrs. Worcester R. Warner welcomed 600 guests to celebrate 1911's New Year. They adorned the entrance with tiny white bells formed in the figures "1911", surrounded by a floral bloom of poinsettias, palms, and ferns. They twined smilax up the broad staircase to guide guests from the first to the third floor and trimmed the halls with fresh flowers. The Warners received in the living room, while their guests mingled in the library and dining room and waiters served refreshments in the third-floor ballroom.[23]

In all seasons, Euclid Avenue wedding parties were heady competition for the high spirits of the New Year's Day tradition, and they were far more frequent due to the size of the neighborhood and Avenue families, each with three to five children (fig. 240). In just two days in 1866, Randall Wade was invited to attend four wedding receptions, two each evening. These were "lively times," he told his father, an understated recognition of his demanding social schedule. But wedding parties seemed to pull the families of this linear neighborhood together. John Hay was impressed on the occasion of Mary Castle and David Norton's marriage in 1876 by the remarkable unity with which "the whole village came together" and by its capacity to make merry and dance.[24] The church ceremony was steeped in the solemn rituals of each denomination, while the wedding reception at the family's Avenue home was liberated by gaiety, good

food, and hearty dancing. The house was thrown open to the hundreds of guests, and only the dining room was reserved for the formal bridal table. Dinners and luncheons for the bride and groom prior to the wedding day were as much a part of the ritual as the ceremony itself. On the day before, the bride hosted a spinster luncheon for her bridesmaids at such a prominent club as the Euclid Avenue Club, and the groom hosted an evening bachelor party for his

Fig. 240. The wedding party. Wedding dinner for Alice Hale Russell and Alfred Gleason Sherman Park (courtesy Mrs. J. Henry Melcher, by G. M. Edmondson).

ushers, often held at the Union Club. For any single wedding, the Avenue's churches, clubs, and homes became the stage set for the celebration, drawing on the services of the city's finest caterers, florists, musicians, dressmakers, and tailors.

Aside from weddings and holidays, the Avenue's residents invested most of their social energies in dinner parties and receptions. And it is no wonder. These sumptuous evenings consumed a remarkable degree of imaginative planning and management and took full advantage of the opulent residences—from the spacious entrance hall, up the sweeping staircase, to the grand ballroom on the third floor. Guest lists were carefully drawn up to bring just the right number and mix of people together. Who should meet whom, and who was owed a reciprocal invitation? In preparing for a dinner reception in 1889, Flora Mather studiously consulted her recent social calendar to draw up the guest list, telling Samuel, "There are certain people, like the Stewart Chisholms, the Alfred Nicks, and the Hitchcocks whom I put down because we've been asked to musicales or evening parties. *Teas* don't count, we paid off all those with one tea last summer." She also invited "some young men" to complement the single young women invited and to have them ready for future dinners or teas. As it was an expensive affair, Flora invited the most people the house could comfortably seat. She decided that 150 guests was a manageable number, so she made up a list of 200, two out of three living on the Avenue.[25]

With so many social events to attend, Avenue hosts made sure that each affair had its own raison d'être and theme. Mr. and Mrs. Amasa Stone hosted a housewarming party in January 1859 for "a throng of old settlers" and "the beauty and fashion of the Forest City" just after their residence was completed. The affair centered around the "spacious and richly finished and furnished salons." The completion of barns and garages gave Avenue patrons another special occasion for which to throw a party. Warren Corning, for one, hosted a lively dance in his new horse barn in 1876. The magnificent structure was finished throughout with hardwood, gas, and brass hardware, inspiring one guest to remark guardedly that it had "all the comforts of an equine home." In 1912, Bessie Miller celebrated the opening of her new, modern garage. She held a grand supper and dancing party for over one hundred guests who gathered in the beautifully appointed auto house. No one even entered the main house during the evening.[26]

Avenue residents' formal celebrations in honor of their architectural creations were exceeded by their fundraising activities. Fashionable balls for favorite charities, rare events among New York's patricians on Fifth Avenue, were quite common among the public-spirited families on Euclid Avenue. But while leading Clevelanders departed from their fellow New Yorkers in their regard for civic duty, they joined them in honoring society's "Four Hundred." Among the annual rituals were the constant round of "coming out" receptions for young ladies, to introduce the dames upon their election into this most elite society. The affairs were hosted by the matriarchs among Cleveland's "Four Hundred," most of whom resided on the Avenue. The afternoon reception for Misses Alice

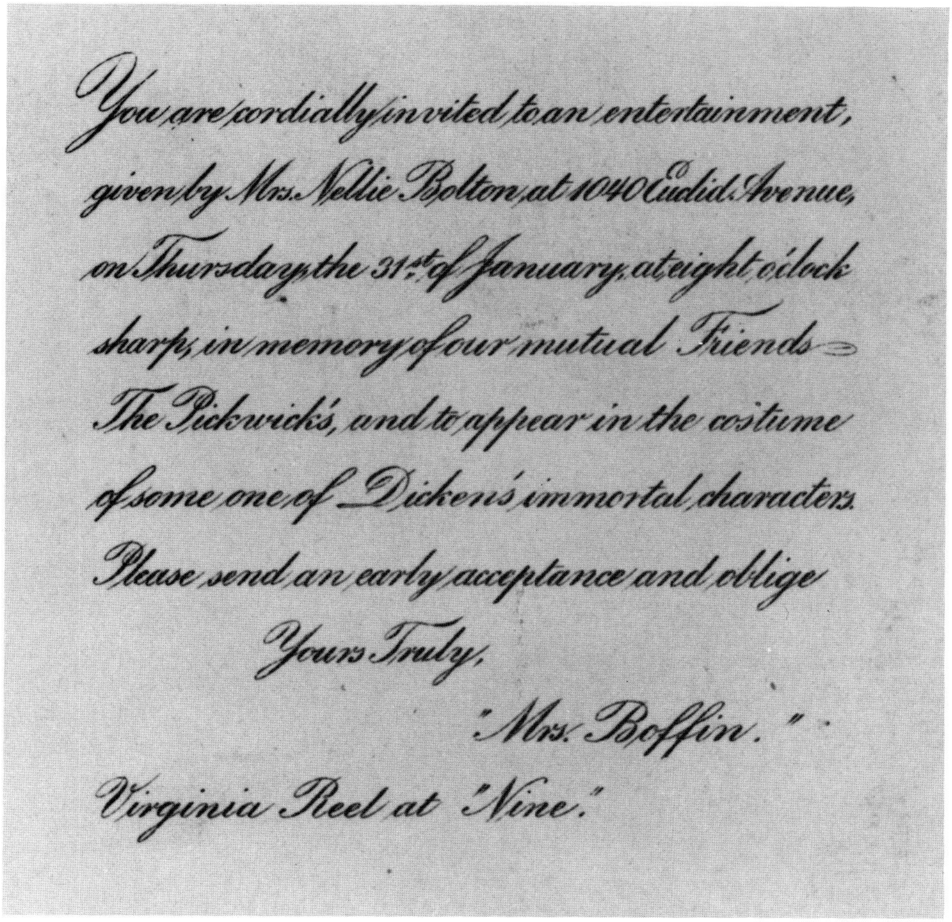

You are cordially invited to an entertainment, given by Mrs. Nellie Bolton, at 1040 Euclid Avenue, on Thursday the 31st of January, at eight o'clock sharp, in memory of our mutual Friends The Pickwicks, and to appear in the costume of some one of Dickens's immortal characters. Please send an early acceptance and oblige Yours Truly,
"Mrs. Boffin."
Virginia Reel at "Nine."

Fig. 241. Invitation to the Dickens party, given by Mrs. Nellie Bolton, a.k.a. Mrs. Boffin (Western Reserve Historical Society).

Russell and Clara Hale in 1896, similar to many, was given by their mothers, Mrs. George Russell and Mrs. Willis B. Hale, and such Avenue ladies as Mrs. Randall Wade, Mrs. Myron T. Herrick, Mrs. Hiram Garretson, Mrs. David Norton, and Mrs. Charles C. Bolton. Together they welcomed 500 guests to meet the young debutantes and their attendants in the Russells' recently remodeled and newly furnished home. In the evening, the young ladies in the receiving party, all students at Miss Hathaway Brown's school, enjoyed a formal dinner alone and then danced late into the night with their male companions.[27]

These rather subdued festivities paled by comparison to Avenue theme parties, fantastic affairs in which all guests were required to dress up in costumes. These really unleashed a jovial spirit in otherwise restrained personalities and were met with rave reviews by guests and onlookers alike. One of these was a Cake Walk party, hosted by Eleanor Hale Bolton in her Euclid Avenue ballroom. The society gossip column in *Town Topics* reported that she "spelled and worded" the invitations to the party in the "negro dialect" and opened the

Fig. 242. *Page 272.* The Old Curiosity Shop, Dickens party (Western Reserve Historical Society).

Fig. 243. *Page 273.* Bleak House, Dickens party (Western Reserve Historical Society).

OLD·CURIOSITY·SHOP

THE·MARCHIONESS	Miss·Edith·Hale	OLD·WOMAN	Miss·Ford
MRS·JARLEY	Mrs·W·H·Boardman	JAPANESE·LADY	Mrs·Chadwick
SALLY·BRASS	Mrs·D·B·Wick	DICK·SWIVELER	Mr·W·H·Boardman
LITTLE·NELL	Miss·Mabel·Burnham	BLUEBEARD	Mr·J·B·Parsons
MARY·QUEEN·OF·SCOTS	Mrs·H·W·Boardman	ROBERT·ELSMERE	Mr·Frank·L·Alcott
MAID·OF·HONOR	Mrs·C·J·Sheffield	SOLDIER	Mr·C·A·Selzer
MAID·OF·HONOR	Mrs·T·A·Kelley	SAMPSON·BRASS	Mr·Douglas·Perkins

BLEAK · HOUSE

LADY · DEDLOCK ·	Mrs · C·F·Brush ·	MR · TULKINHORN ·	Mr · Amos · Townsend ·
MRS · BADGER ·	Mrs · S·H·Chisholm ·	MR · BAGNET ·	Mr · John · Tod ·
MRS · BAGNET ·	Mrs · D·P·Eells ·	MR · BADGER ·	Mr · Wm · Edwards ·
MRS · JELLABY ·	Mrs · J·B·Zerbe ·	MR · GEORGE ·	Mr · S·T·Everett ·
MISS · FLITE ·	Mrs · S·A·Raymond ·	PRINCE · TURVEYDROP ·	Mr · John · Whitelaw ·
SIR · LEICESTER · DEADLOCK ·	Mr · J·Martin ·	MR · SKIMPOLE ·	Mr · C·W·Chase ·
	MR · KENGE ·	Mr · Richard · Parmely ·	

ball with a grand march led by dancing Topsies—red mother hubbards with "blackened" faces, arms, and necks. After an evening of hardy dancing, the guests departed bidding Mrs. Bolton goodnight in "the most approved negro fashion." Her success with this ball inspired her in 1889 to host a Dickens Party for "100 of Cleveland's best known society people in disguise," according to the *Plain Dealer*. This too commenced with a grand march, led by Mr. and Mrs. Turveydrop—neighbors John Whitelaw and Mrs. Mary Brush (figs. 241–43).[28]

A Twelfth Night Party, hosted by Mr. and Mrs. George S. Russell in January 1897, which heralded the close of the English holiday season, brought out the best of Mother Goose's followers. The Russells led off as Father and Mother Goose, and their guests recreated such characters as the "frog who would a-wooing go," Old Mother Hubbard, and Little Bo Peep. Such frivolity as might be expected among less self-consciously formal people was repeated time and again. It was epitomized in a "baby" party at the turn of the century, with guests dressing as infant children and waiters serving champagne in nursing bottles. The free-flowing alcohol assuaged guests' embarrassment, and it also engaged a youthful spirit. Lucia and Charles Otis dressed as eight-year-olds in white dresses, and James and Jessie Hoyt came as a naughty little boy and his nurse.[29]

Formal dinner parties and private receptions, the most common form of socializing, often honored out-of-town visitors to Avenue homes. Among the guests of honor were such eminent statesmen, authors, and industrialists as U.S. presidents, Jacob Riis, William K. Vanderbilt, Andrew Carnegie, and J. P. Morgan. When *Atlantic Monthly* editor William Dean Howells was staying with John Hay in 1879, Hay invited President Rutherford B. Hayes, General James Garfield, Amasa Stone, Henry B. Payne, Mr. and Mrs. William J. Boardman, Samuel L. Mather, and James Mason to meet the journalist with whom he had studied as a boy in Columbus. In turn, Flora Mather accompanied her brother-in-law, then secretary of state, to a private dinner party at the White House in 1905, hosted by President and Mrs. Teddy Roosevelt. She had expected a "dreadfully dull" evening, but to her pleasant surprise, thanks to Mrs. Roosevelt's queenly grace, it turned out to be quite an interesting affair. Those among the twenty guests whom Mrs. Mather enjoyed chaffing with across the table were Mrs. Henry Frick, Mrs. Woodrow Wilson, and Senator Henry Cabot Lodge and his wife, Nannie. Certainly Mrs. Roosevelt's seating arrangement was innocent of any knowledge of the decades-long clandestine love affair between Nannie Lodge and Flora's brother-in-law, John Hay. The liaison, which may have never been consummated, began in the late 1880s when Hay was living alone in the nation's capital, a city that had challenged his genius but which he privately abhorred.[30]

The Hays, Mathers, and their fellow Clevelanders were active in the national area, and had as their companions many of the country's leaders in politics, commerce, and culture. It is not surprising then, since Ohio was the state of presidents in the postwar decades and Cleveland was the most influential city

in Ohio, that quite a few Euclid Avenue residents mixed easily among the nation's leading personalities. They were active in the national scene and in the nationwide network of establishment politics and opulent society (fig. 244).

Fig. 244. A presidential visit. On the doorstop of the residence of Daniel P. Eells, *center*, with President Benjamin Harrison, *right* (Western Reserve Historical Society).

Fig. 245. Coaching day, Four-in-Hand Club preparing to depart for a ride in the country. Charles A. Otis, Jr., residence, no. 3436, *left,* and William H. Boardman residence, no. 3608, *right* (Western Reserve Historical Society, 1890s).

ELEVEN

Life off the Avenue

America's class of socially eminent families was quite congenial among its own. They traveled a lot and saw one another frequently. They met up with each other at resorts and schools and through their endeavors in philanthropy, the arts, and politics. Business was another centralizing force. Most of all, they shared a common ground in their distinguished urban lives, enjoying the fortunes, connections, power, and leisure to strengthen their ties with one another. This milieu linked the nation's grand avenues together (fig. 245).

The School Connection

Educational pursuits loomed large among the concerns of Euclid Avenue families. They invested as much time and money, and certainly more political strength, in advancing the city's public school system and its private institutions as they did in their churches. Western Reserve College and Case School of Applied Sciences were the favorite institutions sponsored by the Avenue's establishment, who reasoned that the presence of good local schools would attract future industry and wealth. Bostonians had Harvard, New Yorkers had Columbia, Philadelphians had the University of Pennsylvania, and Clevelanders had what would one day become Case Western Reserve. The Cleveland Medical College, the first independent college of science and technology west of the Alleghenies, had been founded in 1843 by Leonard Case, Sr., and early Avenue residents Peter Weddell, Samuel Starkweather, Zalmon Fitch, John Woolsey, Henry Payne, Thomas Bolton, and James M. Hoyt. By 1860, it had become a department of Western Reserve College, then based in Hudson, Ohio. Western Reserve, established in 1826, made the important move to Cleveland in 1880, thanks to Amasa Stone's half-million-dollar contribution. Stone changed the name to Adelbert College of Western Reserve University, in memory of his deceased son, and hand-picked the first board of trustees with such confidants as son-in-law John Hay and neighbors William J. Boardman, Col. William Harris, Samuel Andrews, and Liberty E. Holden, who gave his Avenue homesite for the new college (fig. 246).[1] Significant donations by Avenue patrons established the college as one of the finest private universities in the Midwest by the early twentieth century. Consistent with the fine-tuned architectural sensitivities of the university's patrons, the buildings—many the work of Avenue architect

Schweinfurth—created a magnificent Tudor-inspired campus at the eastern entrance to the grand avenue. Jeptha Wade, Samuel Mather, and Franklyn T. Backus underwrote the law school; Henry R. Hatch supported the law library; Dudley P. and Elisabeth Severance Allen were the chief benefactors of St. Luke's Hospital and the Cleveland Medical Library; Flora Mather and Jane Tracy lent their support to the College for Women; and Andrew and Ella Squire gave their 275-acre Valleevue estate to the College for Women for a working farm.

Avenue residents carried these educational convictions through to their own children, whom they encouraged in higher learning at the nation's top preparatory schools and colleges. The absence of an intellectual tradition in the early lives of the Avenue's senior wardens seemed to only heighten their interest in creating one for their children. Such reverence for quality education, manifest as early as the 1860s, departed from the parental ambitions of the mercantile establishment of Chicago headed by Marshall Field and Cyrus McCormick, who placed little value on intellectual activity and higher education, or of patrician New Yorkers, who paid little mind to the quality of the city's public schools.[2] But even while Euclid Avenue parents advanced Cleveland's public educational system for others, they often sent their own children away to private schools and colleges on the East Coast to broaden their horizons and acquire at close range the texts and traditions of their Anglo-Saxon ancestors.

These academic biases, a luxury of the Avenue's comfortable families, might have appeared purely elitist had it not been for the fact that such parents as the Wades, Mathers, and Binghams genuinely believed that their children should profit from the superior education they had been deprived of but could now well afford. For all practical purposes, most of these Clevelanders agreed with Yale University philosopher William Graham Sumner, who maintained that "hereditary wealth [was] the strongest instrument by which we keep up a steadily advancing civilization."[3] Parents were not content to let their offspring rest on the material laurels they could provide, nor did they want them to have to struggle, as they had, to achieve recognition.

Parents prepared their children carefully for entry into the nation's premier colleges. At midcentury, most sent their sons and daughters away to military institutes and private boarding and finishing schools. The newly affluent city had no established preparatory schools. A decade of prosperity and concentrated wealth, however, changed this. Avenue parents personally sponsored the founding of Cleveland's preparatory schools in order to keep their children and those of their peers at home. For boys, they founded Brooks Academy and University School, and Miss Mittleberger's, Miss Guilford's, and Hathaway Brown schools for the girls.

In 1875, Avenue residents John Devereux, Jeptha Wade, Samuel Andrews, and Daniel Eells established Brooks Academy, even though most of their sons were already well beyond secondary school age. The military institute was their model, and a primary role of the Academy was to cultivate disciplined habits as well as scholarship. Brooks was the first private school in Cleveland to introduce regimented drills into its curriculum, giving rise to afternoon spectacles of uniformed battalions and athletic exercises staged on the Devereuxs' front lawn. University School superseded the Academy when it opened in 1890. Founded by a group of Avenue fathers who sought to keep "their sons home during college preparation," this school also emphasized military drills as much as academic and manual training.[4] The founders, notably Samuel Mather, retained architect Charles Schweinfurth to design University's buildings and grounds at Hough and Giddings avenues, to which their sons traveled by chauffeured carriage or streetcar each day. The school had become an Avenue institution by the turn of the century, then as now educating the sons of those among the city's leading families (fig. 247).

For daughters, parents established Brooks School for Young Ladies and Misses in 1876, a pre-collegiate branch of Brooks Academy. A decade after its founding, Anne Hathaway Brown purchased the school and moved it from its original location on the Avenue at Fifty-fifth Street to a townhouse at Twenty-eighth Street. Augusta Mittleberger also opened an exclusive girls school in 1877, located in the house on Prospect and Fortieth streets that Rockefeller owned and had moved off the corner of his Avenue property (fig. 248).[5]

Quite a few Avenue children, girls and boys, attended these respected institutions. Yet in spite of their high caliber, a number of families still favored such Eastern boarding schools as Briarcliff in New York and Andover and St. Marks in Massachusetts. At these academic enclaves, well beyond Cleveland, Euclid Avenue heirs could live amidst the heirs of other socially eminent families, their parents at peace with the knowledge that their offspring were gaining exposure to the national ethos of their class.

Fig. 247. University School football team, 1897 (Western Reserve Historical Society, 1897).

College, too, became an important passage by the last quarter of the nineteenth century, a road that led as much to higher learning as it did to prestigious credentials. Avenue parents, few of whom even graduated from high school, valued this technical pedigree for their sons, if not for their daughters. It was an entrenched convention by the early twentieth century. Yale College in New Haven was probably the most highly regarded, providing many Clevelanders with a link in the national circle of affluent families. In 1890 alone, twenty-seven Clevelanders were among the graduating class.[6] Harvard and Princeton were also highly regarded, even though neither gained the apparent popularity that Yale enjoyed.

Parents seemed to disapprove of college education for their daughters, even though they often excelled in finishing school after high school, if they continued their education at all. Their future roles as wives and mothers, not

Fig. 248. Miss Mittleberger's school photograph (courtesy Mrs. J. Henry Melcher, c. 1885).

professionals, indicated that their careers were "to make the home happy and attractive," as Randall Wade explained it, rather than to be accomplished scholars or managers. Samuel Williamson discouraged his daughter Ethel from entertaining any thought of going to Bryn Mawr, or any other college, even though she was determined to continue her education. This conventional view regarding the higher education of women held forth through the early decades of the 1900s and was adequately accommodated by boarding schools and hovering mothers.[7]

Travels and Seasonal Retreats

Through the decades, Avenue families readily left their urban homes, many for months and even years at a time. They went to the nearby countryside in Bratenahl, Wickliffe, or Little Mountain; to farms in Georgia, Vermont, or Connecticut; to estates in Florida; and many traveled the continent or sailed around the world. Some even went away to live temporarily in other cities because careers in politics or government called them to the state's or nation's capital. Others went simply because they wanted to go elsewhere and had the means to do it.

While most Avenue families clung to their residences most of the year, they also had a genuine love for distant travel. They journeyed throughout America and voyaged across the ocean to Europe, the Middle East, China, and Japan. Young and old happily embarked on extended excursions each year. Affluence afforded the luxury of adventure and their inquisitive enthusiasms provided the driving stimulus. The vast distances and diverse cultures they traversed could be glimpsed through the exotic curios displayed in their houses (and can be seen today in a tour through the Cleveland Museum of Art).

The honeymoon journey was a traditional departure point; it was quite the fashion to take a coaching trip through Europe for a year or more. The Atlantic voyage, departing on an ocean liner out of New York, was part of the affair. Rather than enjoying a rare opportunity to savor the seclusion of one another's company, many honeymooners welcomed chaperoning neighbors and friends to join them on their voyage. Fayette Brown sailed in the 1850s with George Ely and his bride and another newlywed couple who were headed to "some fashionable watering (and liquoring) place." Charles and Lucia Edwards Otis were accompanied by Bishop William Leonard on their London-bound ship, the beginning of an indefinite European honeymoon trip to Paris, to Holland, up the Rhine, and on to Berlin. The young Otises met up with Avenue neighbors throughout their honeymoon—the Outhwaites joined them in London and on to Paris, and the Charles Hickoxes went with them to Cairo. After a year, they returned to their Avenue home to set up housekeeping, having accumulated twenty-seven trunks, several cages of birds, two Irish terriers, and a Skye terrier.[8]

Avenue travelers apparently favored the European grand tour, as did most Americans of means and cosmopolitan tendencies, in which they steeped themselves in the classical traditions of past and present. Even though few on the Avenue could surpass Worcester Warner's nineteen trips to the continent, most were in heady competition with his love for such old-world influences. Charles W. Bingham spent three years in Europe after graduating from Yale—walking through Switzerland, attending lectures in Germany, and mastering the language and customs of France. He returned to Hamburg and Stockholm eight years later for his honeymoon with Molly Payne. Thirty-one-year-old Samuel Mather went to Alhambra, Granada, in 1882 intent on "experimenting with various Spanish wines." Randall Wade, at age thirty-seven, had no definite plans for his remaining six months in Europe except to "spend a month at some German spring to recuperate before starting home." He mused that he might fill up his "intermediate time" enjoying the life of Rome, Florence, Geneva, and the upper Rhine.[9] These were the hard choices of the leisure life.

Twenty years later, Randall's son Homer took his family on two year-long cruises to the Orient on the Wade yacht *Wadena*. The luxury liner was manned with a crew of twenty-three and a battery of quick-firing guns in the event of unfriendly waters. Touring aimlessly around Europe, Homer wrote Samuel

Mather back home that he had never been "so completely and delightfully occupied in doing nothing"; he cruised from Alexandria to Constantinople, along the Asia Minor shore, across the Aegean Sea to Athens, along the Dalmatian Coast to Switzerland, Germany, and then on to Norway. On their second voyage, in 1894–95, the extended family of Homer and Nellie Wade—their daughter Helen, Grandma Wade, Grandma Garretson and her brother George Howe—was accompanied on board by a galley crew of gourmet cooks, on hand to prepare formal dinner parties for local dignitaries and American consular officials at ports along the way. Cruising from Tokyo to Hong Kong, Singapore, Sumatra, Borneo, then through the Red Sea to the Suez Canal and on to Cairo, Greece, Italy, and finally England, the Wades docked frequently to go inland and partake of such local customs as riding elephants, donkeys, and camels. They were even so daring as to go up the Mekong River to the capital city of Saigon, where they were welcomed by the pageantry of South Vietnam's consul and vice consul as the first Americans to make the passage.[10]

Others also ventured far afield to Japan and China. Mr. and Mrs. Feargus B. Squire struck out on a two-year world tour to celebrate Squire's resignation from Standard Oil, first touring Europe then moving on to the Suez Canal, China, Japan, and the southeast islands. Cornelia Warner memorialized her tours through the Near and Far East in her travel guide, "Letters from Afar." Jane Foote Tracy also invited others to *See India with Me* (1928) and *See China with Me* (1930) and took her readers through venturesome expeditions along the 1,200-mile Yangtze River, into Egypt, and across the path of the Trans-Siberian Railroad.[11]

Travels abroad might well have satiated the cultural appetites and leisure time of many affluent Americans, then as now, but not these voyagers. They traveled America's rail lines with the same vigor as they did those of Europe. Many found just as much to discover in the New World as they did in the Old (figs. 249, 250). Honeymooners Henry and Mildred Devereux headed south to New Orleans, then up to Atlanta and Savannah, down to Jacksonville and St. Augustine, and ended up their six-week vacation traveling along the Atlantic coast to New York. In fact, it was Euclid Avenue's own Henry Flagler, Rockefeller's Standard Oil partner, who masterminded the Florida East Coast Railway in the early 1880s, laying the path for his neighbors, and the nation, to journey the east coast of Florida and luxuriate in the sunny seaside resorts of Jacksonville, St. Augustine, Palm Beach, and Key West.[12] Across the continent, the Pacific Coast, particularly California, was another favorite destination, then considered almost a foreign land with its exotic hills and culture.

But even the excitement of these adventures did not abate Avenue travelers' longing for the comforts and conveniences of home. The Wades traveled with an entourage consisting of cooks, servants, a doctor, and a nurse. Mrs. Tracy, who found China's inns to be "horrible in the extreme," brought her own bed, sheets, pillows, food, and servants. She feared that she would "not have stood the trip" otherwise. Most of her neighbors apparently felt a similar need for familiar props; they took along their servants and their friends, traveled in

Fig. 249. *Page 284.* Mr. and Mrs. Ambrose Swasey at Atlantic City (Case Western Reserve University, 1912).

Fig. 250. *Page 285.* Sylvester T. Everett and daughters vacationing at Boulder, Colorado (courtesy E. E. Worthington).

1281

private rail cars, and went supplied with packaged food and water. One traveling party in 1897—made up of Avenue neighbors Will Harkness, Mrs. Barney H. York and her son Roy, Edith Hale, and five of their Cleveland friends—rented a private rail car to take them to Colorado Springs and Mexico. And when Mary Brown, daughter of Fayette and Cornelia Brown, traveled with Mrs. William Boardman in the coach class of a New York–bound train in 1882, she told her mother that it was like being in an "immigrant car." Mary rarely had to endure the company of such persons in close quarters; she felt "surrounded by the most frightful looking people" and was certain that she had been infected by "one or two languages" if not "one or two diseases." Her unease was mitigated only by Mrs. Boardman's company and the bottle of champagne they shared across the miles.[13]

The hardships that Mary Brown and others endured, commonplace to less affluent Americans, suggested the expectations of comfort and luxury that were the staples of their Euclid Avenue lives. Many found such physical pleasures beyond their urban residences at balmy seaside resorts and mountain spas. Often seeking rest in solitude, they went on long retreats to rejuvenate their constitutions. The popular hotels at Saratoga Springs, Hot Springs, Palm Beach, and Bar Harbor were the watering places where fashionable Clevelanders in the 1880s and 1890s lounged, ate, and danced away their ill-health and anxieties.

In much the same way, Avenue families diffused the growing intensity of their urban lives by seeking refuge in bucolic second residences. Such extravagance as could be afforded by the abundance of time and money enabled many of these people around the turn of the century to regain the freedom of open-air vistas—no streetcars, no traffic, no noise, no soot. Most built their country places within a day's carriage drive of their Avenue homes or in the vicinity of local commuter rail lines. They established splinter enclaves among themselves in nearby Mentor and Bratenahl on Lake Erie, or in Gates Mills, Glenville, Willoughby, and Wickliffe around popular horse clubs. Some even went so far afield as to build seasonal homes in Georgia, North Carolina, Florida, Colorado, New York, and Connecticut (figs. 251, 252).

The urge to retreat for extended periods from the downtown street was different from Avenue residents' travel enthusiasms. Touring was a series of animated experiences. In their second homes they sought quiet and relaxation. Charles Otis, Jr., who in 1901 built his Waite Hill summer residence, thirty-acre Tannenbaum Farm, noticed that, like himself, many of his Avenue neighbors "were then beginning to look toward the country with longing eyes, aspiring to be city farmers—town in Winter and the country in Summer."[14] These Clevelanders shared such seasonal mobility with their peers in other cities: Manhattanites built spectacular summer places on Long Island and in Newport; Bostonians established the fashionable watering places in Bar Harbor and other spots on the Maine coast and Cape Cod; Detroit's millionaires went to Grosse Pointe; and New Orleans' wealthy sought the riverside communities on the Mississippi and Lake Pontchartrain. The buildup of these seasonal outposts, temporary as they might have been in the early decades, signaled the beginnings of the exodus off America's grand avenues.

Fig. 251. A summer's day at Wickliffe. *Left to right,* Mr. and Mrs. Andrew Squire, Mrs. Kenyon Painter, Miss Colswell, Mrs. Sheridan (Western Reserve Historical Society, 1913).

Fig. 252. Mildred French (Mrs. Harry K.) Devereux on the porch (Western Reserve Historical Society, c. 1890).

The families of Euclid Avenue, convivial by nature, seemed to settle in groups, as if spawning satellite colonies from the mother Avenue. They also seemed to choose a place because of its leisure-time activity—horse racing, farming, sailing, golf, and the like. But the many families who had been going up to Little Mountain in Mentor for the summer since the 1870s just went to enjoy the outdoors and one another. While some bred horses and ran their own dairy farms, and most slept and dressed in their small frame cottages, all gathered together to spend their days and evenings eating, drinking, and dancing at the big hotels surrounding the mountain (fig. 253). The Little Mountain Club, as it was known, had been organized by Randall Wade and his Avenue neighbors—among them Joseph Perkins, Samuel L. Mather, Charles Hickox, George Worthington, and his father, Jeptha—to finance the popular Avenue retreat and its communal recreation.[15]

Little Mountain was a pleasure ground, *sui generis*. Other families chose a more purposeful setting. Among the most serious horse breeders, the Wades, Hannas, and Devereuxs developed working plantations in Thomasville, Georgia, to raise and race their horses during the winter, as well as provide them with a place to hunt quail and wild turkey in their spare time. Harry Devereux, along with his father-in-law Julius French, also built a farming estate in Wickliffe, about fifteen miles northeast of Public Square, where he went during the summer months to breed his prize horses and raise chickens. The Devereuxs' Nutwood Farm was among the first of twenty summer estates set atop Wickliffe's scenic ridge—all located near the Cleveland, Painesville & Eastern electric line to downtown. Others in the vicinity included Feargus B. Squire's Cobblestone Garth and Frank Rockefeller's Lakeland farm.[16] On the other side of town, the Glenville race track sprouted another summer community of such Avenue horse enthusiasts as Samuel Mather, William Bingham, and Liberty Holden (fig. 254).

These summer and winter enclaves reinforced the eclectic neighborhood tradition, but in different locales rather than along one street. And access by interurban electric rail lines, and later the automobile, put these local country estates within an hour's reach of the Avenue. For some their Euclid Avenue home truly became an urban "townhouse" of grand proportions. The Wades, among the most mobile, returned in April of one year from their winter farm in Thomasville; by June they had settled into their Mentor country place for the summer, stopping off at their Avenue "townhouse" for only about a month in May.[17]

The Consequences of Distance

Travel and seasonal retreats distanced Euclid Avenuers from relatives and friends throughout the year. Boarding school took children out of their homes and away from their parents. The demands of business took men away from their wives and children. Cleveland's capitalists were committed to long hours and often exhausting work. Their success depended on it. If they were not on the road, they were in their offices. These distances were as much self-imposed as they were unavoidable. Regardless, difficulties arose from the disparity be-

tween long absences and natural desires to be together. The greatest of these was loneliness.

Thirteen-year-old Molly Payne went off alone to live with her private tutor in Newburgh, New York. Her days were busy and challenging, but her nights, distant from the warmth of familiar family activities, were often too quiet. She especially felt the absence of the Payne home after receiving a letter from her brother Nathan, later confiding to him, "I cried myself to sleep that night and can not say how many more." Molly's loneliness deepened when she journeyed farther away the next year to Dresden, Germany, to continue her private studies. The Paynes' youngest child lamented her family's apparent abandonment—out of sight, out of mind—when she reminded "the respected inmates of the paternal mansion" of her pain in loneliness: "Just meditate upon the affliction of being *letterless* in this barren land, away from those who have been under the same roof since childhood."[18]

The loneliness was no less for those who remained behind. When John Devereux was away on business in New York or Chicago, Antoinette Devereux

Fig. 254. "Cobbleston Garth"; Feargus B. Squire country residence, Wickliffe, Ohio (*The Country Estates of Cleveland Men*, 1903).

sat alone in their large, lovely house waiting for his return. Her diary was filled with solemn sentiments of loneliness. She wrote on one occasion when John Henry was in Chicago, "lovely day, but very lonely." Another time she mentioned that she was "not feeling at all well this morning, but better in afternoon, till telegram came saying Henry would not return till Monday, made me much worse." Mrs. Devereux was not the only wife who longed for her husband's company. Flora Mather wrote Samuel, "I was very homesick for you all day yesterday, and I've not recovered yet." And Sue Wade wrote her son Randall during one of Jeptha's many absences, "It seems to be my fate to be deprived of sharing my husband's pleasures and enjoyments, or enjoying much of his society. But I will try and bear it patiently."[9]

The wives' loneliness and frustrations in having to manage the households alone could be understood. These women were submissive subjects to their husbands' schedules. The men, however, seemed equally distressed by the time and miles their work wedged between them and their families. Randall Wade expressed this to his wife Anna in one of his many vivid letters from Washington, D.C.:

> *Time*—Twilight. *Place*—third story War Department. *Feelings*—homesick. . . . I get up from my table when my aching eyes tell me it is growing late, look out from my "high position" to the street below and feel myself *almost a prisoner.* . . . I see many people walking, as they would see me if I should leave this room, but they doubtless meet familiar faces—feel that they have pleasant places to visit—perhaps have a *dear loving wife* to rush into their arms in a few minutes where as I would only find that my new boots hurt my feet more than usual, that I was tiring myself without having anything ahead in view to relieve my loneliness, a stranger among strangers, in a strange city.

From the same city a depressed John Hay wrote his brother-in-law Samuel Mather, "I am having a hot and lonely time in Washington just now. The whole family is at The Fells, and the temperature is considerable, and the humidity still worse."[20]

And while long vacations were pleasant for those who went, family members who stayed at home grew lonesome. When Sam Mather was away on his eighteen-month European tour in 1872–73, his father had, at the outset, encouraged him to stay "another winter or year" until he had fully regained his health, following his serious injury at the senior Mather's Michigan mine. But he reminded Sam, "We shall be very lonely without you." When twenty-one-year-old Homer Wade was traveling through Europe in 1878, his grandfather pined about how he "counted the days" since Homer's departure and would "count the remaining days with more and more interest" until his return. Jeptha Wade told his namesake, "We miss you very much and find it indescribably lonesome with you away." The fact that Homer was "well and happy and getting along so pleasantly," however, was steadying consolation for the old man. And when Mrs. Henry Gaylord was vacationing on Coney Island with her neighbors Flora Stone and Mrs. Washington Tyler in 1881, Henry missed his wife so much that he walked in on her unannounced, just hours before she was to leave for New York to meet him.[21]

In the absence of the long-distance telephone, daily—and sometimes more frequent—letters and telegrams helped relieve the loneliness of those at home and the homesickness of those away. Visits by sympathetic neighbors, at home and abroad, also provided some solace. But all of these remained only substitutes for the loved one's presence.[22]

The Club Life

Just as families and friendships bonded this neighborhood, so too did the many and various clubs. They were among the Avenue's venerable institutions, ultimately more so than the residences by the early 1900s. Exclusive city clubs, cultural groups, and fraternal orders were based downtown, some right on the Avenue, and became forceful magnets in pulling residents into the fold of this urban life. They probably even compelled many Euclid Avenuers to stay down-town longer than they might have otherwise. For these Clevelanders, the "Club" was more than an observed or decorative ritual; it was a part of the lifeblood of their street, as much as it was for the blue bloods of New York or the vanguard of Los Angeles. The statutes or missions of the club seemed to have been secondary to the symbolically charged raison d'être, the emotional element that was inherent to club membership.[23]

Club and cultural affiliations linked the Avenue's families with others of their kind in New York, Chicago, Detroit, Washington, D.C., and even London. The "Club," like the "Family," offered a membership card that was honored as equally in one city as in the next; it provided a nationwide network of ready introductions, connections, and residency. The Union and University clubs were probably the most revered nationally, drawing a broad coterie of businessmen and gentlemen throughout the country into an organized fraternity. Distinguished Clevelanders Sylvester Everett and Andrew Squire were welcome in any city's Union Club. And in New York City, it became their platform for entry into the exclusive enclaves of the Grolier, Manhattan, and Lawyers' clubs. In-town or out, for many the social club was a surrogate domicile, a quiet zone between the home and office.

Simply because much of Cleveland's protocol centered around the clubs after the 1880s, the men of the Avenue played as large a role in the conduct of this society as did their wives and daughters, a heinous notion in the female-dominated drawing rooms on New York's Fifth Avenue. Yet for these liberal-minded Clevelanders, who took pleasure in diversity, there was a place for every passion, and every group had its place. Some were guided by a freewheeling social spirit, others by a serious intellectual credo; some were restricted to men only, others were exclusively for women. Whether located on or beyond the Avenue, each club, institutionalized and informal, was an agent in strengthening the fabric of the community.

The Union Club was the leading social and intellectual force in the city (fig. 255). When it was founded in 1872, with Avenue resident William Bingham as its first president, the Club intended to be chiefly concerned with advancing the physical and intellectual aptitude of its male members. In fact, it became much more than just a training forum and quickly expanded to promote a refined society for its elected members. For their first home, Union Club members bought the sedate, pillared residence built by Truman Handy in 1837, an appropriately austere domicile, they believed, "a space where cultivated gentlemen will meet to read and discuss the topics of the day and entertain each other and their friends abroad." Indeed, among the Union Club's many Avenue members, most went there to dine and meet business associates or simply to enjoy the companionship of their colleagues. The dining room was shrouded in an air of serenity and cultivation, a private place where the Avenue's entrepreneurs met daily for lunch, certain as they were of the respectable if not starched service and the presence of only male peers. Women were permitted entry into the inner sanctum after the late 1890s, and then only in restricted areas. But the

Fig. 255. Union Club, 800 Euclid Avenue; originally built as Truman P. Handy residence in 1833 (Cleveland Public Library, 1900).

women did not seem to mind—after all, they had their "off-limits" premises too—and they took pleasure in mocking its self-consciously forbidding presence. They dubbed the new Schweinfurth-designed sandstone structure at Twelfth Street, a strictly sober Renaissance design, "The Mausoleum."[24] Yet male members also found humor in the sanctimonious aura. Such fond names as "The Onion Club," recalled by Horace Weddell and Tom Johnson, are still affectionately used by members today (fig. 256).

Real but rarified respectability also draped the men's literary clubs. The Rowfant Club—patterned after Manhattan's Grolier Club, the Literary Club of Cincinnati, and Boston's Club of Odd Volumes—was founded in 1892 to study

Fig. 256. The new Union Club, 1201 Euclid Avenue; C. F. Schweinfurth, architect, 1905 (Western Reserve Historical Society, c. 1910).

"the technical aspects of bookmaking and collecting." Membership was restricted to men with literary and collecting interests. But even the scholarly earnestness of the Rowfant's mission did not intimidate such members as Ambrose Swasey, Worcester Warner, Andrew Squire, David Norton, and Henry Gaylord from taking a liberal, more lighthearted view of the club's purpose. Warner and Swasey simply enjoyed getting together "with the fellows at Saturday evening meetings." They attended the meetings regularly, but not for a want of intellectual nourishment. In the spirit of their Anglo-Saxon forebears,

these two amiable engineers just liked the club's camaraderie and the intellect of their companions (fig. 257).[25]

    Others—The Arkites, the Cleveland Library Association, the Twentieth Century Club, The Hermit Club, and the Cleveland Sorosis Club for women—also thrived on their founding, scholarly mission. And each, supported as they were by these kindred folks, provided a gregarious but purposeful forum for Avenue members. The sports clubs, catering to Avenue residents' liberal penchant for recreation in the great outdoors, also fit nicely into this pattern. These active Clevelanders would have patently disqualified, if they did not altogether

Fig. 257. The Rowfant Club (Western Reserve Historical Society, 1890s).

reprove, Henry Adams's blanket contention that the nation's business leaders had "forgotten how to amuse themselves" and "the American, by temperament, worked to excess" without diversion. Perhaps Adams thought this was true of his fellow Bostonians, but it was not true of these Clevelanders. Charles Brush had once told his daughter Edna that "work is the real panacea for everything," which did parallel Adams's claim; yet Brush would be the first to board a boat if one of his friends suggested a duck-hunting expedition.[26] Like many of his neighboring compatriots, Brush worked hard and played hard.

Duck hunting, horse racing, fishing, golfing, yachting, and fox hunting were the recreational passions of Euclid Avenue men (figs. 258, 259). Dedicated members of the Hunt Club, the Castalia Sporting Club, and the Winous Point Shooting Club, they were content to sit in rowboats for hours, silently waiting for the elusive bird to fly overhead. Their notations in the Castalia club's daily ledger were priceless; they described numerous two- and three-day boat trips that brought boredom, bodily misery, and, withal, great personal satisfaction. These men, who sometimes brought along their wives and, more often, their children, seemed quite happy to subject themselves to heavy rain, howling wind, bitter cold, and rough seas in pursuit of fowl or fish. Yet during one of these expeditions, John Hay wondered aloud to his skeptical friend Henry Adams why he endured this unpleasant sport, especially considering the meager results.

Fig. 259. Feargus B. Squire tee-ing off (courtesy Barbara S. Vero).

I went to a remote pond in the marsh, and as the water is unprecendently low, we had to push and pull the boat through mud two feet deep a half a mile. We got there at last, after unspeakable trials, built our blind, and waited for ducks; "the tardy ducks that didn't come." . . . I asked, with the immortal Flanagan—"Why am I here?" and got not a satisfactory answer.[27]

One has to wonder why indeed Hay and many of his neighbors subjected themselves to such monotony and self-punishment. Beyond the sport of marks-manship, the answer apparently lay in the club's fraternal environment. To this end, in 1902 members of Castalia wrote a letter to the general membership warning "that the custom of inviting ladies and children to the club has no warrant in the By-laws or in any regulation of the club so far as we know. . . . We conceive that the club is a man's club and not a country club, a hotel, or a sanitarium." The club had been founded in 1878 by Avenue patriarchs Lee Mc-Bride, John Hay, Amasa Mather, Jeptha Wade, and James Rhodes explicitly as a men's social and sporting club. This was the environment that, more than twenty years later, members were intent on preserving. All surviving responses for the 1902 issue affirmed the call for exclusion. The eminent Chicago planner Daniel H. Burnham, then living in Cleveland, replied to the call in his charac-teristically burly manner: "The presence of *a woman or child* always spoils the visit . . . of a busy man. He goes there for *entire freedom from everything that makes any demand on him*." Homer Wade, otherwise diplomatic in mixed company, de-clared, "This is a man's club and the function of inviting ladies and children has been overdone." Another member pronounced, "I am utterly appalled by . . . the entertainment of women and children! This is a *man's* club and should be so maintained."[28] The result was that women and children were permitted entry, but only with members and only on Tuesdays and Thursdays.

In the same spirit of recreational fraternity, Avenue men formed Cleve-land's horse-racing clubs. The most exclusive, if not lively, was the Tavern Club, organized in 1892 by eight friends—all Yale alumni, except one—who met on Saturday nights at The Widow's restaurant on Scoville Avenue to play hearts and drink beer (fig. 260). Inspired by the Onondaga Club in Detroit, the group of boyhood and college buddies—Harry Devereux, William Rhodes, Ed-win Hale, Perry Harvey, Charles Otis, Jr., Addison Hough, and Harry Edwards (the non-Yalie)—decided to form a club. Since all were avid horsemen, they decided it should be a racing club, no new member of which could be taken in without the unanimous approval of the members.[29] The Gentleman's Driving Club was another of these fraternities, this one headquartered at the North Ran-dall Park track and the Roadside Club, where the horsemen assembled after the races for private interludes, lively banquets, and some of the finest dinner spreads in the city. Having among its members the crack amateur reinsmen of Cleveland's elite—its mentor Harry Devereux, Dan Hanna, Henry Chisholm, David Norton, Morris Bradley, to name a few—the club was an active sponsor of the highly competitive national circuit league. In fine tradition, men and women clad in colorful regalia turned out on Sunday afternoons to watch the gentlemen compete.

The men of the Avenue might have appeared to monopolize Cleveland in this most popular of American sports, but not so. As observers, the elegant ladies stole the limelight from their racing husbands and neighbors each time they made an entrance onto the field. And the coaching instinct touched more than a few of the Avenue's ladies, their sporting blood nourished and their society enjoyed in the distinguished Four-in-Hand Club's weekly break parties through-out town (fig. 261). It was the finest coaching club centered on the Avenue and distinguished itself by welcoming women and men alike among its members. Team parties of Avenue residents and their guests turned out on Friday or Sat-urday mornings at the Union Club or the glamorous Hollenden Hotel, the men

in natty grey cutaways and the women in colorful gowns and brilliant parasols. Setting out for a day-long drive, breaks of four to seven teams pranced along the city's tree-lined avenues and through the parks, winding their way out east for a delightful luncheon at the Country Club or Euclid Avenue Club, if not the country home of one of their own—Dan Hanna's in Gordon Park, Edward Merritt's in the Chagrin Valley, Jacob Perkins's on the west shore, or Charles Otis's in Bratenahl.[30]

The arrival of these spectacular tallyhos at the Grand Circuit races, held at the Cleveland Driving Park, became an annual ritual that marked the start of the July meet. The Four-in-Hand Club's trumpeted entrance was renowned for causing "quite a little excitement," as *Town Topics* was fond of remarking. It was worth it for the women looking on in the bleachers just to see the society

Fig. 261. The Four-in-Hand and Tandem Club, on Euclid Avenue near Fortieth Street (Western Reserve Historical Society, 1907).

women draped in their sunny chiffon dresses and wide-brimmed hats.[31] For all the fanfare the Four-in-Hand inspired by its elegant displays, the club's members were truly serious equestrians. Year after year, faithfuls Mr. and Mrs. James Hoyt, L. Dean Holden, William Rice, and Robert York turned out for the long drives and timed relays.

On or off the Avenue, the clubs brought the neighborhood's families together in a variety of settings and activities. They ate together—lunch and dinner—played together, and sat together discussing as broad a range of topics as those that could fill the pages of a modern college catalog. Each club—the Union, the Hermit, the Tavern, the Roadside—strengthened ties and extended the geographic boundaries of Euclid Avenue society. This life of grandeur was as much an institution of social people as it was a panorama of residences. And yet personal pleasures, as great as they might have been, would not deplete Avenue families' civic-minded energies to bring pleasure and improvement to others in the city.

A Tradition of Civic Pride

The energy Avenue residents invested in the larger Cleveland community in fact exceeded that reserved for their own recreation. They had not only the wealth and community pride—and the women, the luxury of leisure time—necessary to direct major philanthropic and cultural endeavors, but collectively they possessed a deep evangelical spirit that appeared genuine by its products. Born out of pious New England roots similar to those among Boston's or Chicago's public-minded society, these Clevelanders were as generous on behalf of others' well-being as they were selfish about their own. They appreciated the fact that they had the means to give something back to the community from which they had prospered so handsomely.

Obviously the funds that supported such civic generosity came from the enormous financial and industrial interests of Euclid Avenue capitalists, as they did for every patrician-sponsored institution throughout America in the postwar decades. The source of these charitable alms was reason for distress, if not outright rejection, on the part of some public reformers who questioned whether the benefactions of so-called "robber barons" should be accepted, thus condoning the standards of their donors. The controversial debate went on for decades and grew in complexity as the power and fortunes of charitable foundations grew. It was even taken up by a federal congressional commission formed around 1915 to investigate the tax-exempt wealth, authority, and freedom from public control enjoyed by such major charities established by John D. Rockefeller, Andrew Carnegie, and others.[32] But the fact remained that absent huge donations from these affluent individuals, much of the public works and research they fostered from the Civil War through World War I would have otherwise not occurred.

Early in his career, Rockefeller stated, "I believe it every man's duty to get all he honestly can, and to give all he can." His Avenue friend Charles Otis, Jr., agreed, recalling a speech by President Lincoln, who said "a man . . . who lives in the city he loves, should love to make that city a better place to live."[33] A solid civic pride indeed permeated Cleveland throughout the nineteenth and twentieth centuries. And Euclid Avenue men and women led the way in consistently contributing their time, energy, and money to the development of the city's civic, religious, cultural, and charitable institutions.

At the civic level, Avenue residents exercised significant influence over the lives of Clevelanders during the nineteenth century through the office of the mayor. Like Chicago's millionaires of the postwar decades, who distinguished themselves nationally as avid public officeholders to further their own private commercial interests, Euclid Avenue men were as entrenched in guiding the city's political system in these years as they were in building its financial and industrial infrastructure.[34] Until 1908, Cleveland's mayor was elected each year. In the seventy-one years between 1844 and 1915, forty-eight of the one-year mayoral terms were occupied by Euclid Avenue men—a remarkable two-thirds. Their control of the mayor's office was reinforced by their neighbors' occupation of city council posts and departmental commission seats. Truman Handy served on the board of education for ten years; Sylvester Everett was city treasurer for fourteen years between 1869 and 1883; Gen. James Barnett and William Bingham each served two years on the city council; and Samuel Mather sat as a commissioner on public improvements during the great park-and-boulevard debate in the mid-1890s.

Mather's declining public influence as a city park commissioner in the 1890s was typical of Avenue residents' diminishing political clout after about 1890. Up to this time, their close alliance with those in local public office helped grand avenue patrons advance their free-market rights as capitalists and residents. They were able to manage the public agenda to protect their private property interests, which during most of the nineteenth century were largely consistent with those of the city. But this happy condition turned around in the 1890s and grew contentious in the early decades of the twentieth century, thanks in great measure to the populist initiatives of Avenue resident Tom Johnson, who occupied the mayor's office during the critical period 1901–9. Johnson, unlike most of his entrepreneurial neighbors, took a dim view of the dominance of capital over labor and favored mass transit access on his residential street. He was a powerful mayor because he promoted the majority interests of Cleveland's population at a time when these initiatives were increasingly at odds with the exclusive, privileged interests of his Avenue neighbors, particularly concerning the protection of Euclid Avenue as a residential haven.

Ironically, Avenue men and women probably enjoyed more consistent influence over a longer period in national affairs than they did in their own city. The Paynes, Boardmans, Hays, Mathers, Wades, Everetts, and Otises, among the most intimately allied, were personal friends of U.S. presidents, from Abraham Lincoln down to Franklin D. Roosevelt, and served in senior administration posts and on various presidential commissions. Whether these Clevelanders had a greater presence in the nation's capital or enjoyed easier access to the White House over more administrations than did their colleagues in New York, Denver, or Los Angeles is unclear. The extent of their involvement, however, Republicans and Democrats alike, was itself extraordinary. Even so, this was not their main venue for advancing the public good. As individual philanthropists they enjoyed greater visibility, and their leadership achieved more for the community.

Meanwhile, the women of Euclid Avenue were the leading purveyors of social betterment. In a manner that would have been astonishing to the indifferent ladies of New York society, many of these genteel women viewed it as their responsibility to manage the social conscience of the city—the city that their fathers and husbands were physically transforming through their businesses. Their benevolence stemmed from Christian bearings and a genuine desire to help those around them who were unable to help themselves. Indeed, these women who came into affluence during Cleveland's industrial buildup in the 1840s through 1870s prevailed as founders of the city's major charitable and social service organizations: dispensaries, hospitals, homes for the homeless, and centers of relief, reform, and education. They gave more than their surplus wealth to reconcile the opportunities of the poor and rich, which would have been a customary approach in their day; they dedicated their personal time and talents to religious, medical, and recreational services for the underprivileged. Such women as Maria Worthington, Rebecca Cromwell Rouse, Martha Steele Perkins, Mrs. Stillman Witt, Jeanne Chisholm, Mary Eells, and Flora Stone Mather stood out as exceptional contributors.[35]

Alcohol abuse was among the chief concerns of Cleveland reformers in the postwar period, as it was for many urban Americans who saw it as the source of vice and dereliction. Mrs. Perkins, wife of Joseph Perkins, was the single greatest force in organizing the Cleveland chapter of the Women's Christian Temperance Union. A devout Christian of Scottish parentage, she was a practicing temperance advocate who made weekly visits to impoverished homes in the river district to plead the cause for reform. In one of her most graphic attempts to spearhead a movement, she led five hundred women in a crusade through town and down to River Street saloons and sailors' boarding houses in 1874, the year in which temperance campaigns throughout the nation sharpened Americans' attentions to the cursed beverage. Through her influence, her husband was able to gain the support of neighbors John D. Rockefeller and Charles E. Bolton, among others, to establish the Temperance Union of Ohio. And together they founded the 1883 campaign committee for the proposed Second Amendment to the Ohio Constitution, which if enacted would have prohibited the manufacture and sale of intoxicating liquors. Even though the vote fell short of a majority, the Perkinses' initiative influenced future plans to tax and regulate liquor traffic in the state.[36]

Flora Stone Mather, a devout Presbyterian, was another of the Avenue women who dedicated her career to aiding the sick and impoverished. Having grown up on the Avenue, daughter of Julia and Amasa Stone, Flora lived in a world far removed from the crowded river district and its commonplace misfortunes. Her parents, however, instilled in their four children not only gratitude for their comfortable lives, but a deep sense of responsibility for those of lesser means. Flora was the most ambitious of her siblings in her lifelong effort to enhance the lives of sick, impoverished, and homeless Clevelanders. She sustained her father's commitment to the Home for Aged Women while herself taking food staples to the sick families she visited each week on Cleveland's west side. She embraced these people as her own. After one visit she told her husband Samuel, "I've been to see one of my sick families again this morning, cholera-morbus, or some form of it seems to be *very* prevalent just now . . . [and] there is terrible mortality among children." Her work was similar to that later assumed by the city's Visiting Nurses Association, a progressive national institution created in 1901 under the auspices of Goodrich House, Alta House, and Hiram House—for all of which she was a founder and benefactor. At the time of her early death from cancer in 1909, she gave the majority of her estate to endow the missions to which she had devoted her life, among them the Children's Aid Society, the Presbyterian Society, the YMCA and YWCA, the Goodrich Social Settlement, and the Cleveland Day Nursery.[37]

The leadership of Mrs. Perkins and Mrs. Mather was truly exceptional, yet their commitments were by no means unique among their Avenue neighbors, many of whom may be credited with organizing the city's chief social service institutions: Hiram House, Goodrich House, the Cleveland Humane Society, the House of Refuge and Correction, the Protestant Orphan Asylum, Alta House, the Bethel Associated Charities, the Cleveland Community Fund, the Gund Foundation. Their initiatives, reaching out to the results if not the roots of poverty, were in their minds not at all contrary to the entrepreneurial interests of their families, nor were they undertaken out of an idealistic sense of noblesse oblige. It was no accident, therefore, that this early philanthropic work formed the nucleus of such national parent organizations as the YWCA, the American Red Cross, and the United Way.

John D. Rockefeller, among the greatest philanthropists in America during the late nineteenth century—though he gave relatively little to Cleveland institutions after effectively divorcing himself from the city of his youth in the mid-1880s—had called for greater management of the millions that supported "this business of benevolence." For himself, as others, administering huge quantities of private wealth had grown into a full-time occupation which called for the expertise of professional trustees, thus marking the creation of such major foundations as the Rockefeller Foundation (1913) and Brush Foundation (1928). Critics assailed these singular institutions for their subservience to donors and unaccountability to public interests. They did indeed subscribe to the founding philanthropist's pet concerns, yet they nevertheless provided essential funds that government agencies could not yet match.[38]

Avenue resident George Gund, for one, who earned his wealth in securities investments and by manufacturing decaffeinated coffee, and then selling the caffeine to the Coca Cola Company, created the $83.5 million Gund Foundation in 1951 to support educational programs for the disadvantaged, the fine arts, and social services. Gund was one of the richest men in Cleveland's history. He established the foundation simply because he wanted to provide opportunities for others, just as the community had provided opportunities for him. Gund believed education, particularly, was at the heart of human and economic development. Having sustained this original mandate, the Gund Foundation today remains the city's second largest foundation and a chief source of funding for innovative community projects.

Gund and many neighbors before him had the means and the vision to shape civic philosophy beyond the political realm on behalf of public interests. Euclid Avenue families also dominated Cleveland's cultural institutions as patrons, benefactors, and trustees, creating in their own image the foundation of the city's museums, symphony, parks, and libraries. They built their greatest legacy at the eastern end of the grand avenue, the magnificent cultural park around University Circle. The ambitions and tastes that shaped this cultural park's growth during the late nineteenth and early twentieth centuries were chiefly those of particular Euclid Avenue men and women who gave their collections, money, and management to the institutions of University Circle

(fig. 262). These limestone buildings became symbolic and architectural monuments in the vision of the Avenue as Cleveland's civic processional.

Jeptha Wade had in 1882 given to the city seventy-five-acre Wade Park, later expanded to 488 acres by land gifts from William J. Gordon's estate in 1893 and from John D. Rockefeller in 1897, as well as the Western Reserve and Case School campuses. In the spirit of American park planning of that day, which subscribed to the ideal that the public environment was incomplete without a museum, Wade dedicated a tract in Wade Park in 1892 for a "College Reservation." In his conveyance to the city, he restricted the use of the property

Fig. 262. University Circle (Western Reserve Historical Society, c. 1940.)

to an art gallery, an open site never to be fenced.[39] Almost a quarter-century later, the Cleveland Museum of Art opened in 1916, designed by Cleveland architects Hubbell & Benes and funded by endowments from the estates of Avenue patrons Hinman Hurlbut, John B. Huntington, and Horace Kelley. Charles W. Bingham, president of The Huntington Art & Polytechnic Trust and the Horace Kelley Art Foundation, managed the joint museum building committee, and William B. Sanders and Jeptha H. Wade II gave sizable donations and portions of their private collections. The Museum, as first conceived by Wade, was, and principally is, an educational institution of the city, a house of art operated for the public. For the early benefactors and trustees, creating an institution of education and social betterment was of prime importance, as it was in all their philanthropy. The patrons saw University Circle as not just a socially desirable playground, a pleasant educational amenity in the park, but also as good business for the city.

The treasury that constituted the core of the art museum's vast collections presented in many respects an encyclopedic survey of Avenue patrons' world tours: the Wades' textiles, jewels, and paintings; Worcester R. Warner's Far Eastern art; David Z. Norton's Japanese prints and objects; Elisabeth Severance Allen's Italian tapestries; and Ralph King's portfolio of original prints and lithographs.[40] These were the most visible gifts by Avenue patrons and others. Less obvious to the eye, however, were in-kind donations, which really laid the foundation of University Circle's institutions. Eleanor Squire, wife of attorney Andrew Squire, organized the Garden Club of Cleveland, as she was the moving force behind the Fine Arts Garden. Mary Castle Norton, wife of David Z. Norton, founded the Musical Arts Association, sponsor of the Cleveland Orchestra, and for years served as an officer of the Cleveland Institute of Music. Ella Burke, wife of Stevenson Burke, chaired the Cleveland School of Art, as she and her husband sponsored many young local artists. And there were many others.

The creation of this campus-in-the-park was a natural extension of Euclid Avenue patrons' vision of their Avenue as a public parade ground. This vision also encompassed the rolling hills of Lake View Cemetery, their permanent residential haven—and another architectural showcase—which spread across 285 landscaped acres north of the Avenue. Euclid Avenue alone, a shaded linear landscape connecting Public Square with University Circle, then Lake View Cemetery and the open country beyond, had become the megastructure of the city's urban landscape.[41]

Fig. 263. Demolition of Leon-
ard C. Hanna residence, 2717
Euclid Avenue (*Cleveland Plain
Dealer*, August 31, 1958).

TWELVE

The Fall of the Grand Avenue,
1895–1950

The Carlins hosted the last dinner dance on the Avenue in March 1950, hailed as the formal farewell to a grand tradition. They and their 100 guests were saluting more than just the Carlins' departure to Shaker Heights; they were memorializing a tradition that had occurred hundreds of times in hundreds of drawing rooms over more than a hundred years. Even though the Avenue had ceased to be a residential neighborhood decades ago, a few families had clung to the glory of the past and a hope for the future. The Carlin affair drew down the curtain once and for all, and the Euclid Avenue story as a grand avenue ended (fig. 263).[1]

Euclid Avenue was envisioned as the grand symbol of this modern American city—Public Square at the western end, University Circle at the eastern, and the residential promenade spanning the four-mile length. Residents invested faith in the permanence of this streetscape when they built their Avenue homes. This was their psychological capital. The pride of place and family name was reflected in the artistic and financial resources they brought to bear in the design, construction, and furnishing of each house. By the mid-1890s, the grand avenue reached its zenith. More than 260 houses lined the linear landscape between Ninth and Ninetieth streets in 1896, six times the forty-five that stood there a half century before. But over the next fifteen years, progressive forces weakened the bonds that shaped the social and architectural neighborhood. Cleveland "had but one Euclid Avenue," architectural critic I. T. Frary eulogized in 1918, "no other street could take its place." But by then, he realized, it was too late to redeem the glory of the past; the progressive forces were too great and well-advanced to resurrect the pride that had been at the heart of the residents' vision through the decades.[2] By 1921 only 130 houses were still standing, and in 1950 the grand avenue's last family left to make their home in the suburbs.

The collective impact of traffic and transit lines on the Avenue, commercial development pressures, extraordinarily high property values, and the buildup of nearby black neighborhoods led to the decline of this residential neighborhood between 1910 and 1950. Over the decades, Avenue residents became less and less devoted to their once unassailable allegiance to the monumental grand

TABLE 15
Commercial Development, 1884–1900

Building	Address	Building Date
Stillman Hotel	1115	1884
Lennox Building	907	1889
Star Theatre	709	1889
The Arcade	510	1890
Euclid Arcade	347	1892
Nottingham Building	427	1893
YWCA	924	1893
Permanent Block	736	1894
New England Building	637	1895
Garfield Building	605	1895
Guardian Savings & Trust	322	1895
Colonial Arcade	530	1899
Williamson Building	201	1900

avenue vision. This changing attitude recognized, consciously or unconsciously, that progress—represented by industry and commerce, ironically, from their own business enterprise—would and probably should shape the future development of the downtown area. These affluent residents were now quite frankly willing and able to move beyond the city's center to their new residential havens in the Heights and along the lake shore. Like most American cities and towns, nineteenth-century downtown Cleveland was fashioned by oligarchic forces, while the twentieth-century city was ruled by democratic and private market forces. In the building of their residential street, Euclid Avenue families led the way through the post–Civil War decades, fought for their vision around the turn of the century, but then acquiesced to popular demand as time went on.

The Park-and-Boulevard Vision

The downtown business district that emerged along the Avenue in the 1870s and 1880s had continued to prosper and expand from its center around Public Square toward the growing residential areas to the east. By the mid-1890s, the length between the Square and Ninth Street was solidly built up with retail arcades, offices, and institutional buildings (figs. 264, 265). New investors had demolished the former residences—the last two came down in 1893—and redeveloped the sites with large-scale stone and brick buildings. Whether a Clevelander's interest was in business, banking, shopping, the theater, or a hotel, this urban district had it all. Builders also transformed the two-block area east of Ninth Street. And in the blocks beyond, such businesses as George Edmondson's photographic studio and the Gage art galleries had taken over former residences, and a few apartment houses had been built on the south side of the street (see table 15).

Fig. 264. The downtown business district; south side of Euclid Avenue between Public Square and Sixth Street. The Arcade, *center*, and Halle Brothers, *right* (Cleveland Public Library, 1894).

In past decades, the Avenue had attracted prospective residents and leisurely strollers because it was the most fashionable downtown street and the most direct route to the east from Public Square. In the 1890s, the fashion and function of the Avenue proved to be powerful magnets for retailers and businesses. These commercial establishments became liabilities for the neighborhood. The local society journal *Town Topics,* a steady proponent of the Avenue's high life, announced in 1896 that the new businesses moving in cheapened the appearance of the grand avenue. It was the "handsomest street in the world," they reflected, "or would be if it were not for some very discreditable buildings erected along it, during recent years, for business purposes."[3]

Mass transit officials were another intrusive faction, relentlessly lobbying
to run the street railway between Ninth and Fortieth streets, the forbidden
length, and adamantly opposed to detouring trolley lines along Prospect, as they
had done since 1862. Thanks to Tom Johnson's impetus, they installed the first
electric streetcars on the Avenue as far as Fifty-fifth Street in 1884 and had
changed over the entire line by 1889.[4] With the enormous profitability of this
new technology, transit factors put even more pressure on city politicians and
Avenue residents to yield the right of way to the streetcars.

Not to be outdone, Avenue residents petitioned the city in 1896 to desig-
nate Euclid a boulevard, which would officially recognize the broad, tree-lined

street for all that it was. Their plan called for integrating the Avenue into Cleveland's park system and controlling its use by a city park-and-boulevard commission. Their intent was to block further commercialization of the Avenue's residential neighborhood. The park commissioners promptly approved the plan to "boulevard" the Avenue between Fourteenth and 105th streets, thus connecting the downtown business district with the pastoral park system four miles to the east. Underlying this picturesque scheme, the plan's sponsors were actually intent on preserving the historic distinction of the grand avenue, the principle of maintaining the country in the city. As it had been manifest by the collective vision of residents over time, and now formally endorsed by the city's park commissioners, the principle embraced the European concept of the grand boulevard connecting urban parks, as could be found in Paris, London, Edinburgh, Glasgow, and Frankfurt.[5]

The park commissioners presented their resolution to city council in November 1896, which distinguished the Avenue as the grand civic processional of Cleveland and the link with the park system around University Circle and Lake View Cemetery:

> Whereas, Euclid avenue . . . has gained a reputation all over the world for its beauty, its magnificent residences, surrounded by beautiful deep lawns, trees, and shrubbery, thereby giving the same appearance of a long and continuous parkway, its reputation thus gained being an extremely important factor in placing the city of Cleveland among the leading cities of this country.

The chamber of commerce, too, largely patronized by gentlemen who lived on the Avenue, lauded the plan for the way it could "contribute to the health, happiness and prosperity of the whole people."[6] It was for the good of all Clevelanders, they believed, adopting a larger view than their self-interests might have warranted. Yet the Chamber's endorsement was really rather farsighted in that it captured the basic intent of future land use and zoning regulations throughout the country.

John D. Rockefeller, the benefactor of Rockefeller Park, also endorsed the parkway plan and recommended further to restrict the Avenue to exclusively "pleasure vehicles," free from all streetcars and commercial traffic. The park commissioners, who agreed with Rockefeller, pointed city officials to other grand avenues—Fifth Avenue in New York and Michigan Avenue in Chicago—where traffic restrictions had not depreciated property values or diminished tax revenues. After a good deal of debate, the city council finally adopted the boulevard plan in April 1897 by a close vote of twelve in favor and ten opposed. It established the park-and-boulevard commission, suggested by Avenue residents the year before, to administer the plan, and it enlisted property owners to pay for it.[7] The council's endorsement, however, turned out to be a hollow victory for Euclid Avenue residents and the park commission. In the end, it turned out to be just a paper approval and was not to be carried out by public powers.

The city failed to take even the first step to commence work on the public project; it never retained the landscape architect who was to design the trolley-free boulevard and work out the logistics for rerouting traffic around the Avenue. In the meantime, the majority of Clevelanders and some council members continued to demand streetcar access along the most direct route between the city's center and the east. Alternate routes were studied, but none matched Euclid's access, that is not until the Van Sweringen brothers opened up the Shaker Rapid Transit line in the 1920s. Transportation was not the only obstacle, however; politics also played a role. City residents, especially those who lived on the west side, were bitter about public money being spent on parks to benefit the wealthy rather than infusing more funds into welfare programs for the poor. The boulevard plan had become a political football. All efforts to move forward were blocked. After three years, in May 1900, council responded to the voice of its constituency and unanimously rescinded the park commission's control of the Avenue.[8] The boulevard plan was filed away deep in the city's archives.

In retrospect, the broader intent of the boulevard plan, beyond creating a promenade and entrance to the parks, was to control the use of private property on the Avenue. Its patrons sought to formalize the residential landscape and its park-like environment. Not without precedent, this effort was one among many around the country in the 1890s and early 1900s inspired by a recognition that economic expediency was threatening to overtake any consideration of long-range planning to guide development. Memorialized nationally as the City Beautiful movement, it constituted a decisive but conservative response by grand avenue patrons in a number of cities to the scale of new commercial buildings that were fundamentally changing the character of their residential streets. The movement's credo was manifest in its purest form in Daniel Burnham's magnificent plans for the 1893 Columbian Exposition in Chicago. The other notable initiative was the 1901 McMillan Plan for Washington, D.C., enacted to restore the character and grand processionals of the 1791 L'Enfant Plan for the nation's capital.

These park-and-boulevard plans envisioned broad, tree-lined avenues to bring light, air, and nature's beauty to urban areas, to make city life more pleasant, and to create an enhanced and unified civic pride. The inherent weakness of such monumental plans, however, as in Cleveland, was the inadequacy of public control over private actions needed to transform the dream into reality. The patrons of these schemes—Euclid Avenue residents were typical in this—generally did not represent the majority interests of the populace and thus were unable to garner the support of voters and public authorities. This was the reason for Cleveland's city council ordering the park commission in 1900 to turn its attention away from Euclid Avenue.

Within two years of repeal of the scheme, however, populist mayor Tom Johnson appointed the now well-known Group Plan commission to create a grand mall surrounded by the city's major public buildings. The mayor's office promoted this plan as serving the public interest, even if it was more grandiose than the park-and-boulevard plan. The origins of the Group Plan arose out of a practical need to replace the cramped and obsolete federal, county, and municipal buildings. The idea for the mall concept specifically was generated by discussions among Johnson's administrators, notably Frederic C. Howe, the chamber of commerce, and the local AIA chapter. Working together, they decided to group Cleveland's major public buildings around a classical central court fronting on the lake, such as those they had seen on their tour of baroque European cities and at the 1893 Columbian Exposition.

Johnson himself, a vigorous advocate of such municipal facilities as mass transit, public baths, and city parks, endorsed the idea on its public merits. The chamber, which financed and had promoted the project since the mid-1890s, endorsed it on its ceremonial merits. In point of fact, many of the chamber members who now backed the Group Plan were among the very Avenue residents— Liberty Holden, Samuel Mather, and Francis Prentiss—who had led the park-and-boulevard campaign five years before. For all constituencies it was viewed as an orderly response to apparent chaotic city expansion. In a manner first affirmed by Baron Haussmann for the monumental projects of Paris, all agreed that the Group Plan was a prudent investment of vast public expenditures— contrary to the Avenue park-and-boulevard scheme's reception—that would be more than returned by attracting new business and wealth to Cleveland.[9]

The designers brought in by the city to create the blueprint for the new civic center were among the best in the national field: Daniel Burnham of Chicago and Arnold Brunner and John Carrere of New York. Burnham, the chief mastermind of the Columbian Exposition plan, expanded his Cleveland clients' vision of monumental civic design to encompass the entire city. He recommended that the city's outlying parks be incorporated into the scheme, specifically via the principal avenues connecting these parks. Burnham focused on Euclid Avenue, ironically, but not surprisingly, as being among the most important processionals (fig. 266). After all, he told his clients who knew all too well, it connected the downtown center with the eastern parks. Under a new guise, the failed park-and-boulevard plan was revived.[10]

The 1903 Cleveland Group Plan was the first so-called City Beautiful plan in the country to be enacted after the 1901 McMillan Plan. Both schemes were only partially completed according to their planners' vision, yet each went a long way to promote the notion that a city's orderly development was as much an aesthetic goal as it was a functional one. While the unsuccessful Avenue park-and-boulevard plan had attempted to realize just this, the Cleveland Group Plan's successful implementation stemmed chiefly from its stated public purpose. Its success was also due to the caliber of its principal designers and the political power of its exponents, notably the mayor's office and the chamber of commerce.

Both Avenue residents and city officials showed considerable foresight in their advocacy of first the boulevard plan and then the Group Plan. The next such efforts in the country came with Burnham's 1905 plan for San Francisco and then the 1909 zoning ordinance for Los Angeles, the first in the country adopted to guide future development. Euclid Avenue residents had recognized the value of the Avenue's landscape and architecture, and they sustained their commitment to the boulevard vision for over a decade. In the first effort, they

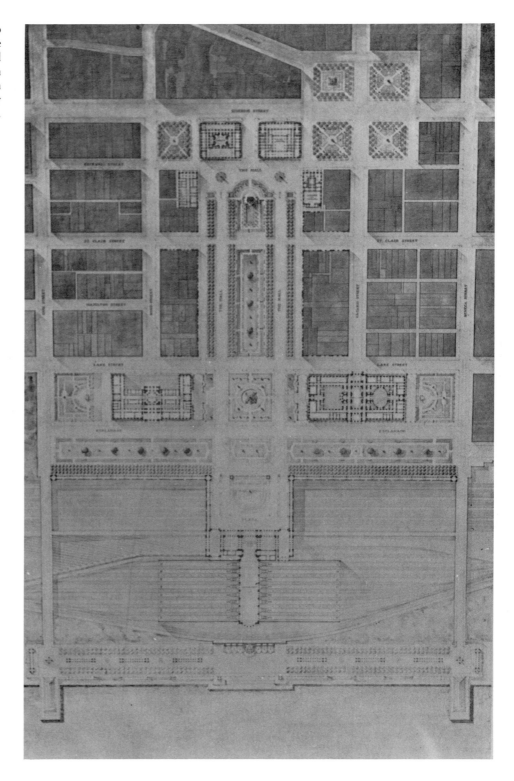

Fig. 266. The Cleveland Group Plan, showing Euclid Avenue and Public Square, *top,* the Mall and proposed Union Station along lakefront, *bottom* (Western Reserve Historical Society, by Group Plan Commission, 1903).

wanted to render permanent the Avenue's principal function, and they looked to an official plan to guide future public projects. Their inability to control by official mandate the future of their own residential street, however, motivated these grand avenue patrons, and those in other cities, to turn their attention to an even grander scale of civic planning, to the city center and its processional avenues.

The Advance of Commerce and Mass Transit

In spite of these efforts, Euclid Avenue remained without peer in its appeal to commercial interests. There was no zoning to regulate or check the movement of commercial development eastward into the residential area. Up to 1929, when the city adopted its first zoning ordinance, the use of land and buildings in Cleveland was controlled only by the doctrine of common law nuisance, a law open to liberal interpretation. In effect, private interests defined the Avenue's principal use and image, particularly those interests that could pay the price of entry. This was no different in 1900 from what Mark Twain had scurrilously portrayed in 1868 as a neighborhood unwelcoming to "poor white trash," only now the contest was between wealthy residents and private businesses.

The soaring value of Avenue property confirmed its lofty commercial appeal and dimmed the prospects of future residential growth. The southeast corner of Ninth Street had steadily increased in value each year between 1865 and 1901, from $9,150 to $500,000; likewise, the corner of Seventy-first Street had appreciated from $80 to $30,000 an acre between 1850 and the early 1900s.[11] Such prices prohibited even Cleveland's most affluent, with a few exceptions, from purchasing land. They could be afforded chiefly by income-producing enterprises (fig. 267).

Such posh retailers as Cowell & Hubbard, Chandler & Rudd, De Klyn's, and Halle Brothers had located on the Avenue as early as the 1880s with an eye for capitalizing on the prestigious address and its affluent clientele (fig. 268). But these were not the only reasons for a retailer to open a store on Euclid between the Square and Ninth Street. Unobstructed frontage on the street railway lines, with access to the masses of downtown commuters who lived in the growing eastern hinterland, was undoubtedly quite profitable. The streetcar magnates certainly thought so. After the East Cleveland Railway had begun running cars between Fifty-fifth and 105th streets in 1889, it next petitioned city council in 1890 to operate a line between Ninth and Twenty-first streets.[12] The proposal was supported by a majority of the affected property owners, mostly businesses, but was adamantly opposed by the Committee of Euclid Avenue Property Owners, mostly residents: Charles W. Bingham, Charles Brush, George Garretson, Leonard Hanna, Samuel Mather, and John Whitelaw. From 1900 to 1908, the committee successfully forestalled further extension of the street railway, both between Ninth and Twenty-first streets and on Millionaires' Row between Twenty-first and Fortieth streets. Meanwhile, the reconstituted Municipal Traction Company, backed by Mayor Johnson, continued to press for the consent of property owners to lay tracks on the entire Avenue. Most residents,

Fig. 268. The William P. and Louisa Southworth residence, Euclid Avenue and Huron Road in 1907, *above;* Halle Brothers' department store on same site in 1908, *below* (*Cleveland Plain Dealer* and Cleveland Public Library).

however, steadfast about preserving the uniform character of the linear grand avenue, were "more determined than ever to prevent the building of these tracks" between Public Square and the city limits.[13]

The Traction company was not the only contingency with which Avenue residents were forced into a sparring match. The Nickel Plate Railroad was also lobbying to build an elevated track across the Avenue at Fifty-fifth Street for the

Fig. 267. *Opposite.* The theater and office district, north side of Euclid Avenue west of Sixth Street. *Left to right,* Guardian Building, Republic Building, Star Theatre (Cleveland Public Library, 1914).

Belt Line. Residents instead proposed a below-grade track. In their view, the "importance and beauty of Euclid Avenue make it desirable that this Avenue should be open and unobstructed." At issue in each of these transit debates was the redefinition of the Avenue to recognize its crucial position in the city's expansion and to accommodate change. Businesses and elected city officials urged change. Residents, steeped in convention and long-term commitment to their exclusive residences and Avenue, defended the status quo. Within seven years, however, compelling pressures by commerce and transit interests overwhelmed the resistance of a diminishing and weakened residential community. In September 1915, the Nickel Plate's overpass at Fifty-fifth Street was built and an electric street railway ran along the full length of the Avenue.[14] This was a critical moment in the life of Euclid Avenue (figs. 269, 270).

A Ghetto Closes In

In truth, other factors besides the street railway were disrupting the residential neighborhood. Thick dirt and pollution from river and railroad industries, choking automobile congestion, and intensified demand for property on the Avenue were just as forceful in disrupting the continuity of this neighborhood as was the street railway. New commercial and institutional buildings were

also dramatically reshaping the scale of the street as the Avenue came to be recognized as the city's premier center of commerce, culture, and institutional life. This role originally had been manifest in the building of residences by Cleveland's business and cultural establishment; theirs was a collective statement, an institution created out of individual acts. Now, as commercial demand for prime property increased in the central city, as the technology of mass transit and the private automobile made travel to prosperous residential areas outside the city easier, and as industrial pollution made for a less attractive living environment in the central city, Euclid's stature as the city's grand avenue diminished. It was no longer the pleasant place to live that it once was, especially for families accustomed to privacy amidst elegant, countrified surroundings.

Something else was also happening around the Avenue that disturbed these affluent, Anglo-Saxon families and, in their view, ultimately compromised their residential haven. A black ghetto was taking shape just to the south of the Avenue, west of Fifty-fifth Street. Up until about 1910, Cleveland's relatively small black population—it constituted less than 2 percent of all Clevelanders—lived in a number of areas throughout the city, having no single district that could be called a neighborhood. The one area in which they did begin to settle at this time, and which soon would become the heart of the emerging black community, was between Euclid and Central avenues and along Scoville and Woodland avenues. But even though about one-third of the city's 8,500 blacks were housed in this crowded district in 1910, they still were a low-income minority living amidst mostly middle-class Italians and Russian Jews.[15] This neighborhood would change dramatically over the next decade.

Between 1910 and 1920, Cleveland's black residents more than quadrupled, from 8,500 to 34,500, with 22,000 blacks migrating to the city from the economically depressed South during the three-year period 1916–19. The black population grew to 72,000 in the next decade. Most settled in the area between the Avenue and the river. The center of the developing black ghetto was around Thirtieth Street and Central Avenue, just two blocks south of the Avenue, where a budding red-light district was also taking shape with its profusion of speakeasies, decaying lodges, and gambling houses. By 1929 the Russians and Italians were moving out, having been replaced by nine out of ten of the city's black residents, who lived in the segregated belt immediately south of the grand avenue down to Woodland.[16]

Even though the city's black families did not suffer such violent racial attacks as did those in Chicago—principally stemming from Cleveland's long-held abolitionist sentiment—urban white residents nevertheless harbored a degree of hostility toward their growing presence, as witnessed by acts of intimidation, some violence, and exploitation in a tight housing market. And contrary to Avenue residents' propertied interests, many Avenue capitalists needed these newcomers to run the vast assembly lines in their booming manufacturing plants. The great black migration between 1914 and 1924, coinciding with the precipitous drop in the number of East European immigrants to the city during the war, was a critical source of inexpensive manual labor.

Blacks clearly presented a dilemma for the Avenue's establishment. Residents resented them moving closer and closer to their exclusive neighborhood, yet at the same time they benefited economically from the cheap labor. Some were also torn between their desire to resist invasion by blacks into their neighborhood and the opportunity to make a profit by subdividing homes into rental apartments, capitalizing on the severe housing shortage by charging these tenants substantially higher rents.[17]

By the mid-1920s, a number of the magnificent houses on the Avenue had been sold and subdivided (fig. 271). Those residents of long standing who remained disliked the downgraded property as much as their new neighbors. This presumably entered into the thinking of Brush, Rockefeller, and Harry Myer, all of whom stipulated that their houses were to be razed immediately after they died; they shuddered at the thought of multiple families occupying their personal havens. The effect of the nearby ghetto on the Avenue's declining grandeur may have also influenced Brush's thinking when, immediately on the heels of the great black migration, he created the Brush Foundation in 1928 to "improve the quality and reasonably limit the number of those who are born." He firmly believed that the world's rapid population growth was threatening civilization.[18]

Avenue residents generally spoke little about the nearby ghetto, and they chose their words carefully when they did. Yet for such wealthy society people as Avenue families unquestionably were, the poor black neighborhood and the

Fig. 271. Rooming houses pro-
liferate, showing "rooms for
rent" in house at left. Looking
east from Seventy-first Street
(Cleveland Public Library, 1937).

vice that invaded it must have diminished their conviction in the future viability of the grand avenue vision. Their commitment to living on the Avenue, previously unshakable, now faltered.

The Price of Grandeur

Still maintaining a lively semblance of grandeur in spite of feeling affronted by urban dirt, streetcars, traffic, commercial activity, and an expanding black community, the families of Euclid Avenue met with another adverse force after the turn of the century, but this one was a real drain on their wealth. Exceedingly high property assessments were bittersweet recognition of the urban street's primacy, a distinction they had consciously sought to create. City officials may have not formally acknowledged the Avenue's value as a residential boulevard, but they certainly did as an enterprising business address and healthy source of public revenues. Property assessments and taxes along the entire length of the Avenue had increased nominally in the late nineteenth century when commerce was in its infancy. But once the Avenue's commercial function had become well established, real estate taxes uniformly skyrocketed 200 percent between 1900 and 1910, and another 300 to 500 percent over the next decade.

The impact on grand avenue residents, still in the majority, was astounding. Sylvester Everett's two-and-a-half acres and Romanesque revival castle at Fortieth Street were valued at $39,000 in 1890 and rose to $604,000 in 1920, increasing his tax payments from only \$1,100 to \$14,000. The combined Payne and Perry holdings at Twenty-first Street went from about \$81,000 at the beginning of the century to over \$2 million twenty years later, a 120-percent increase each year. The Wade properties, likewise, valued at about \$100,000 in 1900, appreciated 934 percent to \$1 million by 1920.[19] These were affluent people, to be sure, many even millionaires, but such a tax burden became too onerous and simply unacceptable. They were outraged by the city's presumption about the price of grandeur. And they were not alone. Commercial property owners—the Statler Hotel, the Cleveland Trust Company, Cowell & Hubbard, the Union Club—also protested.

Land speculation on the Avenue had begun in earnest in the late teens with investors exploiting the perceived commercial value of Euclid property. The city followed the private market and raised assessments to new heights, increasing taxable values along the entire street another 33 percent between 1920 and 1924. This was cause for existing owners to file the first of two major tax appeals in 1925 with the Ohio Supreme Court. It was also cause for both home and business owners to divest, being unable to support the stiff tax burden, and sell their Avenue property. "It is a sad story," said defending attorney Max Goodman to the state tax commission. "There are more vacancies on Euclid Avenue, there have been more business failures and more leases forfeited than on any other street in Cleveland."[20]

Following the inflationary boom of the 1920s, real estate assessments, with most of the value in the land, depreciated during the economic depression in the 1930s—but not enough. In 1937, 146 property owners filed stinging appeals with the city requesting a total reduction in assessments of \$8.7 million. The city's response? It reduced none and instead increased twelve assessments by \$1.8 million.[21] Residents may not have won their tax appeals, but they had another response: moving off the Avenue, razing their residences, and selling the land. In 1934, Homer Wade razed the residence built by his father, Randall. The Everett family could no longer afford to maintain its house and razed it in 1938. The Paynes' Gothic cottage went down in 1947. Other residents donated or sold their homes to tax-exempt, philanthropic institutions. Many of the mansions bought by commercial interests or vacated by the families were demolished during the great urban buildup that began with World War I (fig. 272).

A Change of Heart

Residents' thinking about the Avenue changed dramatically during the grand avenue's declining years. The last house to be built on the Avenue, the Carlins', was completed in 1911. Forty residences were razed around the turn of the century, another ninety came down between 1907 and 1921, and by 1938 only four families remained (fig. 273). The community of shared interests that was centered around the Avenue waned as the street's elegance gradually disappeared. The generation that came of age in the 1910s and 1920s was estranged by the environment their parents had thrived in. This, plus the increasing cost of maintaining a house on the Avenue, utterly destroyed the

Fig. 272. Redevelopment of the Tom L. Johnson residence (*Cleveland Town Topics,* 1909).

collective neighborhood spirit. Generations of schooling and cultivation produced a society of families enchanted by physical beauty. And now they did not like what they saw. The result was an accelerating disintegration of the Avenue's neighborhood order, an atomization of the bonds that had been formed over decades of residency on the grand avenue.

Yet these families apparently did not leave with the melancholy that subsequent generations felt in looking back. The patrons of Euclid Avenue, from the early decades to the last, were on the leading edge in all they did. They were as progressive in business as they were in the architectural drama of their residences and where they chose to live. In establishing the new enclaves in Bratenahl, the Heights, Wickliffe, or Willoughby, they deliberately and increasingly chose to disperse their energies and capital in these other places rather than maintain a singular presence on the Avenue. They moved beyond the Avenue as other interests moved in around them. Their divided loyalties, choices

Fig. 273. The Samuel Andrews palace falls (*Cleveland Town Topics,* 1923).

between the congested urban avenue or spacious suburban enclaves, silenced the advocacy of the majority of Avenue residents about changes on the street. An acquiescence had settled in by the 1920s.

While visitors to the city might have been disappointed by finding the splendid residences that had been Cleveland's pride gradually displaced by aggressive trade, transit lines, inner-city apartments, and recreational enterprise for the masses, the Avenue's patrons had already looked well beyond the Avenue to find homes for themselves outside the downtown area. They shared such mobile tendencies with their American peers, who were moving off the nation's grand avenues in large numbers after 1910 to establish seats of fashion in Tuxedo Park and Scarsdale outside of New York City, along Lake Shore Drive and in Oak Park near Chicago, in Chevy Chase just north of Washington, D.C., and in the Hollywood Hills and Beverly Hills around Los Angeles.

The automobile facilitated the move off the Avenue, the transition from city to suburb (fig. 274). Just as the horse and carriage had enabled affluent Clevelanders in the early nineteenth century to live far from the city's center on Euclid's borderland, the early twentieth-century car freed residents from the practical constraints of distance and rail lines. For most, the automobile bridged the miles between Public Square and their enclaves out east, as far into the country as Gates Mills and Hunting Valley.[22] And while Avenue residents abhorred congestion on their own street, they enthusiastically embraced the auto for their personal use, for it enabled them happily to choose the comforts of nonurban living and commute to their downtown offices, clubs, churches, and

Fig. 274. The automobile on Euclid Avenue. Winslow-Frasch residence, 2409 Euclid Avenue (Western Reserve Historical Society).

Fig. 275. The commercial main street of an American urban metropolis, Euclid Avenue. Looking west from Thirteenth Street (Lake County [IL] Museum, Curt Teich Postcard Archives, c. 1923).

shops. Their diminishing presence only strengthened the potency of underlying forces that were transforming the Avenue (fig. 275).

The rise and fall of Euclid Avenue reflected fundamental aspects about the origins and evolution of Cleveland. A New England austerity—thrift, hard work, and earnest intent—created the city and moved it forward to greater financial and industrial strength. Such families as the Handys, Wades, Worthingtons, Mathers, and Hannas drove their enterprises forward while they cultivated a way of life among themselves that matched the enhanced metropolitanism of the city. But eventually, by the turn of the century, their way of life collided with the industrialism of their own making—the factory smog, the commercial traffic, and the immigrant and black labor crowding into surrounding neighborhoods. The financial ambitions of the capitalists who built the grand avenue brought as many, if not more, commercial changes to Euclid Avenue as they did to any other major street in downtown Cleveland. But while residents possessed financial power to advance economic progress, they ultimately lacked political strength to shape the future of their residential Avenue under siege by market forces. With the grand avenue's declining presence, cohesion among these families—the prime agent of the neighborhood's formation—also weakened. For its residents, Euclid Avenue's life of grandeur had been an end in itself.

The Rise of Cleveland's Main Street, 1910–1950

E uclid Avenue "is the visual testament to the unwillingness of people to work together for mutual advantages," exclaimed the *Architectural Forum* staff writer in 1959.[1] What an interesting counterpoint to testimonials by residents a century before. But after decades of seeking to create a linear showcase, Avenue patrons had succeeded *too* well by the early 1900s in creating a pleasure ground open to all. It had become the downtown main street, the geographic center of the city, and the hub of Clevelander's daily lives (figs. 276, 277).

Reshaping the Avenue

The physical transformation of the Avenue in the twentieth century occurred gradually over five decades, just as the creation of the grand avenue had taken shape in the nineteenth century. The difference now, though, was an absence of a common vision. Each residence built had made the Avenue a more coherent place. Implicitly, the patrons and architects had respected an emerging pattern along the Avenue. But the new commercial buildings going up appeared to be designed in isolation of the world around them, independent statues standing amidst a revolving urban landscape. The modern builders gave little apparent thought to repairing the world around them or building a new one.[2]

The affluent residential neighborhood remained partially intact during the early 1900s, sharing an uneasy coexistence with commerce, transit, and lower-income neighbors. One defiant woman writing in a 1904 *House Beautiful* article defended the grand avenue as "still without peer" in the country, "in spite of the fact that trade and the street cars . . . have encroached mightily on a part once held sacred." Within the decade, however, her defense could no longer be sustained. The new large-scale buildings, some right next door to the houses, were overshadowing the Avenue's residential presence. The last two houses that stood between Public Square and Ninth Street, the Benjamin Strickland and Henry Chisholm homes, were razed in 1893 to make way for the ten-story Garfield building and fourteen-story New England Building, designed by Boston architects Shepley, Rutan & Coolidge (fig. 278). In the first five years of the new century, such projects as the fourteen-story Schofield Building and

Fig. 276. *Opposite.* General Douglas MacArthur's welcome home parade. A crowd of 150,000 well-wishers lined the parade route on Euclid Avenue (Cleveland Public Library, September 1951).

Fig. 277. The crowded retail district, Euclid Avenue near Public Square (Western Reserve Historical Society, c. 1910).

Fig. 278. *Opposite.* The last residences on Euclid Avenue between Public Square and Ninth Street; Dr. Benjamin Strickland house, no. 605, *left,* and Henry Chisholm house, no. 631, *right* (Cleveland Public Library).

thirteen-story Citizens Building dwarfed even Trinity Cathedral and the magnificent residences of Leonard C. Hanna and Lyman H. Treadway, also under construction at the time.[3] Even as commerce was crowding in on the residential avenue, these multimillion-dollar houses and churches were still being added to the neighborhood, injecting new life into the grand avenue.

Even if some Avenue residents appeared to carry on as if the neighborhood was not at risk, others knew better. The churches, just as sensitive as families to life on the Avenue, saw the effect that increasing physical pressures had on the neighborhood's social fabric. Speaking on the occasion of the fiftieth anniversary of the Euclid Avenue Baptist Church, Rev. Charles Aubrey Eaton observed, "The changes of the half century are illustrated by the changes in our surroundings. We used to be a family church, surrounded by homes, in a homogeneous and simple community. Now, we are a downtown church, surrounded by a great heterogeneous population with the family element, falling into a secondary place in our life."[4]

And the architects, who only a few years before had boasted of the fabulous streetscape of houses, now turned their attention to the larger prospects available in the Avenue's new commercial center (see table 16). The *Ohio Architect,* the designers' regional trade journal, directed its readers in 1907 to look at

TABLE 16

Commercial Development, 1900–1920

Building	Address	Building Date
Williamson Building	201–21	1900
John Hartness Brown Building	1001	1901
Citizens Building	850	1903
Union Club	1201	1905
William Taylor Son & Co. Store	630	1907
The Cleveland Trust Co.	900	1909
Hippodrome Building	718	1909
Sterling & Welch Department Store	1225	1909
Halle Bros. Department Store	1224	1910
Swetland Building	1006	c. 1910
Cleveland Athletic Club	1118	1911
Higbee's Department Store	1255	1912
Statler Hotel	1125	1912
Stillman Building	1101	1914
Union National Bank	308	1916
Stillman Theatre	1115	1916
Cowell & Hubbard Building	1301	1919
Bulkley Building/Allen Theater	1501	1920
Keith's Palace Theatre	1621	1922

the lower end of the Avenue as the "Wall Street of Ohio's metropolis." This fresh outlook counted such new banking houses as the Cleveland Trust Company, the First National Bank, the Dime Savings Bank, and the Depositors' Savings & Trust Company. Most residents, too, seemed remarkably indifferent to the street's changed presence. In 1912 Edward Merritt referred to the "two oldest houses on the Avenue," which stood across from the Union Club, as "interesting only historically."[5] They were like dinosaurs on a modern landscape. His letter to his old Cleveland friend Myron Herrick, then U.S. ambassador to Paris, was intoned with whimsy but not alarm (fig. 279).

No matter, commerce, ever advancing, now ruled, not Avenue residents. Sylvester Everett's magnificent property was impeded, in his mind, when in 1910 the Del Prado apartment hotel went up on the lot just east of his mansion. Everett was so enraged that he built a high, spiteful fence to mitigate the overbearing intrusion. In the years following, the great urban buildup that transformed American cities during the spiralling World War I economy decisively changed the image of Cleveland's Euclid Avenue. Viewing this progression in 1917 from a more dispassioned distance than many of his former neighbors, John D. Rockefeller speculated to his friend Worcester Warner that the downtown business center would soon reach Fortieth Street, where his own house stood. Though he had left his Avenue home forty years before, he seemed wistful that his residence's "best use will [then] be for business purposes."[6] Rockefeller was not at all comfortable with this thought, which was one reason he demanded that his house be razed when he died (fig. 280).

Yet even as many of the Avenue's residences were being transformed or demolished by what Cleveland journalist William R. Rose decried as "that most ruthless of wreckers, commercial necessity," the tree-shaded panorama between Twenty-first and Fifty-fifth streets remained largely intact during the 1920s and 1930s. But this stage-set scene masqued changes in the characters. The families were leaving their Avenue homes while the physical facade survived for another generation. By 1928 the four families who remained—the Anthony Carlins, the Amos B. McNairys, the Jacob D. Coxes, and Mrs. Samuel L. Raymond—lived within a six-block area between Thirty-second and Thirty-eighth streets. They were survivors of a vanishing breed of Cleveland society. In 1939, the Coxes

Fig. 279. Interesting only historically; William P. Southworth house, no. 1218, *left,* and Halle Brothers' department store site, no. 1224, *right* (Cleveland Public Library, 1908).

Fig. 280. The razing of John D. Rockefeller mansion; site of new gas station and parking lot (Cleveland Public Library, April 1938).

also left for a nine-acre, lake-front estate, joining many of their former neighbors in Bratenahl.[7]

A Modern Main Street

Visitors and historians of the city have probably pined after the grand avenue's fall far more than contemporary residents, and certainly more than investors. The transformation, a decade or more in the making, startled few locals and seemed a fait accompli, of course, by the mid-1920s. The first zoning map adopted by the city in 1929 confirmed this: The Avenue's entire length was solidly zoned for retail businesses, permitting 175- to 250-foot high structures and apartment houses for an unlimited number of families.[8] The talk of the press and downtown business groups centered on how to make the most of a rosy future for Cleveland's main street. How, indeed?

First, choking congestion had to be fixed. In 1925, Cleveland premiered the country's first electric traffic light at Euclid Avenue's gridlocked intersection with Ninth Street (fig. 281). The odd-looking $15,000 "bird cage" was torn down five years later after it had done little to unravel the mess. Traffic on the Avenue could not be tamed, so the Euclid Avenue Association set about making plans in 1929 to widen the street thirty to fifty feet between Twenty-first and Fortieth streets and run a landscaped parkway down the center. An idea with many lives, the boulevard concept was resurrected. These progressive business-men liked to think of their plan in such glowing munificence as New Yorkers might in making Park Avenue over again: the last word in modernity, "the rest and recreation center of downtown Cleveland."[9]

Four Avenue residents actually contributed land to a thirty-foot setback that fronted the new high-rise project envisioned as the centerpiece of this promenade, the twenty-two-story National Town & Country Club under con-struction at Twenty-fourth Street, the site of Rufus Winslow's former crenelated sandstone pile. But other property owners refused to yield valuable frontage for simply a commercial right-of-way. Nor did the prospective five-star restaurants, luxury hotels, and distinguished fraternities come. Instead the Avenue began to decline in stature, losing its signature as Cleveland's chief transit artery and premier business address.

The spectacular fifty-two-story Terminal Tower project on Public Square, boasting the main terminal of the new Shaker Rapid Transit line out to the eastern region, entirely refocused the heartbeat of downtown back to Public Square when it opened in 1929. The Terminal became the city's transportation hub for electric rapid transit, interurban trolleys, and interstate steam railroads, siphoning business and retail activity off the Avenue and the Burnham-Johnson mall on the lake. The soaring 708-foot Tower—the tallest building in the world outside New York City until 1967—and the fixed rail Shaker Rapid were disas-trous for Euclid Avenue beyond the theater district, around Eighteenth Street, now nothing more than a byway to University Circle. Just as the streetcar and commerce had eroded the soul of the grand avenue, now the Shaker Rapid line was doing the same to the commercial main street.

The Avenue was dead as a transportation way, declared Peter Witt in 1930, son of long-time Avenue resident Stillman Witt. "Provocative nonsense," replied the *Press,* "[it] is not dead and is not going to die." The newspaper argued that thousands of Clevelanders still depended on Euclid Avenue street-cars for the most direct route east out of the city, even if many were inconve-nienced by having to transfer at the new terminal. Premature as it might have been, Witt's prediction came true. A streetcar named "Euclid" traveled the Ave-

Fig. 281. The modern bird cage, the first electronic traffic tower in Cleveland and the United States; at Euclid Avenue and Ninth Street (Cleveland Public Library, 1925).

nue for the last time in April 1952. More than two hundred thousand spectators turned out for the historic event, the largest parade ever staged on the city's preeminent parade ground. It was a celebration to honor the century-old processional and hail the birth of the trolley-free Euclid Boulevard.[10] Sad but true, Avenue residents who had fought for just this in the 1890s had left the Avenue decades before.

With the residents gone and the streetcar gone, less traffic and high property assessments were diminishing the Avenue's appeal, and fewer businesses and investors were willing to take on the risk and expense that a property on the Avenue demanded. Entire blocks were gutted by property auctions and bankruptcy sales (figs. 282, 283). Poorly maintained parking and used car lots mushroomed. "Where Millionaires Reveled Parking Lots Are Blooming," announced one newspaper, while another exposed incidents of racketeering and vandalism. It was a poignant contrast to the 1892 Baedeker's, which placed the grand avenue of magnificent mansions at the top of its visitors' sight-seeing list. Now the 1940 WPA's *Ohio Guide* apologized for the Avenue's current state and instructed tourists to instead go to the city's eastern reaches to find the former patrons' new country estates. Unfortunate though it may have been in its view, the WPA's downtown tour could only describe the Avenue as a ruin, the "symbol of Cleveland's industrial dynasties" that had fallen to "the march of urban forces" (fig. 284).[11]

Fig. 282. Bargains for sale. Former Fayette Brown residence, 3210 Euclid Avenue (*Cleveland Plain Dealer*).

Fig. 283. The James J. Tracy residence in decay, 3535 Euclid Avenue (*Cleveland Plain Dealer,* 1951).

If not the affluent, then who could afford to make a home on the Avenue beyond the business and theater district near the Square? Tax-exempt institutions moved in, as they did not have to pay property taxes and could afford only a second-rate office address. Moreover, they were at the mercy of such beneficence as former Euclid Avenue families could provide. And in fine tradition, these philanthropic-minded patrons happily donated their homes in the 1930s and 1940s to educational and war-related institutions. The long-standing tradition of generosity, which outlived the neighborhood's physical dominion, quite coincidentally preserved sections of the streetscape for one last generation.

Within walking distance of the War Relations Board, located in the Union Commerce Building at Ninth Street, the wartime institutions took up residence in the old homes: the American Red Cross in the former residences of Harry Devereux, Amos McNairy, and Andrew Squire; the Red Cross clinic in William

H. Boardman's old home; and the Soldiers Relief Commission in Orlando Hall's house. Such a concentration of these establishments could be found nowhere else in the city (figs. 285, 286).

By the end of the war, in 1945, the Avenue had gained an institutional signature. And by the end of the decade, educational concerns had also taken up residence on the city's public processional: the Cleveland Bible College in William Chisholm's former home; the Spencerian College in the Daniel Eells mansion; John Huntington Polytechnic Institute in the residence of Charles Otis, Sr. (fig. 287). And of course there was the Union Club at Twelfth Street and the University Club domiciled in the Beckwith-Sterling manse at Thirty-eighth Street. Had the city's institutional life played a primary role in the politics and commerce of Cleveland, as it did in such capital cities as Washington,

Fig. 284. Last remnants of Cleveland's grand avenue. *Lower left,* north side of Avenue between Twenty-first and Thirtieth Streets, showing the Town and Country Club building at Twenty-fourth Street; the former residences of Samuel Mather, no. 2605; Leonard C. Hanna, no. 2717; Hickox-Brown, no. 2727; and William Chisholm, Sr., no. 2827 (Western Reserve Historical Society, 1940s).

Fig. 285. Nonprofit institutions occupy the former magnificent residences. Henry Devereux house, 2525 Euclid Avenue (*Cleveland Plain Dealer*, 1951).

D.C., and Richmond, Virginia, these remaining grand avenue residences might have been protected by a renewed monumental stature, lifted up by the importance of their resident institutions. The foreign embassies saved the spectacular houses on Massachusetts Avenue in the nation's capital, and the regal statues on Monument Avenue kept the spirit of this Virginia grand avenue alive. But the nonprofit institutions of Cleveland's Euclid Avenue, while honored for their civic functions, took a backseat to private capital and industry. The Avenue, too, became a servant of progress to advance the city's chief marketplace function.[12]

Thus when city officials were compelled in 1949 to develop a massive new highway system to absorb the wartime employment boom and ease the downtown traffic gridlock, they redlined the Avenue around Twenty-second Street as one of seven radials feeding into the new innerbelt. The emergency ordinance specified that only those "critical" properties in the path of the eight-lane highway should be acquired.[13] Between 1950 and 1959, the city seized and demol-

Fig. 286. The American Red Cross headquarters; the former Andrew Squire residence, 3443 Euclid Avenue (Western Reserve Historical Society).

ished thirty Avenue houses between Twenty-sixth and Thirty-second streets, for all practical purposes expendable assets in the way of civic progress (see table 17). This mass leveling gutted what little remained of the former neighborhood. It was the grand avenue's final fall.

The innerbelt, opened in 1960, gave rise to a spurt of new hotel and office development in an uneven collection of glass-walled structures. Beyond Twenty-second Street there were mostly rooming houses, filling stations, lunch counters, parking lots, and deteriorating houses and grounds. No architectural landscape here, certainly no grand avenue. The street that had been "the pride and very backbone" of the city, journalist James Lister of *The Clevelander* reported, had become a "honky-tonk." The *Architectural Record*'s 1959 article headlined the Avenue's plight "The Glittering Slum on Main Street." Another

Fig. 287. The American Red
Cross in the former Perry–Bingham residence, no. 2157, *right;*
American Legion headquarters
in the Henry B. Payne residence,
no. 2121, *left* (courtesy Bolton
Family, by G. M. Edmondson,
1918).

TABLE 17
Demolished Residences, 1950–1959

Patron/Resident	Address	Demolition Date
Harry K. Devereux	2525	1952
Orlando Hall	2638	1952
James Parmelee	3036	1952
George Hoyt	3112	1956
Rev. William A. Leonard	3054	1956
Dudley Baldwin Wick	3112	1956
George Hall	3146	1957
Leonard C. Hanna	2717	1958
William Chisholm, Sr.	2827	1958
Charles H. Hickox	2727	1958
George E. Herrick	2435	1958
Daniel P. Eells	3201	1959
Charles W. Bingham	2445	1959
William Bingham	2843	1959

reproach in 1965, by prominent architect Edward Durell Stone, called the former grand avenue "a disgrace."[14] In response, the street's leading patrons of retailers, institutions, and professional businesses and the city combined their efforts to form the Cleveland Development Foundation, the Heart of Euclid Avenue Association, and Euclid Innerbelt Association to establish some unified vision and also subsidize renewal projects. They were in search of an identity for the Avenue.[15] They recognized, as did the developers and architects, that without a city plan and design incentives, the marketplace would prevail, which was, after all, why the grand avenue vision vanished.

Fig. 288. Euclid Avenue in postcards. The Four-in-Hand Club, *top;* the Tom L. Johnson residence, no. 2342, *bottom* (author's private collection).

This city street, like most of America's grand avenues, worked beautifully as an urban neighborhood until its residents were uprooted by economic forces—of their own making—too big to defeat. They lacked sufficient influence because they were excluded from city politics and the civic agenda. As Jane Jacobs maintained in *The Death and Life of Great American Cities* (1961), a city neighborhood survived only when its residents and its function matched the interests of the city, or were at least powerful enough to influence the popular vote. Over time, Euclid Avenue residents' grand avenue life and political interests clashed with those of the majority of Cleveland citizens. And the mobility of Avenue families fractured the neighborhood dominion and group solidarity. Thanks only to the strength of family ties, the currency of the grand avenue has survived in its downtown clubs, churches, and cultural and philanthropic institutions (fig. 288). Withal, the seven houses that stand at this writing are glorious postscripts of Euclid Avenue's historic grandeur.

> Who can tell of the story of that part of Euclid Avenue that sent the fame of Cleveland to the corners of the earth . . . scene of mansions like baronial castles owned by families of almost mysterious wealth, of brilliant events and marriages almost royal in their display?[16]

Euclid Avenue Residents, 1830–1950

Listed Alphabetically

Name	Pre-1906 Address	Post-1906 Address	House Built	House Razed*	Comments
Abbott, Henry S. & Anna	690	2422			
Adams, Charles E.	1493				
Adams, E. E.	2029	8935	1896		Arthur Oviatt, architect
Adams, Ira		8903	c. 1845	1949	
Alcott, Franklyn L.	1176	4820	1866		[Joseph Ireland, architect]
Allen, Dudley P., M.D.	1975	8811	1891–92	1968	Charles F. Schweinfurth, architect
Allen, Luther & Julia B.	1695	7609	1896–97		Meade & Granger, architects
Ammon, Josephine	1939	8615	1889–90		Charles F. Schweinfurth, architect
Andrews, Horace	882	3033	1882–85	1923	Walter Blythe, architect
Andrews, Mrs. Upson A.	1573	7033			
Andrews, Samuel	789	2843	1840		Sold to William Bingham
	882	3033	1882–85	1923	Walter Blythe, architect
Andrews, Sherlock J.	39	400	c. 1833–35		Jonathan Goldsmith and Charles W. Heard, masterbuilders
Arter, Frank A.	1922	8522			Owned in 1907
Arthur, P. M.	1429	6521			
Auld, David, Jr.	1567	7029	1899		Built addition, 1899
Austin, L.	380	1360	1876		
Authwaite	789	2843	1858		William Bingham bought in 1881–82
Avery, Rev. Dr. Frederick B.	634	2240	1838–40		
Avery, John T.	681	2409	1860–70		Wooden porch added, 1876
Babcock, Charles	1961	8705	1896		S. R. Badgley, architect; building permit #24718
Babcock, W. A.	2010	8914			Owned in 1907
Backus, Franklyn T. & Lucy Mygatt	799	2921	1858		Built by George Mygatt; daughter, Lucy Mygatt Backus
Backus, Frederick M. & Nettie E.	578	2044	1860		
Bailey, Daniel K.	2084	9304			Owned in 1907

*Blank space under House Razed column indicates information not available. "No" indicates house still standing.

Name	Pre-1906 Address	Post-1906 Address	House Built	House Razed	Comments
Bailey T. C. & E. B.	946	3450			
Baldwin, Charles C., Judge	1345				
Baldwin, Dudley		2069	1843		Acquired by Mary Payne Bingham
Baldwin, Norman	470	1115	1845		West of Anson Smith House house; two houses west of Twelfth Street
Baley, William	1144	4560	c. 1845–50		
Banning, Dr. Edmund P.		1020	1859		Between Ninth & Twelfth streets on south side
Barnes, O. M.	1089	4111	1866	1882	Simeon Porter, architect; razed for S. T. Everett house
Barnett, James & Maria Underhill	697	2435	1856–57		
Barrett, J. Lawrence	1948	8624			Owned in 1907
Baxter, Harris H., M. D.	1474	6700			
Beckwith, T. Sterling	1023	3813	1866	No	Joseph Ireland, architect
Benedict, Edwin G. & Philena O.	780	2824			
Benedict, George A.	35	605	1838–39	1893	At northeast corner of Bond Street
Bierce, George		8903	c. 1845	1949	
Bigelow, J. J.	1729	7809	1875		
Billings, Frank	758	2728			
Bingham, Charles E. & Isabella	826	3028			
Bingham, Charles W.	611	2157	1901–2	1959	Renovated and enlarged Nathan Perry house; Peabody & Stearns, architects, 1901–2
	707	2445	1883		Peabody & Stearns, architects; Frank Barnum, architect, 1894 alterations; Abram Garfield, architect, 1918
Bingham, Flavel White	122	1220	1836		West of Ursuline Convent
Bingham, William & Elizabeth B.	882	3033	1842–43	1882	Bought John M. Sterling house; sold to Samuel Andrews, 1882
	789	2843	1858		Moved to No. 2843 after sale of No. 3033 to Samuel Andrews
Bishop, Horace A.	1999	8903			Owned in 1907
Bissell, Charles S. & Cynthia	1151	4611	1867		Joseph Ireland, architect
Blair, John	874	3210	1836–37	1904	
Blandin, Judge & Mrs. E. J.	1673	7503	1884–85		Owned in 1907
Blann, A. W.	1160	4712	c. 1875–80		
Blee, Miss	2084	9304			Owned in 1907
Blossom, Dudley S.	595	2121	1849		Formerly Henry B. Payne house
Boardman, Henry W. & Mabel	414	1423	1835		Bought Newell Bond house
Boardman, William H.	950	3608	1891–92		Charles F. Schweinfurth, architect
Boardman, William J.	522	1303	1856		Renovated and enlarged by Boardman, 1860–61; Simeon C. Porter, architect
Bolton, Charles C.	1554	7016	c. 1885		Building permit #10876
Bolton, Thomas	468	1111	c. 1835		Sold to George W. Gardner
	1560	7030	1848–49		
Bond, Newell	414	1423	1835		
Bourne, Benjamin F.	1501	6813	1895		

Name	Pre-1906 Address	Post-1906 Address	House Built	House Razed	Comments
Boynton, Judge W. W.	1781	8021	1884		Coburn & Barnum, architects; S. H. Collister, contractors
Bradburn, Charles			1835	1868	Destroyed by fire, 1868
Bradford, Mary S.	569				
Bradford, William & Mary S.	1604	7122			Frank B. Meade, architect
Bradley, Alvah	1378	6218	1870–72		
Bradley, Morris A.	1621	7217	1886	1988	Owned in 1907
Brayton, Charles A.	789	2843			Owned in 1907
Breed, Rev. Walter R.	1090	4108			Owned in 1907
Briggs, Charles E.	874	3210			Charles Schneider, architect; Charles F. Schweinfurth, original design
Briggs, Pierson D.	1440	6530			
Britton, Bertram	1038	3844			
Britton, Joseph W.	1737	7817	1875		[Levi T. Scofield, architect]
Brooks, Thomas H.	1114	4312	1891		Building permit April 11, 1891, #7198
Brown, Alexander E.	734	2626	c. 1866–70		Owned in 1907
Brown, Fayette	874	3210	1865–66		
Brown, Harvey H.	757	2727	1855–59	1958	Charles Hickox house
Brown, Henry H.	734	2626	c. 1866–70		Owned in 1907
Brush, Charles F.	1003	3725	1887–88	1929	George H. Smith, architect; Louis C. T. Tiffany, interior design
Buell, Mrs. A. M.	574	2002	1888		Coburn & Barnum, architects; house cost $8,000
Bulkley, Charles H.	802	2926			Charles F. Schweinfurth, exterior and interior remodeling, 1890s
Bulkley, R. J.	802	2926			
Burke, Edmund S., Jr.	1183	4915			Owned in 1907
Burke, Stevenson & Ella M.	1171	4811	c. 1882–83		[Levi Scofield, architect]
Burnes, H. D.			1893		Arthur Oviatt, architect
Burnham, Thomas W.	724	2606	c. 1890		Owned in 1907
Burry, John W.	1684	7514			Owned in 1907
Burton, J. Prescott	1524	6912			
Bury, Theodore	626	2051			
Cady, George W.			1890–95		Coburn & Barnum, architects
Canfield, Charles G.	1952	8628	1890		Building permit #5510
Canfield, C. E.	770	2808			
Carlin, Anthony & Mary	885	3233	1911–12	No	Adolph Sprackling, architect
Castle, William & Mary		1211	c. 1855–60	1912	Union Club site
	1631	7301	1897–98		David Z. Norton house
Chadwick, Leroy S. & Cassie	1824	8204	c. 1860–65		
Chamberlain, Selah	371	1351	1856–57		
Chandler, Harrison T.	2173	10007			Owned in 1907
Chapin, Herman	1113	4307	1857		
Childs, Edwin D.	1685	7601			Owned in 1907
Chisholm, Henry & Jean		653	1857–58	1893	Built by Nelson Munroe, 1858; bought by Henry Chisholm
Chisholm, H. A.	2055	9107			Owned in 1907
Chisholm, Mrs. Jean	653	2317	c. 1870		

Name	Pre-1906 Address	Post-1906 Address	House Built	House Razed	Comments
Chisholm, Stewart H.	1006	3730	1891		Sold to Earl W. Oglebay
Chisholm, William, Jr.	962	3618	1895	1960	
Chisholm, William, Sr., & Mary Stone	779	2827	1887–89	1958	Charles F. Schweinfurth, original design; drawing at Western Reserve Historical Society
Christian, George B.	1641	7341	c. 1894		Coburn & Barnum, architects; building permit #19628
	2097	9501			Coburn & Barnum, architects
Christy, Henry C.	2186	10022			Owned in 1907
Clark, Albert	540	1760	1857–58		
Clark, B. H.	1144	4560	1895		A. H. Granger, architect
Clark, Henry F.	770	2808			Owned in 1907
Clark, James F.	399	1415	c. 1855–65		Built by James Clark; bought by W. S. Tyler (son-in-law)
Clark, Mrs. James F.	561	2605	c. 1840		Sold to Jacob Perkins
Clark, Robert H.	946	3450	1895–96		A. H. Granger, architect; building permit #22806
Cobb, Ahira	1379	6305	c. 1870–75		Became The Kensington hotel, c. 1900–1907
Cobb, Lester A.	1369	6211	c. 1882–85		
Cobb, Ralph	1272	5526	1889		Original (unbuilt) design by Charles F. Schweinfurth, No. 1272; drawings at Western Reserve Historical Society; building permits #2531–33
	1361	6203	1887–89		Charles F. Schweinfurth, architect
Coe, Lester M.	1161	4719	1852		Built by William Hart; sold to Zenas King, rebuilt 1865–66; then sold to Lester M. Coe
Coffinberry, Henry D.	971	3609	1865–70		Charles Hopkinson, architect, alterations, 1896; bought from S. Williamson
Collins, G. E.	1010	3738	1872		1896 addition by Arthur Oviatt, architect
Collister, Lucas W.	832	3036			
Colwell, Joseph	852	3122			Owned in 1907
Connelly, D.					Mead & Hamilton, architects
Cooper, George & Druzilla	716	2536	1896–97		Granger & Meade, architects
Corlett, William T., M.D.	553	1953	c. 1882–85		[Levi T. Scofield, architect]
	962	3618	1895	1960	Built annex for medical office and children's room
Corning, Miss Olive	869	3201	1876	1959	
Corning, Warren H. & Helen	869	3201	1876	1959	
Corrigan, Capt. James	1800	8114	1907		1907 remodelling, $10,000 cost; S. & G. Hisch, architects
Cottingham, Walter H.	848	3112	c. 1865–67	1956	Owned in 1907
Cotton, Edwin A.	1939	8615	1889–90		Owned in 1907
Cowing, John P.	1501	6813	1895		Owned in 1907

Name	Pre-1906 Address	Post-1906 Address	House Built	House Razed	Comments
Cowles, Samuel	60	622	1833–34	1906	Jonathan Goldsmith, masterbuilder; sold to Anson Smith, 1842; sold to Ursuline Convent, 1850
Cox, Jacob D., Jr.	468	1111	1880		
	925	3411	1898–99		Charles F. Schweinfurth, architect; original drawings at Western Reserve Historical Society
Crawford, Lemuel		800			West of Ninth Street; west of Gaylord and Scott houses
Crocker, Timothy D. & Eliza Otis	845	3111	1870	1930	Andrew Dall, builder
Crow, David	1572	7032			
Crumb, C. A.		5415	1891		Building permit #6689
Curtis, E. J.			1884		
Cushing, Edward H., M. D.	1160	4712	1875–80		1899 building permit
Dangler, Charles I.	1415	6505			
Dauby, N. L.					Meade & Hamilton, architects
De Klyn, Charles F.	1309	5809			Owned in 1907
De Maeyers, Kate	832	3036	1899		
Del Prado Hotel	1099	4203	c. 1910		
Dempsey, James			1850		
Dennis, H. D.	2045	9007			Owned in 1907
Devereux, Harry K.	713	2525	1889–91	1952	Charles F. Schweinfurth, architect
Devereux, John H. & Antoinette	882	3226	1873	No	Joseph Ireland, architect
Dickson, Frederick S.	595	2121	1847–49		Henry B. Payne house
Doan, E. W.	2102	9506			Owned in 1907
Dodge, George C.		1705	1846		Known as "Strawberry Hill"
Dodge, Henry H.	560	1605	c. 1855	1891	Sold to Gen. Oviatt
Dodge, Lucy A.		1735			
Dodge, Samuel	574	1621	1846	1922	Dodge died 1854
Dow, Prentiss	25	25	c. 1835		
Drake, Francis E.	779	2827	1887–89	1958	Charles F. Schweinfurth, architect; original drawings at Western Reserve Historical Society
Drury, Francis E.	1949	8625	1910–12	No	Meade & Hamilton, architects
Dunham, Rufus	1477	6709	1824	No	
Edmondson, George M.	678	2362			Photographic studio
Eells, Daniel P.	856	1700	1852		
	869	3201	1876	1959	Joseph Ireland, architect; original rendering, "J. Ireland '76"; razed for hotel
Elliott, Dalls	1806	8120	1889–91		Building permit #52301
Ellison, Henry C.	1038	3844			
Ely, George H.	1099	4203	c. 1874–75		
Everett, Charles & Fannie	2575	6801			
Everett, Henry A.	2575	6801			
Everett, Sylvester T.	1089	4111	1883–87	1938	Charles and Julius Schweinfurth, architects
Fanning, M. A.	1759	7913			Owned in 1907

Name	Pre-1906 Address	Post-1906 Address	House Built	House Razed	Comments
Fitch, Zalmon	528	1325			Renovated by King
Flagler, Henry	1003	3725	1872–73	1887	Site of Charles F. Brush house, 1887
Foote, George H.	581	1751			
Ford, H. C.	2089	9409	1860s		Owned in 1907
Ford, Mrs. F. L.	2220	10302			Owned in 1907
Ford, O. D.	2089	9409	1860s		
Foster, Arthur B.	1800	8114	1907		Owned in 1907
Frasch, Herman	681	2409	1878	1926	Levi T. Scofield, architect
French, Julius E.	713	2525	1889–91		Charles F. Schweinfurth, architect; original drawing at Western Reserve Historical Society
Fuller, Augustus		1734	1858		
Gardner, George W.	468	1111	1830s		Formerly Thomas Bolton house
Garretson, George	1000	3716	c. 1865–67		
Garretson, Hiram & Ellen	1000	3716	c. 1865–67		Hiram died 1876
Gaylord, Henry		833	c. 1854–55		West of Ninth Street
Giddings, Charles M.	1554	7016	1843		
Gilbert, John A.	535	1911			Owned in 1907
Gilbert, N. A.	1604	7122			
Gill, Charles H.	1190	5004	c. 1875		Owned in 1907
Gillette, Jonathan		1813	1845–46		West of T. P. Hardy house in 1829; sold to F. M. Osborne?
Goulder, H. D.	1561	7023			
Gowan, Caleb	950	3608	1891–92		Charles F. Schweinfurth, architect
Grandin, J. Wilbert	890	3244			Owned in 1907
Greenough, Malcolm S.	724	2606	c. 1890		
Griffith, Dr. Harry Means	2203	10105			Owned in 1907
Grigg, T. Joshua	2089	9400	1893		Coburn & Barnum, architects
Griswold, Judge S. O.	58	580	1830		West of Samuel Cowles house/ Ursuline Convent; formerly William Shepard house
Gund, George F.	1621	7217	1886		Formerly Morris A. Bradley house
Gundry, John M.	1511	6903	1864		Owned in 1907
Hale, Cleveland C.	1113	4307	1857		
Hale, Edwin B.	1113	4307	1857		
Hale, Edwin V.	1113	4307	1857		
	1501	6813	1895		
Hale, John C.	1520	6910			
	1749	7901	1909–10		Building permit #28701
Hale, Willis B.	1100	4200			
Hall, George	864	3146	1869–70	1957	
Hall, Orlando	742	2638	1865–66	1952	
	1624	7218			
Handy, Truman P.		800	1837	1902	Jonathan Goldsmith, masterbuilder
	521	1829	1841–42		
Hanna, Dan R.	1650	7404	1895		Charles F. Schweinfurth, architect
Hanna, Leonard C.	737	2717	1901–2	1958	Stanford White of McKim, Mead & White, architect
Hannon, J. E.	1524	6912			

Name	Pre-1906 Address	Post-1906 Address	House Built	House Razed	Comments
Harkness, Stephen V.	1420	6508	1866		Simeon Porter, architect
Harkness, William L.	984	3634	1895–98		Bought J. M. Hoyt house; Meade & Garfield, architects; building permits #36905, #38885
Harkness, W. A.	611	2157	1901–2		
Harman, Ralph H.	505	1815	1866		Sold to Earl W. Oglebay
Harrington, B.		400	1866		Simeon Porter, architect; at Hickox Alley
Harris, Col. William	490	1167	1877		Joseph Ireland, architect; razed when Hotel Statler built
Hart, William		1725	1857–58		
Harvey, Edward F.	1150	4608	1896		Building permits #1331, #25504
Harvey, Mrs. H.			1892		Charles Hopkinson, architect
Haserot, Samuel F.	1630	7224	1892–93		Charles F. Schweinfurth, architect
Hatch, Henry K.	1895	8415	1892–94		Charles F. Schweinfurth, architect; building permits #7574, #12962
Hathaway Brown School	768	2802			
Hay, John	506	1235	1875–76	1909	Joseph Ireland, architect
Hayes, Harry E.	1500	6810	1890		Building permit #4774
Heisley, Mrs. Mary Dodge	371	1351	1856–57		Owned in 1907
Herrick, George E.	697	2435	1856–57		
Hickox, Charles	757	2727	1855–59	1958	Heard & Porter, architects
Hoadley, George A.		1201	c. 1835		Jonathan Goldsmith, masterbuilder
Hobart, M. M.	1878	8402			Owned in 1907
Hobbs, Perry L., M.D.	1420	6508	1866		Built by Stephen V. Harkness
Hodge, Judge Orlando J. & Virginia	1096	4120	1850		
Holcomb, James W.	1597	7115			
	1737	7817	1875		
Holden, Liberty	1729	7809	1875		Owned by Lucy L. Thorp in 1881; owned by J. H. Thorp in late 1880s
Hord, A. C.	1650	7404	1895		Dan R. Hanna house; owned in 1907
Hord, John H.	1650	7404	1895		Dan R. Hanna house; owned in 1907
Horner, B. F.	1461	6611			
Horwitz, Henry D.	1755	7911			Owned in 1907
Howe, George W. & Katharine	642	2248	1892–94	No	Coburn & Barnum, architects
Hoyt, George	848	3112	c. 1865–67	1956	
Hoyt, James H.	707	2445	1883		Charles W. Bingham house
Hoyt, James M.	984	3634	1864–65		Sold to William L. Harkness
Hubby, Lester M.	858	3134	1860–65		Owned in 1907
		7040	1868	1868	New house destroyed, 1868
Hunt, Edward P. & Mary	1791	8804	1891		Owned in 1907
Hurd, Harry	574	2002	1888		
Hurlbut, Hinman B. & Jane E.	885	3233	1855–58	1911	Heard & Porter, architects
Hussey, Joseph G.	925	3411	1859–60		Owned in 1907
Ingersoll, J. A.	1517	6907			
Ivison, William C.	1673	7503	1884–85		Coburn & Barnum, architects
Janes, Lorenzo	1845	8221	1845		

Name	Pre-1906 Address	Post-1906 Address	House Built	House Razed	Comments
Jaynes, Hylas	1845	8221	1845		Owned in 1907
Jennings, Gilbert P.		8010	1899		Building permit #30930
Jennings, P. S.			1895		Coburn & Barnum, architects
Johnson, George J.	1110	4220	1855–60		
Johnson, Jonathan		424	1826–30		60-acre farm; Harvey Rice house site
Johnson, Mrs. Philander E.	1490	6720			Owned 1907
Johnson, Tom L.	667	2343	1885–86	1926	George E. Stockley house; remodeled and expanded by Johnson
Jones, Wyndham C.	1692	7608			Owned in 1907
Joseph, M.	2089	9409			Owned in 1907
Kelley, Franklin	1518	6908	1850–52		
Kelley, Herman			1905		Charles Hopkinson, architect
Kelley, Irad		3500	c. 1845		
Kelley, Moses	1518	6908	1850–52		
Kelley, Thomas		1723	1834–35	1897	Jonathan Goldsmith, masterbuilder; next to Harvey Rice house
Kendall, Lyman		540	1833–37		Jonathan Goldsmith, masterbuilder
Kent, Zenas	383	1369	1858		Thomas & Sons, New York City, architects; William McIntosh, builder
Kerruish, Sheldon Q.	1022	3812			Rented
Kerruish, William S.	1022	3812			
Kimball, Samuel H.	1364	6208			
King, Harry W.	1549	7011			
King, J. A.	1325	5800			
King, Ralph	1949	8625	1910–12		Bought Francis Drury house in mid-1920s
King, Zenas	1161	4719	1852		Built by William Hart; sold to King and rebuilt, 1865–66; then sold to Lester Coe
Kinney, George W.	1980	8820			Owned in 1907
Kirk, Frank Martin	1862	8308			Meade & Garfield, architects; remodeled, 1904
Kitchen, Dr. Henry W.	858	3134	c. 1855–60		Owned in 1907
Latimer, E. J.	1517	6907			Owned in 1907
Laurence, Washington H.			1897		Coburn & Barnum, architects
Lawton, L. C.			1891		Coburn & Barnum, architects
Leek, Talmadge W.	1038	3844	1870–72		
Leonard, Rev. William A.	840	3054	c. 1885–90	1956	Coburn & Barnum, architects
Lincoln, Dr. William R.	2146	9810			Owned in 1907
Little, Bascom	1711	7711			Owned in 1907
Little, Hiram H., M.D. & Laura B.	1699	7615	1881–82		Coburn & Barnum, architects
Lovis, S. E.	1487	6719			
Lyman, M.	561	2605	1851–53		Richard Upjohn, architect
Mabley, Dr. H. Clifton	2088	9408			Owned in 1907
McBride, J. H.	1357	6111	1882		Coburn & Barnum, architects
McBride, Lee	1351	6107	1882		Coburn & Barnum, architects
McClymonds, Miss Mary E.	1910	8510			Owned in 1907

Name	Pre-1906 Address	Post-1906 Address	House Built	House Razed	Comments
McIntosh, Henry P.	1641	7341	1894		Coburn & Barnum, architects; building permit #19628
McKenzie, A. C.	1597	7115	1904		
McMillen, Dr. C.	2128	9700			Owned in 1907
McNairy, Amos B.	909	3333	1887–89	1952	Charles F. Schweinfurth, architect
McWilliams, Rev. Thomas S.	1677	7509			Owned in 1907
Malone, Levi H.	1192	5012	c. 1875		
Marshall, George F.		540	1864	1914	Located at southwest corner of Hickox Alley
Marshall, Dr. Isaac	1010	3738	1872		Sold to Otto Miller
Mason, James	1120	4915	1855–57	1918	Neighbors: Samuel Andrews, J. M. Coe, Edwin B. Hale, Stevenson Burke
Mather, Samuel L. & Elizabeth	383	1369	1858		Built by Zenas Kent
Mather, Samuel & Flora	331	1265			Owned in 1907
	727	2605	1907–12	No	Charles F. Schweinfurth, architect
Mather, William G.	383	1369	1858		Built by Zenas Kent
May, Arthur	1666	7418	1907		Charles Hopkinson, architect
Mayer, Adolph	1593	7111	1898		
Meade, Frank B.	1604	7122			
Merritt, Edward A.	930	3424			
Miller, Otto & Elizabeth C. T.	1010	3738	1904		Rented
Miller, S. J.		7103	1881–82		Joseph Ireland, architect; "colonial & modern English style"
Miller, William L.	1635	7335	1882		Joseph Ireland, architect
Millikin, Dr. B. L.	1781	8021	1884		Owned in 1907
Monroe, Nelson		653	1857–58		Sold to Henry Chisholm
Morgan, Alphonse	1939	8615	1889–90		Coburn & Barnum, architects
Morgan, Edmund P.	583	1784	1859		
Morgan, George W.	1848	8302	1889		Coburn & Barnum, architects; building permit #3177
Morgan, William J. & Emily	1939	8615	1889–90		Coburn & Barnum, architects
Morley, Charles H. & Mary L.	794	2908			
Morse, Thomas W.		865	1840–43		
Moses, Charles W. & Mamie H.	2083	9301	c. 1885–89		Coburn & Barnum, architects
Mueller, Otto	1528	6916	1904		Coburn & Barnum, architects
Murfey, G. A.	894	3248			
Murfey, L. A.	894	3248			
Myer, E. W.	645	2263	c. 1866–70	1929	
Myer, Harry E. & Emily	645	2263	c. 1866–70	1929	
Mygatt, George	799	2921	1858		Mygatt, father of Lucy M. (Mrs. Franklyn T.) Backus
Nash, John	660	2330	1840–50		
Nellis, Alfred W. & Mary L.	864	3146	1869–70	1957	
Norton, David Z.	1631	7301	1897–98		Charles F. Schweinfurth, architect; original drawing at WRHS
	1673	7503	1884–85		[Coburn & Barnum, architects]
Oglebay, Earl W.	505	1815	1866		Built by Ralph A. Harman
	1106	3730	1891		Bought Stewart Chisholm house

Name	Pre-1906 Address	Post-1906 Address	House Built	House Razed	Comments
Oliver, John G.	1874	8318			Owned in 1907
Osborn, Alanson T.	653	2317	c. 1870		
Osborn, Henry C.	1415	6507	1904–8		Page & Corbusier, architects
Osborn, Homer W., M.D.	1555	7017	1892		Building permit #10352
Osborn, William	653	2317	c. 1870		
Osborne, F. M.	1648	7348			
Otis, Charles A., Jr.		2200			Rented
	938	3436	1900		
Otis, Charles A., Sr.	857	3133	1868–72	1933	
Otis, Harrison	1114	4312			
Otis, Harrison Gray	1528	6916			Owned in 1907
Oviatt, O. M.	468	951			
Pack, Charles Lathrop	897	3307	1887–89	1952	Charles F. Schweinfurth, architect
Pack, George W.	897	3307	1887–89	1952	Charles F. Schweinfurth, architect; two additions by Schweinfurth, 1906
Painter, John V. & Lydia E.	704	2508			
Painter, Kenyon V.	716	2536	1896–97		Granger & Meade, architects
Parker, Charles B., M.D.	425	1521	1892		Charles F. Schweinfurth, architect
Parmelee, Helen	832	3036	c. 1865	1952	
Parmelee, James	832	3036	c. 1865	1952	
Parmelee, Robert M. & Helen	832	3036	c. 1865	1952	
Parsons, R. C.		1244	1855		West half of double brick house
Payne, Henry B.	595	2121	1847–49	1947	Charles W. Heard, architect
Payne, Mary (Molly)	595	2121	1847–49	1947	Charles W. Heard, architect
Payne, Oliver	595	2121	1847–49	1947	Charles W. Heard, architect
Pennington, Miss	2030	8936			Owned in 1907
Pennock, I. N.	2062	9204			Owned in 1907
Perkins, Douglas	734	2626	c. 1890		
Perkins, Edwin R.	1775	8011	1891		Building permits #1242, #7051
Perkins, Frederick E.	1487	6800			
Perkins, Jacob	727	2605	1851–53	1905	[Richard Upjohn, architect]
Perkins, Joseph	737	2719	1851–53	1904	Richard Upjohn, New York City, architect; Heard & Porter, builders
Perkins, Roger E.	1527	6900			
Perry, Nathan	611	2157	c. 1830	1959	Jonathan Goldsmith, masterbuilder
Pier, L. J.	1401	6407	c. 1855–60		Owned in 1907
Pope, Alfred A.	992	3648	c. 1895–1900		
Powers, M. F.	1621	7217	1886		
Prentiss, Francis F.	1975	8811	1891–92	1968	Charles F. Schweinfurth, architect
Prentiss, Francis J.	464	1107	c. 1843–45		
Prentiss, Miss Lucretia	921	3407	1898–99		Charles F. Schweinfurth, architect
Prentiss, Samuel B.	464	1107	c. 1843–45		
Price, William Albert	1791	7801	1903		Owned in 1907
Price, William H.	1474	6700	1878–80		
Rainey, William J.	1666	7418	1882	1923	Sold to Myron H. Wilson
Ranney, Charles P.	762	2734	1859		Alterations, 1878
Ranney, Henry C.	772	2816			
Ranney, John R.	768	2802			

Name	Pre-1906 Address	Post-1906 Address	House Built	House Razed	Comments
Ranney, Hon. M. P.	762	2734	1859		Alterations, 1878
Ranney, Rufus P.		2728			
Rattle, William J.	1956	8706			Owned in 1907
Raymond, Samuel A.	1030	3826	1845–50		
Rees, William D., M.D.	972	3612	1902?		Building permit #3624
Reese, E. Shriver	1603	7121			
Rice, Harvey		380	1837–42		East of Opera House
Rice, Percy W.	1812	8126	1894		
Rice, W. L.	1673	7503	1890–91		Building permit #5373
Riddle, J. Q.	2026	8932			Owned in 1907
Rockefeller, John D.	1048	3920	1866–68	1938	Built by Francis C. Keith; Simeon C. Porter, architect
Root, Walter S.	1341	6011			
Rose, Benjamin	634	2240	1870		
Rose, William G.			1875		
Rouse, Edwin C.	489	1208	c. 1840–45		
Rouse, Henry	1030	3826	1866–67		
Rummage, Thomas		424	c. 1832		
Russell, George S.	1541	7003	1863–65		
Sackett, Alexander	1353	6700	1852		
Sackett, L. A.	1353	6700	1852		
Sanders, William B.	845	3111	1858	1930	Rented by W. B. White
	857	3133	1868–72		Charles A. Otis, Sr., house (father-in-law)
Saunders, Arnold C.	1645	7407	1892–94		Charles F. Schweinfurth, architect
Savage, James B.	924	3410	c. 1882–87		
Schofield, William B.		822	c. 1847–50		
Scholey, Mrs. George B.	2132	9706			Owned in 1907
Scott, Martin B.	153	830	1858		West of Ninth Street and Henry Gaylord house
Scoville, Oliver			1840s		
Severance, John L.	1975	8811	1891–92	1968	Charles F. Schweinfurth, architect
Severance, Louis H.	1981	8821	1899–1900		F. S. Barnum & Co., architect
Severance, Mary Long	1981	8821	1899–1900		F. S. Barnum & Co., architect
Severance, Solon L.	1981	8821	1899–1900		F. S. Barnum & Co., architect
Sherwin, Henry A.	1437	6529	1898		F. S. Barnum & Co., architect; J. C. Myers, builder
Sherwin, Nelson B.	1805	8117	1859–60		
Sigler, Lucius M.	1616	7214			Owned in 1907
Smith, Anson		622	1834		Judge Cowles house
	490	1167	1840–42		Sold to Capt. Phillips, then William Harris
Smith, Stiles C.	690	2422			
Snider, Martin	1638	7338			
Southworth, William	696	2432	1835–40		
Southworth, William P. & Louisa		1218	1860–61		Owned in 1907
Spencer, P. M.	1421	6513	c. 1885–90		
Sprankle, J. R.					
Squire, Andrew	933	3443	1895		Charles F. Schweinfurth, architect

Name	Pre-1906 Address	Post-1906 Address	House Built	House Razed	Comments
Squire, Feargus B.	1729	7809	1875		1905 building permit; built by Liberty E. Holden
Stager, Anson	1023	3813	1866	No	Joseph Ireland, architect; remodeled, 1912–14, J. Milton Dyer and Henry H. Walsh, architect
Stair, J. Frank	309	1233			
Stanley, John J.	1885	8411	c. 1893–95		Mead & Granger, architects
Stearns, Frank M.	2187	10023			Owned in 1907
Stephens, J. A., M.D.	1477	6709	1824		Formerly Dunham Tavern
Sterling, Elisha T.		4	1845–46		Warham J. Warner, builder
Sterling, Frederick A.	939	3447	1881		George H. Smith, architect
Sterling, John M.	882	3033	1842–43	1882	Sold to William Bingham, Sr.
Stockley, George W. & Olivia D.	667	2343	1885–86	1926	Levi T. Scofield, architect
Stone, Amasa	514	1255	1858	1910	
Stone, Andros B.		1751	1858		
Streator, Dr. Worthy S.	1511	6903	1864		J. M. Blackburn, architect; J. Slatt, construction superintendent
Streator, Mrs. W. S.	2139	9803			Owned in 1907
Strickland, Benjamin	35	605	1838–39	1893	Built by George Benedict
Sullivan, J. J.	1624	7218			
Swasey, Ambrose	1728	7808	1891–92	1939	Richard Morris Hunt, architect
Taintor, Jesse F.	827	3028	1852		Originally built on Sixth Street, then moved to Euclid Ave. in 1867
Taylor, Alexander S.	1926	8604			Owned in 1907
Taylor, Charles	1588	7106			
Taylor, Virgil C.	1468	6620			
Teagle, John	1890	8418			Owned in 1907
Thomas, John	892	3248			Owned in 1907
Tod, John	696	2430			
Tolles, S. H.	1867	8321			Owned in 1907
Topliff, Isaac N. & Frances A.	1452	6602	c. 1885		
Tracy, James Jared, Jr.	852	3122	1903–4		Charles Hopkinson, architect
Tracy, James Jared, Sr.	309	1225	c. 1855–60		
	947	3535	1904–5	1951	Charles Hopkinson, architect
Treadway, Lyman H.	1421	6513	1891		
	2013	8917	1904		J. Milton Dyer, architect
Tyler, Washington S.	399	1415	1850–60		
Upson, Andrew S.	1612	7208			
Vail, G. I.	1621	7217	1886		
Van Tine, W. H.	1806	8120	1889–91		Clarence Arey, architect
Wade, Jeptha, Sr.	1043	3917	1866	1892	
Wade, Jeptha H., Jr.	1017	3903	1866	1934	
Wade, Randall	1017	3903	1866	1934	
Waite, W. H.	521	1829	1841–42		
Walworth, Ashbel & Mary Ann	516	1836	c. 1839–43		Jonathan Goldsmith, masterbuilder; across Euclid Avenue from T. P. Handy house in 1842
Warner, Worcester R.	1722	7720	1891–92		Richard Morris Hunt, architect

Name	Pre-1906 Address	Post-1906 Address	House Built	House Razed	Comments
Wason, Charles W.	1477	6709	1824	No	Owned in 1907; formerly Dunham Tavern
	2069	9209	1862–63		
Waters, A. J.		8926	1880–82		
Webb, J. W. S.	1424	6514			Owned in 1907
Webster, J. H.	790	2902			Owned in 1907
Weddell, Horace P.	902	3304	1872		
	909	3333	1832–33		Jonathan Goldsmith, masterbuilder
Weddell, Peter M.	909	3333	1832–33		Jonathan Goldsmith, masterbuilder
Welch, George B.	1966	8806	c. 1893–95		Meade & Granger, architect
Wellman, S. T.	1965	8803	1896–97		Coburn & Barnum, architects
Wetmore, Russell C.	1915	8517			Owned in 1907
White, Henry Windsor	2031	8937	1898–1901	No	Frank B. Meade, architect
White, Rollin	1467	6619	c. 1865		1907 remodelling; Frank B. Meade, architect
White, Thomas H.	1840	8220	1883	1951	Owned in 1907
White, William B.	845	3111	1890–95		Hubbell & Benes, architects
Whitehead, W. C.	1183	4915			
Whitelaw, John F.	716	2536	1896–97		Granger & Meade, architects
Whittlesey, Miss Caroline	1599	7119			Owned in 1907
Wick, Dudley Baldwin	848	3112	c. 1865–67	1956	
Wick, Henry C.			1884		Clarence Arey, architect; Harris & Grant, builders
	869	3201	1876	1959	
	945	3515	1904		Meade & Garfield, architects
Wick, Lemuel	472	1051			
Williams, S. T.	1956	8706	1896		Coburn & Barnum, architects
Williams, William	43	723	1835–36	1870	
Williamson, Samuel	5	9	1835–37		
	971	3609	1865–70		Sold to Henry D. Coffinberry
Wilson, Myron H.	1666	7418	1882	1923	Owned in 1907; built by William J. Rainey
Wilson, Thomas	2198	10034	1840–50		
Winslow, Alonzo P.	1419	7102	c. 1860–65	1901	
Winslow, Richard	2	2	1832		Levi Johnson, masterbuilder
Winslow, Rufus K.	681	2409	1878	1926	Levi T. Scofield, architect
Withington, Albert L.	1593	7111	1898		Charles F. Schweinfurth, architect
Witt, Stillman	470	1115	c. 1851–52		[Jonathan Goldsmith, masterbuilder]
Woods, John L.	490	1167			
Woolsey, John M.		1211	1837–38		Jonathan Goldsmith, masterbuilder; two houses east of Twelfth Street; next to Hoadley house
Worthington, George	742	2638	1865–66	1952	Owned in 1907
		3635	1852		
Worthington, George H.	1451	6603	1888		Charles F. Schweinfurth, architect; building permits, 1888 and 1891
Worthington, Ralph	1099	4203	1880		

Name	Pre-1906 Address	Post-1906 Address	House Built	House Razed	Comments
Yates, J. V. N.	766	2744			
York, Barney H. & Julia H.	750	2708	1895		Coburn & Barnum, architects
Younglove, Moses C.	614	1921	1857–58		

Euclid Avenue Residents,
1830–1950
Listed by Address

Name	Pre-1906 Address	Post-1906 Address
Winslow, Richard	2	2
Sterling, Elisha T.		4
Williamson, Samuel	5	9
Dow, Prentiss	25	25
Rice, Harvey		380
Andrews, Sherlock J.	39	400
Harrington, B.		400
Johnson, Jonathan		424
Rummage, Thomas		424
Kendall, Lyman		540
Marshall, George F.		540
Griswold, Judge S. O.	58	580
Benedict, George A.	35	605
Strickland, Benjamin	35	605
Cowles, Samuel	60	622
Smith, Anson		622
Chisholm, Henry & Jean		653
Monroe, Nelson		653
Williams, William	43	723
Crawford, Lemuel		800
Handy, Truman P.		800
Schofield, William B.		822
Scott, Martin B.	153	830
Gaylord, Henry		833
Morse, Thomas W.		865
Oviatt, O. M.	468	951
Banning, Dr. Edmund P.		1020
Wick, Lemuel	472	1051
Prentiss, Francis J.	464	1107
Prentiss, Samuel B.	464	1107

Name	Pre-1906 Address	Post-1906 Address
Bolton, Thomas	468	1111
Cox, Jacob D., Jr.	468	1111
Gardner, George W.	468	1111
Baldwin, Norman	470	1115
Witt, Stillman	470	1115
Harris, Col. William	490	1167
Smith, Anson	490	1167
Woods, John L.	490	1167
Hoadley, George A.		1201
Rouse, Edwin C.	489	1208
Castle, William & Mary		1211
Woolsey, John M.		1211
Southworth, William P. & Louisa		1218
Bingham, Flavel White	122	1220
Tracy, James Jared, Sr.	309	1225
Stair, J. Frank	309	1233
Hay, John	506	1235
Parsons, R. C.		1244
Stone, Amasa	514	1255
Mather, Samuel & Flora	331	1265
Boardman, William J.	522	1303
Fitch, Zalmon	528	1325
Chamberlain, Selah	371	1351
Heisley, Mrs. Mary Dodge	371	1351
Austin, L.	380	1360
Kent, Zenas	383	1369
Mather, Samuel L. & Elizabeth	383	1369
Mather, William G.	383	1369
Clark, James F.	399	1415
Tyler, Washington S.	399	1415
Boardman, Henry W. & Mabel	414	1423
Parker, Charles B., M.D.	425	1521
Dodge, Henry H.	560	1605
Dodge, Samuel	574	1621
Eells, Daniel P.	856	1700
Dodge, George C.		1705
Kelley, Thomas		1723
Hart, William		1725
Fuller, Augustus		1734
Dodge, Lucy A.		1735
Foote, George H.	581	1751
Stone, Andros B.	581	1751
Clark, Albert	540	1760
Morgan, Edmund P.	583	1784
Gillette, Jonathan		1813
Harman, Ralph H.	505	1815
Oglebay, Earl W.	505	1815
Handy, Truman P.	521	1829
Waite, W. H.	521	1829

Name	Pre-1906 Address	Post-1906 Address
Walworth, Ashbel & Mary Ann	516	1836
Gilbert, John A.	535	1911
Younglove, Moses C.	614	1921
Corlett, William T., M.D.	553	1953
Buell, Mrs. A. M.	574	2002
Hurd, Harry	574	2002
Backus, Frederick M. & Nettie E.	578	2044
Bury, Theodore	626	2051
Baldwin, Dudley		2069
Blossom, Dudley S.	595	2121
Dickson, Frederick S.	595	2121
Payne, Henry B.	595	2121
Payne, Mary (Molly)	595	2121
Payne, Oliver	595	2121
Bingham, Charles W.	611	2157
Bingham, William & Elizabeth B.	611	2157
Harkness, W. A.	611	2157
Perry, Nathan	611	2157
Otis, Charles A., Jr.		2200
Avery, Rev. Dr. Frederick B.	634	2240
Rose, Benjamin	634	2240
Howe, George W. & Katharine	642	2248
Myer, E. W.	645	2263
Myer, Harry E. & Emily	645	2263
Chisholm, Mrs. Jean	653	2317
Osborn, Alanson T.	653	2317
Osborn, William	653	2317
Nash, John	660	2330
Johnson, Tom L.	667	2343
Stockley, George W. & Olivia D.	667	2343
Edmondson, George M.	678	2362
Avery, John T.	681	2409
Frasch, Herman	681	2409
Winslow, Rufus K.	681	2409
Abbott, Henry S. & Anna	690	2422
Smith, Stiles C.	690	2422
Tod, John	696	2430
Southworth, William	696	2432
Barnett, James & Maria Underhill	697	2435
Herrick, George E.	697	2435
Bingham, Charles W.	707	2445
Hoyt, James H.	707	2445
Painter, John V. & Lydia E.	704	2508
Devereux, Harry K.	713	2525
French, Julius E.	713	2525
Cooper, George & Druzilla	716	2536
Painter, Kenyon V.	716	2536
Whitelaw, John F.	716	2536
Clark, Mrs. James F.	727	2605

Name	Pre-1906 Address	Post-1906 Address
Lyman, M.	727	2605
Mather, Samuel & Flora S.	727	2605
Perkins, Jacob	727	2605
Burnham, Thomas W.	724	2606
Greenough, Malcolm S.	724	2606
Brown, Alexander E.	734	2626
Brown, Henry H.	734	2626
Perkins, Douglas	734	2626
Hall, Orlando	742	2638
Worthington, George	742	2638
York, Barney H. & Julia H.	750	2708
Hanna, Leonard C.	737	2717
Perkins, Joseph	737	2719
Brown, Harvey H.	757	2727
Hickox, Charles	757	2727
Billings, Frank	758	2728
Ranney, Rufus P.	758	2728
Ranney, Charles P.	762	2734
Ranney, Hon. M. P.	762	2734
Yates, J. V. N.	766	2744
Hathaway Brown School	768	2802
Ranney, John R.	768	2802
Canfield, C. E.	770	2808
Clark, Henry F.	770	2808
Ranney, Henry C.	772	2816
Benedict, Edwin G. & Philena O.	780	2824
Chisholm, William, Sr., & Mary Stone	779	2827
Drake, Francis E.	779	2827
Andrews, Samuel	789	2843
Authwaite	789	2843
Bingham, William & Elizabeth B.	789	2843
Brayton, Charles A.	789	2843
Webster, J. H.	790	2902
Morley, Charles H. & Mary L.	794	2908
Backus, Franklyn T. & Lucy Mygatt	799	2921
Mygatt, George	799	2921
Bulkley, Charles H.	802	2926
Bulkley, R. J.	802	2926
Bingham, Charles E. & Isabella	826	3028
Taintor, Jesse F.	826	3028
Andrews, Horace	882	3033
Andrews, Samuel	882	3033
Bingham, William, Sr.	882	3033
Sterling, John M.	882	3033
Collister, Lucas W.	832	3036
De Maeyers, Kate	832	3036
Parmelee, Helen	832	3036
Parmelee, James	832	3036
Parmelee, Robert M. & Helen	832	3036

Name	Pre-1906 Address	Post-1906 Address
Leonard, Rev. William A.	840	3054
Crocker, Timothy D. & Eliza Otis	845	3111
Sanders, William B.	845	3111
White, William B.	845	3111
Cottingham, Walter H.	848	3112
Hoyt, George	848	3112
Wick, Dudley Baldwin	848	3112
Colwell, Joseph	852	3122
Tracy, James Jared, Jr.	852	3122
Otis, Charles A., Sr.	857	3133
Sanders, William B.	857	3133
Hubby, Lester M.	858	3134
Kitchen, Dr. Henry W.	858	3134
Hall, George	864	3146
Nellis, Alfred W. & Mary L.	864	3146
Corning, Miss Olive	869	3201
Corning, Warren H. & Helen	869	3201
Eells, Daniel P.	869	3201
Wick, Henry C.	869	3201
Blair, John	874	3210
Briggs, Charles E.	874	3210
Brown, Fayette	874	3210
Devereux, John H. & Antoinette	882	3226
Carlin, Anthony & Mary	885	3233
Hurlbut, Hinman B. & Jane E.	885	3233
Grandin, J. Wilbert	890	3244
Murfey, G. A.	894	3248
Murfey, L. A.	894	3248
Thomas, John	892	3248
Weddell, Horace P.	902	3304
Pack, Charles Lathrop	897	3307
Pack, George W.	897	3307
McNairy, Amos B.	909	3333
Weddell, Horace P.	909	3333
Weddell, Peter M.	909	3333
Prentiss, Miss Lucretia	921	3407
Savage, James B.	924	3410
Cox, Jacob D., Jr.	925	3411
Hussey, Joseph G.	925	3411
Merritt, Edward A.	930	3424
Otis, Charles A., Jr.	938	3436
Squire, Andrew	933	3443
Sterling, Frederick A.	939	3447
Bailey, T. C. & E. B.	946	3450
Clark, Robert H.	946	3450
Kelley, Irad		3500
Wick, Henry C.	945	3515
Tracy, James J., Sr.	947	3535
Boardman, William H.	950	3608

Name	Pre-1906 Address	Post-1906 Address
Gowan, Caleb	950	3608
Coffinberry, Henry D.	971	3609
Williamson, Samuel	971	3609
Rees, William D., M.D.	972	3612
Chisholm, William, Jr.	962	3618
Corlett, William T., M.D.	962	3618
Harkness, William L.	984	3634
Hoyt, James M.	984	3634
Worthington, George		3635
Pope, Alfred A.	992	3648
Garretson, George	1000	3716
Garretson, Hiram & Ellen	1000	3716
Brush, Charles F.	1003	3725
Flagler, Henry	1003	3725
Chisholm, Stewart H.	1006	3730
Oglebay, Earl W.	1006	3730
Collins, G. E.	1010	3738
Marshall, Dr. Isaac	1010	3738
Miller, Otto & Elizabeth C. T.	1010	3738
Kerruish, Sheldon Q.	1022	3812
Kerruish, William S.	1022	3812
Beckwith, T. Sterling	1023	3813
Stager, Anson	1023	3813
Raymond, Samuel A.	1030	3826
Rouse, Henry	1030	3826
Britton, Bertram	1038	3844
Ellison, Henry C.	1038	3844
Leek, Talmadge W.	1038	3844
Wade, Jeptha H., Jr.	1017	3903
Wade, Randall	1017	3903
Wade, Jeptha, Sr.	1043	3917
Rockefeller, John D.	1048	3920
Breed, Rev. Walter R.	1090	4108
Barnes, O. M.	1089	4111
Everett, Sylvester T.	1089	4111
Hodge, Judge Orlando J. & Virginia	1096	4120
Hale, Willis B.	1100	4200
Del Prado Hotel	1099	4203
Ely, George H.	1099	4203
Worthington, Ralph	1099	4203
Johnson, George J.	1110	4220
Chapin, Herman	1113	4307
Hale, Cleveland C.	1113	4307
Hale, Edwin B.	1113	4307
Hale, Edwin V.	1113	4307
Brooks, Thomas H.	1114	4312
Otis, Harrison	1114	4312
Baley, William	1144	4560
Clark, B. H.	1144	4560

Name	Pre-1906 Address	Post-1906 Address
Harvey, Edward F.	1150	4608
Bissell, Charles S. & Cynthia	1151	4611
Blann, A. W.	1160	4712
Cushing, Edward H., M.D.	1160	4712
Coe, Lester M.	1161	4719
King, Zenas	1161	4719
Burke, Stevenson & Ella M.	1171	4811
Alcott, Franklyn L.	1176	4820
Burke, Edmund S., Jr.	1183	4915
Mason, James	1183	4915
Whitehead, W. C.	1183	4915
Gill, Charles H.	1190	5004
Malone, Levi H.	1192	5012
Crumb, C. A.		5415
Cobb, Ralph	1272	5526
King, J. A.	1325	5800
De Klyn, Charles F.	1309	5809
Root, Walter S.	1341	6011
McBride, Lee	1351	6107
McBride, J. H.	1357	6111
Cobb, Ralph	1361	6203
Kimball, Samuel H.	1364	6208
Cobb, Lester A.	1369	6211
Bradley, Alvah	1378	6218
Cobb, Ahira	1379	6305
Pier, L. J.	1401	6407
Dangler, Charles I.	1415	6505
Osborn, Henry C.	1415	6507
Harkness, Stephen V.	1420	6508
Hobbs, Perry L., M.D.	1420	6508
Spencer, P. M.	1421	6513
Treadway, Lyman H.	1421	6513
Webb, J. W. S.	1424	6514
Arthur, P. M.	1429	6521
Sherwin, Henry A.	1437	6529
Briggs, Pierson D.	1440	6530
Topliff, Isaac N. & Frances A.	1452	6602
Worthington, George H.	1451	6603
Horner, B. F.	1461	6611
White, Rollin	1467	6619
Taylor, Virgil C.	1468	6620
Baxter, Harris H., M.D.	1474	6700
Price, William H.	1474	6700
Sackett, Alexander	1474	6700
Sackett, L. A.	1474	6700
Dunham, Rufus	1477	6709
Stephens, J. A., M.D.	1477	6709
Wason, Charles W.	1477	6709
Lovis, S. E.	1487	6719

Name	Pre-1906 Address	Post-1906 Address
Johnson, Mrs. Philander E.	1490	6720
Perkins, Frederick E.	1500	6800
Everett, Charles & Fannie	1499	6801
Everett, Henry A.	1499	6801
Hayes, Harry E.	1500	6810
Bourne, Benjamin F.	1501	6813
Cowing, John P.	1501	6813
Hale, Edwin V.	1501	6813
Perkins, Roger E.	1527	6900
Gundry, John M.	1511	6903
Streator, Dr. Worthy S.	1511	6903
Ingersoll, J. A.	1517	6907
Latimer, E. J.	1517	6907
Kelley, Franklin	1518	6908
Kelley, Moses	1518	6908
Hale, John C.	1520	6910
Burton, J. Prescott	1524	6912
Hannon, J. E.	1524	6912
Mueller, Otto	1528	6916
Otis, Harrison Gray	1528	6916
Russell, George S.	1541	7003
King, Harry W.	1549	7011
Bolton, Charles C.	1554	7016
Giddings, Charles M.	1554	7016
Osborn, Homer W., M.D.	1555	7017
Goulder, H. D.	1561	7023
Auld, David, Jr.	1567	7029
Bolton, Thomas	1560	7030
Crow, David	1572	7032
Andrews, Mrs. Upson A.	1573	7033
Hubby, Lester M.		7040
Winslow, Alonzo P.	1419	7102
Miller, S. J.		7103
Taylor, Charles	1588	7106
Mayer, Adolph	1593	7111
Withington, Albert L.	1593	7111
Holcomb, James W.	1597	7115
McKenzie, A. C.	1597	7115
Whittlesey, Miss Caroline	1599	7119
Reese, E. Shriver	1603	7121
Bradford, William & Mary S.	1604	7122
Gilbert, N. A.	1604	7122
Meade, Frank B.	1604	7122
Upson, Andrew S.	1612	7208
Sigler, Lucius M.	1616	7214
Bradley, Morris A.	1621	7217
Gund, George F.	1621	7217
Powers, M. F.	1621	7217
Vail, G. I.	1621	7217

Name	Pre-1906 Address	Post-1906 Address
Hall, Orlando	1624	7218
Sullivan, J. J.	1624	7218
Haserot, Samuel F.	1630	7224
Castle, William & Mary	1631	7301
Norton, David Z.	1631	7301
Miller, William L.	1635	7335
Snider, Martin	1638	7338
Christian, George B.	1641	7341
McIntosh, Henry P.	1641	7341
Osborne, F. M.	1648	7348
Hanna, Dan R.	1650	7404
Hord, A. C.	1650	7404
Hord, John H.	1650	7404
Saunders, Arnold C.	1645	7407
May, Arthur	1666	7418
Rainey, William J.	1666	7418
Wilson, Myron H.	1666	7418
Blandin, Judge & Mrs. E. J.	1673	7503
Ivison, William C.	1673	7503
Norton, David Z.	1673	7503
Rice, W. L.	1673	7503
McWilliams, Rev. Thomas S.	1677	7509
Burry, John W.	1684	7514
Childs, Edwin D.	1685	7601
Jones, Wyndham C.	1692	7608
Allen, Luther & Julia B.	1695	7609
Little, Hiram H., M.D. & Laura B.	1699	7615
Little, Bascom	1711	7711
Warner, Worcester R.	1722	7720
Price, William Albert	1791	7801
Swasey, Ambrose	1728	7808
Bigelow, J. J.	1729	7809
Holden, Liberty	1729	7809
Squire, Feargus B.	1729	7809
Britton, Joseph W.	1737	7817
Holcomb, James W.	1737	7817
Hale, John C.	1749	7901
Horwitz, Henry D.	1755	7911
Fanning, M. A.	1759	7913
Jennings, Gilbert P.		8010
Perkins, Edwin R.	1775	8011
Boynton, Judge W. W.	1781	8021
Millikin, Dr. B. L.	1781	8021
Corrigan, Capt. James	1800	8114
Foster, Arthur B.	1800	8114
Sherwin, Nelson B.	1805	8117
Elliott, Dalls	1806	8120
Van Tine, W. H.	1806	8120
Rice, Percy W.	1812	8126

Name	Pre-1906 Address	Post-1906 Address
Chadwick, Leroy S. & Cassie	1824	8204
White, Thomas H.	1840	8220
Janes, Lorenzo	1845	8221
Jaynes, Hylas	1845	8221
Morgan, George W.	1848	8302
Kirk, Frank Martin	1862	8308
Oliver, John G.	1874	8318
Tolles, S. H.	1867	8321
Hobart, M. M.	1878	8402
Stanley, John J.	1885	8411
Hatch, Henry K.	1895	8415
Teagle, John	1890	8418
McClymonds, Miss Mary E.	1910	8510
Wetmore, Russell C.	1915	8517
Arter, Frank A.	1922	8522
Taylor, Alexander S.	1926	8604
Ammon, Josephine	1939	8615
Cotton, Edwin A.	1939	8615
Morgan, Alphonse	1939	8615
Morgan, William J. & Emily	1939	8615
Barrett, J. Lawrence	1948	8624
Drury, Francis E.	1949	8625
King, Ralph	1949	8625
Canfield, Charles G.	1952	8628
Babcock, Charles	1961	8705
Rattle, William J.	1956	8706
Williams, S. T.	1956	8706
Wellman, S. T.	1965	,8803
Hunt, Edward P. & Mary	1964	8804
Welch, George B.	1966	8806
Allen, Dudley P., M.D.	1975	8811
Prentiss, Francis F.	1975	8811
Severance, John L.	1975	8811
Kinney, George W.	1980	8820
Severance, Louis H.	1981	8821
Severance, Mary Long	1981	8821
Severance, Solon L.	1981	8821
Adams, Ira	1999	8903
Bierce, George	1999	8903
Bishop, Horace A.	1999	8903
Babcock, W. A.	2010	8914
Treadway, Lyman	2013	8917
Waters, A. J.		8926
Riddle, J. Q.	2026	8932
Adams, E. E.	2029	8935
Pennington, Miss	2030	8936
White, Henry Windsor	2031	8937
Dennis, H. D.	2045	9007
Chisholm, H. A.	2055	9107

Name	Pre-1906 Address	Post-1906 Address
Pennock, I. N.	2062	9204
Wason, Charles W.	2069	9209
Moses, Charles W. & Mamie H.	2083	9301
Bailey, Daniel K.	2084	9304
Blee, Miss	2084	9304
Grigg, T. Joshua	2089	9400
Mabley, Dr. H. Clifton	2088	9408
Ford, H. C.	2089	9409
Ford, O. D.	2089	9409
Joseph, M.	2089	9409
Christian, George B.	2097	9501
Doan, E. W.	2102	9506
McMillen, Dr. C.	2128	9700
Scholey, Mrs. George B.	2132	9706
Streator, Mrs. W. S.	2139	9803
Lincoln, Dr. William R.	2146	9810
Chandler, Harrison T.	2173	10007
Christy, Henry C.	2186	10022
Stearns, Frank M.	2187	10023
Wilson, Thomas	2198	10034
Griffith, Dr. Harry Means	2203	10105
Ford, Mrs. F. L.	2220	10302

Notes

Prologue
Cleveland's Grand Avenue

1. Published anonymously as a serial in *Century* magazine in 1883 and 1884, *The Bread-Winners'* authorship was privately acknowledged by and publicly credited to Euclid Avenue resident John Hay.
2. Anthony Trollope, *North America*, 162, 167.
3. Robert A. Wheeler, *"Pleasantly Situated on the West Side."*
4. William Ganson Rose, *Cleveland: The Making of a City*, 57, 83, 86.
5. Rose, 334; *Cleveland as It Is*, 102–34. Randall P. Wade to Jeptha H. Wade, Mar. 11, 1867, Cleveland, Jeptha Homer Wade Family Papers.
6. United States Department of Commerce, Bureau of the Census, *1890 Report on Manufacturing Industries in the U.S.*, 154–62.
7. *Leader*, July 16, 1866.
8. *Leader*, Feb. 29, 1872.
9. *Leader;* Nov. 6, 1873; Mar. 24, 28, 30, 1874; John Hay to Henry Adams, May 28, 1888, Cleveland, in John Hay, *Letters of John Hay.*
10. George R. Stewart, *American Place Names*, 158; Warren Uphan, *Minnesota Geographic Names*, 424.

Chapter One
From Buffalo Stage Road to Village "Frog Pond," 1816–1860

1. Rose, 38.
2. Rose, 75; Samuel P. Orth, ed., *History of Cleveland, Ohio* 1: 51; Stewart, 158.
3. Edmund H. Chapman, *Cleveland: Village to Metropolis*, 5; Walter A. Peters, *Names of Cleveland and Vicinity*, 10.
4. *Herald*, Feb. 3, 4, 1827; *Cleveland Press*, Jan. 18, 1917; WPA Records, Ohio Historic Records Survey, Historic Sites of Cleveland Records, Dunham Tavern; Rose, 128.
5. "Notes on Capital Investment in Cuyahoga Roads and Bridges, 1810–1927," vol. 30, p. 267, Clarence H. Hutchinson Papers (primarily his records gathered under auspices of Ohio Historical Records Survey, Works Progress Administration); Rose, 117.
6. Gertrude Van Rensselaer Wickham, *The Pioneer Families of Cleveland, 1796–1840* 2:530. The eastern edge of the village was at Ninth Street, and the corporation limit was at Fourteenth Street.

7. Samuel Dodge received the land from Samuel Huntington, later Ohio's governor, as compensation for building Huntington a frame barn on Superior. The land extended 325 feet along Euclid and north to the lake. Dodge had come to Cleveland from New Hampshire in 1797 and married Nancy Doan in 1803, the daughter of Timothy and Mary Doan. Dodge's residence was razed in 1853 when Seventeenth (Dodge) Street was laid out; S. J. Kelly, *Cleveland Plain Dealer*, Mar. 18, 1937; Aug. 9, 28, 1938; Maurice Joblin, comp., *Cleveland, Past and Present: Its Representative Men*, 220; *Leader*, Oct. 4, 1854.
8. Randall Wade to Jeptha H. Wade II, May 1875, Cleveland; Crisfield Johnson, *History of Cuyahoga County, Ohio*, 243.
9. *City Council Journal D, 1845–48*, Apr. 14, 1847, 237, Cleveland City Council Archives; *City Council Journal F, 1852–57*, July 22, 1852, 62; *Daily True Democrat*, Jan. 12, 1853; Rose, 261; *Ordinance Book A, 1836–57*, Jan. 7, 1851, 176, Mar. 22, 1852, 264.
10. *Herald*, Aug. 8, 1846; Wickham, 1:243; W. R. Rose, *Plain Dealer*, Sept. 27, 1926; *Leader*, Nov. 1, 7, 1855.
11. *Cleveland City Council Journal A, 1836–38*, 56, 247, 259, 328; *Herald and Gazette*, Oct. 19, 1837; *Ordinance Book A, 1836–57*, 60; *City Council Journal B, 1838–40*, 10, 149, 329; Rose, 173.
12. Rose, 187, 220, 241.
13. *City Council Journal E, 1848–52*, July 20, 27, 1848, 29, 31; *City Council Journal F, 1852–54*, Mar. 26, 1852, 7.
14. *Leader*, Aug. 4, Sept. 6, Dec. 5, 1855.
15. *Leader*, June 17, 25, Nov. 4, 1857; May 12, June 17, 1858; Sept. 7, Dec. 21, 1859; Rose, 261, 289; *Cleveland News*, Sept. 23, 1926.
16. *Leader*, May 6, Sept. 1, 1863; May 2, Aug. 14, Nov. 7, 1867; Nov. 26, 1868; Oct. 20, 1869; S. J. Kelly, *Plain Dealer*, Aug. 3, 1943.

Chapter Two
The Finest Avenue in the West, 1860–1875

1. *Leader*, June 25, 1857; May 5, 1858.
2. *Leader*, June 26, 1857; Jan. 27, 1858; July 20, 1866; *New York World*, May 25, 1863, reprint, *Plain Dealer*, June 13, 1946.
3. Trollope, *North America*, 166; Mark Twain to *Alta, California*, reprint in *Leader*, Dec. 19, 1868.
4. *Leader*, May 24, 1865; June 6, Sept. 3, 1870; Oct. 29, Nov. 5, 1873.

5. *Leader,* Dec. 27, 1859; June 5, 1868; *Plain Dealer,* Nov. 1, 11, 1859; Apr. 30, 1862.

6. *Leader,* Oct. 28, 1864; Jan. 1, 1870.

7. *Leader,* Feb. 16, 1861; Apr. 29, May 1, 1865.

8. *Leader,* Jan. 10, 1867; Dec. 28, 1868; Charles Asa Post, *Those Were the Days,* 14–58.

9. *Leader,* Dec. 16, 1868; Post, 19–36, 70; *Cleveland Press,* Aug. 29, 1931; Nov. 2, 1978.

10. Diary, H. K. Devereux, Jan. 12, 13, 1886, Cleveland, Devereux Family Papers.

11. Samuel L. Mather to Samuel Mather, Jan. 13, 1873, Cleveland to Berlin, Samuel Mather Family Papers; *City Council Proceedings,* Jan. 12, 1885, Cleveland City Council Archives; Mary Emma (Betts) Sterling, Jan. 30, 31, 1881, Mary Emma (Betts) Sterling Diaries.

12. Rose, 261, 278; *Leader,* Mar. 15, Dec. 7, 1859; S. J. Kelly, *Plain Dealer,* July 30, 1937.

13. Rose, 318; *Leader,* Aug. 7, 1860; Apr. 24, 1862; Warren Corning Wick, *My Recollections of Old Cleveland,* 88.

14. Wick, 88; *Leader,* editorial, Sept. 10, 1867.

15. S. Frederick Starr, "St. Charles Avenue, New Orleans," Sept. 1989.

16. *Cleveland City Directory,* 1848–49, 1850–51; Rose, 205–6; *Daily True Democrat,* May 21, 1849; Eric Johannesen, "Charles W. Heard," 130–42; Eric Johannesen, "Simeon Porter: Ohio Architect," 177; *Leader,* Apr. 14, 1858; Apr. 20, 1874; Rose, 398.

17. *Leader,* Apr. 3, 1855; Mar. 10, 1859; *Cleveland City Directory,* 1852–53; Rose, 258.

18. *Leader,* Oct. 3, 1868; Apr. 25, June 14, 1869; Oct. 16, 1871; June 29, Nov. 21, 1872; Dec. 14, 1874; S. J. Kelly, *Plain Dealer,* Feb. 19, 1938; Rose, 182.

19. *Leader,* Jan. 1, June 26, Dec. 10, 1855; Dec. 6, Aug. 15, 1856; Aug. 29, 1857; Aug. 7, 1858; *Plain Dealer,* June 3, 1917.

20. Rose, 364, 371; *Leader,* July 4, 1874.

21. *Leader,* Sept. 17, 1872; Aug. 16, 1873; Sept. 6, 1875; S. J. Kelly, *Plain Dealer,* Feb. 14, 1939; Rose, 405.

22. *Leader,* Mar. 3, Dec. 4, 1875; Rose, 406.

23. *Plain Dealer,* Aug. 8, 1874.

24. *Leader,* editorial, Feb. 29, 1872; W. Scott Robison, ed., *History of the City of Cleveland,* 156.

Chapter Three
Urban Townhouses and Country Villas, 1830–1865

1. *Cleveland City Directory,* 1837–38, 1845–46.

2. Frank Barnum, "Architecture," 470.

3. Elizabeth G. Hitchcock, *Jonathan Goldsmith: Pioneer Master Builder of the Western Reserve,* 3, 7, 10.

4. Goldsmith also dabbled in other enterprises. One ill-fated venture centered around his design and patent for a multiple-blade plow. In 1839–40 he took the plow down to New Orleans, where his son Gillett was an architect, to sell and was instead offered 6,000 acres in Texas by General Sam Houston if he stayed to practice architecture. Goldsmith declined the offer and returned to his successful Painesville and Cleveland practices.

5. Talbot Hamlin, *Greek Revival Architecture in America,* 282–83.

6. Wickham, 1:230; Hitchcock, 75.

7. Hitchcock, 75 n. 19.

8. *Plain Dealer,* Sept. 27, 1926; Rose, 186; Hitchcock, 75, 76. *Daily True Democrat,* Feb. 22, 1850.

9. Hitchcock, 71 n. 4.

10. Hitchcock, 80.

11. Rose, 288–89; Grace Goulder, *John D. Rockefeller: The Cleveland Years,* 47.

12. Hitchcock, 78; *Leader,* Sept. 24, 1872.

13. Dunham Tavern, 6709 Euclid Avenue, was originally built in 1824 as a log structure and rebuilt in 1842 as a two-story frame lodge, designed in the Greek Revival manner. U.S. Works Progress Administration, Writers' Program, comp., *The Ohio Guide,* 235–36.

14. See John R. Stilgoe, *Borderland: Origins of the American Suburb, 1820–1939,* 105–10; S. J. Kelly, *Plain Dealer,* Feb. 28, Mar. 4, 5, 10, 1942; Wickham, 2:483; C. L. Kirkpatrick, *Plain Dealer,* Apr. 24, 1921; Rose, 49. The Bolton and Kelley seventy-two-acre property was subsequently divided and sold as five separate house lots.

15. Barnum, 470; *Daily True Democrat,* Mar. 10, 1849.

16. The Payne residence remained in the family for almost a quarter-century after the senator's death in 1896 and was home first to his daughter Mary and her husband Charles W. Bingham, then to their daughters Frances Payne Bingham and Elizabeth and her husband Dudley Blossom.

17. *Dictionary of American Biography,* vol. 7:325–26; Orth, 1:564.

18. *Cleveland City Directory,* 1857, 1858, 1859. Edwin V. Hale, son of E. B. Hale, maintained his father's estate and the family home for years after his parents' deaths. *Leader,* July 10, 1891; *Plain Dealer,* July 10, 1891; Nov. 4, 1904.

19. Richard Upjohn Collection, Joseph Perkins Residence, 1851–53, Original Drawings, (Plans, Oct. 21, 1851–Aug. 11, 1853), Letters (Jan. 27, 1851–Feb. 21, 1853). Upjohn designed Joseph's house, and he is believed to be the architect of Jacob's as well, given their similarities and the fact that the houses were built at the same time. Everard M. Upjohn, *Richard Upjohn: Architect and Churchman,* 128, 200–201.

20. Joseph Perkins account books, Simon Perkins Papers; Joblin, 123.

21. Rose, 250; Mrs. W. A. Ingham, *Women of Cleveland and Their Work,* 183, 189.

22. Ohio was the leading U.S. manufacturer and shipper of clay-brick and pottery products in the late nineteenth century, accounting for 90 to 95 percent of the U.S. industry as measured by the value of products. See *Ohio Architect, Engineer & Builder* 4, no. 2 (Aug. 1904):24.

23. *Leader,* Oct. 12, 1855.

24. See the WPA Records, Ohio Historic Records Survey, Historic Sites of Cleveland Records, Hinman Hurlbut House.

25. Stilgoe, 107–10; *Leader,* Sept. 19, 1859.

26. *Leader,* Apr. 6, 1858.

27. S. J. Kelly, *Plain Dealer,* Mar. 16, 1938; Sept. 12, 1960.

28. *Leader,* Jan. 28, 1858. The prevalence of house fires during the nineteenth century was the chief motivation for instituting building codes in Cleveland in 1888.

29. Telegram, Prof. George J. Bush to Amasa Stone, Jr., June 27, 1865, Yale College, New Haven, Samuel Mather Family Papers.

30. *Plain Dealer,* Jan. 17, 1877; May 12, 1883; Van Tassel and Grabowski, *The Encyclopedia of Cleveland History,* 762–63; Burton Smith Dow III, "Amasa Stone, Jr.: His Triumph and Tragedy," 62–81; Patricia O'Toole, *The Five of Hearts,* 57–58.

31. James F. Ryder to Flora S. Mather, Nov. 22, 1902, 3586 Euclid Avenue; Ella Grant Wilson, *Famous Old Euclid Avenue of Cleveland* 1:120; Rose, 114.

32. Randall P. Wade to Anna Wade, Dec. 18, 1866, Cleveland; J. H. Wade to R. P. Wade, Apr. 2, 1856, Cleveland; R. P. Wade to J. H. Wade, May 10, Oct. 5, 1866, Cleveland.

33. R. P. Wade to J. H. Wade, Sept. 20, 1866, Cleveland; William M. Milliken, *A Time Remembered*, 22; *Cleveland Press*, Oct. 16, 1934.

34. R. P. Wade to J. H. Wade, Sept. 20, 23, Oct. 5, 9, 1866, Cleveland; *Plain Dealer*, July 15, 1878.

35. Jeptha H. Wade, "Sketch of the Life of Jeptha Homer Wade, from 1811–1867," July 1, 1889, was written for J. Homer Wade II, and the original was in the Guardian Trust Company vault.

36. Rose, 374; Jeptha Homer Wade Family Papers.

37. Winsor French, *Cleveland Press*, May 23, 1950.

38. Coburn & Barnum, "Some Selections from the Work of Coburn & Barnum, Architects"; Cleveland Architectural Club, *Annual Exhibition Catalogue*; Ivy Edmondson Starr, interview with author, Princeton, New Jersey, Apr. 14, 1988.

Chapter Four
The Great Age of the Grand Avenue

1. Karl Baedeker, ed., *The United States, with an Excursion into Mexico: A Handbook for Travellers*, 268.

2. John Fiske, *American Political Ideas Viewed from the Standpoint of Universal History*, 14.

3. *Cleveland City Directory*, 1845–46; 1859–60.

4. J. H. Wade to R. P. Wade, Sept. 10, 1870, Cleveland; *Leader*, Mar. 29, 1871; *City Council Journal P*, May 28, July 9, 1883.

5. *London Standard*, reprint, *Leader*, Nov. 7, 1865; Van Tassel and Grabowski, *Encyclopedia*, 415.

6. Stilgoe, 11.

7. Artemus Ward, 1860, reprint, W. R. Rose, *Plain Dealer*, Nov. 27, 1914.

8. *Leader*, Aug. 16, 1855; Apr. 28, 30, 1874. See Mark Girouard, *Cities & People*, 286–91, 170–89.

9. The intent of some Euclid Avenue residents to create assets that would be inherited by their children and grandchildren is noted in letters and diaries of these families, as well as spoken about frequently by descendants in interviews with the author.

10. Diary, John Henry Devereux, 1873; Diary, Antoinette Devereux, 1873; Letterbook, Charles F. Brush, 1887, Charles Francis Brush Papers; Letters between Jeptha H. Wade and Randall P. Wade, Mar.–Oct. 1866.

Chapter Five
Post–Civil War Grandeur, 1865–1885

1. Young, 1.

2. Trollope, 166–67.

3. Barnum, 1:473.

4. Hay, *The Bread-Winners*, 66.

5. *Leader*, Aug. 27, 1864; Joblin, 318.

6. *Plain Dealer*, Mar. 21, 1866; W. R. Rose, *Plain Dealer*, Nov. 5, 1923; S. J. Kelly, *Plain Dealer*, Sept. 25, 1937; Lease, J. D. Rockefeller to Miss Augusta Mittleberger and Cornelia Blakemore, Sept. 1, 1880, Worcester R. Warner Papers. Rockefeller moved the corner house one block down Fortieth Street to Prospect and leased it to Miss Augusta Mittleberger and Cornelia Blakemore for their private girls' school.

7. Allan Nevins, *A Study in Power: John D. Rockefeller*, 267.

8. *New York Times*, Mar. 13, 1915; Nevins, 36–37; *Plain Dealer*, Mar. 21, 1866.

9. Edward Merritt to Myron T. Herrick, June 21, 1912, Cleveland, Myron Timothy Herrick Papers.

10. *Plain Dealer*, Sept. 17, 1972; Worcester R. Warner to John D. Rockefeller, Sept. 16, 1905, Cleveland, Warner & Swasey Papers; Charles Augustus Otis, *Here I Am: A Rambling Account of the Exciting Times of Yesteryear*, 115–17; John D. Rockefeller to Chamber of Commerce members, Jan. 24, 1906, New York, in Otis, 117; *Cleveland Press*, Jan. 29, 1938.

11. *Leader*, Nov. 27, 1867.

12. *Plain Dealer*, Mar. 21, 1866; Rose, 298.

13. R. P. Wade to J. H. Wade, Sept. 16, Oct. 11, 1866.

14. *Leader*, Oct. 17, 1874; S. J. Kelly, *Plain Dealer*, Nov. 16, 1938.

15. Rose, 201; *Leader*, Mar. 27, 1876; Wick, 76–77; Rose, 589; Mary Peale Schofield, "Working File of Cleveland Architects of the Late 19th and Early 20th Centuries."

16. Diary, A. K. Devereux, Mar. 1, 1873, Cleveland; Wade Family Papers; *Leader*, July 27, 1878.

17. See Neil Harris, "Louis Comfort Tiffany: The Search For Influence," in Alastair Duncan et al., *Masterworks of Louis Comfort Tiffany*, 14–42; Marilynn Johnson, "The Artful Interior," Doreen Bolger Burke et al., *In Pursuit of Beauty: Americans and the Aesthetic Movement*, 110–41. For specific references see John Hay to Flora Stone, Feb. 26, 1876, and Flora Mather to Samuel Mather, Apr. 21, 1884; Letter, Charles F. Brush to Herter Brothers, Apr. 6, 1887, Cleveland, Letter-book, 49–54; and Brush to Tiffany Glass Co., Apr. 8, 1887, Letter-book, 57.

18. John Hay to Whitelaw Reid, June 3, 1875, William Roscoe Thayer, *The Life and Letters of John Hay* 1:390.

19. Approximately two-thirds of the builders and carpenters working in Cleveland and on Euclid Avenue in the 1870s and 1880s were foreign immigrants from Scotland, Germany, England, and Austria; *Cleveland City Directory*, 1870, 1880; U.S. Census of Population, 1870, 1880.

20. "Informal Reminiscences of Clarence Hay," John Hay Papers; *Plain Dealer*, Oct. 15, 1983; *Ohio Architect, Engineer & Builder* 4, no. 1 (Jan. 1907): 50.

21. John Hay to Flora Stone, Feb. 26, Aug. 14, 1876, July 10, 1877, Cleveland; Richard Morris Hunt to John Hay, Apr. 7, 1873, New York.

22. J. Hay to F. Stone, Aug. 16, 1877, Cleveland.

23. J. Hay to F. Stone, Aug. 14, 1876, Cleveland. See Barnum, 473; Wick, 36; Wilson 2:8; *Leader*, Nov. 14, 1876.

24. Rose, 449.

25. Rose, 548, 564; "Dan P. Eells . . . account of his life," 1895, Cleveland, Howard P. Eells, Jr., Family Papers.

26. Wilson, 2:12; *Cleveland Press*, Apr. 13, 1959.

27. Rose, 523; Wick, 31: Ralph J. Donaldson, "Untold Tales About Politicians and Newspapermen," 63–64.

28. See Lincoln Steffens, *The Struggle for Self-Government*, 183. Carl Lorenz, *Tom L. Johnson, Mayor of Cleveland*, 126.

Chapter Six
The Age of Robust Prosperity, 1880–1895

1. Diary, Mary Emma Betts Sterling, 1881, undated entry, inside back cover.
2. Carol Hull, "Register," Mary Emma (Betts) Sterling Diaries, May 1971.
3. Nevins, 22–23; Tom Barensfeld, *Cleveland Press,* Dec. 17, 1977.
4. *Cleveland Town Topics,* June 23, 1923; Winsor French, *Cleveland Press,* May 13, 1950.
5. WPA Records, Apr. 3, 1941; *Plain Dealer,* Feb. 28, 1960.
6. "The Architectural Conference," *The Builder* (July 27, 1874), 538.
7. Wilson, 1:64; *National Cyclopedia of American Biography* 9:172.
8. *National Cyclopedia of American Biography* 9:172; *World's History of Cleveland,* 404–6; *Plain Dealer,* Apr. 4, 1931.
9. Vincent Scully, *The Shingle Style and Stick Style;* see also Scully's "Introduction" to *The Architecture of the American Summer: The Flowering of the Shingle Style,* in which he updates and expands the major themes he originally identified in *The Shingle Style.* "Cleveland Building Report," *Inland Architect* 24, no. 3 (Oct. 1894): 29; 13 (July 1889): 104.
10. *Inland Architect* 13:104; Charles E. Jenkins, "Charles F. Schweinfurth," 108, 99.
11. Montgomery Schuyler, "The Romanesque Revival in America," 151.
12. *Ohio Architect, Engineer & Builder* 3, no. 2 (Sept. 1903): 20.
13. J. H. Wade to Mother, Apr. 8, 12, 1883, Cleveland.
14. Jenkins, 107.
15. J. H. Wade to Mother, Apr. 12, 1883, Cleveland; Clay Herrick, *Plain Dealer,* Nov. 6, 1938; Milliken, *A Time Remembered,* 18; Ruth Everett Worthington, "History of Our Family."
16. Rose, 54.
17. Charles W. Bingham House, Peabody & Stearns Collection, thirty-one original drawings and office records; Charles W. Bingham to Messrs Peabody & Stearns, May 1, 1883, Cleveland, Bingham Papers, Bolton Family Private Collection. Julius A. Schweinfurth (1859–1931), Charles's brother, joined Peabody & Stearns in 1879 and was the firm's chief designer by the mid-1880s, probably the most influential of the partners' talented designers until he left in 1892. If there was a connection between the Charles W. Bingham commission of 1882–83 and the Sylvester Everett commission of 1883–87 I have been unable to identify it; however, Peabody and Stearns permitted their designers to moonlight on design jobs, and Bingham might well have introduced Everett to Charles and Julius Schweinfurth. See Holden, "The Peabody Touch." Wheaton A. Holden, interview with author, Millis, Mass., Mar. 29, 1991.
18. The house was built at a cost of $56,000 in 1882–83, and was constructed of red Lake Superior granite shipped from Minnesota. The interior was furnished throughout with hardwood floors, paneling, and carved moldings. *Inland Architect* 13, no. 8 (July 1889): 104. See Charles F. Schweinfurth Plans; Jenkins, 112.
19. Mrs. G. C. Cleveland, "Charles F. Brush House."
20. C. F. Brush to Herter Brothers, Apr. 6, 1887, Cleveland.
21. Wick, 37; unidentified newspaper, Nov. 18, 1888.
22. C. F. Brush, "The Arc-Light," 110–18; Rose, 440, 423, 526, 539; *Scientific American* (Sept. 1929), 141; *National Cyclopedia of American Biography* 21:1–3.
23. *Dictionary of American Biography,* vol. 21, supplement 1: 129–30. Charles F. Brush to Charles Brush, Jr., Dec. 18, 1911; Nov. 26, 1917; Dec. 29, 1917; Sept. 27, 1918; Dec. 6, 1918, Cleveland.
24. *Cleveland Press,* June 16, 1929, Feb. 18, 1971; Worthington, "History of Our Family."
25. See Schweinfurth's Architectural Library. Jacob D. Cox, Sr., *Building An American Industry,* 99, 165.
26. *Cleveland News,* Jan. 23, 1951; Cox-Prentiss House, 3411 Euclid Avenue, original plans, July 1898, Schweinfurth Plans.
27. J. D. Cox to H. C. King, Dec. 1926, Henry C. King Correspondence, Box 20.
28. Regina A. Perry, "The Life and Works of Charles Frederick Schweinfurth: Cleveland Architect—1856–1919," 156–57.
29. *Cleveland News,* Oct. 19, 1950; *National Cyclopedia of American Biography* 21: 375–76.
30. *Plain Dealer,* Jan. 3, 1928; Wilson, 2:220.

Chapter Seven
Imperial Elegance, 1895–1910

1. Paul R. Baker, *Richard Morris Hunt,* 374–76, 380–81; Catharine Clinton Howland Hunt, "The Biography of Richard Morris Hunt." Construction of the Observatory was begun in 1888 and completed in 1893.
2. W. R. Warner to A. Swasey, Apr. 28, 1948, Cleveland; *Cleveland City Directory,* 1918.
3. Warner & Swasey Papers; "Worcester R. Warner," *Case Alumnus,* 3.
4. John G. Rae, "Ambrose Swasey," *DAB* 22:642–43; A. Swasey, "Autobiography," Warner & Swasey Papers.
5. *Inland Architect* 21, no. 3 (Apr. 1893): 42; Eric Johannesen, "George W. Howe's Euclid Avenue," 5–15.
6. Wickham, 2:530; Orth, 2:44–47; *Plain Dealer,* Sept. 15, 1951.
7. *Inland Architect* 26, no. 1 (Aug. 1895): 10; Cleveland Architectural Club, "Annual Exhibition Catalogue," 1896.
8. Clara Tracy Upson, interview with author, University Heights, Ohio, Mar. 11, 1988; *Plain Dealer,* Sept. 15, 1951.
9. *Plain Dealer,* Aug. 6, 1944.
10. Constance Mather Price (daughter of Philip Mather), interview with author, Bratenahl, Ohio, Mar. 12, 1988; Perry, 199.
11. C. F. Schweinfurth to Alfred Stone, Oct. 12, 1896, American Institute of Architects Correspondence; interview with C. F. Schweinfurth by S. J. Kelly, *Massillon News Leader,* Oct. 10, 1892.
12. Jenkins, 81–82; S. J. Kelly, *Plain Dealer,* May 14, 1945; Perry, 72; Molly Mather Anderson (daughter of Philip Mather), interview with author, Oberlin, Ohio, Feb. 15, 1988.
13. Perry, 199; *Plain Dealer,* Aug. 6, 1940; Oct. 22, 1967; Feb. 8, 1969; Feb. 14, 1976; Feb. 23, 1978; Constance Mather Price, (daughter of Philip Mather), interview with author, Mar. 12, 1988; *Ohio Motorist,* Feb., Mar. 1960; Philip Mather to Constance Mather, Nov. 3, 1912.
14. Flora Stone Mather to Clara Stone Hay, Aug. 8, 1908, Cleveland.
15. Restoration of dining room, drawing room, library, reception hall, and master bedroom completed by Dalton, van Dyke, Johnson & Partners, *Plain Dealer,* Feb. 23, 1978.
16. Carle Robbins, "Andrew Squire: A Man and a Portrait," 10; Milliken, *A Time Remembered,* 55, 67; Rose, 572; Perry, 159.

17. Rose, 572; *Cleveland City Directory* (1918); *Plain Dealer,* Jan. 9, 1937; Mrs. Andrew Squire, "The Cleveland Garden Center," Cleveland, 1932, Andrew Squire Papers; *Cleveland Press,* Nov. 23, 1950.

18. See Leland M. Roth, *McKim, Mead & White, Architects; Cleveland Press,* June 24, 1958; May 17, 1975.

19. *Cleveland Press,* Mar. 15, 1950; Johannesen, "George W. Howe's Euclid Avenue," 76–80.

Chapter Eight
The Architects and Builders

1. See Barnum, 473–74. The editors of *American Architect and Building News* acknowledged that the frequent illustration of H. H. Richardson's work had made him a celebrity among his colleagues and the public, and contributed to the widespread popularity of his work. See "Architectural Retrospect," *AABN* 70 (1900): 98; and Mary Woods, "The First American Architectural Journals: The Profession's Voice," 117–38.

2. John Hay to Flora Stone, Aug. 16, 1877, Cleveland.

3. "The Work of Mr. J. Milton Dyer," 392.

4. *Cleveland City Directory,* 1837, 1845, 1850, 1859–60; Richard Klein, "Nineteenth Century Land Use Decisions in Cleveland, Ohio: A Case Study of Neighborhood Development and Change in Ohio City," Table 76, 516–20.

5. I. T. Frary, *Early Homes of Ohio,* 215.

6. *Leader,* Jan. 6, 1865.

7. *Leader,* Oct. 12, 1855.

8. William J. Boardman to Joseph E. Sheffield, Esq., Sept. 28, 1860, Cleveland, Carl Boardman Cobb Private Collection (grandson of William H. Boardman).

9. *Leader,* Mar. 28, 1859; Feb. 23, June 18, Oct. 25, 1875; Aug. 30, 1876; Johannesen, "Charles W. Heard," 130–42.

10. *Leader,* Jan. 15, 1875.

11. Orth, 3:771.

12. Building permit requirements were officially established in 1888, based on legislation introduced by the Cleveland Chapter of the AIA and the Cleveland Builders' Exchange. Most permits which survive in the Cleveland City Hall's Department of Building specify the architect and builder. *Leader,* May 18, 1871; Cleveland Architectural Club, "Annual Exhibition Catalogue," 1896.

13. After Coburn's death in 1897, Barnum turned his attention away from residential design and became the principal architect for the Board of Education; he designed many of Cleveland's public schools in the early 1900s.

14. Benjamin S. Hubbell, "A Great Architect."

15. Jenkins, 81.

16. Perry, 70–71.

17. Hubbell, "A Great Architect."

18. "The Work of Mr. J. Milton Dyer," 391–92.

19. Klein, Table 76, 516–20; *Ohio Architect, Engineer & Builder* 3, no. 1 (May 1903): 12–13.

20. Elroy McKendree Avery, *A History of Cleveland and Its Environs* 3:507–8; Orth, 2:872–73.

Chapter Nine
A Neighborhood of Families

1. Artemus Ward, 1860, reprint, *Plain Dealer,* Nov. 27, 1914; Mark Twain, letter to *Alta, California,* 1868, reprint, *Leader,* Dec. 19, 1868.

2. Wharton, 83.

3. See Frederic Cople Jaher, "Style and Status: High Society in Late Nineteenth-Century New York," 267–80, 455–536; Gunther Barth, "Metropolism and Urban Elites in the Far West," 158–87. Also see Frederic Cople Jaher, *The Urban Establishment: Upper Strata in Boston, New York, Charleston, Chicago and Los Angeles,* 188–262.

4. *Perils of Society,* film and playbill; *Leader,* June 26, 1916; J. B. Van Urk, "The Horse, the Valley & The Chagrin Valley Hunt Club," 157. The film was produced as a benefit for war orphans in France and raised $11,000 in its two-week showing at the Metropolitan Theatre; *Plain Dealer,* Apr. 20, 1977; May 2, 1988.

5. Diary, Randall Wade, Essay on "Fashion," 1855.

6. The occupational profile of Euclid Avenue men is based on an analysis of those who were born 1770–1810 and 1810–40 and who established their careers in the 1830–50s and 1840s–65, respectively.

7. This profile is based on an analysis of demographic material and personal histories, from manuscripts and published sources on Euclid Avenue families, primarily the men, who were born 1840–70 and lived on Euclid Avenue during the period 1865–1900.

8. See Jaher, *The Urban Establishment,* 279–80.

9. This was also true of Chicago's post–Civil War elite who lived on Prairie Avenue, the grand avenue of that city. See Jaher, *The Urban Establishment,* 483, 399–500.

10. Otis, 42.

11. Mary (Molly) Perry Payne to Mary Perry Payne, Oct. 30, 1874, Washington, D.C.; Mary (Molly) Perry Payne to Henry B. Payne, Dec. 6, 1874, Cleveland; Mary Perry Payne to Mary (Molly) Perry Payne, Jan. 9, 1875, Munich, Germany; Mary (Molly) Perry Payne to Charles W. Bingham, Feb. 19, 1875, New York; Jan. 22, 1876, Washington, D.C., Bolton Family Private Collection. Van Tassel and Gabrowski, *Cleveland History,* 97; Wilson, 1:131–33.

12. Unpublished biographies, Carl Boardman Cobb Private Collection, Cleveland.

13. R. E. Worthington, "History."

14. Jeptha Wade to Randall Wade, undated, Cleveland; Randall Wade to Anna McGraw, Mar. 16, 1856, Cleveland; R. E. Worthington, "History."

15. John Hay to John Nicolay, Aug. 27, 1873, Cleveland; John Hay to Whitelaw Reid, Feb. 11, 1881, in Thayer, 1:351, 404.

16. This observation, the author's own, is based on a comprehensive reading of the available diaries, letters, newspaper notices and invitations written by and about Euclid Avenue residents. Flora S. Mather to Samuel Mather, July 26, 1884, Cleveland; Cornelia Brown to Fayette Brown, July 12, 1857, Cleveland, Fayette Brown Papers; Diary, H. K. Devereux, Mar. 24, 1885, Cleveland; Mary (Molly) Payne Bingham to Charles W. Bingham, Mar. 27, 1877, New York City; Cornelia B. Warner to Gentlemen of the Conference, Oct. 16, 1929, Cleveland, Warner & Swasey Papers.

17. Randall Wade to Anna Wade, May 23, 1862, Washington, D.C.

18. Based on the author's review of various house plans and written descriptions. Milliken, *A Time Remembered,* 66.

19. Jeptha H. Wade to Randall P. Wade, Mar. 18, 1855, Columbus; Samuel L. Mather to Samuel Mather, Mar. 13, 1873, Cleveland.

20. Charles F. Brush to Charles F. Brush, Jr., Mar. 14, 1912, Cleveland; Jeptha H. Wade to Jeptha H. Wade II, Oct. 15, 1876, Cleveland.

21. Other families included the Binghams, Boardmans, Brooks, Browns, Cobbs, Devereuxs, Dodges, Eells, Everetts, Garretsons, Hales, Halls, Hannas, Hoyts, Kelleys, McBrides, Millers, Morgans, Otises, Packs, Painters, Parmelees, Perkins, Prentisses, Ranneys, Rouses, Stones, Tracys, Weddells, Whites, Wicks, Wilsons, and Winslows.

22. This profile of servants is based on demographic analysis of 20 percent of Euclid Avenue households in 1850, 5 percent in 1880, and 10 percent in 1900. U.S. Census of Population, 1850, 1880, 1900; interview by author with Mrs. Henry Melcher, granddaughter of Edwin B. Hale, June 15, 1988, Cleveland.

23. Ingham, 188–89; Unpublished biography, Carl B. Cobb Private Collection; Cornelia Brown to Fayette Brown, Oct. 25, 1857, Cleveland; Diary, Antoinette K. Devereux, Feb. 13, 1873, Cleveland; Flora S. Mather to Samuel Mather, Jan. 11, 1889, Cleveland.

24. The description of Euclid Avenue servants' living quarters is based on a review of available house plans and descriptions by family members. Separate servants' houses were built by Edwin B. Hale, Andrew Squire, and Charles W. Bingham.

Chapter Ten
Life on the Avenue

1. Otis, 90–104.

2. Randall P. Wade to Cornelia Brown, Dec. 28, 1865, Cleveland.

3. The term "community" is the author's and is based on the interaction of Euclid Avenue families. The community was not limited exclusively to Euclid Avenue families but they were among the great majority; others lived on Prospect and Superior avenues in downtown and, at the turn of the century, in such eastern "suburban" areas as University Heights, Euclid Heights, and Bratenahl.

4. Charles F. Brush to Charles F. Brush, Jr., Nov. 10, 1911, Cleveland.

5. Samuel L. Mather to Samuel Mather (in Paris), Mar. 13, 1873, Cleveland; John Hay to Robert Lincoln and Whitelaw Reid, Oct. 8, 1889, Washington, D.C.

6. Diary, Mary Emma Betts Sterling, June 27, 1885; Ellen Nickenzie Lawson, "The Gourmet Kitchen"; Flora S. Mather to Samuel Mather, Nov. 14, 1884, Cleveland.

7. John Hay to Flora Stone, Mar. 30, 1876; Apr. 19, 1884, Cleveland; Sept. 2, 1881, New York City; Wick, 85.

8. Diary, Antoinette K. Devereux, July, 1873, Cleveland; Diary, Mary Emma B. Sterling, 1885–86, Cleveland; Flora S. Mather to Samuel Mather, 1880–1900.

9. Leader, Dec. 22, 1856; Nov. 4, 1862; May 3, 1875; Diary, Mary Emma B. Sterling, Feb. 11, 1885, Cleveland; Flora S. Mather to Samuel Mather, Feb. 2–4, 1900, Cleveland.

10. The "Tea and Topics" group, organized by Euclid Avenue women in the early 1900s, became "very jolly" afternoon affairs as they listened to a paper by a fellow neighbor about a notable author, artist or musician. Diary, Antoinette K. Devereux, Feb. 15, 1873, Cleveland; John Hay to Flora Stone, Mar. 2, 1876, Cleveland.

11. Fayette Brown to Cornelia Brown, May 29, 1854, Cleveland, Harvey H. Brown Papers; Samuel L. Mather to Samuel Mather, Aug. 14, 1866, Cleveland.

12. Samuel L. Mather to Samuel Mather, Apr. 21, 1880, Cleveland.

13. Milliken, A Time Remembered, 5; Constance Mather Price, interview with author, Mar. 12, 1988; James J. Tracy, Jr., "Theme Day" essay, Harvard College, 1903, Clara Tracy Upson Private Collection; Worcester R. Warner Papers, July 18, 1908.

14. Ivy Edmondson Starr, interview with author, Princeton, New Jersey, Apr. 16, 1988.

15. Anonymous, manuscript for biography, Mar. 1927, Warner & Swasey Papers; Plain Dealer, Apr. 10, year unknown. In addition to Swasey, John D. Rockefeller was another prolific subject; Edmondson did nineteen portraits of him, before and after Rockefeller started to wear a wig, and was the only photographer with whom Rockefeller ever made an appointment; Plain Dealer, May 6, 1936.

16. Unknown newspaper article (c. 1895).

17. Rose, 135–36, 245, 462, 536, 619; Johannesen, Cleveland Architecture: 1876–1976, 18; "An Uptown Church," newspaper article, source unknown (c. 1901–2).

18. "The First Presbyterian Church Record," vol. 1, no. 2 (Dec. 1, 1879).

19. Euclid Avenue Baptist Church, Historical Sketches: Seventy-Five Years of the Euclid Avenue Baptist Church, Cleveland, Ohio, 1851–1926, 34–41, 110–14.

20. Mary Perry Payne to Mary (Molly) Perry Payne, Munich, Jan. 9, 1875.

21. Leader, June 16, 1874; June 24, 1875; Plain Dealer, July 5, 24, 1878.

22. John Hay to Flora Stone, Jan. 11, 1875, Cleveland; Diary, Antoinette K. Devereux, Dec. 31, 1873, Cleveland.

23. Leader, Jan. 2, 1901; Plain Dealer, Jan. 3, 1911.

24. Randall P. Wade to Jeptha H. Wade, Oct. 16, 1866, Cleveland; John Hay to Flora Stone, Oct. 14, 1876, Cleveland.

25. Flora S. Mather to Samuel Mather, Jan. 14, 1889, Cleveland.

26. Leader, Jan. 7, 1859; Diary, Henry K. Devereux, Apr. 9, 1885, Cleveland; Edward Merritt to Myron T. Herrick (in Paris), June 2, 1912, Cleveland.

27. John Hay to Flora Stone, Oct. 14, 1876, Cleveland; Leader, Dec. 18, 1896; Diary, Antoinette K. Devereux, "Events in Society," undated newspaper article.

28. Town Topics, n.d., 8; Plain Dealer, Feb. 9, 1889.

29. Otis, 68.

30. Rose, 425; Flora S. Mather to Samuel Mather, Jan. 23, 1903, Washington, D.C.; O'Toole, 217–19.

Chapter Eleven
Life off the Avenue

1. Rose, 192, 454.

2. Jaher, The Rich, The Wellborn, 500, 511, 520.

3. William Graham Sumner, The Challenge of Facts, and Other Essays, 43.

4. Rose, 398; Harry Peters, "University School," 4; Rose, 517. Founders of University School included Euclid Avenue residents Samuel Williamson, Samuel Mather, David Z. Norton, J. H. McBride, Charles W. Bingham, and James J. Tracy.

5. Leader, Sept. 7, 1876; Mary (Molly) Payne Bingham to Charles W. Bingham, Dec. 29, 1897, Cleveland; Rose, 410, 415; Lease between J. D. Rockefeller and Augusta Mittleberger and Cornelia Blackmore, 1880, 1889, Worcester R. Warner Papers.

6. Otis, 15.

7. Samuel E. Williamson to Charles W. Bingham, Dec. 29, 1897, Cleveland, Bolton Family Collection; Randall Wade to Anna McGraw, Feb. 5, 1856, Columbus.

8. Fayette T. Brown to Cornelia Brown, June 22, 1850; William A. Leonard to Samuel Mather, Aug. 7, 1894; Otis, 44, 62.

9. Charles Bingham biography, *Payne—Bingham—Bolton Family*, Bolton Family Private Collection, 106; Samuel Mather to Katharine Mather, Mar. 21, 1882, Alhambra Granada; Randall P. Wade to Jeptha H. Wade, Mar. 24, 1871, Rome.

10. J. H. Wade II to S. Mather, June 15, 1892; travel diary, Mrs. Hiram Garretson, 1892–95, Wade Family Papers; Grace Goulder, "A Cruise in the Grand Style."

11. *Leader*, Dec. 1907; *Plain Dealer*, Aug. 6, 1944.

12. Diary, Henry K. Devereux, February–March 1885. See David L. Chandler, *Henry Flagler*, 85–108, 119–28.

13. Jane A. Tracy to Catherine and Lindsay Wallace, Apr. 25, 1915, Clara Tracy (Mrs. David) Upson Private Collection; *Leader*, Jan. 10, 1897; Mary Brown to Cornelia Brown, Apr. 29, 1882, New York City.

14. Otis, 78–79.

15. Wick, 82; Constance Mather Price, interview with author, March 12, 1988.

16. Wick, 84; Thomas A. Knight, *The Country Estates of Cleveland Men*, 71–75.

17. Edward A. Merritt to Myron Herrick in Paris, June 2, 1912, Cleveland.

18. Mary (Molly) Perry Payne to Nathan Payne, June 7, 1868, Newburgh, New York; Mary (Molly) Perry Payne to "Respected inmates of the paternal mansion," Dec. 11, 1868, Dresden, Germany.

19. Diary, A. K. Devereux, May 11, Aug. 5, 1873, Cleveland; Flora S. Mather to Samuel Mather, July 25, 1883, Cleveland; Sue Wade to Randall Wade, undated, Cleveland.

20. Randall Wade to Anna Wade, May 16, 1862, Washington, D.C.; John Hay to Samuel Mather, June 25, 1900, Washington, D.C.

21. Samuel L. Mather to Samuel Mather (in Berlin), Jan. 13, 1873, Cleveland; Jeptha H. Wade to Jeptha H. (Homer) Wade II, Nov. 3, 1878, Cleveland; Flora Stone to Samuel Mather, Sept. 2, 1881, New York City.

22. Randall Wade to Sue Wade, June 1856; W. R. Warner to Cornelia Warner, July 9, 1909.

23. See Eric Hobsbawm and Terence Ranger, eds., *The Invention of Tradition*, 11.

24. *Leader*, Sept. 24, 1872; Diaries, H. K. Devereux; Rose, 387; Worcester R. Warner to Hon. Theodore E. Burton, Mar. 18, 1907; Clara Tracy Upson, interview with author, University Heights, Ohio, Mar. 11, 1988.

25. Eckstein Case, interview with Ambrose Swasey, Cleveland, Feb. 17, 1927.

26. Henry Adams, *The Education of Henry Adams*, 297; Charles F. Brush to Edna Brush, July 28, 1927, Cleveland.

27. Castalia Sporting Club Ledger, 1880–1900, Castalia Sporting Club Records; John Hay to Henry Adams, Oct. 24, 1891, Thayer, 2:88–89.

28. Castalia Sporting Club (including Jeptha Wade II, David Norton, Lee McBride, Charles W. Bingham) to members, Jan. 7, 1902; Daniel H. Burnham to President and Directors of Castalia Sporting Club, undated, (1902); R. P. H. Dunker to President and Directors of Castalia Sporting Club, undated, (1902); J. H. Wade II to Lee McBride, Jan. 9, 1902, Cleveland, Castalia Sporting Club Records.

29. Rose, 540; Otis, 133–34; Newspaper article, undated (c. 1898), in Tavern Club Records.

30. Otis, 194.

31. *Town Topics*, July, 1902; *Plain Dealer*, July 30, 1902; May 31, July 25, 28, 1903; August 3, 1906.

32. See Robert H. Bremner, *American Philanthropy*, 85–133, for a history of charitable giving and philanthropic organizations in the United States from 1865 through 1930.

33. Goulder, *John D. Rockefeller*, 35; Otis, 121.

34. In the postwar decades, 1863–92, about 15 percent of Chicago's public officials were millionaires, and most of them were self-made men. Their civic positions supplemented their business enterprise. After 1870, many were at odds with the majority urban government, moving off-center to positions on the park commission and board of education. See Jaher, *The Rich, The Wellborn*, 501–4.

35. Ingham, 16–19, 109, 197–98; *Leader*, Dec. 20, 1864.

36. Ingham, 183–89.

37. Flora S. Mather to Samuel Mather, July 26, 1884, Cleveland; Flora Stone Mather last will and testament, Jan. 27, 1909, Cleveland.

38. See Bremner, 109–15.

39. Rose, 540.

40. Rose, 742; William M. Milliken, *Born Under the Sign of Libra*, 64–66.

41. See Lake View Cemetery Association, *Historic Lake View Cemetery*. Lake View Cemetery, founded in 1869, was "selected as the last resting place of men and women" of civic prominence, many of whom had lived on Euclid Avenue, including the Wades, Brushes, Hannas, Severances, Andrews, Hays, and Rockefellers. Many of the mausoleums were architectural monuments, just as the houses of Euclid Avenue residents had been. The Wade Memorial Chapel, for example, built in 1898, was designed by prominent Cleveland architects Hubbell & Benes, with the stained glass windows and marble interiors by Louis Tiffany of New York. See Duncan et al. 7–12; Albert Fein, "The American City: The Ideal and the Real," 93.

Chapter Twelve
The Fall of the Grand Avenue, 1895–1950

1. *Cleveland Press*, Mar. 15, 1950.

2. I. T. Frary, "The Passing of a Famous Avenue."

3. *Cleveland Town Topics*, June 27, 1896.

4. *Cleveland Press*, Apr. 2, 1952.

5. *City Council Proceedings*, Dec. 28, 1896, 370–71.

6. *City Council Proceedings*, Nov. 30, 1896, 334; Cleveland Chamber of Commerce to City Council, received Dec. 16, 1896; *City Council Proceedings*, Dec. 21, 1896, 355.

7. *City Council Proceedings*, Dec. 28, 1896, 368–69; Apr. 19, 1897, 499–500.

8. Samuel E. Williamson to Charles W. Bingham, Dec. 29, 1897, Cleveland, Bolton Family Collection; *City Council Proceedings*, May 21, 1900, 48.

9. See Baron Georges Eugene Haussmann, *Theory of Productive Expenditures*.

10. See Thomas S. Hines, *Burnham of Chicago,* 158–73; "The Grouping of Public Buildings at Cleveland," *The Inland Architect* 42 (Sept. 1903): 13–15.

11. Rose, 618, 49.

12. *City Council Proceedings,* Oct. 30, 1882; Apr. 4, 1883; Dec. 29, 1890; *The City Record,* Apr. 9, 1900, Cleveland City Council Archives, p. 491.

13. Committee of Euclid Avenue Property Owners to Worcester R. Warner, Sept. 18, 1908, Cleveland.

14. Alfred Clum, attorney, to Worcester R. Warner, Nov. 17, 1908, Cleveland; *The City Record,* Oct. 13, 1915.

15. Kenneth L. Kusmer, *A Ghetto Takes Shape: Black Cleveland, 1870–1930,* 41–47.

16. Kusmer, 157–65.

17. See *Cleveland Gazette,* May 5, 12, Aug. 18, 1917; May 11, Aug. 17, 1918; *Plain Dealer,* Aug. 4, 1917. Langston Hughes, an eminent black Clevelander, claimed that "the white neighborhoods resented Negroes moving closer and closer—but when the whites did give way, they gave way at very profitable rentals," in Langston Hughes, *The Big Sea,* 27.

18. "The Brush Foundation," 1–4, Charles Francis Brush Papers.

19. Cuyahoga County tax duplicates for twenty-two Euclid Avenue residences, 1890–1950, Cuyahoga County Archives. Based on these assessments, the city was apparently valuing the property's commercial potential: land value constituted at least 90 percent of total property value.

20. *Plain Dealer,* Nov. 11, 1927. Property values for the area between Fourteenth and 107th streets increased from $88.8 million in 1920 to $118.1 million in 1924, a 33 percent increase. The area west of Fifty-fifth Street accounted for a disproportionate amount of the escalation. *Plain Dealer,* Dec. 22, 1925; Apr. 26, 1927.

21. *Cleveland Press,* Jan. 15, 26, Aug. 13, 1937; Samuel E. Williamson to Charles W. Bingham, Dec. 29, 1897, Cleveland.

22. *Plain Dealer,* Nov. 11, 1927.

Epilogue
The Rise of Cleveland's Main Street, 1910–1950

1. Richard J. Miller, "The Glittering Slum on Main Street."

2. See Christopher Alexander, *A Pattern Language.*

3. *Ohio Architect & Builder* 3, no. 1 (Jan. 1904): 41; 4, no. 2 (Aug. 1904): 57–58; Rose, 565.

4. Euclid Avenue Baptist Church, *Historical Sketches,* 39.

5. *Ohio Architect & Builder* 9, no. 2 (Feb. 1907): 49; Edward Merritt to Myron Herrick, 1912, Cleveland.

6. Rose, 461; John D. Rockefeller to Worcester R. Warner, Mar. 8, 1917, New York.

7. W. R. Rose, *Plain Dealer,* Oct. 11, 1918; Milliken, *A Time Remembered,* 1–4; *Plain Dealer,* Jan. 28, 1939.

8. City of Cleveland, Council Committees on Building Code and City Planning, *Zone Maps and Ordinance of Cleveland, Ohio,* Ordinance No. 85681, Jan. 21, 1929.

9. Bill Barrett, *Cleveland Press,* Apr. 2, 1952.

10. *Cleveland Press,* Nov. 13, 1929; Dec. 13, 1930; *Plain Dealer,* Apr. 3, 27, 28, 1952.

11. *Plain Dealer,* May 25, 1934; *Cleveland Press,* May 12, 1952; U.S. WPA, *The Ohio Guide,* 218.

12. Property assessments on Euclid Avenue, 1930–50, reflected the diminished commercial stature, dropping about 35–40 percent between 1920–30 and an additional 40–50 percent each decade between 1930–50. See Cuyahoga County Tax Duplicates, 1920–50, Cuyahoga County Archives.

13. *The City Record,* July 6, 1949, Cleveland City Council Archives, pp. 33–35.

14. James M. Lister, "A Little Story About a Great Street That Is Dying," 8, 31; Christopher Tunnard, "The Glittering Slum on Main Street"; *Plain Dealer,* Sept. 17, 1965.

15. Euclid Innerbelt Association Records; Cleveland Development Foundation Records; *Plain Dealer,* Nov. 22, 1961.

16. S. J. Kelly, *Plain Dealer,* June 10, 1937.

Bibliography

Published Sources

Adams, Henry. *The Education of Henry Adams.* New York: Modern Library, 1918.

Alexander, Christopher. *A Pattern Language.* New York: Oxford University Press, 1977.

Amory, Cleveland. *The Proper Bostonians.* New York: E. P. Dutton, 1947.

Andrews, Wayne. *Americans, Ambition and Architecture.* New York: Free Press, 1947.

"Architectural Retrospect." *American Architect and Building News* 70 (1900): 98.

Avery, Elroy McKendree. *A History of Cleveland and Its Environs.* 3 vols. Chicago: Lewis Publishing, 1918.

Baedeker, Karl, ed. *The United States, With an Excursion into Mexico: A Handbook for Travellers.* Leipzig and New York, 1893. Reprint. New York: Da Capo Press, 1971.

Baker, Paul R. *Richard Morris Hunt.* Cambridge: MIT Press, 1980.

Baltzell, E. Digby. *Philadelphia Gentlemen: The Making of a National Upper Class.* Glencoe, Ill.: Free Press, 1958.

Barnum, Frank. "Architecture." In *A History of Cleveland, Ohio,* vol. 1, edited by Samuel P. Orth. Chicago and Cleveland: S. J. Clarke, 1910.

Barth, Gunther. "Metropolitan and Urban Elites in the Far West." In *The Age of Industrialism in America: Essays in Social Structure and Cultural Values,* edited by Frederic Cople Jaher. New York: Free Press, 1968.

Beard, George M. *American Nervousness.* New York: Putnam's Sons, 1881.

Beautiful Homes of Cleveland. Cleveland: Cleveland Topics Co., 1917.

Beecher, Catharine E., and Harriet B. Stowe. *The American Woman's Home.* New York: J. B. Ford, 1870.

Boorstin, Daniel. *The Americans: The Democratic Experience.* New York: Random House, 1973.

Branca, Patricia. "Image and Reality: The Myth of the Idle Victorian Woman." In *Clio's Consciousness Raised,* edited by Mary Hartman and Louis Banner. New York: Harper & Row, 1974.

Bremner, Robert H. *American Philanthropy.* Chicago: University of Chicago Press, 1960.

Brown, Mrs. M. W., comp. *Cleveland Blue Book.* Cleveland, 1888.

Brush, Charles F. "The Arc-Light." *Century Magazine* 70 (1905): 110–18.

Burt, Nathaniel. *The Perennial Philadelphians: The Anatomy of an American Aristocracy.* Boston: Little, Brown, 1963.

Campen, Richard. *Architecture of the Western Reserve.* Cleveland: Western Reserve University, 1971.

Chandler, David L. *Henry Flagler.* New York: Macmillan, 1986.

Chapman, Edmund H. *Cleveland: Village to Metropolis.* Cleveland: Western Reserve University and Western Reserve Historical Society, 1964.

City of Cleveland, Council Committees on Building Code and City Planning, *Zone Maps and Ordinance of Cleveland, Ohio.* Ordinance No. 85681. Cleveland, Jan. 21, 1929.

Cleveland Architectural Club. *Annual Exhibition Catalogue.* Cleveland: Cleveland Architectural Club, 1896, 1901.

Cleveland as It Is. Cleveland: J. Wiggins & Co., 1872.

Coburn and Barnum. "Some Selections from the Work of Coburn & Barnum, Architects." Cleveland, 1897.

Commander, Lydia K. *The American Idea.* New York: A. S. Barnes, 1907.

Condon, George E. *Cleveland: The Best Kept Secret.* Garden City, N.J.: Doubleday, 1967.

Cox, Jacob D., Sr. *Building an American Industry.* Cleveland: Artifact Printing, 1951.

Cram, George F., J. H. Beers, and J. Q. A. Bennett, comps. *Atlas of Cuyahoga County and the City of Cleveland, Ohio.* Chicago: George F. Cram & Co., 1892.

Croly, Herbert, and Harry Desmond. *Stately Homes in America.* New York: D. Appleton, 1903.

Downing, Andrew Jackson. *The Architecture of Country Houses.* New York: D. Appleton, 1850.

———. *A Treatise on the Theory and Practice of Landscape Gardening.* New York: O. Judd, 1859.

Duncan, Alastair, Martin Eidelberg, and Neil Harris. *Masterworks of Louis Comfort Tiffany.* New York: Harry N. Abrams, 1989.

Euclid Avenue Baptist Church. *Historical Sketches: Seventy-Five Years of the Euclid Avenue Baptist Church, Cleveland, Ohio, 1851–1926.* Cleveland: Euclid Avenue Baptist Church, 1927.

Fein, Albert. "The American City: The Ideal and the Real." In *The Rise of an American Architecture,* edited by Edgar Kaufmann. New York: Praeger, 1970.

Fiske, John. *American Political Ideas Viewed from the Standpoint of Universal History.* Boston and New York: Houghton Mifflin, 1911.

Fitch, James Marston. *American Building: The Historical Forces that Shaped It.* New York: Houghton Mifflin, 1947.

Frary, I. T. *Early Homes of Ohio.* Richmond, Va.: Garrett & Massie, 1936.

———. "The Passing of a Famous Avenue." *Architectural Record* 43, no. 4 (Apr. 1918): 301–2.

Girouard, Mark. *Cities & People.* New Haven: Yale University Press, 1985.

———. *A Country House Companion.* New Haven: Yale University Press, 1987.

———. *Life in the English Country House.* New Haven: Yale University Press, 1978.

Goffman, Erving. *The Presentation of Self in Everyday Life.* Edinburgh: University of Edinburgh Press, 1958.

Gorman, Mell. "Charles F. Brush and the First Electric Street Lighting System in America." *Ohio Historic Quarterly* 70 (1961): 128–44.

Goulder, Grace. "A Cruise in the Grand Style." *Plain Dealer Sunday Magazine,* May 21, 1967, 34–37.

———. *John D. Rockefeller: The Cleveland Years.* Cleveland: Western Reserve Historical Society, 1972.

Gowans, Alan. *Images of American Living.* New York: Harper & Row, 1964.

Grant, Robert. *The Art of Living.* New York: Scribner's Sons, 1895.

Gregory, Frances, and Irene D. Neu. "The American Industrial Elite in the 1870s." In *Men in Business,* edited by William Miller. Cambridge: Harvard University Press, 1962.

Griffith, A. A. "Lighting by Electricity." *Inland Architect and Builder* 1, no. 2 (Mar. 1883): 21.

Gutman, Herbert G. *Work, Culture, and Society in Industrializing America.* New York: Vintage, 1977.

Hamlin, Talbot. *Greek Revival Architecture in America.* New York: Oxford University Press, 1944.

Haussmann, Baron Georges Eugene. *Theory of Productive Expenditures.* Paris, 1850–60.

Hay, John. *The Bread-Winners.* 1883–84. Reprint. New Haven: College & University Press, 1973.

———. *Letters of John Hay and Extracts from Diary.* Vol. 2. New York: Gordian Press, 1969.

Higham, John. "The Reorientation of American Culture in the 1890s." In *Writing American History,* edited by John Higham. Bloomington: University of Indiana Press, 1972.

Hines, Thomas S. *Burnham of Chicago.* Chicago: University of Chicago Press, 1974.

Hitchcock, Elizabeth G. *Jonathan Goldsmith: Pioneer Master Builder of the Western Reserve.* Cleveland: Western Reserve Historical Society, 1980.

Hobsbawm, Eric, and Terence Ranger. *The Invention of Tradition.* Cambridge: Cambridge University Press, 1983.

Holden, Wheaton A. "The Peabody Touch: Peabody and Stearns of Boston, 1870–1917." *Journal of the Society of Architectural Historians* 32, no. 2 (May 1973), 114–31.

Hopkins, G. M., comp. *City Atlas of Cleveland, Ohio.* Philadelphia: G. M. Hopkins Co., 1881.

———. *City Atlas of Cleveland, Ohio, and Suburbs.* Philadelphia: G. M. Hopkins Co., 1912, 1920–21, 1932–37.

Hubbell, Benjamin S. "A Great Architect." *Town Topics,* Nov. 15, 1919. Reprint. *AIA Journal* 8: 139–40.

Hughes, Langston. *The Big Sea.* 1940. Reprint. New York: Hill and Wang, 1963.

Huyett, M. C. "Mechanical Heating and Ventilation." *Inland Architect* 23, no. 5 (June 1894): 50.

Hyde, G. A. "The Dunham Tavern." *Annals of the Early Settlers' Association* 6, no. 3 (1912): 67.

Ingham, Mrs. W. A. *Women of Cleveland and Their Work: Philanthropic, Educational, Literary, Medical and Artistic.* Cleveland: W. A. Ingham, 1891.

Jackson, John Brinckerhoff. *American Space.* New York: W. W. Norton, 1972.

Jacobs, Jane. *The Death and Life of Great American Cities.* New York: Random House, 1961.

Jaher, Frederic Cople. "Industrialism and the American Aristocrat: A Social Study of John Hay and His Novel *The Breadwinners." Journal of the Illinois State Historical Society* 65, no. 1 (Spring 1972): 69–93.

———. *The Urban Establishment: Upper Strata in Boston, New York, Charleston, Chicago and Los Angeles.* Urbana: University of Illinois Press, 1982.

Jaher, Frederic Cople, ed. *The Rich, the Wellborn and the Powerful.* Urbana: University of Illinois Press, 1973.

Jenkins, Charles E. "Charles F. Schweinfurth." *Architectural Reviewer* 1, no. 3, Sept. 30, 1897.

Joblin, Maurice, comp. *Cleveland, Past and Present: Its Representative Men.* Cleveland: Fairbanks, Benedict & Co., 1869.

Johannesen, Eric. "Charles W. Heard: Victorian Architect." *Ohio History* 77, no. 4 (Autumn 1968): 130–42.

———. *Cleveland Architecture: 1876–1976.* Cleveland: Western Reserve Historical Society, 1979.

———. "George W. Howe's Euclid Avenue." *The Gamut* 25 (Winter 1988): 5–15.

———. "Simeon Porter: Ohio Architect." *Ohio History* 74, no. 3 (Autumn 1965): 169–90.

Johnson, Allen, and Dumas Malone, eds. *Dictionary of American Biography.* 11 vols. New York: Scribner's Sons, 1929, 1930, 1944, 1958.

Johnson, Crisfield. *History of Cuyahoga County, Ohio.* Philadelphia: D. W. Ensign, 1879. Reprint. Evansville, Ind.: Whipporwill Publishers, 1984.

Johnson, Marilyn. "The Artful Interior." In *In Pursuit of Beauty: Americans and the Aesthetic Movement,* edited by Doreen Bolger Burke et al. New York: The Metropolitan Museum of Art and Rizzoli, 1987.

Jones, Howard Mumford. *The Age of Energy.* New York: Viking, 1971.

Kaufmann, Edgar, ed. *The Rise of an American Architecture.* New York: Praeger, 1975.

Kennedy, James Harrison. *A History of the City of Cleveland.* Cleveland: Imperial, 1896.

Knight, Thomas A. *The Country Estates of Cleveland Men.* Cleveland, 1903.

Kostof, Spiro. *American by Design.* New York: Oxford University Press, 1987.

Kusmer, Kenneth L. *A Ghetto Takes Shape: Black Cleveland, 1870–1930.* Urbana: University of Illinois Press, 1976.

Lake, D. J., comp. *Atlas of Cuyahoga County, Ohio.* Philadelphia: Titus, Simmons & Titus, 1874.

Lake View Cemetery Association. *Historic Lake View Cemetery.* Cleveland: Lake View Cemetary Association, n.d.

Lawrence, Ruth, ed. *Payne, Bingham, Bolton and Allied Family Histories Genealogical and Biographical.* New York: National Americana Publication, 1954.

Lawson, Ellen Nickenzie. "The Gourmet Kitchen." *Northern Ohio Live,* Dec. 1989, 28–29.

Lister, James M. "A Little Story About a Great Street That Is Dying." *The Clevelander,* Apr. 1952.

Lorenz, Carl. *Tom L. Johnson, Mayor of Cleveland.* New York: A. S. Barnes, 1911.

Loth, Calder, and Julius Sadler. *The Only Proper Style.* Boston: New York Graphic Society, 1975.

McCray, R. Y., ed. *Representative Clevelanders.* Cleveland: Cleveland Topics Co., 1927.

McKelvy, Blake. *Rochester: The Flower City, 1855–1890.* Cambridge: Harvard University Press, 1949.

Miller, Richard J. "The Glittering Slum on Main Street." *Architectural Forum,* Apr. 1959.

Milliken, William M. *Born Under the Sign of Libra.* Cleveland: Western Reserve Historical Society, 1977.

———. *A Time Remembered.* Cleveland: Western Reserve Historical Society, 1975.

Morse, Kenneth S. P. *Cleveland Streetcars.* Part 2. Baltimore: n.p., 1964.

Mumford, Lewis. *The Brown Decades, 1863–1895.* 1931. Reprint. New York: Dover, 1971.

National Cyclopedia of American Biography. Vols. 9, 21. New York: James T. White, 1907, 1931.

Nevins, Allan. *A Study in Power: John D. Rockefeller.* New York: Scribner's Sons, 1953.

Orth, Samuel P., ed. *History of Cleveland, Ohio.* 3 vols. Chicago and Cleveland: S. J. Clarke, 1910.

Otis, Charles Augustus. *Here I Am: A Rambling Account of the Exciting Times of Yesteryear.* Cleveland: Buehler Printcraft Corp., 1951.

O'Toole, Patricia. *The Five of Hearts.* New York: Clarkson Potter, 1990.

Payne, William. *Cleveland Illustrated.* Cleveland: Fairbanks & Benedict, 1876.

Persons, Stow. *The Decline of American Gentility.* New York: Columbia University Press, 1973.

Peters, Harry. "University School." In *A History of Cleveland and Its Environs,* vol. 1, edited by Elroy McKendree Avery. Chicago: Lewis Publishing, 1918.

Peters, Walter A. *Names of Cleveland and Vicinity.* Cleveland: Western Reserve University, 1927.

Post, Charles Asa. *Those Were the Days.* Cleveland: Caxton, 1935.

Potter, David. *People of Plenty.* Chicago: University of Chicago Press, 1934.

Raymond, Julia. *Recollections of Euclid Avenue.* N.p., [1936].

Robbins, Carle. "Andrew Squire: A Man and a Portrait." *Town & Country,* July 27, 1928, 10.

Robison, W. Scott, ed. *History of the City of Cleveland.* Cleveland: Robison & Crockett, 1887.

Rose, William Ganson. *Cleveland: The Making of a City.* 1950. Reprint. Kent, Ohio: Kent State University Press, 1990.

Roth, Leland M. *McKim, Mead & White, Architects.* New York: Harper & Row, 1983.

Sanborn Map Company. *Cleveland, Cuyahoga County, Ohio.* Vols. 1–5. Chicago: Sanborn Map Company, 1886–1951.

Schuyler, Montgomery. "Concerning Queen Anne." *American Architect and Building News* 1 (Dec. 16, 1876): 404–5.

———. "The Romanesque Revival in America." *Architectural Record* 1, no. 2 (Oct.–Dec. 1891): 151–98.

Schwartz, Barry. "The Social Psychology of Privacy." *American Journal of Sociology* 73 (1968): 741–52.

Scully, Vincent. "Introduction." In *The Architecture of the American Summer: The Flowering of the Shingle Style,* edited by Robert A. M. Stern. New York: Rizzoli, 1989.

———. *The Shingle Style and Stick Style.* New Haven: Yale University Press, 1971.

Starr, S. Frederick. *Southern Comfort: The Garden District of New Orleans, 1800–1900.* Cambridge: MIT Press, 1989.

Steffens, Lincoln. *The Struggle for Self-Government.* 1906. Reprint. New York: Johnson Reprint, 1968.

Stewart, George R. *American Place Names.* New York: Oxford University Press, 1970.

Stilgoe, John R. *Borderland: Origins of the American Suburb, 1820–1939.* New Haven: Yale University Press, 1988.

Sumner, William Graham. *The Challenge of Facts, and Other Essays.* Edited by Albert G. Keller. New Haven: Yale University Press, 1914.

Thayer, William Roscoe. *The Life and Letters of John Hay.* 2 vols. New York: Houghton Mifflin, 1908.

Thernstrom, Stephen. *The Other Bostonians: Poverty and Progress in the American Metropolis, 1880–1970.* Cambridge: Harvard University Press, 1973.

Townsend, Helen de Kay, comp. *The Cleveland Blue Book and Social Register of Cleveland, Ohio.* Cleveland: Helen de Kay Townsend, Dec. 1903, Apr. 1907.

Trollope, Anthony. *North America.* 1861–62. Reprint. New York: Knopf, 1951.

Tunnard, Christopher. "The Glittering Slum on Main Street." *Architectural Forum,* Apr. 1951.

United States Department of Commerce Bureau of the Census. *1890 Report on Manufacturing Industries in the U.S.* Washington, D.C.: Government Printing Office, 1895.

United States Works Progress Administration, Writers' Program, comp. *The Ohio Guide.* New York: Oxford University Press, 1940.

Uphan, Warren. *Minnesota Geographic Names.* St. Paul: Minnesota Historical Society, 1920.

Upjohn, Everard M. *Richard Upjohn: Architect and Churchman.* New York: Columbia University Press, 1939.

Van Tassel, David D., and John J. Grabowski, eds. *Cleveland: A Tradition of Reform.* Kent, Ohio: Kent State University Press, 1986.

———. *The Encyclopedia of Cleveland History.* Bloomington: Indiana University Press, 1987.

Vaux, Calvert. *Villas and Cottages.* New York: Harper & Brothers, 1857, 1864.

Veblen, Thorstein. *The Theory of the Leisure Class.* 1899. In *The Portable Veblen,* edited by Max Lerner. Reprint. New York: Viking Press, 1948.

Wade, Richard C. "Urbanization." In *The Comparative Approach to American History,* edited by C. Vann Woodward. New York: Basic Books, 1968.

Ward, William. "The Relations of the Architect to the Client." *Inland Architect* 6, no. 2 (Sept. 1885): 15.

Warner, Sam Bass. *Streetcar Suburbs: The Process of Growth in Boston, 1870–1900.* Cambridge: Harvard University Press, 1976.

Welter, Barbara. "The Cult of True Womanhood: 1820–60." *American Quarterly* 18 (Summer 1966): 151–74.

Wharton, Edith. *The Age of Innocence.* New York: D. Appleton, 1920.

Wheeler, Robert A. *"Pleasantly Situated on the West Side."* Cleveland: Western Reserve Historical Society, 1980.

Whiffen, Marcus. *American Architecture Since 1780: A Guide to the Styles.* Cambridge: MIT Press, 1969.

Wick, Warren Corning. *My Recollections of Old Cleveland.* Cleveland: Carpenter Reserve Printing Co., 1979.

Wickham, Gertrude Van Rensselaer. *The Pioneer Families of Cleveland, 1796–1840.* 2 vols. Cleveland: Evangelical Publishing House, 1914.

Weibe, Robert. *The Search for Order: 1877–1920.* New York: Hill and Wang, 1967.

Wilson, Ella Grant. *Famous Old Euclid Avenue of Cleveland.* 2 vols. Cleveland, 1932, 1937.

Woods, Mary. "The First American Architectural Journals: The Profession's Voice." *Journal of the Society of Architectural Historians* 48, no. 2 (June 1989): 117–38.

"Worcester R. Warner." *Case Alumnus* (Oct. 1929): 3.

"The Work of Mr. J. Milton Dyer." *The Architectural Record* 20, no. 5, Nov. 1906.

World's History of Cleveland. Cleveland: The Cleveland World, 1896.

Wortman, Marlene Stein. "Domesticating the Nineteenth-Century American City." In *Prospects,* edited by Jack Salzman. New York: Burt Franklin Press, 1977.

Young, Agatha. *Light in the Sky.* New York: Random House, 1948.

Archival Sources

American Institute of Architects Correspondence. AIA Archives, American Institute of Architects, Washington, D.C.

Annals of Cleveland Newspaper Abstracts, 1816–76. Manuscript Collection, Western Reserve Historical Society, Cleveland.

Barnett, James. Papers, 1861–1906. Manuscript Collection, Western Reserve Historical Society, Cleveland.

Bolton Family. Private Collection. Cleveland.

Brown, Fayette. Papers, 1841–91. Manuscript Collection, Western Reserve Historical Society, Cleveland.

Brown, Harvey H. Papers, 1879–1905. Manuscript Collection, Western Reserve Historical Society, Cleveland.

Brush, Charles F. Picture Group, 1870–1975. Manuscript Collection, Western Reserve Historical Society, Cleveland.

Brush, Charles Francis. Papers. Special Collections, Freiberger Library, Case Western Reserve University, Cleveland.

Burton, Theodore Elijah. Papers, 1876–1928. Manuscript Collection, Western Reserve Historical Society, Cleveland.

Castalia Sporting Club. Records, 1878–c. 1950. Manuscript Collection, Western Reserve Historical Society, Cleveland.

Cleveland Building Permits, 1888–1910. Cleveland City Hall.

Cleveland City Council Archives, 1836–1960. Cleveland City Hall.

Cleveland Development Foundation. Records, 1954–69. Manuscript Collection, Western Reserve Historical Society, Cleveland.

Cleveland, Mrs. G. C. "Charles F. Brush House." Feb. 1930. Historic Ohio Home Series, Library, Western Reserve Historical Society, Cleveland.

Cleveland Ordinances, 1836–57. Cleveland City Hall.

Cobb, Carl Boardman. Private Collection. Chagrin Falls, Ohio.

Cuyahoga County Surveyor's Records, 1823–93. Cuyahoga County Archives, Cleveland.

Cuyahoga County Tax Duplicates, 1890–1950. Cuyahoga County Archives, Cleveland.

Decker, Edgar. Photograph Collection. Manuscript Collection, Western Reserve Historical Society, Cleveland.

Harry K. Devereux Family. Picture Group. Manuscript Collection, Western Reserve Historical Society, Cleveland.

Devereux Family Papers, c. 1808–1932. Manuscript Collection, Western Reserve Historical Society, Cleveland.

Dickens Party. Picture Group. Manuscript Collection, Western Reserve Historical Society, Cleveland.

Donaldson, Ralph J. "Untold Tales About Politicians and Newspapermen." Edited by George Condon and John Huth. 1984. Library, Western Reserve Historical Society, Cleveland.

Edmondson, George Mountain. Photograph Collection. Cleveland Public Library.

Howard P. Eells, Jr., Family Papers, 1840–1978. Manuscript Collection, Western Reserve Historical Society, Cleveland.

Euclid Avenue. Picture Group, 1865–1970. Manuscript Collection, Western Reserve Historical Society, Cleveland.

Euclid Avenue Congregational Church. Records, 1822–1970; Picture Group. Manuscript Collection, Western Reserve Historical Society, Cleveland.

Euclid Innerbelt Association Records, 1961–68. Manuscript Collection, Western Reserve Historical Society, Cleveland.

Sylvester T. Everett Family Papers, 1891–1953, 1976. Manuscript Collection, Western Reserve Historical Society, Cleveland.

Four-In-Hand and Tandem Club Company. Records, 1902–8; Meet Book, Picture Group. Manuscript Collection, Western Reserve Historical Society, Cleveland.

I. T. Frary Collection. Picture Group. Manuscript Collection, Western Reserve Historical Society, Cleveland.

Garretson, George A. Picture Group, 1898–1919. Manuscript Collection, Western Reserve Historical Society, Cleveland.

Hanna Family Papers, c. 1830–1900. Manuscript Collection, Western Reserve Historical Society, Cleveland.

Hay, John. Papers. Manuscript Division, Library of Congress, Washington, D.C.

Herrick, Myron Timothy. Papers, c. 1880–1935. Manuscript Collection, Western Reserve Historical Society, Cleveland.

Historic American Buildings Survey. Prints and Photographs Division, Library of Congress, Washington, D.C.

Historic American Buildings Survey, Cleveland, Ohio. Picture Group. Manuscript Collection, Western Reserve Historical Society, Cleveland.

Hodge, Orlando John. Papers, 1822–1913. Manuscript Collection, Western Reserve Historical Society, Cleveland.

Hunt, Catherine Clinton Howland. "The Biography of Richard Morris Hunt." Undated (post–1895). Prints and Drawings Collection, The Octagon Museum, American Architectural Foundation, Washington, D.C.

Richard Morris Hunt Collection. Prints and Drawings Collection, The Octagon Museum, American Architectural Foundation, Washington, D.C.

Hutchinson, Clarence H. Papers. Ohio Historical Records Survey, Works Progress Administration, 1930s. Manuscript Collection, Western Reserve Historical Society, Cleveland.

King, Henry C. Correspondence. Oberlin College Archives, Oberlin, Ohio.

McKibben, W. Jeanne. "The Allen-Severance Connection." Unpublished paper, Jan. 6, 1988, Oberlin, Ohio.

McKim, Mead & White Collection. The New-York Historical Society, New York City.

Samuel Mather Family. Papers, c. 1872–1945; Picture Group. Manuscript Collection, Western Reserve Historical Society, Cleveland.

Necrology File, 1850–1950, 1951–75. Library, Western Reserve Historical Society, Cleveland.

Norton, David Z. Family Picture Group; Residence Picture Group, 1910–39. Manuscript Collection, Western Reserve Historical Society, Cleveland.

Otis, Charles Augustus. Papers, c. 1920–53; Picture Group, 1910–50. Manuscript Collection, Western Reserve Historical Society, Cleveland.

Otis-Sanders Residence. Picture Group, 1933. Manuscript Collection, Western Reserve Historical Society, Cleveland.

Peabody & Stearns Collection. Fine Arts Department, Boston Public Library, Boston.

Perils of Society. Film and playbill, 1916. Picture Group. Manuscript Collection, Western Reserve Historical Society, Cleveland.

Perkins, Joseph. Account books. Simon Perkins Papers, 1801–1919. Manuscript Collection, Western Reserve Historical Society, Cleveland.

Post, Charles Asa. Papers, 1917–41. Manuscript Collection, Western Reserve Historical Society, Cleveland.

Rockefeller, John D. Papers. Rockefeller Archives Center, Pocantico Hills, North Tarrytown, New York.

Rowfant Club. Records, 1891–1973; Picture Group. Manuscript Collection, Western Reserve Historical Society, Cleveland.

Schofield, Mary Peale. "Working File of Cleveland Architects of the Late 19th and Early 20th Centuries." Microfilm, c. 1979. Library, Western Reserve Historical Society.

Schweinfurth, Charles F. Architectural Library. Fine Arts Deparment, Cleveland Public Library.

Schweinfurth, Charles F. Architectural Plans, 1880s–c. 1900. Manuscript Collection, Western Reserve Historical Society, Cleveland.

Scofield, Levi T. Architectural Plans, c. 1866–1910; Family Picture Group. Manuscript Collection, Western Reserve Historical Society, Cleveland.

Severance, John L. House Architectural plans. Business Office, Cleveland Health Museum.

Squire, Andrew. Papers, 1855–1943. Manuscript Collection, Western Reserve Historical Society, Cleveland.

Starr, S. Frederick. "St. Charles Avenue, New Orleans." Unpublished paper, Sept. 1989, Oberlin, Ohio.

Sterling, Mary Emma (Betts). Diaries, 1872–92. Manuscript Collection, Western Reserve Historical Society, Cleveland.

Swasey, Ambrose. Papers. Special Collections. Freiberger Library, Case Western Reserve University, Cleveland.

United States Census of Population, 1830–1910, Cuyahoga County, Ohio. Library, Western Reserve Historical Society, Cleveland.

Richard Upjohn Collection. Avery Architectural and Fine Arts Library, Columbia University, New York.

Upson, Clara Tracy (Mrs. David). Private Collection. University Heights, Ohio.

Van Urk, J. B. "The Horse, the Valley & The Chagrin Valley Hunt Club." 1947. Library, Western Reserve Historical Society, Cleveland.

Wade, Jeptha H. "Sketch of the Life of Jeptha Homer Wade, from 1811–1867." Unpublished paper, July 1, 1889, Edward Everett Worthington Private Collection, Kirtland, Ohio.

Jeptha Homer Wade Family. Papers, 1837–1925; Picture Group. Manuscript Collection, Western Reserve Historical Society, Cleveland.

Wade, Randall Palmer. Journal, 1870–71. Manuscript Collection, Western Reserve Historical Society, Cleveland.

Warner & Swasey. Papers. Special Collections, Freiberger Library, Case Western Reserve University, Cleveland.

Warner & Swasey. Picture Group, 1900–1978. Manuscript Collection, Western Reserve Historical Society, Cleveland.

Warner, Worcester R. Papers. Special Collections, Freiberger Library, Case Western Reserve University, Cleveland.

Williamson, Samuel, Jr. Papers, 1820–80. Manuscript Collection, Western Reserve Historical Society, Cleveland.

Ella Grant Wilson Collection. Picture Group. Manuscript Collection, Western Reserve Historical Society, Cleveland.

Works Progress Administration (WPA) Records, Ohio Historic Records Survey, 1930s. Manuscript Collection, Western Reserve Historical Society, Cleveland.

Worthington, Ruth Everett. "History of Our Family." Undated. Edward Everett Worthington Private Collection, Kirtland, Ohio.

Newspapers and Periodicals

American Architect and Building News.
Architectural Reviewer.
Cleveland City Directory, 1837–1920.
Cleveland Gazette.
Cleveland Plain Dealer.
Cleveland Leader.
Cleveland News.
Cleveland Press.
Cleveland Social Directory, 1885, 1886.
Cleveland Town Topics.
Daily True Democrat.
Herald and Gazette.
Herald.
Inland Architect.
Massillon News Leader.
New York Times.
Ohio Architect, Engineer & Builder.

Dissertations and Thesis

Dow, Burton Smith, III. "Amasa Stone, Jr.: His Triumph and Tragedy." Master's thesis, Western Reserve University, 1982.

Klein, Richard. "Nineteenth Century Land Use Decisions in Cleveland, Ohio: A Case Study of Neighborhood Development and Change in Ohio City." Ph.D. diss., The University of Akron, 1983.

Perry, Regina A. "The Life and Works of Charles Frederick Schweinfurth: Cleveland Architect—1856–1919." Ph.D. diss., Western Reserve University, 1967.

Index